The Body in Culture, Technology and Society

Theory, Culture & Society

Theory, Culture & Society caters for the resurgence of interest in culture within contemporary social science and the humanities. Building on the heritage of classical social theory, the book series examines ways in which this tradition has been reshaped by a new generation of theorists. It also publishes theoretically informed analyses of everyday life, popular culture, and new intellectual movements.

EDITOR: Mike Featherstone, *Nottingham Trent University*

SERIES EDITORIAL BOARD
Roy Boyne, *University of Durham*
Mike Hepworth, *University of Aberdeen*
Scott Lash, *Goldsmiths College, University of London*
Roland Robertson, *University of Aberdeen*
Bryan S. Turner, *University of Cambridge*

THE TCS CENTRE
The *Theory, Culture & Society* book series, the journals *Theory, Culture & Society* and *Body & Society*, and related conference, seminar and postgraduate programmes operate from the TCS Centre at Nottingham Trent University. For further details of the TCS Centre's activities please contact:

Centre Administrator
The TCS Centre, Room 175
Faculty of Humanities
Nottingham Trent University
Clifton Lane, Nottingham, NG11 8NS, UK
e-mail: tcs@ntu.ac.uk
web: http://tcs.ntu.ac.uk

Recent volumes include:

Critique of Information
Scott Lash

Liberal Democracy 3.0
Stephen P. Turner

French Social Theory
Mike Gane

Sex and Manners
Cas Wouters

The Body in Culture, Technology and Society

Chris Shilling

SAGE Publications
London • Thousand Oaks • New Delhi

First published 2005

Published in association with Theory, Culture & Society, Nottingham Trent University

SAGE Publications Ltd
6 Bonhill Street
London EC2A 4PU

SAGE Publications Inc
2455 Teller Road
Thousand Oaks, California 91320

SAGE Publications India Pvt Ltd
B-42 Panchsheel Enclave
Post Box 4109
New Delhi – 100 017

British Library Cataloguing in Publication data

A catalogue record for this book is available from
the British Library

ISBN 0 7619 7123 8
ISBN 0 7619 7124 6

Library of Congress Control Number Available

Printed in India at Gopsons Paper Ltd, Noida

Contents

Acknowledgements

Philip A. Mellor and Keith Tester have been valuable sources of support and critical insight, while this study has also been improved by the comments of Ian Burkitt, Mike Hardey, Caroline New and Pauline Leonard. At Sage Publications, Chris Rojek provides all the encouragement and good advice one would want from an editor, and thanks also to Ian Antcliff and and Kay Bridger for their assistance during the production process. The *Theory, Culture & Society* editorial group continue to provide valued support for my work, while the Faculty of Humanities and Social Sciences of the University of Portsmouth granted to me a period of sabbatical leave so that I could complete this book. The support that I have received since starting this project, which has been several years in the making, also came in other guises. I am extremely grateful to Xulong Lee for his ongoing help and expertise, and thanks also to Richard Gulliver for his assistance. Max and Katie made this period of time so much more fun than it would otherwise have been, while I want to dedicate this book to my wife, Debbie, for her love, friendship and support.

1

Introduction

Social theories of the body have exerted an enormous influence on the social sciences and humanities in the past two decades. From being a subject of marginal academic interest, the intellectual significance of the body is now such that no study can lay claim to being comprehensive unless it takes at least some account of the embodied preconditions of agency and the physical effects of social structures. In sociology, discussions of embodiment pervade general theoretical works and specialist sub-disciplinary studies. Indeed, a recognition that its subject matter includes thinking, feeling *bodies*, rather than disembodied minds unaffected by their senses and habits, has become central to the sociological imagination. Despite these advances, however, clear portraits of the body's status, generative capacities, and receptivity to structural forces, remain frustratingly elusive within most accounts of contemporary society.

It is against this background that this book is intended to be a theoretical and substantive contribution to the study of the body, as well as to social theory and sociological research more generally, and is addressed to the problems that still confront this area. In what follows, I aim to do the following: (a) account for the enigmatic nature of embodiment in social theory; (b) suggest that classical sociological writings converged around a hitherto neglected view of the body as a *multi-dimensional medium for the constitution of society*; (c) critically examine recent approaches to the subject; and (d) undertake a series of substantive analyses of the body and the economy, culture, sociality and technology. These four aims are related in that this classical convergence, that I characterize as a form of corporeal realism, provides us with a framework that can be used to reduce the analytical elusiveness of the body and overcome some of the theoretical limitations of recent approaches. It also allows us to investigate the strongly held concerns about the subjugation of the embodied subject that characterize these recent approaches. This opening chapter is designed to explore in more detail the enigmatic nature of the body in social theory, before outlining the framework adopted in this study and introducing the reader to the main themes informing the rest of the book.

The Rise of the Enigmatic Body

In accounting for the ubiquitous yet elusive nature of the body in modern thought, the first aim of this book is to examine how the physical subject has come to possess an exceptional academic popularity, yet still seems to fade away when we ask the question 'What is the body?'. In terms of its popularity, there has been a breathtaking explosion of interest in the subject of the body since the early 1980s. However, academic interest was stimulated initially by social trends and analyses which helped position the body as significant to a range of *other* subjects of established intellectual significance. Several strands of social thought and analytical perspectives assisted this early rise of the body, and it is important to revisit and re-examine the most important of them here as they help explain why embodiment became so ubiquitous yet remains such a contested and slippery subject. This rise of interest in the body represents the *centrifugal* stage in the recent development of the area as it attaches the subject to a wide variety of disparate agendas. It contrasts with the somewhat more *centripetal* trend that has emerged in recent years (when several broad perspectives emerged as dominant resources for examining embodiment) that I examine later in this Introduction, but has not yet receded completely and continues to inform developments in the area.

First, analysts of consumer culture highlighted the commercialized body as increasingly central to people's sense of self-identity, a shift that was associated with a corresponding change in the structure of advanced capitalist societies in the second half of the twentieth century. During this period, there was a move away from the focus on hard work in the sphere of production coupled with frugality in the sphere of consumption, towards an ethos which encouraged hard work *and* hedonistic consumption (Featherstone, 1982). The body's status as ubiquitous sign in advertising culture, and the proliferation of production oriented toward leisure, helped promote an emphasis on the achievement of an appearance and a degree of physical control commensurate with the display of a hyper-efficient 'performing self'.

Theorists of consumer culture analysed these developments through the related prisms provided by Tönnies's *Gemeinschaft/Gesellschaft* distinction and Durkheim's mechanical/organic solidarity distinction. Pasi Falk (1994: 12–13, 36), for example, argued that the boundaries of the late modern self had become detached from the bonds of collective physical rituals, and centred around individualizing consumption acts focused on the 'bodily surface and its sensory openings'; a development clearly associated with the rising influence of consumerism. This distinction between the collectively determined body of the pre-modern era, and the individualized body of the late modern era, also underpinned the studies of Giddens (1991) and Turner (1984); analyses which focus in very different ways on the socio-political contexts in which consumer culture developed. They suggested that the body was increasingly 'on show' as *the* vehicle of consumption, and that social status was linked to the visible exteriors of the physical self. This emergence of a topographical approach to the *flesh as appearance* was seen as emptying the body of its traditional Christian significance as a container of sin, and promoting it as a form of physical capital (Bourdieu, 1978).

The second perspective that contributed to a flourishing and diverse interest in the body was the rise of 'second wave' feminism. From the 1960s onwards, feminists emphasized through a critical interrogation of the biological sex/cultural gender divide that there was nothing natural about women's corporeality which justified their public subordination (Oakley, 1972). They argued that menstruation and pregnancy, for example, provided no reasonable grounds to discriminate against women in education or politics. Thus, the body uncovered by feminist studies was a biologically sexed body which *should* have few social consequences, but which had been defined within patriarchal society as determining women's life chances.

Feminist writings highlighted how the body had been used as a means of discriminating against women. Because of the 'male stream' history of writing on the subject, however, feminists did not seek initially to place the body at the centre of social thought. Philosophers had traditionally associated men with freedom and the mind, and women with 'unreason associated with the body' (Grosz, 1994: 4). Women were seen as '*more* biological, *more* corporeal and *more* natural than men', and therefore more suited to the world of private than public existence (ibid.). Despite this ambivalent view of embodiment, feminism contributed much towards the popularity of body studies. Eisenstein (1988) and W. Williams (1997) traced the legal history of the female body as male property, while Mackinnon (1989) highlighted the bodily bases of female oppression through the construction of 'compulsory heterosexuality', and Irigaray (1988 [1977]) and Kristeva (1986) examined the marginalization or 'erasure' of female sexuality in male culture. Feminists have also placed on the agenda the project of 'reexploring, reexamining, notions of female corporeality' (Grosz, 1994: 14), have interrogated the body within sexuality, ethics and standpoint epistemologies (e.g. Haraway, 1994 [1985]), and have constructed imaginative metaphysical conceptions of the female body as 'fluidity'. It is the sexually different body that feminists have highlighted, though, and the idea of embodiment as providing humans with certain common capacities and frailties tended to fade in their discussions.

The third set of concerns that increased the prominence of the body involved a growing awareness of changes in modes of *governmentality*, changes which highlighted human physicality as an *object* of various forms of control. Instrumental here was Foucault's (1970, 1979a, 1979b) analysis of how modernity's creation of 'man' was accompanied by a shift in the target of governmental discourses (the fleshy body gave way to the mindful body as a focus of concern); in the object of discourse (preoccupation with matters of death was replaced by interest in structuring life); and in the scope of discourse (the control of anonymous individuals gave way to the management of differentiated populations). The eighteenth century witnessed a large increase in discourses on sexuality, for example, which linked the sex of individual bodies to the management of national populations (Foucault, 1981), while the twentieth century was characterized by a continued shift away from negative forms of bodily repression towards positive forms of exhortation in which embodied subjects were encouraged to structure their lives in particular ways.

This focus on governmentality painted a picture of a relatively passive and undifferentiated set of bodies subject to institutional control. It highlighted the spaces that contained, the rules that constrained, and the forces that operated on and through bodies. Teaching hospitals were instrumental in developing medical norms, for example, and subjected distinctive types of sick bodies to different types of treatment (Armstrong, 1983, 1995). This particular concern with physicality also cast its spotlight on the problems governments faced in dealing with large numbers of bodies in the contemporary era. There are millions more people across the globe for governments to manage today than there were a thousand years ago. Declining infant mortality rates and increasing life expectancies in the West, medical advances, and the rise of diseases such as HIV/AIDS requiring long-term care, have also increased massively the costs associated with controlling bodies. In summary, while issues of governmentality helped stimulate academic interest in the body, the body they resurrected was objectified as a statistic, a problem, or a target of control. It became meaningful when it impinged on the operation of government, and faded away when it lived, experienced and intervened in life outside of nodes and networks of power.

Technological advances which contributed to a growing uncertainty about the 'reality' of the body constituted a fourth analytical concern that raised the profile of this subject. Advances in transplant surgery, *in vitro* fertilization and genetic engineering increased control over bodies, but instituted a weakening of the boundaries between bodies and machines that prompted some to reconceptualize humans as cyborgs. These same developments appear to have thrown into radical doubt our knowledge of what the embodied subject is. The principle of individuality accepted by Enlightenment thought depended on identifying what was unique to a person across the contingencies of date and location, yet the potential malleability of the body threatens such constancies. The Human Genome Project, for example, heralds the start of an era in which all aspects of embodiment are theoretically open to alteration, while (at the time of writing) surgeons are close to being able to carry out face transplants (operations which would further destabilize the notion of any constant visible self). In this context, it is hardly surprising that post-modernist writings have abandoned the modernist project of 'knowing' what the body is. The body for them becomes a 'blank screen' or 'sign receiving system' ever open to being (re)constructed by social forces beyond its control (Kroker and Kroker, 1988). Alternatively, in the work of Deleuze and Guattari, it has been transformed into an elusive 'body without organs' (Goodchild, 1996). The 'decentring' of the subject is, apparently, complete.

If technological advances encouraged analysts to focus on the 'uncertain body', this has not always resulted in a post-modern concern with 'cyborgs' or 'disappearing bodies'. These advances have also been analysed in terms of their aesthetic and sensual consequences by those unhappy with attempts to erase the facticity of the embodied subject. It has been suggested, for example, that the destabilization of our knowledge of bodies does not signify a 'dissolution' of the body, but a loss of psychological 'basic trust' or 'ontological security' (Berger, 1990 [1967]; Giddens, 1991: 45–7). Alternatively, the supposed instability of the body has been associated with the revival of effervescent experiences of the sacred in a modern world in which the profane has become banal (Mellor and Shilling, 1997). By placing the 'uncertain body' within such social and corporeal parameters, these writings relativize the relativistic claims of post-modern writings. The body may have become more malleable, but it is our feelings about the body, rather than the physicality of the body itself, that have been undermined.

The fifth major analytical concern that continues to both increase the popularity of the subject, and tie the growing interest in the body to other intellectual agendas, involves those academics who viewed the subject as a conceptual resource which could assist them in advancing their discipline. In the case of sociology, theorists used the body to avoid the over-socialized conception of the individual associated with Parsons's (1991 [1951]: 541–2, 547–8) focus on values (which portrayed the body as merely a sub-system of the action system), and the unrealistic assumptions of rational choice theory (which holds that actors cognitively establish goals before acting, and views the body as a permanently available instrument of action immune to frailty, chance, and epiphany). Conceptions of 'creativity' (Joas, 1996), of 'human being' (Archer, 1995), and of an 'embodied interaction order' (Shilling, 1999), for example, have sought to provide conceptions of embodiment which are resistant to being collapsed into any unidimensional view of social action or structurally determinist analysis of society. In these cases, the body constitutes an overlooked element of social reality whose capacities have important implications for disciplinary analysis.

These five strands of social thought/analytical concerns have done much to stimulate and maintain the rise of interest in the body since the 1980s, but they approached and defined the subject in very different ways. The body was a surface phenomenon which had become a malleable marker of commercial value subject to the vagaries of fashion for theorists of consumer culture. It was a sexed object that had been used as a means of justifying women's subordination for feminists. It was an object that had been rendered passive by changing modes of control for Foucauldian analysts of governmentality. The body was changed into an uncertain and even a rapidly disappearing remnant of pre-technological culture for those interested in the meeting of meat and machines which had occurred with the development of cyborgs. Finally, it became a positive conceptual category for those concerned with addressing theoretical problems in their own discipline. Within each of these analyses, the spotlight rests on certain aspects of the body, leaving others obscured.

These disparate concerns are reflected in the enormous number of studies to have appeared on the subject since the 1980s.[1] The sheer quantity of this work has been received as evidence of the healthy establishment of a new field of study. Writings on the body have challenged the assumption that 'society operates upon us intellectually and consensually rather than directly upon our bodies' (O'Neill, 1985: 48), have established several new sub-disciplinary areas of study, and have made general contributions to social and cultural theory. Nevertheless, 'the body' remains one of the most contested concepts in the social sciences: its analysis has produced an intellectual battleground over which the respective claims of post-structuralism and post-modernism, phenomenology, feminism, socio-biology, sociology and cultural studies have fought (e.g. Howson and Inglis, 2001). Tied to competing agendas, and against the background of the huge diversity of body studies, varying aspects of embodiment are foregrounded, allowing others to fade into the background. This has the effect of making the body recede and slide from view, while undergoing a series of metamorphoses that render it unrecognizable from one incarnation to the next. Of course, in any sociological study of the body, attention will at times focus on structures and norms, and the constraining and shaping potential of these phenomena. To this extent we should expect there to be a temporary and justified 'fading' of the body within limited portions of such analyses, but this is quite different from the wholesale loss of the body and its generative capacities that we find in so many studies on the subject. More generally, the body appears for many to have become a mere metaphor through which particular concerns can be pursued. In this context, it is increasingly difficult to define the body or to even say what was being examined within the field. In two of the best-known studies on the subject, for example, Bryan Turner (1984: 8) concludes that the body may appear to be solid, yet is 'the most elusive, illusory ... metaphorical ... and ever distant thing', while Judith Butler (1993: ix) admits that in 'trying to consider the materiality of the body', she 'kept losing track of the subject'.

The under-determined body

If we are to account for this ubiquity and elusiveness, we need to understand how it was possible for interest in the body to be stimulated by such diverse intellectual projects, and for the subject to be defined in such different ways. The main reason for this is that the body has not been subject to a strong tradition of positive conceptual appropriation within Western thought. While philosophy had historically imparted the body with a good deal of negative content, this left contemporary writers seeking to invest it with theoretically productive and positive meanings with a high degree of latitude.

The negative view of the physical flesh dominant in Western thought can be traced to ancient Greece. *Soma* (which subsequently came to mean 'body') referred to the corpse, while Socrates argued that lasting happiness came not from the (perishable) body but through the (immortal) soul; a division later mapped onto that between the 'irrational passions' and 'rational thought' (Snell, 1960 [1948]). More generally, Greek ethics held that the soul's aspirations should be guided by a self-control termed 'healthy thinking' which opposed itself to the inevitable 'sufferings' of the bodily instincts and emotions. This philosophical approach marginalized the importance of the body, by suggesting that it was the *mind* that made us truly human. While there were important exceptions to this denigration of the body, negative views on the subject were strengthened further during some of the key events that ushered in the modern world. The Protestant Reformation and the Enlightenment were especially important in this respect.

The religious wars which followed the Protestant Reformation of the sixteenth century created a situation in which the protagonists of modern philosophy faced political intolerance, the dogmatic claims of rival theologians, and views of the body which frequently associated it with irrationality and sin. In this context, a 'Quest for Certainty' became increasingly popular among philosophers as a path to establishing truths which were ubiquitous, universal, timeless, and independent of the vagaries of people's bodily dispositions and emotions (Toulmin, 1990). This Quest was based on the rational, non-partisan powers of the mind, and was exemplified by Descartes. Descartes claimed that the essence of our humanity subsisted in our (noble) ability to think, while our bodies inflicted (ignoble) emotions on us (Toulmin, 1990: 134–5). In distrusting the senses, he argued that 'I am ... only a thing that thinks', and that 'my mind ... is entirely and truly distinct from my body and may exist without it' (Descartes, 1974: 105, 156). Hobbes objected to many of Descartes' formulations and proposed a radically different philosophy based on the body and centred around the problem of order (the problem of how it is that people can live together without social life degenerating into violence). However, even here, the body was conceived of as a liability, propelling people into self-aggrandizing actions which could lead into a war of all against all.

The eighteenth-century Enlightenment did little to ameliorate these negative views of the body. Despite its intellectual diversity, the dominant tendencies within Enlightenment thought viewed individuals as rational, cognitive authors of their own actions (Cassirer, 1951; Hamilton, 1992). For example, one of the most famous philosophers associated with the Enlightenment, Immanuel Kant (1964 [1785]), devalued the body and desire as motives for action, and rejected the possibility that criteria for the good are grounded in the natural properties of humans. Instead, Kant (1985 [1797]: 56) argued that humans were rational beings and that the 'good' was attained when individuals transcended nature and complied with the categorical imperative.

I have already mentioned that there were exceptions to this denigration of the body. It was not only Hobbes, but such figures as De Maistre, Feuerbach, Nietzsche and Husserl, as well as those associated with sociology such as Marx, Durkheim, and Weber, who have been identified as important contributors to a 'hidden history' of body relevant writings (Turner, 1991a; Shilling, 1993). As the twentieth century progressed, however, this history was governed by two main trends in relation to the subject which failed ultimately to consolidate theoretically productive views of human embodiment.

On the one hand, it was only a small, albeit a growing number, of thinkers for whom the body possessed a positive role in the creation of social life. Marcel Mauss (1973 [1934]) examined the corporeal foundations of human agency in his analyses of 'techniques of the body', analyses which also highlighted how social processes could help structure the deepest recesses of people's physical being. Maurice Merleau-Ponty's (1962) phenomenology suggested that our bodies provide us with our 'opening onto', our 'vehicle of being in', and our 'means of communication with' the world, while Erving Goffman's (1963) concern with 'shared vocabularies of body idiom' highlighted the importance of the body's appearance and management for the creation of a social self and for the maintenance of social interaction. The diversity and relative infrequency of such contributions, however, meant that the positive conceptual significance of the body remained under-determined.

On the other hand, this under-determination of the body was reinforced within sociology by the work of Talcott Parsons. Parsons was the twentieth-century's most influential interpreter of sociology, yet his vision of the discipline generally suppressed and marginalized the significance of the body in the work of previous theorists. It did this by constructing a view of the discipline which took as its negative referent Hobbes's 'utilitarian' solution to the problem of order. Parsons (1968 [1937]) rejected Hobbes's analysis of what motivated social action, and developed an alternative, normative solution to the problem of order. Crucially, he also suggested that there existed a coherent sociological tradition that had already replaced Hobbes's concern with bodily passions with a more realistic concern with common value integration. This reinterpreted Durkheim's writings about bodily collective effervescence, for example, as an analysis of shared values and normative integration. In one sweeping move, Parsons obfuscated the significance of the body to classical sociology.

What is essential about this background for our purposes is that it enabled contemporary theorists to impart 'the body' with productive, highly varied capacities more easily than would have been possible for a concept over-determined by a strong tradition of positive theoretical usage. As we have seen, since the rise of interest in the subject from the 1980s, different intellectual agendas defined the body in widely contrasting ways and invested it with incompatible roles. The body was annexed as a 'blank screen' on which the effects of culture were 'written', as a constructor of identities, as a marker of irreducible difference, as a receptor of governmental micro-powers, as a vehicle through which the mind/body, culture/nature and other 'binary oppositions' which characterized traditional social thought could be overcome, and as the physical seat of all experience. The body, it soon became clear, could be all things to all people. If the body's malleability as a sign contributed to its popularity in academic thought, however, it also contributed to its elusiveness. There seemed to be no agreement about *what* the body was, or *how* it should be analysed.

Classical Foundations

This conceptual under-determination of the body is clearly of great importance in understanding how the subject became so ubiquitous and elusive in
contemporary social thought. However, if we wish to stabilize our understanding of the capacities of the body, a necessary step if we are to make theoretical advances within the field of body studies, there is much to be gained
by undoing Parsons's suppression of the body. In this context, the second
aim of this book is to recover the centrality of the body to sociology. This
will not involve a simple review of sociological writings relevant to the body.
I am not concerned here to summarize generally what a whole range of classical theorists have written about the body. This has been undertaken previously and does not actually capture how the body underpinned so many key
concepts and writings within the sociological tradition. Instead, I seek to
highlight a hitherto neglected convergence in how several classical figures
analysed the body.

Parsons (1968 [1937]) is the best-known exponent of a convergence thesis in sociology. His focus was on social action and he suggested that there
existed within diverse sociological writings common foundations for a non-
utilitarian, 'voluntaristic theory of action'. Parsons's writings continue to be
criticized for their interpretive inaccuracies and have been largely, and
somewhat unfairly, rejected as a useful resource for body studies. What contemporary interest in embodiment has overlooked, however, is the possibility that certain classical writers may converge not necessarily in their
treatment of action, as Parsons suggested, but in terms of how they conceptualize the body as both productive of, and receptive to the powers of, society.[2] This convergence can be said to exist in the theories of Marx,
Durkheim and Simmel, and it is on their writings that I shall be concentrating in order to construct the theoretical framework utilized in this book.
This is not just because they have unexpectedly complementary things to
say about the body, but because they each provide us with ethically
informed criteria (concerned respectively with exploitation and oppression,
with the collective enhancement of individual powers, and with the effects
of rationalization and the individual development of personality[3]) against
which it is possible to assess the position of bodies in the contemporary era.

Huge differences separate Marx, Durkheim and Simmel. Their writings
are conventionally viewed as being theoretically incompatible (significantly
because they stem from opposing philosophical traditions), yet I want to
contend that this assessment needs to be modified as each converges around
a view of the body, and embodied experience, as a *multi-dimensional medium
for the constitution of society*. Thus, while Durkheim is indeed distinctive in
beginning with the theoretical and moral primacy of the collectivity as a culturally constituted, *sui generis* reality, and looked to the possible rise of a
moral individualism that could provide a suitable framework for an
advanced capitalism (Durkheim, 1984 [1893]), he also viewed the body as
a source and recipient of a collective symbolism that possessed the capacity

to incorporate individuals into the moral life of the group. Similarly, while Simmel attributes primacy in theoretical and moral matters to the (inter-acting) individual, he analysed the body as a source of dispositions con-ducive to the formation of embryonic social forms which could stimulate in individuals socially binding emotions (Simmel, 1971 [1908a]). Simmel (1990 [1907]) also articulated how these forms could coalesce within the money economy into existentially suffocating structures that stimulate cyn-icism, reserve and a blasé attitude, while insisting that the physical vitalism of human life retains the potential to transcend existing forms (Simmel, 1971 [1918b]). Finally, while Marx combined elements from different the-oretical traditions in focusing on the relationship between social class, the marketplace of competitive individualism, and the possibilities of collective emancipation, he viewed the body as a source of economic relations and developed a deep concern with the destructive bodily effects of capitalism (Marx, 1975 [1844]; 1968 [1848]). These effects could 'fit' workers to restrictive jobs within the market place, but could also form the basis for class struggle and social change.

If we isolate what these analyses have in common, in order to make their convergence clearer, we can identify three similar elements in their views of the body. First, Marx, Durkheim and Simmel each suggest that the body possesses properties that are a *source* for the creation of social life. In con-trast to post-structuralist views of the embodied subject as 'a cultural arti-fact' (Harré, 1983: 20), this recognition of the body as a source of society insists that our bodily being is an active, generative phenomenon not totally given by the properties of society. More generally, what we can take from this idea that the body is a source of society is that the embodied subject is possessed of an intentional capacity for making a difference to the flow of daily life, and of socially creative capacities resulting from its sensory and mobile character which are not always directly accessible to individual con-sciousness. This notion of the body as a source of society suggests that there is a causal link travelling from basic human capacities towards social struc-tures that sometimes operates *irrespective* of the conscious intent and thought of the subject.

Second, the body also serves in part as a *location* for the structural prop-erties of society. Marx focuses on the structural properties of the economy, Durkheim on the structural properties of cultures, and Simmel on the 'structural' properties that are social forms, yet they each examine how these structures locate themselves on the bodies of subjects. They recognize that while society is built upon the embodied characteristics of humans, it cannot be explained on the basis of its existing bodily members and pos-sesses the power to 'react back' upon these bodies. Society stimulates and helps develop in us certain needs and abilities at the expense of others. It also sediments itself in the bodies of its members by encouraging appear-ances, habits and actions that can 'belie or override our conscious decisions and formal resolutions', and classifies as valid certain bodies while labelling others as deviant (Connerton, 1989: 72). More generally, this idea that the body is a location for society suggests that we need to take seriously a family of closely related ideas associated with the body being developmentally and physically shaped and constrained, temperamentally and dispositionally directed, presentationally managed, and actively encouraged to act in certain ways rather than others. Recognizing that the body is such a location, therefore, suggests that there is also a causal link travelling from society to the body, though not one of complete determination (the body does not lose all of its creative capacities simply because societal structures shape some of the dispositions and appearances of embodied subjects).

The third element in this analytical convergence between Durkheim, Simmel and Marx involves their acknowledgement that interaction between the body's generative capacities and the existing structures of society has important consequences for the subsequent development of both human potential and the social environment. The body is not only a source of and location for society, but is a vital *means* through which individuals are *positioned* within and *oriented towards* society. The sensory and sensual engagement of embodied subjects with the structural properties of social life can either attach them in particular ways to their environment, or distance them from it. These responses, and their resulting outcomes, re-form the body in ways which can either enhance or diminish people's potentialities, and Marx, Durkheim and Simmel each possess specific concerns about the effects of modernity on people's embodied character. This process of positioning – involving a physical attraction to, or revulsion from, social institutions – also constitutes the basis on which social systems persist or degenerate.

This approach to the body as a multi-dimensional medium for the constitution of society is developed in different ways, and through different terminologies, in the writings of Durkheim, Simmel and Marx. As I focus on them in this study, Marx is predominantly concerned with the structural properties of economic (including material/technological) factors, Durkheim with the structural characteristics of culture (including ritual and symbolic phenomena), and Simmel with the structural elements of society he refers to as 'social forms' (which pattern interaction). Nevertheless, it remains the case that each theorist views the body as a *source of*, a *location for* and a *means* by which individuals are emotionally and physically positioned within and oriented towards society. The notions of source, location and means are thus 'umbrella' terms, referring to a range of closely related concepts, but their general meaning and relational status are clear: they refer respectively to the generative properties of the body, to the social receptivity of the body, and to the body's centrality to the outcomes of interaction between (groups of) embodied individuals and the structural features of society.

The theoretical implications of this approach towards the body can be clarified further by exploring how it is based upon a version of what I shall refer to as *corporeal realism*. There is a long tradition of writings on realist philosophy and scientific method, a tradition which constitutes an influential (if internally differentiated) trend in the social sciences and which has been developed recently by Roy Bhaskar and others into forms of critical realism (for excellent introductions to key debates regarding realism, see Keat and Urry, 1982; Sayer, 2000). Some of these realist works have tended to marginalize the body, but if we take seriously the implications key realist principles have for the analysis of embodiment it is possible to explicate the central features of a corporeal realist approach towards the body–society relationship as outlined in the convergence thesis. In what follows, then, I am not concerned with engaging with the philosophical complexities of realism, or even with outlining here the full range of implications that realism could have for an analysis of the body, but with isolating in the briefest and simplest of terms its central features.[4] My reason for doing this is to help formalize and extend what is of value in the convergence thesis outlined above, and to provide a framework for the substantive studies that follow later in this study.

Corporeal realism

Corporeal realism is distinct from its realist counterparts insofar as it identifies the body–society relationship as the core subject matter of sociology. However, it is based on long-standing realist conceptions of (a) the ontologically stratified character of the relationship between the structural forces, institutions and roles which constitute society, on the one hand, and the people who inhabit society on the other; (b) the need for a temporal element to social analysis (which enables one to analyse the interaction over time of the generative properties of the body and the constraining features of society without reducing one to the other); and (c) the potentially critical import of this approach towards social analysis. I shall deal with each of these in turn.

First, corporeal realism has at its centre an ontologically stratified view of the world which insists that the body and society exist as real things, that cannot be dissolved into discourse, possessed of causally generative properties. Dealing with society first, while corporeal realism positions the body as central to its concerns, it recognizes social structures as *emergent* phenomena. Society consists of economic classes, bureaucracies, legally sanctioned roles, and social norms, for example, that contain properties that are fundamentally different from the desires and actions of embodied subjects. People do not create anew the society in which they live, but confront it as a given structure and are 'always acting in a world of structural constraints and possibilities that they did not produce' (Bhaskar, 1998: xvi). A nation's language, demographic structure, housing stock, available sources of energy, and levels of road congestion, for example, pre-exist each new generation and set the parameters in which bodily development, action, and health/illness occurs. This is why Margaret Archer (1995: 135) refers to society as a 'vexatious fact', a description of its facticity which draws on Comte's recognition that the majority of actors are dead and Marx's argument that the legacy of past generations weighs heavily on the actions of the living. The extant features of society do not simply include the structural conditions in which embodied action occurs, but include cultural norms and values that can potentially shape the behaviour of the generations that confront them. If we accept the premise that humans possess a relatively weak instinctual structure and are biologically 'unfinished' to a greater extent than other animals, it is possible to see how we are predisposed towards and require social norms and structures to survive and prosper (Honneth and Joas, 1988). This means that the body has to be conceptualized, in part, as a location for societal structures.

Recognizing society as an emergent phenomenon does not, however, marginalize the significance of the embodied subject in the body–society relationship. Just because the body is a location for the pre-existing structural parts of society does not mean that embodied subjects can be reduced to society or lose their capacities for creative action. As Andrew Sayer (2000: 13) notes, 'the interaction of the social with the physical' still 'needs to be acknowledged'. This can be accomplished, in line with the realist espousal of a stratified ontology, by insisting that the embodied subject, and not just society, is an emergent phenomenon (Archer, 2000). Thus, in contrast to socio-biologists (who reduce individuals to the status of 'survival machines' for genetic matter; Dawkins, 1976), or evolutionary psychologists (who hold that our behaviour is 'hard wired' as a result of selective pressures that impart the brain with a particular modular architecture adapted to the needs of survival), corporeal realism also insists on viewing the *embodied subject* as an emergent, causally consequent phenomenon and an important objects of analysis *in its own right*.[5] It is important to elaborate briefly on the basis on which this judgement is made.

The case for recognizing the body as an emergent, socially generative phenomenon is crucial to the viability of corporeal realism. While recognizing that the human body is made up of distinctive parts (genes, blood, bones, etc.), this approach insists that its actions cannot be reduced to these parts. This is because the embodied subject is possessed not only of a physical boundary and a metabolic network, but of feelings, dispositions and an embodied consciousness which emerge through its evolution and development as an organism and which together enable humans to intervene in and make a difference to their environment, to exercise *agency* (Capra, 2002). Even Darwin viewed the physical organism *as a whole* as the basic unit of evolutionary competition. This conception of the embodied subject contrasts with cognitive conceptions of the individual that prioritize the thinking mind to the exclusion of the feeling body, and is concerned to highlight how the basic, often pre- or non-conscious, bodily conditions of existence and propensities (given to us by evolutionary processes which change only slowly in the *longue durée* of human existence; Braudel, 1973) may be an enduring source of certain structures. Marx, Durkheim and Simmel did not have access to contemporary biological research and evolutionary thinking, but they each recognized the body as an emergent phenomenon that

is central to the generation of society. They held that the fundamental physical make-up and physiological properties of human being provide us with
both the need and the capacities to intervene in and mould our natural and
social environment in certain ways, and that the physical dispositions and
habits we acquire while engaging in such activities are consequential for the
viability of existing social structures. This means that the establishment and
endurance of particular structures are likely to be affected by the affinity, or
lack of affinity, they possess with the conditions of human embodiment. It
is no accident, for example, that every known human society that has
existed for any length of time has produced patterns of work and sociability, tools and other technologies, games or sporting rituals, and music: these
structures exist, albeit in widely different forms, because they possess a
deeply rooted foundation in bodily needs and capacities. As I shall explore
later in this book, their existence and longevity are connected inescapably to
people's embodied capacities, and make it necessary to conceptualize the
body not just as a location for, but as a generative source of society.[6]

The first key element of corporeal realism, then, is the idea that in dealing with the body–society relationship we are dealing with emergent,
causally consequential phenomenon. Structures and embodied subjects are
not identical: the former are often crystallized within social roles, legal codes
and material artefacts, for example, and these possess very different properties than the people upon whose actions their future depends (Bhaskar,
1989: 35; Archer, 1998: 200). Theories of the body–society relationship
should not seek to account for the body exclusively in terms of its social
construction, or for society in terms of its corporeal construction. As structures contain emergent properties, it is just as unacceptable to analyse and
explain them purely with reference to the actions of living individuals (as in
rational choice theory) as it is to account for the beliefs and actions of individuals exclusively with reference to structures (as in structuralism).

The second and third key elements of corporeal realism can be summarized much more briefly. Second, this approach entails that in order to avoid
analytically conflating what are different types of phenomena, it is important to incorporate a *temporal component* to social analysis (Archer, 1988,
1995). This means that if we want to understand the relationship between
embodied actors and society, it is necessary not only (a) to identify how the
body may be generatively associated with the emergence of social structures; but also trace over time (b) how established structures form a context
for embodied action and have the potential to shape people's bodily actions
and habits; and (c) how the generative capacities of embodied subjects actually interact with these structures and either reproduce or transform them
(and therefore establish the conditions in which the next generation of bodies develops, senses and acts). Existing research on the body may limit our
capacity to reproduce this temporal dimension in its totality. Nevertheless,
any corporeal realist interrogation of literature on the subject can be sensitive to which of these temporal elements is addressed by discussions of the
body and can evaluate these discussions accordingly.

Third, I want to suggest that corporeal realism can and should be *critical*. In this respect, the recent development of a specifically critical realism by Bhaskar has been concerned mostly with the valuation of *cognitive* truths, and of uncovering those institutions and conditions that give rise to false beliefs or that undermine the individual's capacity to engage in the process of communication and the pursuit of truth (Bhaskar, 1989). However, such criteria are insufficiently attentive to the body. As Caroline New (2003: 60) points out, 'It is not only because health', for example, 'is conducive to *discourse* that we value it … It is rather because health, and other goods, are relevant to human flourishing in a wider sense; to all sorts of agency, not only the capacity to communicate discursively.' While it may be difficult to agree on a specific notion of human flourishing, the minimal principles underlying the critical criteria informing corporeal realism involve the avoidance of harm to the embodied subject. As Sayer (2000) argues:

> It is not unreasonable to argue that some acts are wrong because they involve damage to biological and psychological powers … for example, lobotomy or clitorectomy can be argued to be wrong on the grounds that removing organs or parts of them deprives victims of important biologically based capacities, which contribute to human flourishing and happiness.

In conclusion, this approach to the body as a multi-dimensional medium for the constitution of society is *corporeal* because it puts the body at the centre of its concern with social action and structures. Social action is embodied, and must be recognized as such, while the effects of social structures can be seen as a result of how they condition and shape embodied subjects. This approach is also *realist* as it recognizes a distinction between (embodied) action and social structures (by attributing bodies with their own ontology, irreducible to society), and because it acknowledges the importance of examining their interaction over time. The fact that Marx, Durkheim and Simmel all feature prominently in my explication of this approach does not compromise its realism. The significance of emergence and interaction has been firmly established in the cases of Marx and Durkheim (Collier, 1998; Creaven, 2000; Sawyer, 2002), although these exist alongside radically different interpretations of their work, and I shall suggest in Chapter 2 that it also characterizes Simmel's writings despite prevailing views of him as a methodological individualist. Each are concerned with the structural properties (of the economy/technology, of culture, and of social forms) that constitute society, and recognize that these properties emerge from, but are irreducible to and can react back upon, their embodied creators. Finally, this view of the body as a multi-dimensional medium is also critical because it is concerned with evaluating the effects particular societies have on human potentiality. Marx, Durkheim and Simmel do not converge in their assessment of the precise effects of the rationalized world of capitalism on embodied subjects. Marx was predominantly concerned with how the social inequalities and oppressions surrounding the economic system stunted embodied human potential. Durkheim was interested in how participation within a cultural community could enable individuals to transcend the ego-istic pole of their *homo duplex* nature and become moral beings possessed of socially enhanced capacities. Simmel's concern was with the development of individuality and sociality, and he was acutely conscious of the ambiva-lent effects that social forms had on the flourishing of personality. Nevertheless, each of them sensitizes us to issues that are of great impor-tance in arriving at a critical assessment of the relationship between the body and society.[7]

Dominant Theories of the Body

This corporeal realist approach to the body as a multi-dimensional medium for the constitution of society provides a powerful resource for the field, but extracting it from the writings of classical figures requires a considerable work of reconstruction. Despite the importance of the body, the main con-cerns of Marx, Durkheim and Simmel revolved around modern industrial society. This is why the body still sometimes faded within their writings to an absent presence (Shilling, 1993), and why it was possible for Parsons to suppress the status of the body in their work and for it to lie dormant as an object of study for so long. In this context, the third aim of this book is to provide a critical overview and interrogation of the most important recent approaches towards the subject.

Having dealt with the centrifugal tendencies central to the rise of inter-est in the body, this moves us to the centripetal trend in this area. For all its diversity, three theoretical approaches have emerged as dominant forms of explanation within the field of body studies. While none of them manages to hold onto the view of the body as a multi-dimensional medium for the constitution of society, they do provide us with an unprecedented focus on the body as the apparent object of study. Furthermore, despite their enor-mous differences, they each express a deep concern about the fate of the embodied subject in the contemporary era that reinforces and builds on the concerns of Marx, Durkheim and Simmel, and warrants further investiga-tion. Social constructionist analyses of the *ordered body*, action or phenom-enologically oriented approaches towards the *lived body*, and conceptions of the body in *structuration theory* now represent the most influential ways in which the social significance of the body has been conceptualized. They also continue to set agendas which steer much writing in this area yet, ulti-mately, serve to increase still further the elusiveness of the body.

Social constructionist analyses of the ordered body view human physi-cality as an object produced and regulated by political, normative and dis-cursive regimes. They focus on the body as a location for society, implying that it is only through such an approach that we can appreciate the over-whelming structuring powers of the social system. Studies which developed this view did much to initiate and consolidate the form taken by the corpo-real turn in social theory. Thus, Bryan Turner's (1984) structuralist *The Body and Society*, and later post-structuralist studies such as Judith Butler's

(1990) *Gender Trouble* and (1993) *Bodies that Matter*, established the *governmental management* of the body as key to the external environment in which social action occurs. The influence of Michel Foucault is readily apparent in such studies. Foucault (1977) conceives of the body as 'the inscribed surface of events' and as 'totally imprinted by history'. There are no irreducible 'essences' that define people's identity or actions for all time, just 'inscriptions' of identity which change over time.

Theorists concerned with the governmental environment in which the body is controlled have not relied exclusively on Foucault, but combined his insights and methods with those of other thinkers. Turner's (1984) study, for example, is heavily steered by Parsons and Hobbes as well as by Foucault. Similarly, Butler's (1993) concern with the 'heterosexual matrix', which positioned the body as an object and target of gendered power relationships, drew on Austin and Althusser in arguing that individuals are 'hailed' to perform particular subject positions. Despite their common interest in how the body is governed, then, such theorists directed their analyses, via an array of writers, towards a variety of subjects including sexual and 'racial' difference, medicine, and the performativity of identity (e.g. Diamond and Quinby, 1988; Sawicki, 1991; Case et al., 1995; Turner, 1995; Gatens, 1996; Phelan, 1997; Richardson, 2000). Social constructionist analyses tend to be united, however, by a political concern with the subjugation of bodily diversity and creativity in the contemporary era.

These theories were effective in illuminating how the body was ordered and inscribed by power relations, but frequently remained silent about how the body could be a source of the social, and about the 'lived experience' of embodied action. They also tended to erase any ontological existence the body had apart from society, thus making it impossible to evaluate institutions in terms of their beneficial or detrimental effects on the body. In response to this lacuna, the 1990s witnessed a rise in studies about 'the body's own experience of its embodiment' which viewed the opportunities and constraints of action as given by the 'problems of bodies themselves' (Frank, 1991: 43). Drew Leder's (1990) focus on the lived experience of instrumentally rational action is an important example of this genre. His conception of the 'absent body' suggests that the body ordinarily 'fades' and 'disappears' from our experience when we are engaged in purposeful action, yet abruptly reappears as a focus of attention when we are ill or in pain. In contrast, Iris Marion Young's (1980, 1998: 147–8) feminist phenomenology highlights the daily foregrounding of the female body within patriarchal societies in a manner which ladens women's bodies with immanence, while Arthur Frank (1995) has drawn on experiential accounts of the prominence of the body during illness in analysing how a 'pedagogy of suffering' can result in a new ethics of relating to others.

Accounts such as these drew on phenomenology, on existentialist and on interactionist resources, to portray the body as a *source* of society. It is the phenomenology of Merleau-Ponty, however, that has been most influential in shaping calls for a 'carnal sociology', the founding assumption of which being that '"self", "society" and "symbolic order" are constituted through the work of the body' (Crossley, 1995: 43). For Merleau-Ponty (1962: 136), embodied subjects develop direction and purpose on the basis of the practical engagements they have with their surroundings and through the intentionality they develop as a result of the situatedness of embodied existence. This emphasis on the determining rather than determined nature of our embodiment, and on the universal bodily basis of meaning and knowledge, constitutes a major challenge to structuralist and post-structuralist theories. Despite its ostensible focus on the 'lived body', however, there is a paradox within phenomenology. Having been interpreted as analysing how people experience their bodies, this tradition is actually concerned with the bodily basis of experience. As Leder's (1990) study illustrates, it is quite possible, therefore, for the body to fade away within a phenomenological account of people's practical experiences of the world. What I find fascinating about Leder's study, though, is that its focus on the normal body as a latent, disappearing body can be interpreted as a comment on the fate of the body under the instrumental rationality that is so dominant within modernity. In this context, his study can be read as a work that raises fundamental concerns about the body's fading significance within modernity and, to this extent, has limited parallels with its social constructionist counterparts.

These analyses of the ordered and 'lived' bodies provided the field with alternative lines of development, but replicated what many saw as a long-standing and debilitating division between theories of structure and agency (Dawe, 1970, 1979). Structuration theories developed as a means of overcoming this opposition. Based on assumptions about the mutually constituting nature of social structures and actions, the body was central to structuration theory's vision of society. Pierre Bourdieu and Anthony Giddens are the most influential proponents of this theory of social life, while Elizabeth Grosz provides us with a different, feminist analysis of the mutual constitution of the body and dominant norms of sexuality. Despite their differences, each of these theorists claimed that the body was a recipient of social practices *and* an active creator of its milieu. In Bourdieu's theory of social reproduction, the body is shaped by, yet also reproduces, class inequalities. The embodied dispositions that people acquire during their upbringing 'continuously transform necessities into strategies, [and] constraints into preferences' (Bourdieu, 1984: 190). Giddens's (1991) conception of 'high modernity' provides us with a different version of how the body and the social principles characteristic of society are mutually determining: the contingency of the contemporary social world is incorporated into and reinforced by the contingency of the body. Grosz's (1994) view of the sexual body as both constituting and constituted is again quite different. Using the topographical image of the Möbius strip (the inverted three-dimensional figure eight), she explores how the body provides a morphological basis for sexual difference, yet is also structured (both internally and externally) by the inscriptive powers of sexual norms.

Structuration theories provide us with a 'middle way' between social constructionist accounts of governmentality and phenomenological accounts of 'lived experience'. The body, in short, is a means through which individuals are attached to, or ruptured from, society. Whether they provide us with viable alternatives, however, is questionable. While Bourdieu (1984: 466) asserts the facts of changing bodily dispositions, his argument that the *habitus* operates at the level of the subconscious makes it difficult to see how individuals can escape from the dispositional trajectory assigned to them. The emphasis Giddens places on changeability and reflexivity, in contrast, invests the body with an unlikely 'lightness of being'; it is a durable resource rather than a frail, inescapable part of existence, and can be reinvented by the individual alongside their reflexively constituted narratives of self. Finally, despite her concern to identify possibilities for change, Grosz's focus on the body's sexual specificity, and the additional 'investments of difference' made by society into the interiors and exteriors of bodies, seems to ensure the continuation of opposing male and female identities. Putting these difficulties aside for a while, however, each of these analyses can be interpreted as raising, once more, deep concerns about the body's productive capacities. For Bourdieu, Giddens and Grosz, the body has become subordinated respectively to the imperatives of social class, cognitive reflexivity and sexual difference.

Mediating Theories, Mediating Bodies

Social constructionist theories of the governed body, action and phenomenological accounts of the lived body, and structuration theories have provided us with systematic theoretical alternatives, demonstrated the ubiquity of the body as a subject, and imparted to the field an identity. These are considerable achievements. However, their opposed ontological and epistemological assumptions served ultimately to increase the body's elusiveness. They variously demanded of the body that it justify the argument that society constructs what are normatively presented to us as 'natural' identities, that the body is the seat of all experience, and that social structures are absorbed and actively reproduced by embodied subjects. While focusing variously on the body as a location for, as a source of, and as a means for the positioning of individuals within their environment, none allows room for the embodied subject's multi-dimensional implication in all three of these processes. It is one thing to acknowledge the body's importance as a location on which the structures of society inscribe themselves, as a vehicle through which society is constructed, or as circuit which connects individuals with society, but any comprehensive theory of the body needs to take account of *all three* of these processes.

More constructively, each of these dominant contemporary approaches contains important insights about the body's implication in the modern world by raising deep concerns about the loss of significance and creativity of the embodied subject. As such, these writings suggest there is a need for substantive studies which assess whether contemporary developments in society really are subjugating the embodied subject. Thus, while the classical convergence around a form of corporeal realism provides a valuable framework through which to undertake substantive investigations of the body, the overt concerns of more recent approaches, as well as those evident in the writings of Marx, Durkheim and Simmel, can usefully steer the direction of these studies.

Exploring Bodies

The three dimensions of the body's status as a medium for the constitution of society identified in this chapter have been treated separately for analytical purposes in order to clarify the corporeal realist approach adopted in this study. They should not be considered mutually exclusive options or totally separate 'functions' of the body, but constitute instead co-existing moments in, or dimensions of, an ongoing process that manifests itself over time. The advantage of corporeal realism is that it provides us with an analytical way of gaining access to and examining the flux of socio-natural life. It is the erasure of certain of these dimensions of the body that results in the various forms of reductionism that afflict the dominant contemporary approaches examined above and, more generally, is why neither naturalistic views of the body nor their social constructionist alternatives can provide adequate conceptions of the relationship between the body and society (Shilling, 2003).[8] Recognizing the body's significance as a multi-dimensional medium for the constitution of society is, of course, only a starting point for further analysis. The balance between these ongoing aspects of its existence as a source, location and means undoubtedly shifts over time depending on a number of variables. A truly comprehensive analysis of these factors, furthermore, will require detailed biological and evolutionary investigations, as well as sociological analysis, into the generative properties of the body. Sociologists can certainly take these into account, by recognizing them and refusing to overlook their significance, but will almost inevitably have more to say about the effects of society on the body. There is nothing wrong with this. Corporeal realist analyses can start with and concentrate on society as long as they do not analytically collapse what is physical, material and biological about the body with social structures. It is also absolutely vital to recognize that the bodies of different groups of people are variously generative of and receptive to societal structures. An appreciation of social stratification is as important to body studies as it is to social theory more generally. The bodies of men and women, white people and black people, able-bodied and those characterized by physical disabilities, and adults and children, for example, have long been differently positioned within society. Such issues feature in subsequent chapters.

Chapters 2 and 3 develop the theoretical groundwork for this book by establishing in more detail the convergence thesis in the writings of Marx,

Durkheim and Simmel, and by interrogating the disparate theories of, and common concerns raised by, contemporary approaches to the body. Having established a case for a corporeal realist view of the body as a multi-dimensional medium for the constitution of society, Chapters 4–8 investigate the concerns evident in recent studies by undertaking a series of substantive analyses into the relationship between the body and various societal structures. Each chapter is organized into sections which reflect the distinctions made by corporeal realism and deals sequentially with the body as a source of, a location for, and a means of positioning the body within, society. This allows me to provide an overview of and to analyse those writings which concentrate on one or other of these features of the body, while making it clear that none provides the whole picture of the body–society relationship. Each chapter then concludes with an assessment of whether the concerns raised by recent studies are valid by asking if developments in the contemporary era really are subjugating the capacities and potentialities of human subjects.

These substantively informed discussions consist of broad general overviews and assessments. They draw on the mountain of body relevant work published in recent years, but place these studies within, and interpret them on the basis of, a realist schema which facilitates substantive analysis of the interaction between the embodied subject and society. Individual chapters analyse Working Bodies, Sporting Bodies, Musical Bodies, Sociable Bodies, and Technological Bodies. I have chosen these subjects as they constitute important issues in their own right (with music, in particular, being a subject that has been unjustifiably marginalized in the area), and because they cover the economic/technological, cultural and social concerns of those classical theorists whose work has been drawn on in establishing the convergence thesis central to this study. Finally, Chapter 9 concludes by explicating the consequences of this study for future empirical research and for the concerns of recent theories about the fate of the body in Western societies. The body has served as an enormously productive focus for theoretical and empirical work over the past two decades, but this has resulted in an increasingly fragmented field of studies. In this context, the conclusion makes the case for a consolidation of body studies around an agenda that can impart a greater degree of coherence to the subject.

Notes

1   Apart from those who have sought to construct an area of body studies (e.g. Turner, 1984; Frank, 1991; Synnott, 1993; Shilling, 1993), publications have highlighted the social and medical consequences of interactions between culture and biology (e.g. Hirst and Woolley, 1982; Freund, 1982; Turner, 1991a; Wilkinson, 1996, 2000; Elstad, 1998; Newton, 2003a, 2003b; Williams et al., 2003; Williams, 2003a, 2003b), the structural, communicative, political and interpretive dimensions of embodiment (e.g. Johnson, 1983; O'Neill, 1985), and genealogies of contemporary forms of embodiment (Feher et al., 1989; Laqueur, 1990; Sennett, 1994; Sawday, 1995; Hillman and Mazzio, 1997; Mellor and Shilling, 1997). In addition, feminist and post-modernist writings have examined the power relationships surrounding female and male patterns of embodiment, while theorists have sought to construct a new body ethics (e.g.

Butler, 1990, 1993; Diprose, 1994; Grosz, 1994; Frank, 1995; Kirby, 1997; Shildrick, 2002). Others have studied the senses and the embodied nature of emotions (e.g. Scarry, 1985; Howes, 1991; Classen, 1993; Bendelow and Williams, 1998; Burkitt, 1999; Craib, 1997; Shilling, 2002), and critically interrogated traditional Western conceptions of the mind/body relationship (Burkitt, 1991, 1999, 2002; Crossley, 2001). There has been a flourishing of work on the relationships between ageing, masculinity, femininity and the body (Davis, 1995; Featherstone and Wernick, 1995; Connell, 1995; Peterson, 1997; Watson, 2000), on health, illness, disability, reproductive genetics and the body (e.g. Turner, 1995; Freund and McGuire, 1991; Peterson and Bunton, 2001; Seymour, 1998; Ettorre, 2002), and on the 'lived experience' of the body subject (e.g. Young, 1980, 1998; Crossley, 1995, 2001; Wacquant, 1995; Nettleton and Watson, 1998; Ahmed and Stacey, 2001). Other writings have examined the medical management of bodies (Martin, 1987, 1994), cultural geographies of embodiment (e.g. Rodaway, 1994; Ainley, 2001; Bale and Philo, 1998; Nast and Pile, 1998), the bodily bases of community and religion (e.g. Bynum, 1987; Brown, 1988; Mellor and Shilling, 1994; Coakley, 1997), post-colonial bodies (Ahmed, 2000; Holliday and Hassard, 2001), and the embodiment of philosophy (e.g. Burkitt, 1999; Lakoff and Johnson, 1999). There has also been a rapidly growing interest in the consequences of biotechnologies for self-identity (e.g. Haraway, 1994 [1985]; Heim, 1992; Kimbrell, 1993; Featherstone and Burrows, 1995).

2   Although it does not deal with the body, Levine's (2000) article on newly identified convergences in the writings of classical sociologists illustrates how productive it can be to pinpoint areas of agreement and consensus between apparently incommensurate writings.

3   Weber contends with Simmel as *the* theorist of rationalization, but Simmel's (1990 [1907]) analysis of the money economy lays realistic claim to being an unparalleled study of the effects of rationalization on modern human personality (see Turner, 1986). Furthermore, while Weber tends to denigrate affectual and habitual action, Simmel places more value on the socially productive effects of bodily contents and drives.

4   As my concern is with outlining the basic principles of what I refer to as corporeal realism in order to facilitate substantively informed analyses of the body, a further, more detailed, exposition of this approach will be the subject of a future study. In terms of existing work that contributes to the construction of a corporeal realism, Margaret Archer's (2000) *Being Human* provides us with the most developed example of this type of approach. Distinctive approaches towards the development of corporeal realism can be found in the writings of such figures as Benton (1991), Doyal and Gough (1991), Soper (1995) and New (2003). The realist approach has also gained ground in neurology as well as in medical sociology and other areas in a manner which suggests that a broadly corporeal realist approach towards the body–society relationship may become increasingly influential in the future (e.g. Sawyer, 2001). In the area of medical sociology, for example, the application of Bhaskar's and Archer's writings to the issues of health, illness and the body appears to be gaining significant influence (e.g. see Wainwright and Forbes, 2000; Scambler and Scambler, 2003; Williams, 2003).

5   Evolutionary psychology is currently the most influential naturalistic approach towards the body and has sparked furious debate between its proponents and social scientists. While the former dismiss sociological explanation by inaccurately suggesting that there exists a Standard Social Science Model which views the mind as a blank sheet on which culture imprints its patterns oblivious to the effects of evolution, some of its opponents seem to reject even the possibility that *any* elements of our behaviour might be 'hard-wired' as a result of evolutionary influence. Prominent contributions and overviews to this debate include Segerstrale (2000) and the collection edited by Rose and Rose (2000). In recent years, however, recognition of the importance of biology and evolution by sociologists working inside and outside of the sociology of the body (e.g. Elias, 2000 [1939]; 1991a, 1991b; Hirst and Woolley, 1982; Freund, 1982; Benton, 1991; Shilling, 1993; Birke, 1999; Burkitt, 1999) have at least placed these issues on the sociological agenda. This is reflected by the recent sociological collection by Williams, Birke and Bendelow (2003) entitled *Debating Biology*.

6   Corporeal realism does not entail the assertion that everybody's body is absolutely

identical, but does require us to accept that similarly embodied humans share certain physical powers and socially generative capacities. Nor, as I shall emphasize shortly, does it rule out the idea that bodily potentials are mediated by society. It is simplistic and unhelpful to suggest that we have to conceptualize the body–society relationship as governed either by biological essentialism or by social constructionism (Shilling, 1993, 2003; Sayer, 2000).

7   Durkheim's concern with community and Simmel's interest in individuality can be viewed as complementary rather than contradictory if we accept Durkheim's point that individuality can be enhanced via incorporation into the collectivity, but also recognize Simmel's point that too much immersion in a collectivity can blunt the individuality of the subject. Durkheim and Simmel may analyse the individual–society relationship from different starting points, but Durkheim also recognized, in his studies on suicide and the division of labour, the problems for individuals when their identities became submerged within that of the collectivity.

8   Naturalistic views perceive the biological body as a source of identity and society, immune to the influence of social, cultural or technological factors. As such, they are unable to appreciate the body as a location for non-corporeal processes or, as a result of being unable to recognize the social environment's interaction within the body, as a means through which individuals are positioned within and oriented towards society. Social constructionist views also fail, but for the different reason that they view the body as an empty vessel filled, and even created, by the determining forces of society. While focusing on the body as a location, such approaches are unable to appreciate its significance as a source of society, or, as a result of not being able to recognize the physical body's interaction with society, as a means by which people are positioned within and oriented towards the environment.

2

Classical Bodies

This chapter advances the thesis that it is not only possible to develop significant approaches to the body–society relationship from the writings of classical social thinkers, but that several of the most important of these thinkers converged around a theory of human embodiment as a *multi-dimensional medium for the constitution of society*. This theoretical approach, I argue, is underpinned by a form of corporeal realism, a realism that resides at the heart of what are otherwise very different visions of social life yet which allows us to examine the interaction between bodies and society. Such an approach to the interaction of bodies and society can be characterized as highlighting a partial process of mutual determination between human physicality and the social environment. However, it also insists that the 'flesh' and cultural/economic/social structures each possess distinctive properties which means that neither can be reduced to the other.

If we wish to understand how this convergence has remained hidden from contemporary theorists, and what is required for us to recover its various dimensions, it is necessary to appreciate the enormous impact that Thomas Hobbes and Talcott Parsons exerted on the foundations and content of sociology. Hobbes shaped the intellectual context in which the philosophical foundations underpinning sociology were established. He conceptualized the 'problem of order' that preoccupied the discipline (the problem of how it is that individuals can live together without social life degenerating into violent chaos) 'with a clarity which has never been surpassed' (Parsons, 1968 [1937]: 93), and sought a solution to it by proposing a thoroughly corporeal conception of social science. Parsons, in contrast, did much to forge the modern content and direction of sociology by developing an alternative, normative solution to the problem of order, and by arguing that there already existed a sociological tradition that rejected Hobbes's concern with bodily passions in favour of a more realistic focus on common *value* integration.

I begin by examining Hobbes's and Parsons's diametrically opposed visions of social analysis, before explicating the convergence thesis that lies at the heart of this chapter by focusing on the writings of Karl Marx, Emile Durkheim and Georg Simmel. These authors have produced major works, frequently cited as central to the sociological tradition, which are usually seen as incommensurate. They emerge from different philosophical backgrounds, are articulated through distinct terminologies, espouse separate visions of society, and therefore constitute a stringent test for the demonstration of convergence. Marx's work is marked by the optimism of a revolutionary seeking to 'anchor the quest for transcendent freedom in worldly realities' (Levine, 1995: 221). Durkheim's is based on an organic model of collective life, central to French thought, in which society enables individuals to override their egoistic dispositions within a moral community. Simmel's analyses reflect a German philosophical focus on the individual's capacities for self-directed action, and a melancholy associated with what he sees as the 'tragic' character of modern life. Despite these very significant differences, Marx, Durkheim and Simmel each position the body as methodologically key to the relationship between social action and society, and each work (implicitly or explicitly) with a *homo duplex* model of embodiment which allows them to recognize the body as an ontologically stratified phenomenon which cannot be reduced to society. In what follows, I focus on how Marx highlights the importance of the relationship between the body and economics/technology, on how Durkheim focuses on the body and culture, and on how Simmel explicates the relationship between the body and sociality. In each case, the body is viewed as a *source* of these dimensions of society, as a *location* on which the effects of society are inscribed, and as a *means* through which these agentic and structural processes interact, position people within, and orientate them towards, society.

From Corporeal Social Science to Normative Sociology

The story of modern social theory's dealings with the body starts with Hobbes, a thinker whose influence is such that it has been suggested that 'all the philosophical traditions that undergird the disciplines of modern social science ... consist of elaborations, revisions, or replacements of the Hobbesian conception of social science' (Levine, 1995: 121). Writing in the aftermath of civil war in England, Hobbes extended to the whole of social life the Galilean view that the universe consisted of a field of atomic motions. In so doing, he proposed a corporeal social science which began by conceiving the dispositions and capacities of the human body in terms of perpetual *movements* and natural *passions*. The individual constituted a 'body in motion', and the 'essential natural feature' of humans was not their potential for nobility, justice or rationality, but 'the appetites and aversions that motivate their actions', sustain thought, and determine intellectual and moral character (Gardiner et al., 1937: 184; Hobbes, 1962 [1650]; Levine, 1995: 272). In particular, the two primary passions that informed human bodies-in-motion were 'a perpetual and restless desire for power' and the concern to avoid violent death (Hobbes, 1914 [1651]). It is these passions of self-aggrandizement and self-preservation that account for Hobbes's depiction of the 'state of nature', and explain the necessity for, and the eventual emergence of, civil society.

The social outcome of the first major human passion, the desire for self-aggrandizing power, was mediated by the essential *scarcity* of resources. This scarcity meant that while many individuals 'have an appetite for the same thing', in the 'state of nature' it is only the 'strongest' who can possess it. This situation brings about conflict and, eventually, anarchy. Embodied life is governed by ceaseless competition, 'griefe' rather than 'pleasure', a 'desire to hurt' and a 'Warre of every one against every one' in which 'every man has a Right to every thing: even to another's body' (Hobbes, 1914 [1651]: 64–7; 1962 [1650]: 114–15; 1991 [1658]: 40). If the first major bodily passion leads to an instinctual hell, however, the passion for self-preservation inclines people to transfer their power to an absolute sovereign and thus to institute an 'artificial body which provides the framework in which the real bodies of men can find security and peace' (Turner, 1984: 88). This is Hobbes's utilitarian solution to the problem of order and, with the institution of this absolute sovereign, his conception of social science as an analysis of the relationship between individual bodies and the social body was complete. The social implications of this corporeal science were as devastating as they were clear: given the unchangeable properties of the human body, any realistic conception of the 'good society' could not concern itself with realizing the 'highest potentialities of humans', but had to restrict itself to 'the ways and means of creating a state free from warfare' (Levine, 1995: 127).

Having formulated the problem of order with such power and simplicity, Hobbes's writings proved hugely influential. Subsequent British, French and German conceptions of social science felt obliged to attempt to refute his work. Furthermore, many actually followed Hobbes in positioning the body at the very centre of social science, even if they proposed very different conceptions of human nature. Hobbes's formulations went against the dominant Cartesian strand in Western philosophy, however, and increasingly became a *negative* referent against which apparently more productive rules for social analysis could be developed. It was in this context that Parsons's construction of a sociological tradition attributed to the body a very different, marginal status.

Parsons argued that Hobbes's relevance for sociology lay in providing the classic statement of the problem of order (which remained relevant to the discipline), and the utilitarian solution to this problem (which was unworkable and did not remain relevant to the discipline). The implications that Parsons took from this critique of utilitarianism proved particularly damaging for the position of the body within sociology. Utilitarianism suggests that individuals are essentially slaves to their passions, the ends of which are random, and that they seek to maximize (through a limited, self-interested form of rational action) acquiring the goals of their passions. Having characterized the embodied individual as driven by passions, however, Parsons points out that utilitarianism has to introduce elements outside of its core assumptions in order to account for social order (Parsons, 1968 [1937]: 92). Hobbes's own solution 'involves stretching, at a crucial point, the conception of rationality beyond its scope in the rest of theory, to the point where the actors come to realize the situation as a whole instead of pursuing their own ends' and agree to transfer power to a sovereign (ibid.). This leads Parsons (1968 [1937]: 93–4) to argue that 'a purely utilitarian society' would be chaotic, unstable and could not be realized in reality. He goes on to conclude that utilitarianism could not account for empirically existing cases of social order, and that its corporeal starting point must, therefore, be mistaken.

Parsons's engagement with the Hobbesian problem of order, which has been widely criticized for its interpretive inaccuracies, led him to expel the body from the core features of his account of the individual–society relationship. This expulsion, Parsons argued, was entirely consistent with previous writings in the sociological tradition: Durkheim and Weber (and also Pareto and Marshall) shared the view that social order was achieved through the existence of a common value system. They used different terminologies to express this view, and analysed different aspects of this value system, but each developed the 'outline of what *in all essentials*, is the same system of generalised social theory' (Parsons, 1968 [1937]: 719). Durkheim developed the insight that individuals acted on the basis of moral obligation, for example, while Weber's analysis of the Protestant ethic focused on the value elements in human action.

Parsons's marginalization of the body from the history of sociology was maintained in his own conception of sociology as the study of voluntary (rather than embodied) action that took place in relation to the dominant norms of a society. This is exemplified by what he considered the key concept in sociology, the 'unit act'. As John Scott (1995: 35–6) summarizes, 'the unit act is the sociological equivalent of the particle in classical mechanics. It is … the most elementary way of conceptualising human action and the building block for larger systems of action' and provides us with the basis of Parsons's anti-Hobbesian view of the individual–society relationship. The unit act consists of five elements. These include an *actor*, an *end* (a 'future state of affairs toward which the … action is oriented'), situational *means* over which the actor has control, and situational *conditions* which are not controllable (Parsons, 1968 [1937]: 44). Finally, and most importantly, the means employed by the actor in order to reach a particular end are not chosen at random but are guided by *norms* (ibid.). As Parsons (ibid.: 45) concludes, 'What is essential to the concept of action is that there should be a normative orientation.'

The body is almost invisible in this formulation. It is confined to being part of the hereditary conditions of action and is made residual in relation to Parsons's key concern with normative action. Parsons is concerned with the *subjective* understandings of the actor and the extent to which norms enter into that understanding, while action no longer occurs as a result of bodily passions or dispositions but as choices motivated by social norms (Parsons, 1968 [1937]: 47; 1951: 541–2, 547–8). Specifically, action concerns 'those aspects of human behaviour … involved in or controlled by culturally structured symbolic codes' (Levine, 1991: 192). Parsons's rejection of corporeal social science is complete. Sociology should concern itself with culturally patterned actions, egos and selves, while the physical organism (conceived of as merely a limiting condition to human life) should be left to the biological and physical sciences.

The Body as a Multi-Dimensional Medium for the Constitution of Society

Parsons did more than any other figure in the history of the discipline to identify a 'sociological tradition' and frame the major problems that shaped sociology during the twentieth century. It is frequently assumed that his legacy is no longer significant for a discipline that is now more concerned with difference, diversity and conflict than it is with norms, values and social systems (Shilling and Mellor, 2001). However, the body has yet to be included fully within sociology. In particular, while various attempts have been made to recover the subject for the discipline, the writings of Marx, Durkheim and Simmel remain under-utilized. Bryan Turner's (1984) frequent references to Marx have not been followed up by an investigation into the value of his work for body theory. Durkheim is often marginalized, being viewed as an analyst of 'social facts' who overlooks the lived experience of embodiment (cf. Falk, 1994; Mellor and Shilling, 1997; Shilling, 2004a). Simmel's writings occupy an even lower profile, despite the relevance of his work for studying the emotions and the senses (cf. Tester, 1998a, 1998b; Stewart, 1999: 13). This is a serious lacuna as it has prevented body theorists from recognizing a convergence in the work of these figures, a convergence that provides us with a highly productive way of conceptualizing the body and a framework which can guide substantive studies in the area.

The body as a source of society

Marx, Durkheim and Simmel have been viewed as conceptualizing the social environment as an autonomous, self-sustaining system (Althusser, 1969; Lukes, 1973; Turner, 1986). While Simmel is often portrayed as a methodological individualist (or interactionist) who rejected the notion of 'society', his conception of the money economy provides a vision of the economic basis of social life possessed of an obduracy worthy of a Durkheimian 'social fact' and a pervasiveness and consequentiality that stand comparison with Weber's vision of 'mechanical capitalism' (Turner, 1986). What each of them has written about the physical capacities and experiences of individuals, however, suggests that the body plays an independent and essential causal role in the formation of societal phenomena. The body is an important source of society as a result of those capacities and dispositions which enable it to transcend its natural state and create a social environment.

Marx's view of the embodied subject emerges from his attempt to overcome the one-sidedness of idealist and materialist philosophies which conceive of humans exclusively as mental beings or as determined fully by life circumstances. His alternative begins with real human beings engaged in sensuous, practical activity. It is the embodied nature of humans and the unfolding of their senses onto the environment that both connects them to, and leads to the development of, the natural and social worlds (Colletti, 1975: 280). In terms of being connected to the world, Marx (1975 [1844]: 390]) argues that our 'corporeal, living, real, sensuous' being means we have an inescapable need for natural objects and social relationships that reside outside of ourselves (see also Engels, 1968 [1925]: 356). Hunger, for example, is the acknowledged need of the body for an external object, and also propels people into combining with others in order to produce their means of subsistence (Marx, 1968 [1849]: 80). In terms of the human ability to develop the world, the idea that people engage practically with their environment through labour is key to Marx's writings. Our bodies may be part of nature, but they must also actively 'oppose' themselves to nature by 'setting in motion arms and legs, head and hands', the 'natural forces' of the body, in order to provide for their natural and social needs (Marx, 1954: 173). According to Engels (1968 [1925]: 348]), it is the hand as *the* organ of labour that is of utmost importance to the development of our environment. The productive capacities of the hand emerge through its ability to invent and manipulate increasingly complex tools, while its gestural use is key to the cultivation of social relationships. As the hand acquires new techniques and skills, furthermore, it can even exercise the 'degree of perfection required to conjure into being the pictures of a Raphael, the statues of a Thorwaldsen, the music of a Paganini' (Engels, 1968 [1895–6]: 355).

It is not just the hand that is central to this process for Marx and Engels. The 'highly complex' embodied properties of humans as a whole predispose them towards a productive relationship with the environment, equipping individuals with the powers of intentional practical activity that 'unites the labour of the hand with that of the head' (Marx, 1954: 476). It is this practical embodied consciousness that distinguishes humans from other animals; imparting labour and the social relationships surrounding it with 'an ever-renewed impulse to further development', and ensuring that social actors possess the capacity to actively create, and not just be passive recipients of, society (Marx, 1975 [1844]: 329, 1954: 173; Engels, 1968 [1895–6]: 357). The existence of economic activity in society, then, is not the voluntary product of individuals making more or less constrained choices in relation to the circumstances they face at a particular time. Instead, it constitutes the outgrowth of capacities that humans have by necessity to exercise as a result of their embodied nature.

Durkheim also viewed the social and natural worlds as complementary and, especially in his later work, analysed the body as an essential source of society. Illustrated most comprehensively in relation to Australian aboriginal societies, Durkheim's vision of the body was intended to be part of an explanation which revealed the universal, culturally embedded mechanisms leading to the creation of *all* societies. Durkheim expresses this creativity in his argument that the body 'conceals in its depth a sacred principle that erupts onto the surface in particular circumstances' (Durkheim, 1995 [1912]: 125, 138). Manifest via cutting, scarification, tattooing, painting, or other forms of decoration, these eruptions produce a bodily symbolism that helps create a shared moral whole by enabling individuals to recognize others as participants in a common culture. Indeed, symbols associated with the body possess a special intensity in Durkheim's work because of his realization that without the body there can be no life and no society (Janssen and Verheggen, 1997). This vital generative link between the body and society has, furthermore, been recognized by communities through the ages. Historically, people have surrounded the body with a series of totemic prohibitions and imperatives in an attempt to control and steer its productive powers (Durkheim, 1995 [1912]: 125, 138).

Durkheim's work enables us to see that the cultural life of society, like its economic activities, is neither completely arbitrary nor the product of voluntary choices disconnected from the embodied being of its participants. Instead, it possesses a deep affinity with the body's capacity for generating a sacred symbolism; a symbolism that was itself productive of a space in which individuals were able to transcend their self-oriented impulses and join with others as common participants in collective life (ibid.: 125, 138, 233).

Simmel's primary concern is with social interaction rather than the economic foundations or symbolic order of society, but he still conceptualizes the body as a productive source of those social and cultural forms in which interaction and sociality occur. Like Marx and Durkheim, this is because Simmel recognizes the body as being possessed of generative properties that make it a corporeal basis for society. Specifically, the embodied individual is characterized for Simmel (1971 [1908a]: 23) by drives, dispositions and purposes which include erotic, religious and aggressive impulses, and motives of gain, defence, attack and instruction. It is these bodily 'contents' which *propel* individuals towards others, into being for others, with others, or against others, and which constitute an essential stage in the initial assembly of forms (Simmel, 1971 [1908a]). *Social forms* originate in the elementary points of contact between individuals when glances or pleasantries are exchanged, emotional responses are stimulated, conversations are begun, and reciprocal mental orientations are established. It is here that threads of social life emerge and begin to bind people together. *Cultural forms*, in contrast, emerge when individuals' practical bodily immersion in the world is interrupted. Here, the experiencing self divides into a self-conscious subject and an object that confronts itself with 'protocultural' forms in seeking to solve the problem with which it is confronted. This process, grounded in practical bodily activities, provides a foundation for thought which can potentially result in a shared framework for social interaction (Levine, 1971). Social and cultural forms may develop and coalesce into increasingly rigid 'structures' within the context of the money economy, but the body is their definite source: life's bodily contents strive to produce forms which allow for their expression.

The specific manner in which the body constitutes a source for the constitution of society varies for each of the above theorists. For Marx, the bodily needs and capacities of the individual both necessitate and mean that they are able to intervene in their natural environment, engage in social relationships, and start to create economic and social structures. For Durkheim, the body contains the power to transcend itself because of its generation of a sacred energy that facilitates the emergence of a cultural or symbolic order. For Simmel, the body's life contents energize individuals to engage with others in particular social forms by equipping them with particular drives and motives for action, while it is people's practical, intentional activity that results in the creation of problem-solving techniques and the development of socially valid knowledge. Nevertheless, these 'needs', 'energies', 'drives' and 'purposes' have in common the property that they both require and enable human physicality to transcend its natural existence. The body stands, for Marx, Durkheim and Simmel, as a central source for the creation of society. Social structures *per se* are not alien to people, nor are they the creation of entirely voluntaristic cognitive choices, but in many cases possess a deep affinity with the central embodied characteristics of human being.

The body as a location for the social

In line with the corporeal realism underpinning their writing, Marx, Durkheim and Simmel each attribute the body with characteristics that are productive in relation to society (and, as I shall discuss later, that cannot be reduced to, or eradicated entirely by, society), but none view society as reducible to its embodied members. Society constitutes a *sui generis* reality and each new generation confronts it as a given reality possessed of its own processes, norms and structures. Schools, for example, constitute structural parts of society as a result of incorporating positions (e.g. teacher/pupil) related to each other in a hierarchical order, cultural practices (revolving around a curriculum which sanctions the incorporation and exclusion of culturally distinctive forms of knowledge), and technological resources (e.g. desks, computers). In this context, the embodied subject is not just a more or less active source of, but is also a prime *location* for the economic, cultural and social structures that constitute society. What I mean by this is that the body is variously *receptive* to the effects of society (in that its habits and appearances are, in part, moulded by society) and *constrained* by the parameters of its social environment: it variously has inscribed on it the effects of economic relationships, is a site for the expression of social symbolism, and is the material on which the fixity of forms becomes established. The major social positions within schools, to continue with the above example, are associated with legal obligations regarding teaching a particular curriculum and attendance, while the sociology of education has long established the socializing effects that the curriculum content and organization have on the bodies and minds of its charges.

Marx's writings on economics are characterized by a particularly acute sense of social structures as emergent phenomena. While he recognizes that social relations and technological means of production are created by embodied subjects, Marx also insists that the economic creations of generations past imprint themselves on the bodily being of generations present (Marx and Engels, 1977 [1846]; Marx, 1968 [1852]: 96). People make history, 'but they do not make it under conditions chosen by themselves, but under circumstances directly encountered, given and transmitted from the past' (Marx, 1968: 96). This sense of the body as a recipient of social practices is exemplified in Marx's writings on capitalism in which it sometimes appears as if there has been a complete reversal of people's creative relationship with their environment. Capitalism *alienates* embodied individuals from their practical activities and denies them all but their most basic needs.

Marx's (1975 [1844]: 325) concept of alienation is key to his account of how the economic structures of society locate themselves on the bodies of individuals. The general meaning of alienation refers to an environment in which individuals forfeit control of their physical activity, and become estranged from their essential humanity. In capitalism, alienation is associated with four major features of economic activity. By separating the products of labour from their producers, capitalist labour alienates individuals by removing them from an essential part of their species life and also from their relationship with the natural world. As the extraction of surplus labour is intensified, and physical and mental work becomes a mere means for the sustenance of life, individuals are also alienated from their bodies (a theme which was developed later by Marcuse's [1955] deliberations on the 'surplus repression' that characterizes capitalism). The extension of the division of labour has related consequence. Quoting with approval Adam Smith's 1776 analysis of the deleterious effects of the division of labour, Marx (1954: 342) highlights how the development of specialized skills promotes a limited dexterity or expertise at the expense of other capacities and virtues, and eventually results in individuals becoming 'as stupid and ignorant as it is possible for a human creature to become'. Finally, the addition of increasingly advanced technology to the labour process turns workers into appendages of machines, and estranges individuals from each other (Marx, 1975 [1844]: 329–30, 1968 [1848]: 41).

Comparing capitalism to a vampire that sucks the blood of its prey, Marx (1954: 76, 244) describes how this alienation depletes the energies of the brain, nerves, muscle and senses. Having emphasized how human nature develops through the receptive unfolding of all the senses onto the world, Marx argues that capitalism blunts the species capacities that separate humans from, and elevate them above, animals. At best, life begins for workers when their labour has ended (ibid.: 327). This restriction of sensuous experience and expression is exacerbated by the ubiquity of private property within capitalism. Private property imparts need and enjoyment with an egoistic nature; a process which 'has made us so stupid and one-sided that an object is only *ours* when we have it', and which replaces '*all* the physical and intellectual senses' with the single, estranged 'sense of *having*' (ibid.: 351–3). The conditions of capitalism burrow ever deeper into the bodily being of social actors, disfiguring and reconstructing them according to a logic over which they have apparently lost control. This loss of control is not, however, total and Marx is keen to emphasize that embodied humans retain the potential to perceive the causes of their oppression and engage in revolutionary action.

The body also serves as a location for society in the work of Durkheim, though he does not share Marx's diagnosis of capitalism. Society, as we have seen, is expressed through its symbolically expressed cultural order for Durkheim. These symbols are not just generated by bodies, however, but become situated on the body. Durkheim argues that the image-imprinted-on-flesh 'is in fact, and by far, the most important' mode of representation that exists. It is because bodies 'share in a common life, [that] they are often led, almost instinctively, to paint themselves or to imprint images on their bodies that remind them' of this life (Durkheim, 1995 [1912]: 233). Tattooing, 'the most direct and expressive means by which the communion of minds can be affirmed', exemplifies this 'instinct' and occurs within clans or tribes 'apart from any reflection or calculation' (ibid.: 233–4).

Durkheim's colleague, Marcel Mauss, built on this analysis by examining how social techniques that are both traditional to and effective within a society become ingrained through apprenticeships into the capacities and habits of the body. For Mauss (1973 [1934]: 71–2) 'there is perhaps no "natural" way for the adult' to manage their body and, therefore, 'each society has', and has to have, 'its own special habits' pertaining to the body. These techniques are transmitted by initiation and education in which the surfaces of the body are penetrated and in which social symbolism enters the heart of the individual's physical self. As Durkheim (1995 [1912]: 211) argued, in order for any society to exist, the life of the group must become 'organised within' individuals. These body techniques remain vital to modern societies because their transmission involves an 'education in composure' congruent with the needs of a specialized society (Mauss, 1973 [1934]: 86). The cultural structures of society shape the behaviour of people's bodily being in a manner which can increase (but not guarantee) the likelihood of them acting in a way that is congruent with the reproduction of those structures.

Simmel's writings highlight how embodied experience constitutes the location on which the increasing fixity of social forms is played out. We have described how, for Simmel, emotional dispositions propel individuals towards others, initiating the inception of social and cultural forms which allow for the expression of 'life contents'. However, these forms are also *structuring* principles: irrespective of the motivations bringing individuals together, it is possible to identify forms such as conflict, the family, and sociability that impose a pattern on interaction. This means that while forms initially constitute an outgrowth of life's expression, they soon become stabilized and develop into autonomous traditions or institutions which acquire 'fixed identities' and 'a logic and lawfulness of their own' (Simmel, 1971 [1918a]: 375). This inevitably distances them from the dynamic that created them, yet deeply shapes the experiences of individuals. Simmel cites marriage as an example of this: emerging as an expression of love, the individual emotions and motives underpinning this form may fade and shift. The form of marriage remains, however, playing out its asymmetrical expectations and interactional constraints on husband and wife (Oakes, 1984).

If social forms locate themselves on embodied interactions, acting as constraints on the creative life contents of individuals, this does not affect everyone equally. As one of the few classical sociologists to develop a sociology of the sexes, Simmel argues that male forms of behaviour claim superpersonal validity in an objective culture in which men perceive their own perspective on social life to be 'rooted in the eternal order of things' (Coser, 1977). Anticipating feminist critiques of this 'male order', Simmel suggests that men seek to manage the fragmenting demands of modern life by developing a psychic mechanism which enables them to separate public from private life, using women as a counterweight to their own dissociative tendencies (Tijssen, 1991). More generally, however, the rationalization of life characteristic of the money economy in Simmel's work exerts an enormously constraining effect on the emotions of women and men, stimulating a tendency to distance the self from emotional expression and to develop a cynicism towards life. The rationalizing effects of the money economy locate themselves on people's lives in a way which encourages a calculative attitude. Strong emotions are tempered and the variety of life tends to be blunted by the need to constantly assess and weigh the consequences of every social act.

Marx and Durkheim have clear views of the body as a physical entity on which social structures or cultural symbols are inscribed, while Simmel concentrates on how forms become located within the emotional interactions and experiences of individuals. Nevertheless, each theorist is acutely aware of how the creations of embodied subjects become emergent phenomena which can sometimes dominate people's subsequent actions, and traces how the societal environment locates itself on the flesh and blood lives of its inhabitants. Thus, each of them is concerned not just with how the body is a source of society, but with how its fundamental characteristics make it receptive to and constrained by society. The body, in other words, is a prime location for social structures.

The body as a means of positioning individuals within the social

Having examined the body as a source of and a location for society, Marx, Durkheim and Simmel were also concerned to evaluate the outcomes of the interaction between people's creative dispositions and capacities, on the one hand, and their receptivity to, and ability to be constrained by, social forces, on the other. They recognized that this interaction serves to position people within and orientate them towards society in different ways: it can variously attach them to or distance them from society. This interaction also has the effect of re-forming certain elements of the bodily character of individuals in a way that can enhance or constrain human potentialities, and results in outcomes that contribute to the reproduction or transformation of social structures. In examining the outcomes of the relationship between the body and society, Marx focused on how the lived experiences of capitalism resulted in either ideological misrepresentation of the system, and further damage to the bodily capacities of workers, or an awareness of its exploitative nature, an awakening of people's species capacities, and pressures for social change. Durkheim was interested in how interaction between the individual and the effervescent energies stimulated by the group could result in the incorporation of individuals into a moral order and an associated enhancement of people's capacities for action, or a separation of individuals from the group and an associated shrinkage in their bodily capacities. Finally, Simmel's concern was with how interaction between individuals and particular forms of sociality either allowed for the expression of life's contents, and the creation of new forms appropriate to the changing needs of humans, or resulted in the stagnation of human experience and expression.

Marx's analysis of the body as a location for capitalism raises the question of how individuals could possibly tolerate this alienating economic system if they possessed any remaining agentic capacities. The answer to this question, which suggests that even the bodies of the oppressed continue to be productive and complicit sources of the economic system they inhabit, lies in Marx's analysis of the interaction that occurs between experience and 'ideology'. While ideology may conjure up images of distorted ideas more than it does lived experience, Marx employs the term to reveal how the material conditions surrounding people's sensory existence can produce 'inverted' forms of consciousness (Larrain, 1979). As Marx and Engels (1977 [1846]: 47]) note, 'If in all ideology men and their circumstances appear upside down as in a camera obscura, this phenomenon arises just as much from their historical life process as the inversion of objects on the retina does from their physical life-process.' Specifically, it is the difference between the lived *appearance* and *essence* of capitalism that leads people to misrecognize the conditions determining their lives: the economy operates on the basis of a series of exchanges which appear equitable even though they are not (ibid.: 64). Thus, the social relations of production and contents of waged-labour seem to be natural economic arrangements, rather than means of extracting surplus labour, while the value of commodities appears to be an inherent part of their character instead of incorporating the results of exploitative relations of production. This is because a worker will seemingly receive a 'fair' day's wage for a 'fair' day's work for a job which, however unpleasant, seems to be a necessary part of a specific productive process, while the products of this labour incorporate raw materials which, fetishistically, appear to possess a value over and above the work invested in them (Marx, 1954: 77). These appearances are reinforced, furthermore, by the ruling class's capacity to present self-serving ideas as impartial representations of reality (Larrain, 1979: 46).

The interaction between the body and capitalism does not, however, necessarily attach individuals permanently to this socio-economic system. While perceptions of capitalism's obduracy are reinforced as long as the possibilities for overcoming its social relations of production, and ultimately inefficient use of the technological means of production, remain latent, economic crises can alter these circumstances (Marx, 1968 [1849]). As capitalism spreads across the globe, opportunities for exploiting new world markets fade. In this context, economic downturns result in increasingly acute crises, wages fall and unemployment rises, while the productive potential of society remains underdeveloped as the means of production continue to be utilized for the creation of exchange values rather than use values (ibid.: 181). The lived experience of these circumstances becomes increasingly inimical to the ideological appearance of capitalism, and forms instead the corporeal basis for the emergence of a revolutionary consciousness and practice. Workers eventually have 'nothing to lose but their chains' by engaging in revolt (Marx and Engels, 1968 [1848]: 63). In these circumstances, from being a means for the attachment of individuals to capitalism, bodily experience can become a vehicle for *social transformation*.

For Marx, this transformation involves a revolution in both the socioeconomic system and in people's bodily being. Under a communist system, in which transformed social relations allow the productive powers of capitalism to be utilized to their full, necessary labour time is minimized and people no longer have to devote themselves to an exclusive sphere of activity. In this body-friendly society, Marx looks forward to a time in which one can in principle 'hunt in the morning, fish in the afternoon, rear cattle in the evening, criticize after dinner ... without ever becoming hunter, fisherman, herdsman or critic' (Marx and Engels, 1977 [1846]: 54). The one-sided specialist is replaced by the all-round individual able to experience their body as a means of species realization rather than a mere instrument and object of labour.

Durkheim's (1995 [1912]: 217) analysis of the interaction between the body and society is informed by a view of the circulation of energy between individuals and the collectivity. Properly incorporated into the cultural collectivity, the individual can be enhanced by this energy, yet this is not an automatic or guaranteed process, and it is possible for individuals to become disconnected from social groups, devitalized, and reduced to a physical shell of their potential being. In terms of incorporation, Durkheim talks of individuals being attached to a community through the ritual generation of collective effervescent energies that 'fix' emotions to common cultural symbols. This effervescence is a social force, akin to a 'sort of electricity', that connects people to the symbolic circuitry of society (ibid.: 213, 217). Its power serves to substitute the world immediately available to an individual's perceptions for another, moral world in which people can interact on the basis of shared understandings (Durkheim, 1973b [1914]). Collective effervescence thus structures the inner lives of individuals and enables a social group to know and feel itself to be a moral community (Durkheim 1995 [1912]: 221–3, 229, 239).

The attachment of individuals to society, when it occurs, contributes both towards social reproduction and a beneficial increase in the powers of the embodied subject. For Durkheim, being joined to a collectivity helps us by 'thrusting us into the nourishing milieu of society' and encourages set ways of responding to situations which release us 'from an incessant search for appropriate conduct' (Durkheim, 1973c [1925]: 37, 40, 73). Even in modernity, the advancing division of labour, with its attendant 'cult of the individual', leads to 'the glorification not of the self but of the individual in general', a sentiment associated with the extension of rights and respect for personal differences (Durkheim, 1973a [1898]: 48–9). This cult, manifest through the diversity of bodily identities developed in the contemporary era, expresses a variety which 'binds us all to each other', prompting individuals to 'reach outside' themselves in looking to others as a means of adding 'to the energy' they possess (Durkheim, 1973a [1898]: 48–9, 53; 1995 [1912]: 427).

Productive attachment was not automatic, however, and the outcome of interaction between embodied subjects and cultural collectivities remained dependent on a periodic recharging provided by the energetic effervescence of group life. When the positive interaction between the individual and group weakens, the symbolic order of society loses the energy that gave rise to it and the reality it incarnated (Durkheim, 1995 [1912]: 217, 342). Durkheim had genuine worries that this weakening was occurring in his lifetime, and emphasized in his lectures on education that collective representations must be given 'enough color, form and life' to stimulate moral action among children (Durkheim, 1973c [1925]: 228–9). Ideas had become weakened from the collective forces that sustained them and Durkheim's (1973c [1925]: 222, 229) interest in education was part of a wider concern to reattach the two in order to develop the altruistic over the egoistic elements of bodily nature. This was because the effects of a reduction in the energy that joined individuals to society could be devastating to society and to the capacities and dispositions of the embodied subject. As well as encouraging dangerous forms of 'centrifugal' nationalism, which seek to stimulate loyalty by encouraging artificial and potentially dangerous sectarian sentiments (ibid.: 77), individuals could 'fall out' of society altogether. As Durkheim's (1952 [1897]) study of suicide illustrates, this could result in a loss of thirst for life itself. Egoistic suicide, for example, is associated with an absence of meaning and an 'excessive individualism' in which the individual loses the support of that collective energy that attaches them to society (ibid.: 209–11). Life seems empty and 'the bond attaching man to life relaxes because that attaching him to society is itself slack' (ibid.: 214–15). The positioning of the body in society, in short, can either enhance or dangerously diminish the capacities of the embodied subject and the cultural milieu they inhabit.

Simmel's (1950) work offers an immediate contrast to that of Durkheim by focusing initially on how emotions generated by interactions between individuals, rather than between individuals and collectivities, attach people to particular forms and shape the development of their personality. Furthermore, Simmel's conception of interaction as involving a bodily sacrifice is diametrically opposed to Durkheim's vision of collective occasions adding something to the energies of individuals. Interaction constitutes a process of exchange between individuals for Simmel and, for it to continue, individuals have to expend personal energy in the form of shows of affection, willingness to 'take turns' and repair 'gaffes' in conversation, and so on. These represent a giving up of something belonging to the individual, and illustrate for Simmel that there must be a certain sacrifice of the self for social forms to exist (Simmel, 1990 [1907]: 82).

If sacrifices made in interaction are a loss to the individual, however, Simmel argues that their exchange stimulates social emotions such as 'gratitude' and 'faith' which bind individuals together and contribute towards the reproduction of society. Gratitude is an internalized, emotionally experienced 'moral memory of mankind' (Simmel, 1950: 388). It originates when someone receives in interaction any sacrificial good – be it material or non-material – such as a complement or a gift, and imposes on that individual a moral obligation to 'reach out' to others (ibid.: 388–9). While gratitude may become an echo of past relationships, Simmel emphasizes its resilience: gratitude ties together different elements of society via microscopic but infinitely tough threads and society would break apart in its absence (ibid.: 388–9, 395, 392). Faithfulness, in contrast, links fluctuating individual impulses to the form of a relationship even after the feeling or motive that initiated that relationship ends. Irrespective of the motives for establishing a relationship, the exchange of sacrifices that marks its development may stimulate a deeper and pervasive inner feeling of faithfulness, making the individuals-in-relation hold fast to one another. Its importance is such that Simmel (1997 [1912]: 170) argues that our 'capacity to have faith in a person ... beyond all demonstrable evidence ... is one of the most stable bonds holding society together'.

These forms of attachment to society are not an unmitigated good for the individual, however, and nor are they guaranteed. They are not necessarily good because the development of individuality – a supreme value for Simmel (Levine, 1995: 208) – can be retarded as well as nurtured by continuing to participate in the same social forms. The experience of routine reaches a point where it can stifle growth and exclude the benefits to be gained from confronting novelty and diversity. Thus, while people have bodily predispositions to interact with others, and need to do so in order to develop themselves, sociality can also compromise their individuality and development by requiring communication to occur around common norms (Simmel, 1990 [1907]). These forms of attachment are not guaranteed because of the corroding effects of the money economy and the metropolis. Money, its creation, circulation and multiplication, becomes the *raison d'être* of the modern world. It is pursued in an economy which works according to abstract and differentiated principles involving just the calculative and acquisitive elements of the individual. While this situation allows people to enjoy unprecedented levels of personal freedom, by liberating them from membership of a single community and from judgements based on their background, it also threatens their significance, prominence and individuality (e.g. Simmel, 1971 [1903]: 324). This is because money levels by turning qualitative into quantitative differences. Everything is seen as having a price and as possessing a value that can be expressed in monetary terms, and this situation stimulates the development of a *cynical* attitude towards morality and the development of personality. In previous eras, an individual's attempts to better or enrich themselves, or to cultivate actions informed by a set of coherent values, might be associated with religious or noble motivations. The modern cynical attitude, in contrast, views such behaviour as thinly veiled attempts to acquire monetarily valuable forms of distinction.

These circumstances are consolidated by the primary environment in which money is pursued, the metropolis. The built environment of the metropolis is characterized by a quantity and velocity of stimuli which overwhelm the sensory capacities of humans. This prompts the individual to reduce the effect of the fluctuations of the external milieu by reacting intellectually, thus intensifying conscious life and withdrawing from full sensory life, and through the adoption of a blasé attitude. Here, the embodied subject apprehends everything as 'being of an equally dull and grey hue, as not worth getting excited about' (Simmel, 1971 [1903]: 325; 1990 [1907]: 256). This encourages an indifference towards events and a reserve towards people which can result in unprecedented feelings of loneliness and low self-esteem (Simmel 1971 [1903]: 334, 1990 [1907]: 255, 491, 512).

The blasé attitude may facilitate survival in modernity, and constitute a toleration of this order, but it is associated with a fundamental weakening of social emotions, such as faithfulness and gratitude, that bind people together within social forms. It is not just individual personality that is eroded for Simmel, then, but social life itself. Nevertheless, Simmel (1971 [1918b]) also insists that the vitalism of human life retains the potential to transcend existing forms, thus providing a potential source for social change. When forms such as those dominating modernity become experienced as ossified and drained of vitalism, there is an emotionally felt need for new forms more in tune with an individual's development (Simmel, 1971 [1908a]; 1971 [1918b]; 1971 [1908c]: 352). In his discussions on religiosity and youth, indeed, Simmel (1971 [1918b]: 393) talks of the desire of life 'to transcend all forms and to appear in its naked immediacy'. The body may be a means of attaching the individual to 'society', and of dulling its potentialities, but it retains its agentic properties and its capacity for contributing towards the supersession of the status quo.

Marx's, Durkheim's and Simmel's conceptions of the body as a means of positioning individuals within society differ in detail and in terms of their political consequences, but they converge in terms of three central conclusions. First, each attributes great importance to the interaction that occurs between the body and society. These phenomena possess distinctive properties but are moulded and altered by the effects they have on each other. Second, each argues that this positioning has profound consequences for the enhancement or diminution of people's bodily potentialities. While people's bodily capacities and dispositions are not entirely determined by society, the form they take is deeply affected by the social milieu in which they live and this has a profound impact on their development. Third, each recognizes that those human experiences that variously *attach* people to or *distance* them from their social milieu have important consequences for the continuation or transformation of particular social formations.

Bodies Doubled

In conceiving of the body as a multi-dimensional medium for the constitution of society, the writings of Marx, Durkheim and Simmel propose stratified ontologies of human embodiment which are embedded in, but irreducible to, specific social milieux. This stratified ontology is a vital underpinning for their view that the body is characterized by properties which are generative of society, and which are not eradicated by the tendency for other aspects of the embodied self to be shaped by society. Because of the importance of this stratified ontology to the convergence thesis sketched in this chapter, I want to explore it here in more detail. My argument will be that each theorist operates, implicitly or explicitly, with a *homo duplex* model of embodiment which facilitates their wider approaches towards the body–society relationship.

Marx's concern with the body is explicit and often extensive (Synnott, 1991: 73), but his ontology of embodiment has to be explicated from an apparently contradictory conception of human needs as natural and as socially constructed (Heller, 1974; Levine, 1995). On the one hand, Marx strongly emphasizes the natural fixity of various human needs. He adapts Feuerbach's term 'species-being' in discussing the essential characteristics of human being and, in *The German Ideology*, argues that fixed needs must always be satisfied as the first human act (Marx, 1973 [1939]; see also McLellan, 1980: 243). In this respect, the needs of the body clearly constitute a source of basic individual action, action designed to secure food and water, shelter and security, which involves the formation of associated social relations. These features of Marx's work allow commentators like Norman Geras (1995: 153–4) to argue that the 'notion of an enduring human nature served Marx as a standard of normative judgement' in evaluating historical progress (see also Heller, 1974). Others have made similar points: Marx's early and later writings were informed by an 'unwavering acceptance of the stability and reality of the human being' (Nisbet, 1993 [1966]: 286–7), and 'ethical evaluations of the degree to which social structures' enable people to fulfil their basic needs and 'realize an ideal of authentic being' (Venable, 1945; O'Neill, 1972: 119; McLellan, 1980: 77).

On the other hand, Marx also insists upon the *historical determination* of human need. This focus on the apparent malleability of embodied being finds support from what Chris Arthur (1977: 21) refers to as 'the most fundamental idea in *The German Ideology*, which is discovered in the 1844 *Manuscripts* and is assumed by *Capital*', the idea that 'man produces himself through labour'. This focus on the malleability of the body is evident in

Marx's criticisms of the abstract conceptions of 'man' proposed by political economists, and empty conceptions of human rights which ignore historical circumstances. It is also explicit in his comments on the relative character of desire and pleasure which 'spring from society; we measure them, therefore, by society and not by the objects which serve for their satisfaction. Because they are of a social nature, they are of a relative nature' (Marx, 1968 [1849]: 83). These features of Marx's work clearly highlight the body's status as a location for society, and have allowed commentators to argue that he espoused a *relativistic* conception of need. Thus, Coser (1971: 44) claims that 'Marx was a relativising historicist', while Sayer's (1994) argument that human needs are made and remade according to social conditions.

Donald Levine (1995: 221–2) suggests that these contrasting parts of Marx's work reveal a contradiction that arises from his effort to anchor a vision of transcendent freedom in this-worldly realities. Nevertheless, they are not incompatible if we accept that Marx was exploring two sides of an ontologically stratified *homo duplex* model of humanity. Humans are natural beings, possessed of fixed needs which must be met if people are to preserve themselves as natural beings, but humans also possess the capacity to add to and partly *transcend* this natural state. They do this by becoming social beings who fulfil their natural needs in a variety of culturally specific ways and who develop new needs unrestricted to the maintenance of life. As Marx (1973 [1939]: 92) argues, 'Hunger is hunger, but the hunger gratified by cooked meat eaten with a knife and fork is a different hunger from that which bolts down raw meat with the aid of hand, nail and tooth.' This capacity of humans to transcend their natural state extends, as it does with Durkheim, to sensory experiences and sensitivity. For Marx (1975 [1844]: 353), 'the *senses* of social man are different from those of non-social man', and the cultivation of these senses is a thoroughly historical phenomenon. This socialization of need and nature does not, however, make irrelevant relatively fixed needs, which are forged by long-term processes of human evolution, and nor does it stop providing one basis on which Marx evaluates socio-economic systems (Creaven, 2000). An individual deprived of, or condemned to struggling for, life's necessities is thrown back on their natural, essentially animal, existence, and is alienated from the economic system that has reduced them to this existence (ibid.: 327). Indeed, it is precisely because capitalism continues both to generate and tolerate hunger, disease and squalor, and to warp the sensory development of even the privileged, that Marx condemns it as a system. In contrast, it is with the future development of a communist society that bodily potentialities can be properly 'humanized'. It is only under these conditions, in which it is possible to pursue the cultivation of rich needs in an non-alienated existence, that the senses can be developed in a manner conducive to 'human gratification' (ibid.: 353).

In contrast to Marx, Durkheim (1973b [1914]) develops an explicit model of *homo duplex* which categorically distinguishes between people's natural bodily existence and the embodiment of social capacities. Durkheim begins by noting that humans have, in every age, been aware of the duality of their nature and have traditionally expressed this through the idea that they possess a this-worldly, profane, physically limiting body, and a transcendent, sacred soul (ibid.: 151). Instead of dismissing these beliefs, Durkheim suggests that they capture the tension between our individual and social existence: the reality that humans are both egoistic and moral beings. Humans possess an *individual* bodily being constituted by their drives, appetites and sensory impressions which 'are necessarily egoistic: they have our individuality and it alone as their object'. However, they also possess the capacity to transcend themselves and to be a source of, and develop on the basis of, *social* categories and emotions (Durkheim, 1995 [1912]: 151). During the 'normal' processes of its maturation within society, the individual, egoistic pole of *homo duplex* is increasingly subordinated to its social and moral characteristics: the individual body becomes attached to, and partly transformed by, the social body.

Durkheim focuses on the costs and benefits that accrue to the individual as a result of their bodily nature being a source of both egoistic impulses and of cultural life. Dealing with the costs first, he argues that we can never be 'completely in accord with ourselves for we cannot follow one of our two natures without causing the other to suffer' (Durkheim, 1973b [1914]: 154). We do not, in other words, offer our bodies voluntarily as a source of society (Durkheim, 1995 [1912]: 316). Instead, our sensuous nature attaches us 'to the profane world with every fibre of our flesh', and provides an ongoing source of friction which can stimulate social change (ibid.). We can only pursue moral ends, which have as their object the collectivity, by offending 'the instincts and the penchants ... most deeply rooted in our bodies. There is not a moral act that does not imply a sacrifice' (Durkheim, 1973b [1914]: 152). The very possibility of society, indeed, depends on physical, emotional, and psychical pain. This pain is not just associated with the denial of the egoistic elements of our instincts, but with the fact that the symbolic order of society that humans produce 'can never succeed in mastering our sensations and in translating them completely into intelligible terms. They take on a conceptual form only by losing that which is most concrete in them, that which causes them to speak to our sensory being and to involve it in action' (ibid.: 153).

Despite the fact that Durkheim clearly explicates the painful dimensions of the body's status as a source of society, this is not simply a negative constraint on the individual (Durkheim, 1995 [1912]: 321). He also shows how this society locates itself subsequently on individuals in ways which *benefit* them. Indeed, the positive integration of individuals into the symbolic order of society is facilitated by the fact that embodied agents need society to survive as much as society needs individuals to exist. This is because the symbolic order of society liberates the agent from the enslavement they suffer from the asocial pole of their *homo duplex* nature (ibid.: 151, 211). First this symbolic order enables individuals to subjectively recognize that they possess the capacity to exercise agency. It emancipates the individual from the limits of their individual sensory impressions – by placing a distance between them and immediate physical stimuli – and equips them with a capacity for 'thinking and acting conceptually' in line with communal norms (Durkheim, 1995 [1912]: 12, 151, 159, 274–5; 1973b [1914]). As Durkheim (1995 [1912]: 370) argues, 'man could not have arrived at the idea of himself as a force in charge of the body in which it resides without introducing concepts borrowed from social life into the idea he had of himself.' Second, the symbolic order also increases massively the capacity of individuals for actually effecting change. This is because common cultural symbols are the result of an 'immense cooperation' and a 'multitude of different minds' (ibid.: 15), and reflect a store of knowledge that possesses a 'very special intellectuality that is infinitely richer and more complex than that of the individual distilled in them' and can facilitate productive interventions in the environment (ibid.). Third, the symbolic order imparts a dignity and a sacredness to the individual. As Durkheim (ibid.: 229) argues, society conceives the individual 'as being endowed with a *sui generis* character that insulates and shields him from all reckless infringement – in other words, that imposes respect'. This collective notion that the individual is sacred also provides the basis for the 'cult of the individual' that Durkheim (1984 [1893]) suggests will characterize the *conscience collective* of societies possessed of a highly developed, 'normal' division of labour.

This stratified ontology of embodiment is not simply used by Durkheim to highlight the internally divided nature of human beings, but allows him to assess the degree to which people are attached to or repelled from society, and to explore whether particular societies enhance or diminish people's bodily potentialities. This is clear in his studies on suicide and the division of labour: analyses in which he establishes that societies tread a fine line between supplementing and stifling the bodily capacities of individuals. Abnormal forms of the division of labour, and the major types of suicide identified by Durkheim, illustrate how individuals can be damaged when this balance is not achieved.

Simmel constructed a radically different sociology to that of Durkheim, yet also developed a *homo duplex* model of the individual. Embodied subjects are characterized for Simmel by a distinction between individualized mental forms and pre-social contents and impulses on the one hand, and social emotions and reciprocated mental forms, on the other (Simmel 1971 [1908a]: 24, 1950: 315). The individualized and pre-social elements of life are a creative source of forms. The evolution of our physical and psychological structures repeatedly reaches stages in which available energy levels initiate a period of social and cultural change: the 'flux' and 'stream' of life ensure there is a constant 'reaching beyond' current boundaries and limitations (Simmel, 1971 [1908c, d]; 1971 [1918b]: 362, 364). Individuals also have an inherent cognitive creativity according to Simmel. The mind organizes the appearances of reality, through its own categories, into its own forms, and thus actively transforms the chaos of the world into a series of unifying pictures, images and sentences (Levine, 1971: xxxvii). Finally, people also possess what Simmel refers to as a 'moral soul'; a pre-social but biologically and socially transcendent religiosity that instils in individuals the need and potential to develop a coherent personality (Simmel, 1997 [1904]).

If pre-social impulses, individualized forms and the moral soul invest life with vitalism and creativity, it should already be clear from my previous discussion of Simmel's writings that these sources of invention can only express themselves through social and cultural forms. It is by participating in collective forms that individuals develop their social potentialities and personalities. The 'doubled' nature of the embodied individual remains, however, and is exemplified by Simmel's analysis of the 'tragedy' of modern life: individuals need forms to enable them to develop, yet their individuality is constricted, blunted and frustrated by these same forms.

Simmel's stratified ontology of embodiment also enables him to examine the interaction between people's bodily dispositions and capacities, and those forms which locate themselves on the interactions and personalities of individuals, and to evaluate how these forms affect human potentialities. In terms of the body–society interaction, Simmel may highlight the tragedies of culture and sociality but he also points out that the essential vitalism of human life ensures that there will always be dimensions of human existence and experience undetermined by society. The contents of human life and drive towards individuality add imponderables to social roles, and a creativity and unpredictability to action. Individuals continue to lead a 'doubled' existence in Simmel's work. They are never fully incorporated into social interaction, nor fully identical to their associates (Simmel, 1971 [1908b]; 1971 [1908c]: 252). Life is never completely congealed into forms as it constitutes 'a continuous stream', a 'boundless continuity', and a 'flux without pause' which overflows and transcends the limits of society (Simmel, 1971 [1918b]: 173). In terms of how this situation enhances or diminishes people's bodily potentialities, Simmel did more than perhaps any other sociological theorist to highlight the contrasting tendencies of the modern world. Modernity provides individuals with unprecedented opportunities for development, yet makes it impossible for them to pursue all these possibilities or to be sure that they have chosen the right way to develop their personalities.

Marx, Simmel and Durkheim converge not only in proposing a theory of the body as a multi-dimensional medium for the constitution of society, as it is presently constituted, but in underpinning their theory with a stratified ontological model of embodiment, which supports this theoretical view of the body–society relationship. Such conceptions of embodied being may prove unacceptable to body theorists concerned to use the body as a way of removing all dualisms in social thought. Nevertheless, in contrast to biologically essentialist views of the body, or conceptions of the subject as offering us 'over-socialized' analyses of social experience and action (Wrong, 1961), they view the embodied individual as an organic continuum existing both *in* and *outside* of society as it is presently constituted. This provides the basis of the corporeal realism that exists in their writings. The body has a natural basis, yet possesses basic characteristics that enable it to transcend itself and create social phenomena which take on their own properties and processes in the form of society. Once established, society can shape the bodily characteristics of its inhabitants, and this provides Marx, Durkheim and Simmel with the means of evaluating whether specific social formations enhance or diminish the potentialities of their members. Thus, Marx devoted considerable attention to how waged labour within the capitalist mode of production involved quantities and intensities of work that had oppressive consequences for the species-being of humans, and resulted in inequalities that limited people's opportunities to combine with others and develop their capacities. Durkheim was concerned with whether individuals had the opportunity to join with others in a moral community possessed of the capacity to take them beyond themselves and increase the cognitive and cultural resources at their disposal. Simmel examined the extent to which social forms were able to facilitate the development of human personality and individuality. He expressed concerns about the effects of the metropolis and the money economy on personality, and traced a tendency towards reserve, cynicism and the blasé attitude that was deeply debilitating for human development.

Conclusion

The convergence theory I have traced out is limited: it concerns the significance of the body to the constitution of society and does not imply that the general analyses of Marx, Durkheim and Simmel are compatible. I am also deliberately applying this convergence thesis to all humans. Feminist analyses have pointed out the gendered character of some of the writings of Marx, Durkheim and Simmel, yet this does not invalidate utilizing creatively what is productive in their work to our species as a whole. Indeed, in contrast to the contemporary tendency in body studies to focus on difference at the expense of what humans share as a single species living in a single world, the convergence thesis that can be taken from their work provides us with a form of corporeal realism that recognizes what people possess in common while also focusing on how social forces can locate themselves differentially in distinctive groups within society to create social inequalities. The balance between the body serving as a source, location and means undoubtedly shifts depending on a number of variables, and it is important to be clear about whose bodies are most productive of, or constrained by, society at any point in time. Nevertheless, we cannot capture the body's ubiquity by referring to it exclusively as a creator of, a product of, or a means for the reproduction of, society, or by focusing exclusively on difference. In terms of its general analytical conception, human bodies need to be defined sociologically through their three-fold character.

This conception of the body as a multi-dimensional medium for the constitution of society reverses the relatively disembodied conception of the individual–society relationship that Parsons proposed as being central to sociology. It is important to note, however, that despite the body's significance to the work of Marx, Durkheim and Simmel, it was not the topic of central concern. Embodiment sometimes faded to an 'absent-presence' in their writings on modernity, appearing at times to occupy a fixed relationship to its surroundings. The conditions in which Marx, Durkheim and Simmel lived were also very different to those that face us in the present. It is simply not possible to apply their substantive writings wholesale to the contemporary era. In this context, it is important to examine the contributions made by those writings that have emerged since the explosion of interest in the body during the 1980s. What is of particular interest in this respect is that the most powerful and influential body theories have sought to develop particular aspects of the body–society relationship into all-embracing theories that at least appear to place embodiment at the very centre of social theory.

3

Contemporary Bodies

Introduction

Diverse centrifugal tendencies may have dominated the development of body studies for much of the 1980s and early 1990s, but these were gradually accompanied by a centripetal trend in which particular approaches became increasingly popular and even dominant resources. While these approaches drew on classical writings, they were concerned to integrate previous themes with recent insights in order to outline a new range of perspectives on the body–society relationship. The range of issues covered by these contemporary approaches grows ever wider, but from a theoretical point of view they can be clustered around three characteristic positions: (1) social constructionist analyses of the *ordered body*; (2) action and phenomenologically oriented approaches towards the *lived body*; and (3) conceptions of the body in *structuration theory*.

These three approaches are not the only ones to have informed the diverse field of body studies. Nevertheless, they have foregrounded the body as central to social theory, have been particularly influential in establishing the parameters of body theory and in setting agendas for its development, and have explored the significance of embodiment within the contemporary era. During an age in which governmental techniques of power have become increasingly pervasive, when identities appear to be more fluid than ever before, when the pace of social change has reached unprecedented levels, and when issues such as gender and sexuality have become central to the sociological imagination, they represent timely attempts to reassess the body–society relationship.

In what follows, I shall argue that each approach usefully develops certain elements of the body's multi-dimensional relationship with society explored in the previous chapter, but that the one-sidedness of these developments means that they ultimately disallow for the dynamism and interplay that characterize corporeal realism. While these contemporary approaches raise important ethical issues about the fate of human potentialities, they tend to go too far in implying that there has been a blunting of human experience and creativity and that the body has lost the agentic powers it used to possess as a source of society. In conclusion, I suggest that these ethical concerns highlight the need for substantive investigations into the body–society relationship, even if these investigations need to be informed theoretically by corporeal realism rather than by structuralism, phenomenology or structuration theory.

Social Constructionist Analyses of the Ordered Body

Social constructionist analyses of the ordered body did much to initiate and consolidate the form taken by the corporeal turn in social theory. They sought to deconstruct conventional notions of the human organism's biological immutability by viewing physicality as an object regulated and even produced by discursive regimes, highlighted the pervasiveness of government power in the contemporary era, and reflected the control exerted over our lives by the political system. As such, they identified and focused on the body's receptivity to, and capacity to be constrained by, society, as that feature of corporeality which had become of defining significance in the contemporary era.

The roots of these social constructionist theories are diverse, and they reach back to such figures as Malthus and Nietzsche, Durkheim and Austin, Goffman and Althusser. While the writings of Thomas Hobbes and Michel Foucault at least appear to have proved most significant in shaping their overt assumptions, however, the (sometimes unannounced) presence of Parsons remains significant. In exploring the parameters and influence of these theories, I examine Bryan Turner's structuralist account of 'bodily order', and Judith Butler's post-structuralist writings on the ordering power of the 'heterosexual matrix'. Turner's and Butler's writings may appear to have little in common, and Turner (1996) is critical of Butler's conception of the body. Nevertheless, their analyses converge in so far as Butler (1990, 1993) focuses on two of the systemic problems identified by Turner, the restraint of desire and the presentation of self. Butler's specific interest may be the cultural enforcement of heterosexuality, but she remains, like Turner, centrally concerned with the ordering and regulation of bodies.

Structuralism and the ordered body

Bryan Turner (1984) recognizes the significance of Hobbes to the history of body studies, and bases his work on a reinterpretation of the problem of order. He characterizes this problem with reference to Hobbes's argument that the multitude of bodies propelled by appetites and aversions would collide without adequate regulation, yet views Hobbes's position as overly individualistic and as neglecting the ways in which societies are 'structured by social class, ethnicity, status groups or gender' (Turner, 1984: 89). Having concluded that 'Almost every aspect of Hobbesian materialism is now open to question', Turner (ibid.: 89–90) nevertheless suggests that it is possible to 'rewrite Hobbes in order to produce a theory of social order which starts out from the problem of regulating bodies'.

Turner (ibid.: 91) argues that the Hobbesian problem of order has four related dimensions which imply that all social systems must ensure: (1) the reproduction of populations through time; (2) the regulation of populations in space; (3) the restraint of desire as an interior body problem; and (4) the representation of bodies in social space. While the issues of desire and representation appear to be tasks facing the individual, Turner views them as intrinsic to the functioning and reproduction of social systems. Turner then proceeds to examine a mode of control, a dominant theorist, and a paradigmatic disease associated with each dimension of the government of the body. Thus, *population reproduction* was historically managed by a system of delayed marriage and patriarchal households, a system analysed by the eighteenth-century theorist, Malthus. Masturbation was the 'disease' which resulted from the breakdown of the body under the demands of moral purity. The *regulation of populations in space* has been accomplished by a panopticism which developed during the eighteenth century when urbanism was seen as a threat to elite culture. Rousseau's argument that population concentrations undermine natural compassion places him as the theorist of this problem, while agoraphobia emerged as a term describing a (gendered) fear of leaving home in these circumstances (Turner, 1984: 107–8). The *restraint of desire* involved the patriarchal regulation of female sexuality and operated through a general ideology of asceticism encouraging the delay of sexual gratification. Weber's (1991 [1904–5]) 'Protestant ethic thesis' traces the development of asceticism, while hysteria was likely to affect women unregulated by a married sexual life governed by the aim of reproduction. Finally, the *representation of bodies* refers to the societal need for stability in terms of how people represent themselves in social space. Goffman is the theorist of the presentation of self, while anorexia nervosa expresses the breakdown of the (usually female) body under the pressures of presentation.

Turner's approach demonstrates the importance for governmentality of the corporeal environment. His accomplishment is to position the body as an object that can never be neglected or marginalized by any comprehensive social theory. The immense scope of Turner's 'core problems' approach also has the benefit of identifying a ready-made list of authors (from Hobbes to Foucault) and subjects (from religion to patriarchy) that can forge the parameters of body studies. Having learned how bodies become ordered as physical objects, however, we gain little sense of the body as a vehicle of individual action or lived experience, or as a source of society. Turner actually condemns phenomenology for providing 'an individualistic account of embodiment from the point of view of the subject' which is 'largely devoid of historical and sociological content' (Turner, 1984: 54). Sociologically, he insists, 'the body' should be examined as 'socially constructed and socially experienced' (ibid.). Nevertheless, the power of this account lies in its suggestion that the body–society relationship is not one in which the partners enjoy equal significance. Instead, the body exists as a location for society, and it is our responsibility to explore how the constraining and moulding effects of social systems leave their (gendered) marks on individuals.

Post-structuralism and the deconstructed body

Judith Butler's thesis suggests that embodied individuals are turned into cultural beings as a result of what she calls the 'heterosexual matrix'. This matrix is a cultural imperative which demands that bodies present themselves on the basis of a stable sex/gender system 'oppositionally and hierarchically defined through the compulsory practice of heterosexuality' (Butler, 1990: 151). In arguing that sex and gender do not exist prior to, but only emerge through, discourse, Butler takes her major inspiration from Foucault. Foucault appears to be a well-suited ally of body theory. Having described his work as constituting a '"history of bodies" and the manner in which what is most material and vital in them has been invested' by various 'discursive formations' (Foucault, 1981: 152), his analyses of discipline, punishment and sexuality have proved influential for body theory.[1] Feminist writers, in particular, have drawn on his work in pursuing the argument that discourses are intimately involved in the production of gender differences (e.g. Nicholson, 1990; Sawicki, 1991; McNay, 1992; Wittig, 1992). Butler is not uncritical of Foucault, and also draws on the work of Althusser, Freud, Derrida, and theories of performativity. Nevertheless, the main strategy informing her two major body studies involves deconstructing the opposition between normative gender (as product and cultural) and the sexual body (as foundational and natural) by reiterating the Foucauldian argument that 'sex', 'body', 'gender' and 'identity' are equally constructed and ordered by the dominant matrix of heterosexuality.

Butler's (1990) *Gender Trouble* argues that gender emerges through the discursively determined activity of stylized acting; 'a set of repeated acts within a highly rigid regulatory frame that congeal over time to produce the appearance of substance' (ibid.: 33). Referring us to Esther Newton's anthropological study of female impersonators, Butler (ibid.: 136–7) argues that 'the structure of impersonation' revealed in drag highlights 'one of the key fabricating mechanisms through which the social construction of gender takes place'. The signs of an apparently fixed, naturally sexed bodily identity are nothing more than the products of performativity (ibid.: 136). The gendered body, in short, 'has no ontological status apart from the various acts which constitute its reality' (ibid.: 136).

Butler's (1993) *Bodies that Matter* shifts the focus from the category of gender to the category of sex, and seeks to avoid the somewhat immaterial body that characterized her previous book (Bordo, 1998; Hekman, 1998). Butler proposes to do this by rejecting the constructionism that informed *Gender Trouble* and by proposing 'a return to the notion of matter', yet this rejection is more apparent than real (Butler, 1993: 9). 'Materiality', she argues, does not refer to physical or biological facticity but is simply a process which produces the 'effect' of corporeal boundaries and surfaces (ibid.: 9), while 'sex' refers to the discursively constituted materiality of the sexed body. The materialization of sex in the body involves regulatory norms which 'hail' subjects to assume subject positions supportive of the 'heterosexual imperative' (ibid.: 1). Specifically, ideological and repressive institutions participate in the 'girling' of the infant, a 'founding interpellation' reiterated to produce a 'naturalized effect' which sets boundaries and norms (ibid.: 7–8). This hailing is enormously powerful. It constitutes the individual subject both discursively, in language, and socially, and is 'reiterated by various authorities and throughout various intervals of time' (ibid.: 8; 1997: 153).

Butler's work has proved extraordinarily influential in rethinking the sex/gender/body distinctions in feminist theory and in highlighting the restrictive boundaries of the heterosexual subject positions made available to women. While her writing is by no means uncritical of Foucault's analyses, however, it shares with them the problem of being unable to conceptualize the body as a *material* phenomenon. In conceptualizing the body as 'always already' constructed by discourse, the body fades as a material and phenomenological entity whose distinctive dimensions might otherwise be conceptualized as variously open to discursive reconstruction depending on their social and cultural context. Butler even expresses doubts about whether feminists need talk about the materiality of sex, as 'language both *is* and refers to that which is material', and admits that in seeking to consider the materiality of bodies, she found herself moving to other domains and neglecting this issue (Butler, 1993: ix, 29, 68). Butler's work also shares with Foucault's writings the problem of being unable to conceptualize the body as something which is irreducible to extant power relations or as a phenomenon which constitutes a source of society. Butler emphasizes that the construction of the sexed body takes place over time, that its performative nature means that 'gaps and fissures' open, and that there is always something surplus to the 'norm' that can undermine its successful inculcation (ibid.: 10). Far from being based within the pre-conscious generative capacities of the body, or the voluntaristic practices of embodied persons, however, this 'resistance' is produced by the heterosexual matrix and is, therefore, always tied to the dominant source of power in society. To the extent that it can be said to exist, 'agency' is 'immanent to power, and not a relation of external opposition to power', and is most evident in the restricted realm of speech (Butler, 1993; 4, 15; 1997: 155). The disappearance act is completed. Flesh-and-blood bodies are dissolved within the magical linguistic powers of the heterosexual regime.

The precarious ontology of the body within Butler's work is an undoubted problem, but her writings highlight the concern that our gendered physical *performances* are socially ordered and should not be viewed as natural, unchanging expressions of a fixed, pre-social bodily identity. Like Turner, she challenges us to think about the extent to which our bodies have become a location for (gendered) norms that prevent our physical capacities and dispositions from being a creative source of the social world we inhabit.

The constructed character of constructionism

Social constructionist theories of the ordered body instituted an 'epistemological break' from common-sense thinking, radically challenging the idea that the body constitutes a natural base on which the superstructures of self and society are founded. By examining how the body is controlled and regulated, they drew attention to the fact that power can be exercised on and through bodies, and thus revealed the partiality of theories which focus on ideas, ideologies and norms at the expense of the physical dimensions of social control. Nevertheless, these constructionist theories are based on a methodological objectivism that overlooks human experience and agency. They also replace biological essentialism with a social reductionism which collapses the body into society. The body remains a *recipient* of social practices, a location for the social system, and disappears as 'a vital organism which is experienced subjectively' (Soper, 1995: 135). In highlighting the importance of the body's receptivity to and capacity to be constrained by society, social constructionism tends to eclipse the body's significance as a source of the social world. One of the reasons for this, in the work of Turner and Butler, is the respective influences of Talcott Parsons and Louis Althusser.

Parsons has rarely been seen as a productive influence within the sociology of the body, but his theories of action and the social system inform key social constructionist assumptions. These include the idea that the significance of bodies lies in their capacity to be socialized and activated by the social system, and the view that the cultural values underpinning this system provide us with the key to understanding the relationship between embodied identity and social order. Furthermore, Parsons's analytical division of the body into sociologically relevant and irrelevant matter can also help us understand why theories of bodily order view embodiment from the perspective of society rather than from the lived experience of a biological organism. According to Parsons's normative sociology, the body was important to the social system mostly as a constraining sub-system of action that needed to be socialized in order to maximize the functional capacity of society. Other body issues, he suggested, could safely be omitted from the discipline (Parsons, 1991 [1951]: 541–2, 547–8). These remarks make Parsons an unlikely progenitor of the sociology of the body (see Chapter 2). Indeed, it is over four decades since Denis Wrong (1961) urged the discipline to avoid Parsons's 'over-socialized' and disembodied conception of the individual by starting from the suggestion that 'in the beginning there is the body'. However, far from rejecting his influence, Turner's (1984) theory of 'bodily order' sought to increase the analytical prominence of the body *within* a Parsonian framework. Bodies were no longer a sub-system of action, but became *the* environment in which individual and governmental action occurred and set the 'core problems' that social systems had to manage. The problem with this formulation, in its attempted combination of the fundamentally opposed methods of Hobbes and Parsons, is that it at once makes bodies *all important* and of *no importance*. They are all important because they provide the essential context for governmental and social action, yet they are of no importance because of their status as passive objects on which action is exercised.

Turner (1991a, 1996: 30) has revised his work in light of such criticisms by developing foundationalist perspectives which recognize that the body possesses 'biological and physiological characteristics' and distinguish between how the body is *classified*, what the body *is*, and how it is *experienced*. Such revision seems essential. If we do not have some idea of our body's own needs and abilities at a particular time, we ignore thousands of years of socio-natural evolutionary history and are unable to judge whether an institution or a society is good or bad for our well-being. As Kate Soper (1995: 138) argues, if we reject the idea of bodily pleasures and pains that are irreducible to discourse,

> we remove the objective grounds for challenging the authority of custom and convention, and must accept that it is only on the basis of personal preference (or prejudice) that we can contest the 'necessity' of a practice such as clitorectomy or foot binding, [or] challenge the oppression of sexual minorities.

It may seem ridiculous to associate Butler's feminist work with the normative sociology of Parsons (there is no mention of him in her writings), but the 'heterosexual matrix' appears to exemplify the operation of those norms Parsons saw as key to sustaining the family and the sexual division of labour within American society. Butler's route to these conclusions draws explicitly on Althusser, but her concern with ideological interpellation and the hailing of apparently infinitely malleable embodied subjects has a very similar effect. By depriving the body of its own ontological substance in order to expose the partiality of the heterosexual norms that recruit individuals to patriarchy, Butler deprives herself of any material basis on which to object to the effects of these social standards or any source of resistance and social change. Radical analyses of the body such as Butler's may have been promoted with the aim of 'freeing up the subject from the policing of cultural norms' but they end up ceding to culture the right to arbitrate on matters bodily (Soper, 1995: 138).

Social constructionist approaches have highlighted the importance of taking the body seriously as a location for society. With the present age described as a 'runaway world' in which people find it increasingly difficult to exercise control over their external environment, it is important to give due weight to the powers of social structures and norms (Giddens, 1990). In doing this, however, contemporary theories of the ordering and regulation of bodies have tended to erase any possibility of the body being a source of society. By denying the body any ontological materiality, furthermore, these perspectives leave themselves bereft of any physical grounds on which to examine the interaction between the body and society over time or to make judgements about the impact of particular social formations on the potentialities of their inhabitants. These are very real limitations, but theories of the ordered body do reflect a strong sense that our physical capacities and dispositions are no longer able to contribute creatively to the construction of society. Their case may be over-stated, but the suggestion that the parameters of human experience and creativity have been restricted in the contemporary era needs taking seriously.

Action and Phenomenological Approaches towards the Lived Body

In an attempt to rescue lived experience and individual action from their occlusion within structuralist and post-structuralist theories of the governed body, there were calls during the mid-1990s for a 'carnal sociology' that would operate on the assumption that '"self", "society" and "symbolic order" are constituted through the work of the body' (Crossley, 1995: 43). Crossley's articulation of that demand was timely as it coincided with a growing feeling that while theories of the body illuminated the *Körper* (the structural, objectified aspects of physical being), they had yet to come to grips fully with the *Lieb* (the living, feeling, sensing, and emotional aspects of bodily experience) (Csordas, 1994; Stoller, 1997). Expressed in the terms used in this study, it was time to move away from an exclusive focus on the body as a location, and to give prime attention to the body's role in being a source of the subject, of experience, and society.

Various sociological perspectives place experience and action at their centre (Dawe, 1979), but the drive towards carnal sociology was most influenced by *phenomenological* views of the 'lived body' (e.g. Jung, 1996). Phenomenology identified the body, rather than social structures, as the condition of our experience and our conscious orientation to the world (Marcel, 1951), and insisted that the body was not separate from the mind but formed 'the medium of all perception' (Husserl, 1989 [1929]: 61). It is the phenomenology of Merleau-Ponty that has exerted most effect on the sociology of the body (e.g. Young, 1980, 1998; Crossley, 1995, 1996, 2001; Nettleton and Watson, 1998). After examining some of the key concepts used in Merleau-Ponty's conception of the body as a source of society, I highlight the difficulties phenomenology has in taking into account the body's receptivity to, and ability to be constrained by, society. I then interpret Drew Leder's ground-breaking analysis of the 'absent body' as an attempt to rectify this failing, and as unintentionally raising deep concerns about the subjugation of bodily experience in the modern rationalized world.

Phenomenology and the experiencing body

Merleau-Ponty (1962: 160) rejected the idea that bodies could be seen exclusively as objects. Instead, he saw them as sites for subjectivity and consciousness: the body constitutes our active 'vehicle of being in' the world and provides us with a point of view on and situated experience of our environment. This emphasis on the bodily basis of meaning and knowledge constitutes a major challenge to structuralist and post-structuralist theories. Far from being given in advance of our existence, phenomenology suggests that the structure and meaning of the world and the integrity of objects are 'achieved through the medium of body experience' (ibid.: 30, 229). Embodied subjects develop direction and purpose not because of the influence of governmental or discursive regimes structurally removed from individual reach, but on the basis of the *practical* engagements they have with their surroundings and through the *intentionality* they develop as a result of the situatedness of embodied existence (ibid.: 136).

The idea that humans are lived, intentional body subjects, always practically oriented towards the world, assumes that individuals gradually become integrated, coordinated, and aware of their capacities and limitations. This sense of somatic unity has several preconditions and it is important to outline them if we are to appreciate contemporary applications of Merleau-Ponty's work within the field. These preconditions include the development of our body schema, our capacity for motility, and the sensory media through which we are able to engage with the world.

The *body schema* is central to Merleau-Ponty's conception of our bodily unity, and refers to a general pre-conscious awareness of our body's position 'in relation to the vertical, the horizontal, and certain other axes of important coordinates of its environment' (ibid.: 117, 123).[2] This schema develops slowly in humans, from its fragmented state in infancy, yet is crucial to the spatial sense we have of our bodily selves.

Our capacities for *motility*, 'a project towards movement or "potential movement"', further orientate the body in space (ibid.: 234). Motility accomplishes an extension of the body schema, through the incorporation of new skills and new objects, which enables us to expand the quantity and quality of our movements and to exercise agency. By developing expertise in the use of objects, we effectively embody new means of projecting ourselves onto the world. In learning to type, for example, the 'key-bank space' is incorporated into 'bodily space' in a manner which allows us to communicate with others (ibid.: 145). Similarly, the tennis player's racquet, the painter's brush, and the sculptor's chisel become extensions of limbs. It is through these objects, or tools, that the tennis ball can be felt and directed, the texture of the paint touched, and the surface and density of material sensed. These extensions of the body schema are especially apparent in cases of disability where a major sense, such as sight, has been lost. 'The blind man's stick has ceased to be an object for him, and is no longer perceived for itself; its point has become an area of sensitivity, extending the scope and active radius of touch, and providing a parallel to sight' (ibid.: 143).

If the body schema and motility are integral components of the lived body subject, the above example illustrates the importance Merleau-Ponty also attached to our *sensory media*. Our senses provide the world, and ourselves, with 'thickness', facticity, and meaning: sensory perception occurs in the world and constitutes this world for us (Edie, 1963: xviii). As we move through the world, our active, intentional relationship with the environment involves an intercommunication of the senses as they open themselves up to a particular object or setting (Merleau-Ponty, 1962: 229). Visual perception is of primary importance in this process, providing subjects with an opening

55

onto, and a culturally framed perspective on, a perceptual field which stretches around them (Crossley, 1995: 47). It is not just sight that provides the conditions for the lived, intentional subject, however, but our senses of touch, smell, hearing and taste which enable us to open ourselves onto, and effectively create, our environment.

Merleau-Ponty provides us with a powerful account of the universal subjective features of bodily existence that involve us in the constitution of our natural and social world. He recognizes that the body possesses an objective existence (e.g. Merleau-Ponty, 1968), but it is his writings on the lived body as a subject which have proved most influential in stimulating body theory's increasing concern with experience. This is because Merleau-Ponty's (1962: 198–9) focus on the bodily basis of experience enables theorists to get away from views of the individual as either physical automata, permanently receptive to the ordering powers of political or discursive regimes, or as subjects defined by 'pure consciousness'. In their place, Merleau-Ponty analyses how our awareness of the world is actively embodied, constituting a 'being-towards-the-thing through the intermediary of the body' which enables us to be an active source of the world around us and to invest that world with a particular emotional patterning (ibid.: 106, 138, 189, 203).

Phenomenology redirects our attention to the body's significance as a source of the self and of society. Despite its recognition that the body can at times be an object for others, however, this approach has no developed conception of how the body can be shaped by social relations and contexts, or how its somatic experiences provide a means through which particular body–society relationships can serve to attach people to or alienate them from their social milieu. Thus, body theorists indebted to Merleau-Ponty have faced a dilemma. On the one hand, they have sought to integrate his work with that of a variety of theorists who provide a more effective examination of social context and structure (Crossley, 1996, 1998, 2001). Alternatively, they have suggested that phenomenology's valuable concern with lived experience and social action (including how the capacities and dispositions of the body constitute a source of society) is just what theorists should concentrate on, and have accused sociology of erasing this concern (Howson and Inglis, 2001). The implication here is that analysts of the body should embrace the phenomenological concern with the body as a source of self and society, and abandon sociology's disproportionate concern with the flesh as a location for the social.

The absent body

There is a paradox within phenomenology. Having been interpreted by many theorists as analyses of the 'lived body', of how people experience their bodies, the work of Merleau-Ponty and others within this tradition is actually concerned with the bodily *basis* of experience. It is quite possible, therefore, for the body to fade away within a phenomenological account of how the capacities and dispositions of the body are a source of society and shape people's practical experiences of the world. Drew Leder's (1990) theory of the 'absent body' exploits this characteristic of phenomenology in his account of how the body is experienced during purposeful or instrumental action. In so doing, I want to suggest that Leder's account can be interpreted not as a universalist account of the lived body, but as a troubling phenomenological analysis of the body's status as a location for the effects of a highly rationalized society in which instrumentalist action is prized and rewarded above other forms of behaviour.

The starting point of Leder's (1990) thesis is that the body ordinarily 'fades' and 'disappears' from our experience when we are engaged in that purposeful action that creates our environment and governs our daily routines, yet can abruptly reappear as a focus of attention when we are ill or in pain and when our bodies are at their least socially productive. Phenomenology needs to account for these different states of 'body consciousness', Leder suggests, by constructing an explicitly layered account of embodiment which recognizes the contrast between functioning efficiency and corporeal absence, and organic malfunction and corporeal presence. He begins with the relationship between purposeful action and corporeal disappearance:

> When reading a book or lost in thought ... I experientially dwell in a world of ideas, paying little heed to my physical sensations or posture. Nor is this forgetfulness restricted to moments of higher-level cognition. I may be engaged in a fierce sport, muscles flexed and responsive to the slightest movements of my opponent. Yet it is precisely upon this opponent, this game, that my attention dwells, not on my own embodiment. (Leder, 1990: 1)

By assuming that normal human action is purposeful action, Leder is able to argue that our daily lives are most commonly marked by the subjective absence rather than the presence of the body. In interrogating the relationship between organic malfunction and corporeal presence, however, he develops his thesis by exploring how pain, illness and other states can make the body *reappear* with a vengeance. Utilizing the Greek prefix 'dys' (signifying 'bad', 'hard' or 'ill' and deployed in an adapted form in 'disfunctional'), Leder (1990: 84) employs the term *dys-appearance* to refer to when the body reappears as a thematic and sensory focus of our experience in a pathological or deviant form. Bodily dys-appearance alienates us from the world and assumes several different forms (Buytendijk, 1974). Pain can 'take our breath away', rupture us from purposeful activity, and make us acutely aware of our body as a 'thing', demanding our attention. We can, indeed, become lost in a world of pain whose parameters consist of a highly restricted body image shot through with stabbing, piercing, searing agony (Scarry, 1985; Williams, 1996). Our rational calculations and activities can also be completely overwhelmed by the experience of passion, fear or anxiety, or may be interrupted by the simple development of our body (Smith, 1992: 12, 134). During a girl's first period, or the breaking of a boy's voice, for example, a bodily 'state' foregrounds itself forcefully within experience.

The self-consciousness associated with 'slips' or 'gaffes' during interaction provides another example of the (emotional) dys-appearance of the body. The body can reappear to us here through an embarrassed consciousness of a reddening face or a stuttering voice (Goffman, 1956a, 1956b). Socially caused dys-appearances of the body can even lead to ill health. The cultural pressures on women to achieve an 'ideal' body shape have been associated with anorexia nervosa, for example, while the tensions involved in a society which values self-control, productive labour *and* hedonistic consumption have been linked to bulimia (Turner, 1984; Leder, 1990: 99).

Leder's account of how the body can fade from, and reappear within, experience resonates with Merleau-Ponty's writings but is not uncritical of them (Leder, 1990: 20, 33). First, he agrees with Merleau-Ponty that social- ized adults usually have a tacit command over their bodies which enables them to perform actions without reflecting on every physical movement made. The more effectively our balance and sensory perception operate, indeed, the more the body tends to disappear from our phenomenological experience of living (ibid.: 41–3). Second, he also follows Merleau-Ponty in arguing that the successful acquisition of new skills is usually dependent on them becoming fully incorporated into the body at a *pre-conscious* level. Third, he highlights how a phenomenological account should be able to show that the process of engaging in an activity, such as reading, requires that countless skills and motor schemata remain unused. Even 'the percep- tual organ remains an absence or nullity in the midst of the perceived': the reader does not see the eye which enables her to read (ibid.: 13–26). Fourth, in an analysis which reveals aspects of the body ignored by Merleau-Ponty, Leder points out that our internal visceral organs provide an example of 'depth disappearance'. Our internal organs do not usually provide us with the degree or specificity of information that our surface senses do. We may be suffering from dangerously high hypertension, for example, without being aware of our condition, and without it interrupting our reading (ibid.: 26, 43, 53). This 'depth disappearance' raises an important related point. We are frequently subjectively unaware of various evolutionary developments and physical potentials which are crucial to our capacities as human beings. These physical qualities are often overlooked by phenomenological accounts, yet they surely need to be taken into account in any comprehen- sive theory of the body. Finally, Leder differs from Merleau-Ponty in terms of the precise nature of his focus on the phenomenological experience of purposeful action. The body only fades for Leder when it has become suffi- ciently *rationalized* to be engaged in instrumental action and is actually *engaged in* such action. Thus, Leder's account can usefully be read as an eth- ically worrying explanation of what happens to bodies when they become locations for the effects of a highly rationalized society. It should not, how- ever, be read as an analysis of the universal features of embodiment. There are several reasons for this.

To begin with, Leder's suggestion that bodies become visible only when socially or physiologically pathological appears to project the logic of instrumental rationality onto the experience of embodiment. As in Parsons's (1991 [1951]) analysis of the 'sick role', the body becomes prominent only when illness or other malfunctions disturb that purposeful action prized by modern social systems. Yet there are good reasons for thinking that it is precisely when our bodies are at their most creative that we possess a heightened awareness of them (Joas, 1996). It is when we are confronted with a practical problem that requires a novel solution that we often become acutely conscious of our bodies' positioning, capacities and inventiveness. Our bodies may fade from consciousness when we are engaged in instrumentally rational action, but this is action that is routinized, oriented towards the known, and mostly reproductive of a particular practice. Translated into the terms of this study, our bodies fade from experience when they have become a location for the effects and normalized practices of a rationalized social system. If Leder's account of experience is indeed becoming more widespread within modernity, then it can be seen as a damning indictment of the fate of embodiment in the current era.

Leder's vision of the latent body is also partial as it seems to model itself upon the bodies of those whose capacities display the greatest affinity with a highly rationalized society, those healthy males in their middle years not subject to the bodily processes involved in menstruation, pregnancy, ageing, illness and decay. Iris Young (1980), for example, argues that instead of being characterized by intentionality, bodily unity, and transcendence, the typical modalities of feminine movement exhibit an *inhibited* intentionality, a *discontinuous* unity, and an *ambiguous* transcendence (see also Laws, 1990). Leder (1990: 86) acknowledges there is something to this criticism of bodily absence, but his central thesis remains unchanged. There is little suggestion that the body can become a major, prolonged focus of attention in its 'normal' state; that it can become a sensual vehicle for creativity or an explicit site for individual development. Again, this reflects something deeply worrying about the tendencies Leder has focused on.

Finally, this view of the normal body as one that has become a location for the effects of rationalized society, is reflected by the cultural and historical specificity that forms a background for, yet fades away within, Leder's study. Leder's disappearing body is one that has been absorbed into the logic of performativity governing affluent societies, yet is immune to any characteristics that may disrupt this performativity. Thus, the flows of peoples between regions characteristic of post-colonial societies provide regular, foregrounded encounters with 'corporeal otherness' that are associated in part with new forms of racism (Ahmed, 2000). Furthermore, given the global inequalities that continue to mark our planet, hunger, disease and fear are part of daily life for millions across the globe, entering into the 'normal' state of their embodied existence. Here, it might be more applicable to talk of the much rarer emergence of the healthy, fully functioning body as a process of *appearance* rather than disappearance.

A return to sociological bodies?

Phenomenology usefully refocuses our attention on to some of the capacities of the body that enable it to be a source of the self and of society. As such, it helps extend the classical concern with this feature of the body, and also addresses that which is marginalized within constructionist accounts of the ordered body. If phenomenology is generally less convincing when it comes to explaining how the body is also receptive to, and able to be constrained by, society, or in analysing the outcomes of interaction between the body's agentic capacities and societal structures, Leder's account of the absent body can be interpreted as a provocative view of experience which presupposes the dominance of a rationalized, instrumentalized society. It is during *instrumental action* that a sufficiently fit and healthy body (not in need of refreshment or toilet) can temporarily fade from view. Seen in this light, Leder's work can be taken as a reason for expressing deep concern about the dominance of instrumentality that has reduced the parameters of our bodily experience. The body may be a productive source of society in Leder's account, but it is only instrumentally productive: the expressive and creative capacities of human embodiment fade from view.

Conceptions of the Body in Structuration Theory

Theories of the ordered body and phenomenological accounts of the lived body provided the field with alternative lines of development, but were not the only ones to shape the parameters of body studies. Conceptions of the body in structuration theory suggest that theories which make a stark distinction between external structures and the agentic living subject are unhelpful and invalid as they posit an unbridgeable dualism between the body as a location for and a source of society. This dualism, they suggest, disallows us from recognizing that the bodily bases of action and structure are instantiated in each other. Anthony Giddens is the best-known exponent of structuration theory, but Pierre Bourdieu's long-standing concern with the body can also be classified in this way.[3] Finally, Elizabeth Grosz's conception of the sexed body as a Möbius strip – the inverted three-dimensional figure eight – provides us with a quite different, feminist interrogation of the mutual constitution of the body and (patriarchal) society.

Each of these theorists seeks to retain a sensitivity to the bodily basis of action and identity *within* its social contexts. However, I shall suggest that the body and society do not just interact with one another in these accounts, but are mutually constituted by one another to the extent that it becomes difficult to disentangle them or to attribute them with distinctive properties that would allow us to track their interaction over time. Because of this, there is a tendency for the positioning of the body within society to appear fixed and unalterable. I begin with the work of Bourdieu as he has been described as the 'sociological heir' of Merleau-Ponty, and seeks to retain the insights of phenomenology by relating subjectivity to the historical conditions of its emergence and development (Wacquant, 1992: 20).

Habitus, *field and social reproduction*

Bourdieu's (1990c [1980]) statement that 'The body is in the social world but the social world is in the body' reveals his assumption that the embodied actor is both indelibly shaped by, and an active reproducer of, society. Bourdieu develops this position, which underpins his work, by critically engaging with the objectivism associated with structural analysis of the ordered body, and the subjectivism associated with phenomenological writings on the body subject. He argues that while objectivism fails to apprehend that bodily experiences are a precondition of, and are inscribed within, social institutions, the subjectivism associated with phenomenology is unable to address the existence and development of the contexts in which experience occurs (ibid.: 25). In his interview-based study of 'social suffering', for example, Bourdieu (1999: 613, 620) rejects the unacceptable method of assuming experience from structural conditions, and the simplistic phenomenological 'projection of oneself into the other'. Instead, he seeks to relate the experiences, appearances and accounts of individuals to the social conditions which gave rise to them (Bourdieu, 1990c [1980], 1984, 1999).

The principles informing Bourdieu's approach are developed through the key conceptual distinction he makes between the 'social field' and *habitus*. Social field refers to a set of dynamic organizing principles, ultimately maintained by social groups, which identify and structure particular categories of practices that occur within a social space (e.g. education, art, sport, economics). Social fields 'are the products of a long, slow process of autonomization' (Bourdieu, 1990c [1980]: 67). Their development allows us to trace the contours of an age which is increasingly specialized into social sectors organized on the basis of their own specific logics, and is no longer characterized by a relatively undifferentiated community. Each social field has a relative autonomy from other fields, and bestows values on social practices according to its principles of internal organization and recognition.

Characterizing society in terms of its multiple social fields reflects Bourdieu's view that contemporary social life is not governed by a single, overarching culture, system, or logic of capital, but is constituted by organized spaces which each possess their own regulative principles. The social fields of fashion and sport, for example, operate on the basis of distinctive rules and recognize distinctive forms of capital which establish the parameters in which individuals enter into and compete within them (Bourdieu, 1986). If social fields locate themselves on the bodies of those entering their space, they do not constitute completely determining structures but are characterized by a measure of contingency which allows space for individual variation (Bourdieu, 1990b). The rules which structure a field can always be reflected upon and negotiated. If this room for manoeuvre exists, though, why is it that Bourdieu views social life as so patterned, regular and stable? The reason for this, as Loic Wacquant (1992: 18) points out, is related to the significance he places on the conceptual relationship that pertains between social field and the *habitus*.

The *habitus* is a socially constituted system of 'durable, transposable' dispositions which provides individuals with class-dependent, predisposed ways of categorizing and relating to both familiar and novel situations (Bourdieu, 1990c [1980]: 53). The *habitus* is formed in the context of people's social locations, and inculcates in them a set of tastes and a 'worldview' based on, and reconciled to, these positions (Bourdieu, 1981, 1984). Specifically, it installs in the human organism 'schemes of perception, thought and action' derived from the social fields inhabited by individuals (Bourdieu, 1990c [1980]: 54). This process of installation is not necessarily experienced as oppressive or restrictive, and its results are frequently embraced by individuals (Bourdieu, 1981). The working-class lads examined in Paul Willis's (1977) *Learning to Labour*, for example, celebrated the masculine practices of their fathers' manual work culture and incorporated its valuation of physical toil and skill into their approach towards school. Rejecting academic work as 'feminine' – a judgement which reflects the social oppositions between manual and mental work, men and women – they effectively helped create the conditions of their future subordination within the workplace.

The concepts 'social field' and '*habitus*' are central to Bourdieu's attempt to transcend the subject/object and structure/agency dualisms. Social fields are not autonomous 'social facts', but depend for their continuation on the social practices of groups and individuals. Similarly, the *habitus*, being 'the social embodied', makes people 'at home' in the fields they inhabit (Bourdieu, 1984: 190; 1992: 128). There is an 'almost miraculous encounter between the *habitus* and a field', Bourdieu (1990c [1980]: 66) suggests, which is analogous to the soccer player who has a 'feel for the game' and is able to anticipate and participate in its flow without engaging in conscious reflection. More generally, this 'fit' means that the *habitus* legitimates institutions by encouraging people to recognize as valid the 'performative magic' of ritual, dress and actions which make particular individuals appear to be the flesh-and-blood incarnation of social roles (ibid.: 57).

Bourdieu's analysis of social fields and the *habitus* suggests that structural and agentic factors are interdependent and mutually reinforcing of the conditions that facilitate their reproduction. The interaction between the body and society involves a mutual determination which harnesses physical capacities and dispositions to the reproduction of the status quo. The body, in short, has become a *means* for the attachment of the individual to society (and of society to the individual). This is evident in Bourdieu's analysis of the class-dependent development of *practical sense* and *physical capital*.

Bourdieu's (1990c [1980]: 69) analysis of practical sense suggests that there exists a bodily common sense that causes people to act in accordance with the possibilities and constraints given by their social circumstances.

This circuit connecting individuals to society involves an 'implicit pedagogy' which can place the 'most fundamental principles' of a culture beneath the reach of consciousness and into 'the primary experiences of the body' (ibid.: 69, 71). Examples of this process can be seen in the reproduction of gender differences through the 'fixing' of highly charged cultural meanings onto the basic anatomical differences dividing the sexes (ibid.: 71). The mutual accommodation of structure and agency evident in practical sense is also evident in the associated development of physical capital. Bourdieu suggests that individuals develop a taste for acquiring bodily appearances, competencies and performances that raise their stock within those social fields most likely to reproduce their existing social status (Shilling, 2003: 111–30), while the amount of body work done on the body by different classes in order to enhance self-presentation is 'proportionate to the chances of material or symbolic profit they can reasonably expect from it' (Bourdieu, 1984: 202).

Bourdieu's concern with the structuration of the body and society seeks to combine the insights of structuralism and phenomenology while avoiding their limitations. In attempting to do this, however, he ties action and experience to structures. While Bourdieu protests that the *habitus* does not imply a structural determination of individual action, he continues to argue that it produces in people a voluntary acceptance of their social circumstances. While Bourdieu asserts the facts of changing bodily dispositions, his argument that the *habitus* operates at the level of the subconscious, 'beyond the reach of introspective scrutiny or control by the will' (ibid.: 466), makes it difficult to see how individuals can escape from the dispositional trajectory assigned them. In virtually every sphere of social life examined by Bourdieu, we find a near perfect fit between the *habitus* and the social field instead of a genuine, causally consequential interaction between the embodied subject's creative powers and existing societal structures. Thus, practical sense and physical capital, the sports chosen, the foods eaten, the careers aspired to, the films watched, the cultural preferences expressed, etc., all represent a homology between a group's *habitus* and the position of practices or objects within the relevant social field. This is despite the fact that Bourdieu (1990c [1980]: 108) formally identifies 'rational and conscious' principles of action which are meant to provide an alternative to the *habitus*. Not only do these principles appear to be foundationless, constituting highly residual categories within his theory, but they rarely disturb this more habitual form of action (Shilling, 2004b).

In contrast to theories of the ordered body, the embodied individual is active in Bourdieu's work. Nevertheless, this subject is active on the basis of a relationship between the social field and *habitus* which mitigates against change, makes a virtue out of necessity, and reproduces their conditions of existence. If such a theory effectively disallows for the prospect of change, however, it can once again be said to reflect real concerns that the modern world is stifling the creativity of humans and allowing the body to be productive of social phenomena only when it is serving to help reproduce the status quo.

Reflexivity, identity and the body

Giddens's structuration theory has proved as influential within body theory as it has in sociology generally (e.g. Burkitt, 1992, 1999; Shilling, 1993; Hancock et al., 2000), informing conceptions of the body as a project and arguments about the increasingly close association between self-identity and the exterior of people's bodily selves. Giddens, like Bourdieu, views the body as both shaped by social structures and as an active reproducer of them. However, Giddens's early writings on the subject pay more attention to the natural organism as a constraint on social action, while his later studies focus on the body's transformation within modernity into a vehicle and an expression of reflexivity.

In *The Constitution of Society*, Giddens (1984) emphasizes how the body constrains individuals. Individuals have first to acquire a 'basic trust' in their own motility and environment before they can even exercise their bodily capacities, while the physical design and sensory qualities of the human organism impose 'strict limitations' on social agency (Giddens, 1984: 111). These constraints do not, however, make the body unimportant. In relation to agency, the ability to intervene in daily life is dependent on the bodily conditions surrounding the spacing, timing and significance of interpersonal encounters (Giddens, 1984: 41). In relation to structures, what Giddens (1979: 5; 1984: 26, 41) conceives of as 'rules' and 'resources' are only instantiated in practice, and reproduced by, embodied subjects (Giddens, 1984: 111). The significance Giddens attributes to the body, indeed, is reflected in his judgement of Erving Goffman as a 'systematic social theorist' (Giddens, 1988). For Giddens (1991: 56), Goffman's analyses of the interactional techniques involved in 'turn taking', 'make work', and the presentation of self demonstrate the skills involved in becoming a 'competent agent' and the structural rules and resources implicated in social action. It is the body that provides the essential means through which individuals are connected to society.

If Giddens (1984) suggests that the body imposes a natural constraint on individuals, even if it remains of great importance for the structuration of social life, a much more voluntaristic tone permeates his later analysis of the body in modernity. Here, he argues that while in traditional societies the body used to be governed by processes 'only marginally subject to human intervention', modernity has liberated individuals from nature (Giddens, 1991: 102). The body is no longer 'an extrinsic "given", functioning outside the internally referential systems of modernity', but has become 'drawn into the reflexive organisation of social life' to the extent that we are 'responsible for the design of our own bodies' (Giddens, 1991: 7, 98). Thus, the development of cosmetic and transplant surgeries, developments in DNA replication, and the rapid advance of 'cybertechnologies' have all facilitated the body's colonization by individual choice and social technology (Kelly, 1994; Featherstone and Burrows, 1995; Heim, 1995).

In this context, the body becomes a much more malleable part of the circuit connecting individuals to society: it is the cognitively *reflexive* monitoring and changing of action that have acquired a unique significance for the exercise of agency and the fate of 'structures' (Giddens, 1990: 36–45). It is our reflexive life plans and our increasingly reflexive engagements with lifestyle politics and risks, for example, that determine our social actions (Giddens, 1994, 1998). Similarly, self-identity, 'the self as reflexively understood by the person in terms of her or his biography', is maintained by the 'capacity to keep a particular narrative going' (Giddens, 1991: 53). Finally, love and intimacy have become ethereal affairs in late modernity, involving mutual disclosure, communication and the maintenance of individual autonomy, and eschewing bodily passions which colonize the mind and may threaten the transcendence and even 'erasure' of the self (Giddens, 1992: 90, 94; cf. Bataille, 1962). In contrast to the likes of Bourdieu and Mauss, there is for Giddens no 'deep self' located in a set of 'body techniques' or an intransigent *habitus*, but an almost infinitely flexible body that is involved in the positioning of the individual within society.

Giddens's 1984 study usefully demonstrates the embodied basis of both agency and structure, and it seems to me that this is the essential point that needs to be taken from structuration theory, but the body fades from view in his later writings. The reason for this is that it is absorbed into, and defined by its function as, a location for an all-powerful, internally referential, reflexivity. In an analysis which has a surprisingly Cartesian character for someone concerned with the body's importance, it is cognitive reflexivity, the parameters of which are defined by the reflexive character of society, that is of most importance in determining how individuals acquire knowledge and make decisions. While the bodily remains tied to reproducing the status quo in Bourdieu's writings, it is worn lightly by Giddens's late modern subjects and can be reinvented by the individual alongside their reflexively constituted narratives of self.

Despite the undoubted insights of Giddens's later analysis, it is characterized by major problems. Its conception of the body as controlled by reflexivity severely restricts the extent that we can recognize its continued productive significance for the reproduction or transformation of structural rules and resources. People's sensory engagement with structures is vitally important as they can exert an important impact on whether they *feel* at ease with, and tend to reproduce, the 'rules' and 'resources' most readily accessible to them, or experience them as unpleasant, undesirable and worthy of transformation, yet Giddens's focus on reflexivity marginalizes emotional experiences and expressions (Shilling and Mellor, 1996). Similar to Leder (1990), the body tends to reassert itself in Giddens's analysis only when it 'breaks down'. Pain, illness, the emergence of addictive behaviours, or the confrontation with death, for example, can effect this by highlighting a body that is out of control in a world dependent upon control (Giddens, 1991: 202–3). There is little sense of the non-pathological dispositions and tastes one finds in Bourdieu's work. These are very real limitations, yet despite the celebratory dimensions of Giddens's analyses (related to his endorsement of reflexivity as a central aspect of 'third way' politics in the contemporary era of globalization), they can also be interpreted as depicting an era which has neglected and marginalized the socially productive elements of human embodiment. The reflexive powers of society and the reflexively competent individual have entered into a mutually determining relationship which seems to allow no positive room for the capacities and dispositions of enfleshed subjects.

Sexuality: the interiors and exteriors of embodiment

Elizabeth Grosz provides us with a very different form of structuration theory, shifting focus away from the individual–society relationship and towards the mutual structuration of the body and sexuality. In place of such concepts as the '*habitus*' and 'reflexivity', Grosz employs the Lacanian topographical image of the Möbius strip (the inverted three-dimensional figure eight) which she uses to illustrate how 'through a kind of twisting or inversion' the psychic interiors and fleshy exteriors of the body relate to each other and to the dominant social norms of sexuality.

The structure of Grosz's major 1994 study, *Volatile Bodies*, is organized so as to reflect this concern with the mutual structuration of the interiors and exteriors of bodies. Its first half focuses on how the body is constituted from 'the inside out'. Grosz discusses psychoanalytic, neurological and phenomenological accounts in support of her argument that the body is not simply 'given' to the individual but must be 'psychically constituted in order for the subject to acquire a sense of its place in the world and in connection with others' (Grosz, 1994: xii). As we do not have a complete view of our body and its potentialities (we only usually glimpse our bodies as we live our daily lives), this view must be built up through the interior psychological resources at our disposal. Grosz examines the development of these resources by engaging with Freud's (1923) analysis of how the ego emerges from the id 'through a gradual process of differentiation initiated by the organism's confrontations with reality', Head's and Schilder's writings on body schema, and Merleau-Ponty's analysis of the reciprocal effects of touching and being touched. By placing great store on the argument that the interiors of our bodily being are in fact shaped by the organism's confrontation with social reality, however, she lays the ground for the establishment of a correspondence between the psyche, the body and culturally constituted sexual norms (Grosz, 1994: 27).

In its second half, *Volatile Bodies* interrogates sexuality from 'the outside in' by examining how society's impact on the corporeal surfaces of the body affects the subjectivity of the individual. Grosz utilizes theorists of 'corporeal inscription' (Nietzsche, Foucault, and Deleuze and Guattari) in tracing how sexual difference is printed on our bodies via 'pedagogical, juridical, medical and economic texts, laws, and practices' (ibid.: 117). Such practices have very real effects and, for Grosz (ibid.: 205), the 'fluidity and indeterminacy of female body parts, most notably the breasts but no less the female sexual organs' are 'confined, constrained, solidified, through … temporary or permanent means … by clothing or … by surgery' in male culture. Normative practices inscribe the subject with a sexually specific and agentically limiting identity.

It is through these contrasting views (the sexual constitution of the body from within and without), that Grosz's view of the structuration of the body and sexuality unfolds. Her study may be 'a literal patchwork, written in pieces, many of which do not fit easily together' (ibid.: xiii), but it develops a distinctive view of how the body and dominant norms of sexuality are mutually constitutive. This process of structuration is at its most visible in her analysis of body image. In living the body from 'inside out', the morphology of the male and female body exerts an inevitable effect on how individuals psychically perceive their embodied selves. As Grosz (ibid.: 58) argues, 'It seems incontestable that the type of genitals and secondary sexual characteristics one has (or will have) must play a major role in the type of body image one has.' At the same time, this conception of the physical self is also inevitably linked to 'the social meaning and value [attached to] the sexed body' (ibid.).

Grosz seeks to combine a wide variety of resources in demonstrating that the sexual body both structures our view of 'male' and 'female' identities, and is structured by extant social norms. As with other structuration theories, she is opposed to both biologically essentialist views of the body as completely determining of people's identities, and socially constructionist analyses which conclude that sexual difference 'is purely a matter of the inscription and codification of somehow uncoded, absolutely raw materials' (ibid.: 190). In contrast to Butler, therefore, Grosz is determined to hold on to a view of the materially sexed body. As she argues, '[t]he body is constrained by its biological limits' and 'the kind of body inscribed' makes an essential 'difference to the meanings and functioning of gender that emerges' (ibid.: ix, 58, 187). Society does not exert its effects on a corporeal 'blank page', but etches them on specific materials which contribute to the kind of physical 'text' produced (ibid.: 191).

Grosz's study constitutes a radical extension and partial reconstruction of structuration theory into the field of gender, yet fails to escape from the wider problems of this approach in relation to its insistence on the simultaneously constituting and constituted nature of the (sexed) body. Grosz does not over-emphasize the body's malleability (as with Giddens's focus on individual reflexivity), or its determination (as with Bourdieu's notion of the *habitus*), but she does veer between these two positions without establishing any criteria which allow us to judge which of them is valid at a particular time. Thus, on the one hand, Grosz (1994: 58, 188–90) opposes the idea that sexual difference is forged out of undifferentiated bodies. On the other hand, Grosz (ibid.: 203) denies that women are ontologically different to men: dominant conceptions of women's sexual identity stem from social inscription and there is nothing essential about sexual difference. Grosz admits that the tension in her writing may be the result of strategic priorities, but ultimately leaves us with a correspondence theory which posits an equivalence between the interiors and exteriors of the body, and dominant sexual norms, yet which cannot explain how this correspondence emerged. We are left with a body that is positioned by, and unalterably tied to, the sexual norms of society.

Unstructuring structuration theory

Margaret Archer (1988, 1995) has accused structuration theory of engaging in 'central conflationism', a form of reductionism in which structures and agents are tied together so closely that it is impossible to examine their separate properties or how they affect each other over time. The problem here is not that the body and society *partially* mutually constitute each other, I would suggest, but, as Archer (1995: 87) puts it, that they 'are effectively defined in terms of one another'. Structuration theory seeks to hang on to the (sometimes sexed) body as an irreducible component of social reality. When it succeeds, however, the defining features of the physical flesh soon become defined *entirely* in terms of society. This is the case for Bourdieu and for sections of Grosz's study. When it fails, the body disappears into the reflexive powers of the mind. This is the case with Giddens's later writings in which cognitive reflexivity has come to define what it is to be human. Ultimately, it seems that this approach to the body–society relationship is no more successful than structuralist theories of the governed body or phenomenological accounts of the lived body in recognizing the multi-dimensional nature of the body's relationship with society. More productively, however, it does raise similar concerns to these perspectives about the significance of the body within contemporary society. For Bourdieu and Grosz in particular, the body's positioning within society seems to leave it irredeemably attached to dominant structures of social class or sexuality that stifle human potentiality.

New Directions?

Contemporary theorists of the body have done much to place embodiment at the centre of social theory. Each of the approaches I have examined in this chapter, moreover, focuses on something of enduring significance to the analysis of embodiment and society. Social constructionist theories of the ordered body draw our attention to how power is exercised on and through bodies, and have distanced sociological thinking about embodiment from naturalistic, biologically reductionist analyses. They have, in short, developed our appreciation of how the body constitutes an important *location* on which society imprints itself and through which it is able to exercise influence and power. Action and phenomenological approaches have demonstrated the importance of the body as the basis for the exercise of agency and the lived experience of social actors. Sociology will not capture the complexity of the body by viewing it simply as a physical object, they suggest, but needs to recognize how the organism is our vehicle of being in, experiencing and creating the world in which we live. If we combine this with an appreciation of how certain evolutionary developments and bodily capacities may be out of reach of phenomenological introspection, we can appreciate their contribution towards advancing our understanding of how the body constitutes a vital *source* for the creation of society. Furthermore, Leder's phenomenological theory of the absent body takes this insight in a different direction by sketching out a theory of experience within a society dominated by the principles of instrumental rationality. Finally, conceptions of the body in structuration theory seek to position human physicality (or, in the case of Giddens's later work, human reflexivity) as a central part of a circuit connecting the individual to society. Social actors both create their social milieu, through the capacities and facilities of their bodies, and are shaped by the impact their social location exerts on their bodies. If we reject their tendency to conflate the embodied subject and society, and focus instead on the genuine interaction between these phenomena, structuration theories can remind us that the body constitutes a *means* through which individuals are attached to, or ruptured from, society (although the body becomes decreasingly significant to this process for Giddens).

These are very real insights and it would be rash to dismiss one in favour of another of these theories. Nevertheless, by advancing their analyses in the context of different and frequently opposing philosophical and sociological principles, the cumulative effect of these approaches has been to invest the body with a partiality and elusiveness identified in the opening chapter. Theories of the ordered body let the individual's active and experienced body fade from view. Phenomenologically informed theories tend to occlude the effect of structures on the experiences of individuals (though we can interpret Leder's work as rectifying this problem), and, ironically, sometimes converge with structuralist approaches when suggesting that the body fades from view during purposeful action.[4] This fading is perhaps inevitable in sociological studies which focus for a time on the significance of social structures, but needs to be counterbalanced in such analyses by a return to the embodied subject. Structuration theories, despite their attempts to combine a concern with the body's significance for structure *and* agency, frequently collapse these together in analyses when the body tends to oscillate between the dead weight of structure and the lightness of reflexive choice. The centripetal trend in body studies, in short, has done little to reduce the elusiveness of the body in social thought.

In attempting to avoid these problems, body theorists associated with these contemporary approaches have tended to employ one of four main strategies. First, they have simply added to their preferred theories concepts or accounts which seek to address those issues or elements of embodiment marginalized within these writings. This is clearly Turner's preference as he includes a concern with 'the phenomenology of experience' as a corrective to 'the underlying structuralism' of *The Body and Society* (Turner, 1996: 33;

Turner and Wainwright, 2003). Bourdieu has also done this in identifying principles of action which differ from those based in the *habitus*. Such an approach has the advantage of starting from a developed position, while at the same time seeking to 'stretch' that approach to take into account elements of the body it previously ignored. However, it runs the risk of creating a proliferation of residual categories which cannot be explained by the primary concepts of the theory. Turner (1996), for example, adds to his concern with the body as a flexible classificatory system a recognition that there are foundational aspects of our physicality which provide a basis for the analysis of lived experience. Nevertheless, this leaves unanswered the questions of how these perspectives actually fit together, and when and how dominant views of the body may actually change the materiality of the body and people's experience of their bodies. Such additions remain outside of the prime, positive features of his theory.

Second, there is the argument that a preferred approach *really can* take into account the body as an object and a subject, and its relevance for structure and agency. This is Crossley's (1995) interpretation of Merleau-Ponty as a flexible theorist who can reconcile the dualisms apparent in sociological theories of the body through his treatment of the body as subject and object. Such an approach is, in many ways, the easiest option and has the advantage of allowing us to concentrate on refining and developing a single theoretical paradigm. However, Crossley's endorsement of Merleau-Ponty has developed through the introduction of quite disparate and arguably incommensurate theorists such as Habermas, Foucault and Bourdieu. The attempt to analytically stretch a structuralist approach to the body is also fraught with tension. Butler's post-structuralism seeks to recover the materiality of the body, for example, but eventually retreats from this quest in favour of a continued focus on the constructing powers of the 'heterosexual matrix'.

Third, there have been attempts to start afresh by rejecting existing approaches in body theory, and by pursuing a quite separate programme based upon a different philosophical starting point, defining the body and its social consequences anew. Bryan Turner's theory of human rights based on an ontology of bodily frailty can be categorized in this way, representing a radical reappraisal of the importance of physical weakness (if not bodily potentialities) for a universal approach towards social existence (Turner, 1993; Turner and Rojek, 2001; Turner, 2003). However, this option can be seen as overlooking some of the advances that the major existing theories of the body have made in this area, as well as serving to undermine the identity that body studies has developed.

A fourth way of responding to the current diversity in the field of body studies is to accept the body's elusiveness in social thought and to recognize that its enigmatic character is most usefully tied to the development of diverse theoretical traditions. These traditions can be seen as providing different resources for the pursuit of different analytical tasks. Again, there is something to be said for this option. Focusing on the body has led to advances within diverse areas of study and has provided historically marginalized modes of thought, such as 'queer' and lesbian studies, with a substantive vehicle through which the importance of their endeavours has been more widely recognized. This proliferation of theories on the body also provides apparently tailor-made perspectives that can be used to interrogate a wide range of subjects. Simply accepting the proliferation of theories, however, provides no ground upon which cumulative advance might be accomplished within the disparate field of body studies, and threatens to exacerbate the problem of the body's elusiveness.

There is, however, a different approach that can be taken to the theories we have examined in this chapter. I want to maintain that while contemporary studies are characterized by significant theoretical limitations, they heighten our sensitivity to various aspects of the body's multi-dimensional relationship with society. If we are to incorporate their insights within a more comprehensive framework while avoiding their theoretical excesses, however, this cannot be accomplished by 'taking together' incommensurate paradigms (a problem with Turner's [1996: 33] suggestion that he incorporate a focus on the 'phenomenology of experience' as a corrective to 'the underlying structuralism' of *The Body and Society*). It must also avoid the associated problems of completely conflating distinct socially productive and socially receptive capacities of the body, a step which loses the theoretical means to account for the interaction that occurs between bodies and society (Archer, 2000). If we manage to overcome these obstacles, then it is also easier to take seriously the deep ethical concerns expressed by contemporary theories. These suggest that the body–society relationship has undergone a transformation in the modern era which has limited the socially generative significance of human physicality and restricted the scope of human experience and creativity. This is reflected in the focus on governmentality and constraint evident in social constructionist theories of ordered bodies, in what I have characterized as Leder's phenomenology of the rationalized body engaged in instrumental action, and is evident in the difficulty that structuration theories sometimes have in conceptualizing the properties of the body apart from the structural 'rules' and 'resources' that dominate society.

In this context, the substantively focused chapters that follow take as their starting point the corporeal realist approach developed in the convergence thesis outlined in Chapter 2; the idea that the body is a multi-dimensional medium for the constitution of society. In my opinion, this approach remains the most theoretically convincing account of the body–society relationship. It builds on the notion of the body as a socio-natural entity that both shapes as well as being shaped by society (Shilling, 1993, 2003; Burkitt, 1999), is non-deterministic, makes an analytical distinction between the body's capacities and dispositions, on the one hand, and society as an emergent phenomenon, on the other, and makes it possible to evaluate the effects of a particular social system on the bodily being of its members. This evaluation reflects the concerns of contemporary body theorists mentioned above. Following Marx, Durkheim and Simmel, it will also pay particular attention to the effects that economic/technological, cultural and social structures have on inequality and oppression, on whether the relationship between the individual and group is life-enhancing, and on the extent to which dominant structures allow for the enrichment of individuality and personality.

The chapters that follow are organized into separate sections concerned with the body as a source of and a location for the sectors of society under consideration, and with how the interaction between the body's productive properties and society's structures positions people within their wider environment. While structural constraints and norms form the focus of the 'body as a location' sections, subsequent considerations of the body as a means through which people orientate themselves and others in society prevent the body from fading within these accounts. This organization not only makes theoretical sense in terms of corporeal realism but allows us to group together a variety of literature which can throw at least some light on how the body might be considered to be a productive creator of society, to be shaped, constrained, inscribed or enhanced by society, and, finally, to be affected by the actual outcomes which result from interaction between the body and society.

Notes

1 Foucault's position changes significantly in his later volumes on the history of sexuality, in which individual agency and the material body come more into view, but problems of discursive reductionism characterize what have been the most popular developments of Foucault's analyses.

2 The intentionality with which the body schema is associated can even provide an explanation for the much discussed phenomenon of phantom limbs. For Merleau-Ponty (1962: 81), to have a phantom limb is to 'remain open to all the actions' of which the limb was capable, to 'retain the practical field which one enjoyed before mutilation'.

3 Bourdieu's primary concern may be to transcend the philosophical opposition between subjectivism and objectivism rather than reconcile structure and agency (Wacquant, 1992: 3), but these are related divisions. There is a tendency for subjectivist approaches towards social life to focus on the motivations and processes informing action, with objectivist perspectives concentrating on the regularities and patterns associated with structures that surpass the perspectives of individuals.

4 Leder's work can even help account for why structuralist theories of the ordered body ignore 'lived experience'. If experience fades into the background during purposeful action, then a rationalized society is likely to exacerbate this recession.

4

Working Bodies

Introduction

My substantive investigations into the body–society relationship begin with the subject of work. The social relationships surrounding the workplace and the contents of work have been central to classical concerns about the development and subjugation of human potentiality, and remain key to contemporary debates about the embodied character and organization of society. While definitions of the subject remain contested, I want to suggest that a comprehensive examination of the relationship between work and the body needs to take account of two major, related issues. The first concerns the *official* activities involved in, and the social context surrounding, waged labour, and has been the subject of numerous sociological and historical studies. These have ranged from investigations into how 'clock time' was used to discipline factory operatives during the Industrial Revolution, to studies of the organization of work and the norms that have solidified gender inequalities in occupations, to a concern with how the fast-changing character of the contemporary labour market has promoted personal insecurity (e.g. Thompson, 1967; Crompton and Mann, 1986; Beck, 2000; Hassard et al., 2000). Such literature has not always focused on the *physical* character of labour. Indeed, the body has only recently moved centre-stage within academic analyses of the subject. Nevertheless, these studies provide us with sufficient information to reflect on how people's 'reciprocal jostlings' with the organization and machinery of work shape the development of embodied identities and the workplace (Scarry, 1994: 51).

The second issue raised by the relationship between work and the body concerns the labour that people 'do' on and for their bodies in order that they can survive and function adequately. Much of this work cannot be categorized under the heading of waged labour. 'Body work' (Shilling, 1993: 118), has been marginalized in traditional accounts of work, but has recently become a popular topic in the sociology of the body (e.g. Seymour, 1998; Gimlin, 2002) and consists of three distinctive types of activity. These are job-related, cultural, and reproductive forms of body work. *Job-related* body work refers to those *unofficial* tasks involved in maintaining the embodied self as viable within the environment of waged labour. This is distinct from the activities that individuals undertake, or the body techniques they acquire, as a formal part of their employment, but covers such things as 'make work' (relieving the pressures of a job by giving off the impression of working while actually doing something else) and forms of emotional and mental 'escape' practised in order to cope with repetitive tasks (Goffman, 1969 [1956b]; Roy, 1960). Ethnographically informed studies of the workplace have done much to identify the various forms of job-related body work (e.g. Ditton, 1979; Cavendish, 1982). *Cultural* body work, in contrast, is concerned with how individuals present themselves as acceptable subjects in everyday life. Norbert Elias (1983) and Erving Goffman (1969 [1956b], 1963) have demonstrated that individuals must become skilled in the arts of 'impression management' if they are to maintain their status in society, while Durkheim's (1995 [1912]) analysis of collective effervescence and ritual provides us with a sociological theory of the construction of cultural norms informing this type of body work. Cultural body work mirrors some of the forms of self-presentation to occur within jobs, but it is not determined by economic considerations. As Goffman's (1983) analysis of the 'interaction order' suggests, it emerges as a result of the demands in managing physical copresence wherever it occurs. Finally, *reproductive* body work is closely related to domestic labour. It includes catering for one's own and other people's basic bodily needs for sustenance and physical care, and covers such matters as child-bearing and caring, food preparation, and providing emotional support to others. Women have traditionally undertaken most of this work, and feminists have been its most prominent theorists (e.g. Oakley, 1974a, 1974b; Hartmann, 1979). Nevertheless, it is not gender-exclusive and includes the tasks undertaken by all who attempt to maintain a minimally functioning physical self. Washing, brushing one's teeth, and seeking help from a doctor when necessary are all examples of reproductive body work, and illustrate why this type of body work cannot easily be contained within the traditional, highly gendered, category of domestic labour.

Having distinguished analytically between waged labour and body work, it is important to recognize that in practice these activities overlap and are sometimes interrelated. Thus, Marxist-feminists have demonstrated that it is difficult to make an absolute distinction between productive and reproductive work (e.g. child-rearing provides the next generation of workers while food preparation helps renew the energies and strength of individuals belonging to the current workforce). This point has been reinforced over the last few decades by the growth of jobs in the beauty, cosmetic surgery, and health and fitness industries that consist of monitoring, working on, and moulding other people's bodies (Gimlin, 2002). Waged labour and cultural body work can also affect each other. It has long been recognized, for example, that working-class cultures of masculinity impact on the forms of resistance and cooperation displayed by shop floor operatives, and that the masculine emphasis placed on physical strength and presence is utilized within a range of jobs that involve dealing with violence (e.g. Benyon, 1973; Monaghan, 2002). Finally, waged labour and job-related body work have become increasingly interrelated, with firms now seeking to manage and direct those parts of the worker that were once seen as private and non-essential to the job in hand. Employers have, for example, shown a growing interest in the emotional states and expressions of their employees (phenomena also traditionally related to cultural and reproductive body work), and have sought to incorporate these capacities into the formal requirements of various jobs (Hochschild, 1983; Streans and Streans, 1986).[1] The incorporation of sexualized reproductive work is also evident in this development. Certain leisure service industries, for example, demand that women (but also sometimes men) modify and use their bodies in explicitly sexualized ways (Adkins, 1995). Women working in 'Olde English Pubs' in theme parks, for example, are required to wear revealing dresses and engage in flirtatious behaviour with customers. If the boundaries between waged labour and body work have weakened, however, it is still useful to maintain an analytical distinction between them. This distinction allows us to remain sensitive to the real differences which exist between the varied types of activity undertaken by most people in their daily lives, and enables us to trace how overlap and interaction between these forms of work have changed over time.

Given the breadth of issues involved in the relationship between the body and work, this chapter has to be selective. To keep discussions manageable, I have decided to focus on how the changing conditions of waged labour have affected the body, and on how these same conditions have eroded the boundaries between paid work and body work. This choice is not arbitrary. Body studies have tended to neglect the subject of waged labour in favour of issues concerning culture and consumption, and this chapter is intended to help rectify that imbalance. The next section examines the body as a source of our need and capacity to work on our environment and ourselves. It does this by looking at some basic evolutionary issues concerned with tool use, and by examining how the malleability and creativity of the physical self provide a source of those 'techniques of the body' which shape the depths of our bodily being (Mauss, 1973 [1934]). I then examine how the body serves as a location for the effects of waged labour, on the one hand, and reproductive and cultural body work, on the other, by surveying the major characteristics of nineteenth-century industrialization and later 'Fordist' and 'post-Fordist' regimes. The penultimate section analyses three contrasting assessments of the outcomes that have emerged as a result of the interaction between the body's generative capacities and the structures of waged labour by examining how the body has been seen variously as a means for the attachment of individuals to, and their alienation from, typical forms of work within these regimes. This section is also attentive to the changing content and role of job-related body work. The conclusion summarizes the relevance of these changes for Marx's, Durkheim's and Simmel's respective concerns with social inequalities and the development of community and individuality within the modern era, and asks whether contemporary body theories are justified in suggesting that there has been a major erosion of the body's generative capacities.

The Body as a Source of Work

Social theory has long rejected biologically essentialist explanations of the human predicament, but its most insightful proponents have also recognized the physical implications that follow from the need we have to establish a productive relationship with our organic selves and the wider natural environment. As we saw in Chapter 2, Marx and Engels capture the importance of the body in this respect when arguing that our biological nature determines the 'first historical act' people must undertake. The fact that we are embodied beings means that we must secure our means of subsistence by satisfying our basic needs for food, drink, warmth and shelter before we can engage in other activities, and that we possess the physical capacities to pursue the satisfaction of these needs (Marx and Engels, 1977 [1846]: 48; Marx, 1954: 173). Other needs can subsequently be created by humans, but it is these fundamental physical requirements and capacities that ensure that the body remains a source of 'productive' work. Within capitalism, securing the means of subsistence can increasingly be undertaken only within the parameters of waged labour: people must sell their labour for a wage and use this wage to secure the necessities of existence.

The body is not a static source of work, however, but provides a corporeal basis for its conduct that has changed over the course of history as a result of the evolutionary development of our ancestors into a species of tool users.[2] The limited bipedalism of early men and women enabled them to use stones and sticks as rudimentary tools, and this encouraged the body to develop in ways that provided the corporeal foundations for what we now recognize to be characteristically human forms of work. As Hirst and Woolley (1982: 14) argue, the use of hands to hold implements not only created evolutionary pressures 'in favour of modifications in the structure of the hand to allow more effective manual movements, greater precision and dexterity, but also in favour of a more erect posture and a greater facility for bipedal movement on the ground'. This is because upright posture and bipedal locomotion frees the hands to use implements on the move, while efficient bipedalism makes possible specialized hunting as well as providing the basis for efficient gathering and harvesting.

Once established, our capacities for tool use mean that the manner in which we intervene in our environment can be more creative and 'open' than it is for other animals. In this context, the precise methods through which we establish a relationship with our material environment are not *instinctually* determined, but are established by our physical *problem-solving* encounters with the land and our prey (Joas, 1996). Over the course of time, individuals find certain techniques successful, habituate them into their working lives, and pass them on to future generations as norms of managing bodily interventions in the environment (Mauss, 1973 [1934]: 70, 73, 76). This standardization saves individuals time, and allows them to draw on a tried and tested repertoire of bodily actions which contain a reservoir of social knowledge and represent an embodiment of social data. By acquiring these techniques, 'the knowledge upon which people act undergoes an explosive expansion' (Elias, 1991: 90).

Upright posture, bipedal locomotion, manual dexterity, and the capacity to reflect practically upon the techniques we are using to undertake a task may be taken for granted these days, but it is worth remembering that they constitute the essential physical source for contemporary forms of work now undertaken within waged labour. If the body's needs and capacities provide an essential source of waged labour, however, its essential characteristics also mean that we have to engage in, and are capable of undertaking, job-related body work. Our bodies are not automata, but can be unpredictable, frail, and vulnerable to making mistakes. There is always a performative element involved in undertaking a technique: the possibility of slips and errors means that its successful execution is not guaranteed. This contingency means that individuals must always be ready to engage in additional, 'unofficial' tasks in order to carry out formal work. Extra effort may be needed to complete a task, over and above that presupposed by its purely technical execution, and individuals sometimes find that their bodily limitations mean that they have to engage in a careful management of the impressions they give off to those around them. One may find it difficult to keep up with the rate of work set by a team paid on the basis of daily productivity, for example, but it may be necessary to hide this difficulty in order to keep one's position within that team (Goffman, 1969 [1956b]).

Our organic selves also constitute a source of *cultural body work*. The 'openness' and flexibility that characterize humans' relationship with their environment may be advantageous in relation to undertaking productive work, but it has also been associated with an erosion of our instincts that poses a problem for human identity (Honneth and Joas, 1988). In this context, cultural body work is necessary for humans if they are to possess symbolically meaningful physical identities (ibid.). The forms of presentation developed by a group allow individuals to recognize others as familiar and 'safe', or as strangers who may pose risks to their lifestyle and existence, for example, while the ritual marking of physical variables associated with sex and age have traditionally been sanctioned as ways of differentiating between individuals within a group (Simmel, 1971 [1908b]; Mauss, 1973 [1934]: 72, 76; Elias, 1994; Durkheim, 1995 [1912]).

Finally, while the 'first historical act' (having to work in order to produce the means of subsistence) may be associated with the body having become a source of what is now organized as waged labour, another circumstance 'which, from the very outset, enters into historical development' involves the propagation and care of the human species (Marx and Engels, 1977 [1846]: 49). Reproductive body work is vital to the continued existence of humans, and people have historically engaged in various types of social relationship in undertaking it, albeit relationships in which women have tended to assume the major responsibilities.

The body has been portrayed in this section as a fundamental source of work. As it is our modality of being in the world, and is a relatively malleable vehicle of existence, it both requires and enables us to undertake physical, cultural and reproductive work on our environment and ourselves in order to survive. However, the body is not only an active, generative phenomena in relation to these activities. The body techniques that emerge as a result of their success in helping people procure the means of subsistence, for example, are not set in stone. Individuals may feel uncomfortable with or incapable of executing smoothly certain techniques, while others may cease to be effective in the face of environmental or technological changes. Furthermore, practical success is not the only basis on which this imitation occurs: learning involves a process of *prestigious imitation* in which individuals copy actions conducted by respected others within the community (Mauss, 1973 [1934]). As Mauss suggests, body techniques consist of *social norms* as well as biological (and psychological) capacities. This demonstrates that the body is not just a source of work, but can also serve as a location for communal norms which help determine how individuals intervene in their environment. Related points can be made about other forms of body work. While human bodies impose on people an elementary division of labour in terms of the capacity to give birth, this simple fact cannot account for the norms that have historically stipulated that women should carry out most of the tasks involved in reproductive body work (Rubin, 1975). Similarly, the simple need to wash ourselves cannot explain the multitude of religious and cultural prescriptions that have surrounded this and related acts concerned with the basic maintenance of our physical selves (Foucault, 1988a). Norms clearly enter into the organization of these activities and appear to have the capacity to inscribe themselves on the bodily dispositions of those subject to them.

The Body as a Location for the Effects of Work

If the body is a source of work, the social relations entered into, and technological forces produced in securing the means of subsistence, come to develop internal relations (such as the employer–employee roles) and properties (such as prescribed methods and tools to be used in executing a task) that are irreducible to the individuals who created them. New generations confront these pre-established roles, artefacts and obligations as structures which can appear to have an inescapable effect on their bodily being. The effect of these structures can be illustrated from even the most cursory analysis of work in the pre-industrial and industrial eras, work which varied in terms of its locations, hours, rhythms and techniques. In pre-industrial societies, workshops were frequently attached to the home, enabling productive and reproductive work to be combined. The length of the working day differed according to the season and hours of daylight, and the division of labour was elementary compared to the specialization with which we are now familiar. The shift to industrialization brought about major changes in the character and context of work, geographically and organizationally separating waged labour from reproductive work, and imposing new rhythms, demands and differences on the human body.

This section will discuss these changes before focusing on later shifts in labour that began to occur in the twentieth century during what became known as the transition from 'Fordist' industrial organization to 'post-Fordist' information-based and service-oriented economies. While the complex nature of these changes are not easily accounted for by the 'binary histories' conjured up by Fordism and post-Fordism (Gilbert et al., 1992: 9), these terms remain useful 'ideal type' indicators of how waged labour has altered over the last century. I then look at how this transition has impacted on the other types of body work undertaken by people. If the industrial era strengthened the boundaries between waged labour and reproductive body work, we are now living at a time when processes of commodification are reducing the distinction between waged labour and other forms of body work.

Industrialization

E.P. Thompson (1980: 218) characterized the crucial experience of the Industrial Revolution in terms of 'changes in the nature and intensity of exploitation', yet these changes in the bodily demands of labour were not accomplished easily. The creation of an industrial workforce was associated with physical coercion and an associated reorganization of space and time. In terms of *physical coercion*, the development of early modern industry was associated with prisons, workhouses and orphanages (Engels, 1958 [1845]; Braverman, 1974). These sites could supply a captive labour force and provided vivid examples of the fate that awaited individuals unable to survive in the new industrial marketplace. More generally, the labouring bodies of those drawn from urban crafts, cottage industries, or from the surplus population of the countryside, had to be disciplined in order that their pre-existing work rhythms and patterns of working sociability (which were incompatible with the demands of rationalized forms of production) could be regulated (Roberts, 1992: 103). Factory employers used beatings and other physical punishments in an attempt to banish idleness from their adult and child employees. While it is important not to over-estimate the novelty of physical force in the development of industrialization (it operated as a far more important factor in previous systems of production such as slavery), the role it played during this era has led one study to conclude that 'the modern industrial proletariat was introduced to its role not so much by attraction or monetary reward, but by compulsion, force and fear' (quoted in Pollard, 1965: 7).

The disciplining of workers' bodies was not accomplished purely on the basis of overt physical coercion, but relied heavily upon an associated *reorganization of space and time*. In terms of *space*, Foucault (1979a) highlights how modern factory production enclosed, partitioned, and ranked bodies in order to facilitate their functional productivity. The *enclosure* of bodies within factories confined work to a particular space, a space that visibly belonged to the employer and over which the labourer had no rights. This altered the context of work, and had a particular impact on those women whose domestic and working responsibilities used to be discharged in and around the home. As (waged) work came to be carried out in its own exclusive site, there was an entrenchment in the relationship between reproductive body work and the sexual division of labour; an entrenchment that had a lasting, detrimental effect on the inclusion of married women in the workforce (McBride, 1992: 70). Manufacture supplemented this process of enclosure by *partitioning* individuals in a manner which reduced sociality and helped neutralize the dispositions groups brought with them into the workplace. This isolation of employees assisted employers in acquiring knowledge about and controlling their labour force. Foucault illustrates this with reference to the Oberkampf printing manufactory at Jouy, in France. Its ground floor contained 132 tables, arranged in two rows, and at the end of each table stood a rack on which printed material was left to dry. This arrangement of bodies and machinery meant that the supervisor could, by walking up and down the central aisle, reduce unproductive communications and observe the individual's presence, application and quality of work. The organization of space also allowed bodies to be *ranked* and compared according to their 'skill and speed' so that workers could be distributed and circulated within the productive process in order to maximize output (Foucault, 1979a: 143–4). Such arrangements formed a 'grid' whereby the labour process was articulated according to its basic operations and to 'the particular bodies, that carried it out', and did much to facilitate the 'individualising fragmentation of labour power' characteristic of factory production (ibid.: 145).

If the reorganization of space facilitated the disciplining of workers' bodies, so too did the transformation in the experience of *time* that occurred during the Industrial Revolution (Thompson, 1967). The clock, it has been suggested, was as important as the steam engine to the Industrial Revolution 'since it facilitated the synchronisation and control of activities across space' (Grint, 2000: 8). By allowing owners of factories to organize and measure work in terms of hours spent on the job, the clock rationalized the bodily rhythms of work that had previously been irregular and determined by the time of year (Hassard, 1996). Time was not just used to discipline workers, but became the key meter through which the commodification of labour occurred. It provided the basis on which individuals sold their embodied labour to capital, and the basis on which capitalists extracted surplus value from workers (Marx, 1954). Time was money and employers sought to extract from labourers as much working time from the day as was possible, even to the extent that factory operatives were sometimes reduced to snatching a few hours of sleep on the shop floor between shifts. As women and children began to replace men in mechanized jobs where brute strength was not a consideration, time became even more important. It was clear that the length of time an individual could put into work often dominated other considerations such as their age or sex: physical stamina grew in importance over strength. This is why there were such struggles over the length of the working day, and why the Factory Acts defined restrictions on work not just in terms of age but in terms of time spent on the job (Engels, 1958 [1845]). The long working day taxed people's stamina to its limit and made it increasingly difficult to undertake other forms of body work necessary for social well-being and physical health.

The cumulative impact of these disciplinary mechanisms involving physical coercion and the reorganization of space and time are summed up by E.P. Thompson. The factory system demanded 'a transformation of human nature' by routinizing the '"working paroxysms" of the artisan or outworker' until they were 'adapted to the discipline of the machine' (Thompson, 1980: 397). This is not to say that it always succeeded in turning the vagaries and diversity of embodied individuals into common units of production, but there were indisputable and major changes in the bodily impact of work. For Engels (1958 [1845]: 39), the factory system treated workers like machines, removed from them 'the last trace of independent activity', and resulted in them being worn down by injuries, diseases and deformities. Poor health and early death were the usual effects of years spent in the cramped and unhealthy conditions of factories, while the bodies of child labourers suffered in such industries as glass manufacture from stunted growth, eye problems, rheumatism and bronchial problems (ibid.: 234). The body was worn down by being positioned as a location for the highly deleterious structures of economic work.

In visiting its harsh effects upon the bodies of workers, industrialization also changed the activities to which they were suited. E.P. Thompson investigates this issue by looking at the differences between skilled and semi-skilled jobs, on the one hand, and the heavily manual labouring jobs that still existed at the base of industrial society, on the other. The former involved 'steady methodical application ... forethought, and punctilious observation of contracts; in short, the controlled paying out of energies' (Thompson, 1980: 437). Heavy manual work, in contrast, 'required a spendthrift expense of sheer physical energy – an alternation of intensive labour and boisterous relaxation which belongs to preindustrial labour rhythms' (ibid.). The point of this comparison is that once disciplined into 'the controlled paying out of energies', working bodies were no longer suited to the demands of heavy manual work. This is why English employers requiring that type of labour would often look to Irish immigrants. Not only were they cheaper than their domestic counterparts, but their bodies had not yet been subjected to the regulated, constant routines that had debilitated the English physique (ibid.). In this case, as in others, the body is shown to have been deeply shaped as a result of it being a location for the effects of industrialization.

Industrialization was accompanied by a restructuring of time and space as a means of reforming bodies in line with the needs of rationalized methods of production, but these methods were refined by the scientific management movement and consolidated by the rise of Fordist mass production methods in the early twentieth century. Because of the importance of scientific management and Fordism in determining the demands placed on wage labouring bodies for most of that century, it is to them that we now turn.

The rise of scientific management and Fordism

Scientific management was based on the work of F.W. Taylor and originated in the USA during the 1890s. It assumed that the processes of work could be broken down into constituent parts which could then be standardized, timed, separated into tasks concerned with conception and execution, and devolved to those most competent at undertaking them. By taking these steps, it held, businesses would be able to restructure jobs and eliminate time-wasting in order to enhance productivity. The organization of work was thus treated 'as a technical problem whose solution could be obtained by following the canons of science, [and] by applying the criterion of efficiency' (Barley and Kunda, 2000: 311).

This technical, rationalized view that scientific management displayed towards the organization of work incorporated within it a very similar view of the body. The worker was not simply a physical entity, to be disciplined through the organization of space and time, but should be seen as a mechanism that could be articulated precisely to the parts and rhythms of a scientifically assessed production process. This image of a human–machine system anticipates later debates about cyborgs, and one of the ways in which it was articulated was through the creation of industrial prostheses for disabled workers which sometimes literally fixed limbs to machines (Rabinbach, 1990). The creation of fully rationalized bodies, however, remained some way from realization. As F.W. Taylor put it, 'the greatest obstacle' that stood in the way of maximizing production on the part of the workers was 'the slow pace which they adopt ... marking time as it is called' (cited in Rabinbach, 1990). This is why scientific management sought to help employers deconstruct the jobs undertaken by workers. If work could be fully rationalized, so too should the labouring body. The ambition was that inefficiencies and wasted energies would be removed, and the working body made into a location for pure productivity.

The uptake of scientific management was slow at first, and met with considerable opposition, but eventually proved so influential that Braverman (1974) concluded that 'it is impossible to overestimate' its importance in shaping the contemporary labour process. Much of the reason for Braverman's judgement concerns the sympathetic industrial context in which scientific management flourished; a context initiated by Henry Ford's pioneering launch in the early twentieth century of mechanized mass production and moving assembly lines. 'Fordism' became a term used to characterize the combination of assembly line technology and organization developed by Henry Ford and the principles of efficiency central to scientific management, and dominated debates about industrialization in the post-Second World War period. It was associated with large increases in productive capacity and output, with a Keynesian welfare state that provided the infrastructure and investment necessary to underpin this productive system, and with high levels of employment. The most significant means through which the embodied worker was disciplined within Fordism involved having to keep pace with the assembly line.[3] The relentless motion of the productive process dictated the speed at which factory operatives had to work, and this attempt to organize the rhythms of the working body around the rhythm of the assembly line was still evident in Huw Benyon's classic 1973 study, *Working for Ford*.

Benyon's research provides a detailed empirical report on what had become the archetypal factory form within this epoch of mass production. He reports that all Ford's workers had to come to terms with the incessant motion and physical demands of the assembly line. Those whose job it was to fit gear boxes, for example, put a great strain on their backs which could result in permanent damage, while the work involved in installing suspension units had led to haemorrhages. More generally, the repetition, boredom and pressures of assembly line work added up to a 'painful' experience which left operatives feeling estranged from their bodies and minds, and burdened by the need to engage in job-related work concerned with restoring personal morale. As one of the stewards at the Ford factory explained:

> The point about this place is that the work destroys you. It destroys you physically and mentally. The biggest problem for people is getting to accept it, to accept being here day in and day out. So you've got low morale from every point of view. You're inflicted with a place of work and you've got to adapt because it won't adapt to you. (quoted in Benyon, 1973: 188)

The Fordist era of mass production did not remain static in its attempts to organize the bodies of wage labourers. Direct physical coercion declined during this era, but the rationalization of time and space were stepped up as ways of disciplining the working body. Nevertheless, these constraints continued to operate predominantly on the *exteriors* of people's bodies and, with some notable exceptions, strong boundaries continued to exist for full-time workers between home and work, leisure and work, and 'freedom' and 'unfreedom'. As time passed, it was no longer acceptable for employers to monitor the home lives of their employees or to dictate how they should present themselves outside of the workplace. Local communities, furthermore, provided people with strong norms of cultural body work, as well as relatively stable networks of social relationships, which made available to them sources of identity apart from those associated with the workplace. If the differentiation of social space that had occurred since industrialization generally removed productive work from the home environment, however, developments in post-Fordism challenged these boundaries.

Post-Fordism

Fordism revolutionized the productive capacity of the economy, but during the last few decades of the twentieth century there was growing talk of economic 'crisis'. This crisis in Fordism was associated with a reduction in productivity gains, an increase in union unrest centred around intensified working conditions, a decline in profitability associated with taxation levels, rising unemployment, the oil crisis, changing consumption patterns, and the impact of cheaper overseas producers (e.g. O'Connor, 1973; Amin, 1994). It was accompanied in Western countries by a loss of traditional, male-dominated heavy industry. Coal mining, the steel industry, dock work and ship-building all declined in response to global competition and the rise of alternative sources of power and raw materials.

If Fordism represented the height of the industrial age, it became popular to suggest that its demise was accompanied by the growth of a 'post-Fordist' system. According to its most influential commentators, post-Fordism developed in response to the possibilities provided by computers, robotics and microchip technology in production, and constitutes an economic system in which information has become an increasingly valuable commodity. Post-Fordism is characterized by a system of 'flexible specialization' in which information technology, contracting out, fast turnovers of small batches of goods, and differentiated companies operating in and around market niches become increasingly prominent (e.g. Piore and Sabel, 1984). Even when large-scale production continued to dominate consumer markets, it was suggested that firms were becoming more flexible in their organization of work, while smaller and more widely dispersed plants enabled companies to move production to where costs were cheapest and unions ineffective (Stanworth and Stanworth, 1991). These developments challenged the dominance, if not the existence, of the classical Fordist factory. They altered the security and content of work, and exerted a closely related effect on the experiences of many labouring bodies.

The most influential recent studies which seek to develop our appreciation of what has become key to the post-Fordist world of work suggest that previously secure patterns of employment have been undermined. In their place, they argue, there has been a radical *individualization* of work, a growth in *unemployment,* and an increase in *part-time, temporary, and insecure jobs* (e.g. Sennett, 1998; Beck, 2000). Such claims have been greeted with scepticism by many, but there is a growing amount of evidence to support at least some of them. In terms of the individualization of work, the fastest-growing sector of the American labour force consists of people who work for temporary agencies (Sennett, 1998: 22). In Britain, two-thirds of the self-employed (a sector of the labour force successive governments have viewed as a major vehicle of growth) work alone. In terms of the growth of part-time work, the OECD and the International Labour Organization identified a rapid spread of such work in nearly all industrialized countries during the 1980s and 1990s. Part-time jobs made up at least 40 per cent of the total number of jobs in industrialized countries by the beginning of the 1990s (Beck, 2000: 56). In terms of insecurity, the rate of involuntary dismissal has doubled in the past twenty years for men in their forties and early fifties in the US and UK, while there has been a strong tendency for men from their mid-fifties to face redundancy and to be effectively removed from the labour force in the USA, the UK, France and Germany (Sennett, 1998: 92–5). Such insecurity is not without precedent (Mills, 1953), but it has intensified. According to Sennett's (1998: 22) estimate, for example, 'a young American with at least 2 years of college can expect to change jobs at least 11 times in the course of working, and change his or her skill base at least 3 times during those 40 years of labour' if they are to remain employed.

These conditions have produced what Beck refers to as a new 'political economy of insecurity' in which the foundations of stable jobs and stable communities have broken down. Even for the apparently prosperous middle classes, he suggests, 'attractive, highly skilled and well paid full-time employment is on its way out' and is being replaced by an a 'nomadic multi-activity' marked by 'endemic insecurity' (Beck, 2000: 2–3). The work society has, apparently, reached its limits and is confronted by a fundamental paradox: 'on the one hand, work is the centre of society around which everything and everyone revolve and take their bearings; on the other hand, everything is done to eliminate as much work as possible' (Beck, 2000: 14).

The body continues to serve as a location for these changes, but the direct corporeal consequences of post-Fordist developments have become increasingly diverse. The low-paid employees of fast-food restaurants such as McDonald's (who have to rationalize their actions in line with the demand to make standardized products in the shortest possible time), for example, present a striking contrast to highly paid creative designers in the fashion industry (responsible for innovation and setting standards of 'taste'). Nevertheless, it is possible to make several points about how the structures of waged labour have come to locate themselves on the bodies of workers in this era in comparison with the Fordist era.

First, the post-Fordist developments outlined above are experienced as changes mostly by the *male* labour force. Women have long occupied a disproportionate number of part-time, temporary and insecure jobs as they have sought to combine waged labour with bringing up children and other reproductive body work (Dex, 1985; Beechey, 1987; Walby, 1997). If the notion of a lifelong 'career' is now becoming less applicable for men as well as for women, we may be witnessing a feminization of working patterns for the mass of the working population. More people now have to engage in 'nomadic' activity in which productive body techniques cannot be acquired once and for all, but have to be monitored for their continuing effectiveness and relevance, and changed over the course of their work histories (Beck, 2000). While Willis (1977) and Bourdieu (1981) wrote about how the development of a stable working *habitus* fitted people to pre-existing jobs, analysts of post-Fordism suggest that era is now passing. If work is becoming a 'project' – to be pieced together in increasingly contingent and creative ways – so too must the productive body; as something to be worked on in order to ensure that it retains value within the fields of waged labour. Furthermore, for growing numbers of people the time has perhaps gone when any single 'career' can provide the prime constituent of embodied identity. Instead, identity may be becoming increasingly reliant on the cultural and reproductive body work undertaken *outside* the formal labour force. It may be that this is why the body's appearance, size and shape have in recent decades become so central to people's sense of self, a development which perhaps heralds a feminization of approaches towards the body alongside a feminization of working patterns.

Second, waged labour often now requires a greater degree of flexibility from employees; a flexibility which makes considerable demands on their bodily capacities. Factory and office production schedules increasingly require workers to vary their times of paid work according to fluctuations in demand, and have recently led to a considerable increase in nightwork. In the British labour market alone, one in seven workers (four million people) worked at least some night shifts as part of their regular jobs by 2003. This figure had increased by half a million since 1998 and is exposing more and more people to the higher incidence of heart problems and gastrointestinal complaints associated with nightwork (Obi, 2003). Such problems are not equivalent to the exploitation faced by workers during the early decades of industrialization, but they have clearly grown in recent years.

Third, while factory work has declined in the advanced capitalist West, significant numbers of people still work in full-time jobs characterized by the discipline of the assembly line. It is not just that factory work continues to be a significant form of employment, but that other workplaces exhibit strong continuities with the classical Fordist image of work. Typical here are the call centres and tele-sales centres that have become especially prominent since the 1990s in banking, insurance and other financial services. These have been referred to as 'electronic panopticons' which are more oppressive than the 'tyranny of the assembly line' (Fernie and Metcalf, 1998), and which allow workers' output to be 'measured and monitored to an unprecedented degree' (Bain and Taylor, 2000: 17). Furthermore, while physical injuries from heavy manual labour may have become less common, repetitive strain injury has become a growing concern for those engaged in jobs characterized by monotonous physical routines (Arksey, 1988). We should also remember that despite the narratives of progress associated with recent writings on the organization of work (Piore and Sabel, 1984), immigrant workers in particular continue to provide a cheap and readily exploitable source of labour that has been utilized in domestic service and casualized employment across the United States and Europe. Service sector jobs still provide millions of minimum wage positions that force many individuals to work extra shifts, and take extra jobs, just to pay their rent, utility and food bills (Ehreneich, 2001; Toynbee, 2003).

Fourth, in other sectors of the economy, the increased importance of image and presentation of self in the workplace has placed a heavy burden on personal appearance, expanding the incursion of waged labour into the realm of body work (e.g. Adkins, 1995). In jobs where this applies, employees can no longer be concerned simply with the immediately negative effects of work on their bodies. Instead, they must cope with the demands of being positively exhorted to embody the image of fitness associated with efficiency and productive capacity. The ageing body faces a particular problem in this respect. In contrast to those cultures in which age is associated with wisdom, the capitalist West tends to view age as a sign of burnout, incapacity and incompetence (Hepworth and Featherstone, 1982). Youth is valued as a productive resource, and the cultivation of a lean body (trimmed of any 'unproductive' excess) has become a key part of marketing the self in the commercial world (Sennett, 1998). Job-related body work has increased in this respect, making the cultural monitoring and reproductive care of one's body a key ingredient for success and even survival in many workplaces.

In short, while factories, call centres and tele-sales centres show that externally imposed discipline retains a central role in many jobs, other changes associated with post-Fordism have increased the importance of *internal* bodily discipline. If individuals must reskill in order to maintain their employability, combine jobs, work on keeping their appearance as youthful and attractive as possible, and be alert to new threats and opportunities in the labour market, self-controls and motivations become increasingly significant. These centre around an internal determination to control one's bodily appearance, to evaluate one's own skills in relation to current trends and local opportunities, to update these skills, and to learn to change one's lifestyle and even place of residence. The costs of not cultivating this internalized discipline, of relying on the supposed stability of a 'secure' job, are illustrated by the IBM computer programmers in Sennett's (1988) study. Sennett (1998: 132) relates how these individuals were made redundant and retrospectively admitted that they could and should have taken more seriously the changes occurring in the computer industry, foreseen the possibilities provided by the Internet, and reskilled accordingly. In the absence of such action, simply adhering to the externally structured discipline of the workplace resulted in redundancy.

Changing patterns of body work

The shift from Fordism to post-Fordism not only changed many of the conditions of waged labour, but is also clearly associated with alterations in the form and content of body work, and in the boundaries that traditionally separated waged labour and body work. I have touched on these issues in the above discussion, but it is important to expand on some of the more important of them here and I shall do that by focusing on reproductive and cultural body work (I shall turn my attention to job-related body work in the next section).

In terms of *reproductive body work*, the spatial and temporal separation that industrialization instituted between home and labour did much to entrench a sexual division of domestic labour. It was deemed a woman's place to look after the bodily needs of men and children within the family home, yet women were often confronted with the 'double burden' of waged labour and reproductive body work. The normative idea that women's embodied being was 'naturally' suited to domestic and caring work, moreover, continued to inform the jobs available to them in the Fordist era. Whole sectors of caring and service work were dominated by a female workforce, and there remained a strong segregation between 'women's' and 'men's' occupational classifications by the close of the twentieth century (Hartmann, 1976; Cockburn, 1983; Walby, 1986, 1997; Reskin and Roos, 1990).

Millions of women still have to work a 'second shift' of domestic labour on returning from waged labour (Hochschild, 1989). In the post-Fordist era, however, there has also been an individualization and commodification of reproductive body work, and a growth in its scope. Several factors have contributed to the recent accentuation of individualization. The number of people living in single person households has increased, especially among the professional middle classes. In England and Wales, for example, it has been estimated that one-person households will make up one-third of all dwellings by 2020 (Hall et al., 1999). Divorce rates have also risen sharply over the last century, while the average age of marriage has increased as has the time at which women have their first baby. There has also been something of an erosion in the traditional gap that exists between the sexes in educational achievement which has helped more women achieve economic independence from men (Walby, 1997). Such factors may not have abolished gender inequalities, but they have led to an individualization in body work, the most noticeable outcome of this being an increase in the amount of body maintenance that men have to do for themselves.

There has also been a growth in the commodification and scope of reproductive body work. Feminists have long highlighted the economic costs of housework, and there has been a growth in small firms oriented to undertaking domestic work for those who have the money but do not have the time (or a partner) to do it. Furthermore, the increased emphasis placed on image and appearance in the contemporary market place has been associated with a proliferation of jobs which maintain and care for all aspects of people's bodily being. In the sphere of health and fitness, personal trainers and dieticians devise routines and regimes to help individuals get fit and lose weight. Even those not convinced by the ideal of cultivating the perfectly healthy, beautiful body find it easier to pay at least token respect to this ideal by engaging in limited forms of exercise or therapy (Crawford, 2000; Gimlin, 2002: 50–72). The popularity of alternative and complementary medicine has also grown enormously as individuals seek to supplement conventional Western medicine by turning instead to specialists in acupuncture, herbalism, podiatry, and cranial osteopathy (Select Committee on Science and Technology, 2000). In the sphere of personal relations, dating agencies and commercial Internet sites now seek to provide for the emotional, as well as the physical, needs of men and women (Hardey, 2002). The commercialization of sex has also accelerated in recent years (759 million porn movies were rented in the USA during 2001 compared with 410 million in 1991) (Seager, 2003), with the growing respectability of mainstream pornography helping to create 'stars' out of its 'actors'. Here again, the body is ruthlessly subjected to the rationalized demands of work, with women's orifices having to be readily available for penetration and men having to provide erections, and ejaculate, on demand (Stoller and Levine, 1993). The marketization of reproductive body work is also reflected in pregnancy and childbirth. For those whose work schedules are too busy to take time out for childbirth, it is now possible to 'rent a womb'. Finally, this general extension and commodification of reproductive body work are reflected in the profusion of lifestyle counsellors who help individuals view their bodies as organizations whose inputs and outputs, needs and priorities, should be approached as rationally as they would be in any commercial enterprise.

The changes in *cultural body work* that have occurred during the shift from Fordism to post-Fordism are also significant. Industrialization tended to increase the hours individuals had to work in order to secure their means of subsistence, but working-class culture thrived despite such deprivations. Community and sporting activities developed in which individuals established firm interactional norms which, in turn, shaped political protests against working conditions (Thompson, 1980). Such norms were inflected with a cultural idiom that was not only working class, however, but was based on a particular form of masculinity. The most acceptable and prestigious forms of cultural body work reflected masculine culture, and while men's management of their bodies during social interaction was seen as an indication of their superior character and integrity, women's was viewed as an expression of their limited physical nature (Tseelon, 1995). The dominant norms of cultural body work during the nineteenth and twentieth centuries were not just classed and gendered, but were also predicated upon a *white* corporeality which excluded people of colour. In these circumstances, as Frantz Fanon (1984 [1952]: 110) argues, consciousness of the body for black people in particular could become 'a negating activity' which filled the body's space with uncertainty, with a 'third-person consciousness', and with an awkwardness which pervades every physical action.

These cultural body norms preceded Fordism, but maintained their force during that era. While their influence has not disappeared in post-Fordism, however, any single racial norm of bodily appearance or cultural norm of interaction has lost something of its ability to signify membership of a distinguished moral community. This is partly because of the rapid internationalization of ethnic styles. As Paul Gilroy (2000: 21) argues, 'The perfect faces on billboards and screens and in magazines are no longer exclusively white', while in certain areas of corporate and social life 'some degree of visible difference from an implicit white norm' may be prized as a sign of 'timeliness, vitality, inclusivity, and global reach'. Mediated interaction has also contributed to the limited decline in the extent to which direct physical copresence signifies membership of a moral community. Communications by email, text and telephone have increased massively over the past few decades and, while interactional customs do develop around these forms of contact (Hardey, 2002), they have increased those occasions on which *physical* co-presence and cultural body norms do not determine people's status. These occasions have not, however, prevented certain norms from continuing to dominate certain types of cultural body work undertaken by people.

It is not just because of the demands of work in the formal economy that men and women, irrespective of their class or race, still face great pressure to develop well-honed bodies, shorn of excess. Dominant cultural images of the ideal body associate physical maintenance with moral worth and individuals clearly find it difficult to ignore this corporeal indicator of value. Furthermore, the sheer numbers of women undergoing cosmetic surgery suggest that these norms continue to be gendered and have penetrated more deeply into the body. In the USA during 2001, for example, over 216,000 women underwent breast augmentation (an 114 per cent increase since 1997) while 88 per cent of all cosmetic procedures were performed on women (Seager, 2003). Since over 385,000 liposuction procedures were also performed in 2001 (an 118 per cent increase since 1997), together with 117,000 face-lifts, and over one million collagen injections (ibid.), it would be hasty to conclude that the demands associated with cultural body work have become anything other than more onerous in the contemporary era.

The shift from Fordism to post-Fordism seems, then, to be associated with changes in body work as well as in waged labour. The boundaries between these forms of work appear to have weakened at the same time that cultural norms of appearance have, in certain respects, become more demanding. While the reorganization of waged labour and the statistics on plastic surgery detailed above provide examples of how many bodies have indeed become a location for these changes, it would be dangerous to assume that structural pressures associated with the workplace and norms of appearance have obliterated the creative potentialities of the human body. Instead, it is important to examine the various ways in which the generative capacities of embodied subjects have interacted with, and in some cases resisted, these structures.

The Positioning of Working Bodies

One of the central arguments of this study is that the body cannot be conceptualized adequately as an entirely passive location for social or cultural inscriptions. Not only do embodied subjects often possess the capacity to resist the effects of external structures, but the properties of the body serve *actively* to dispose them favourably or unfavourably towards these conditions (precisely how active or creative bodies are within different working environments is, of course, a matter for empirical investigation). In what follows, I shall explore briefly three visions of the outcomes of the interaction between the body as a source of, and a location for, the structures of work; visions which impart the body with different degrees of generative efficacy. The section begins by summarizing the writings of classical theorists on the subject, before looking at empirical research into worker resistance during industrialization and Fordism, and concluding with analyses of the increasing significance of emotion work in the post-Fordist labour market. The focus will be on waged labour, but I shall also suggest that these visions of working life imply that job-related and other forms of body work have become increasingly incorporated into the formal requirements of the work-place.

The first vision is associated with the writings of Marx, Durkheim and Simmel. Despite their differences, these figures converged in suggesting that the interaction between embodied agents and the structures of the economy could temporarily 'fit' people for their jobs. Marx (1975 [1844]) analysed the working-class experience of labour as a wearing, repetitive denial of life which alienated individuals from themselves, their species being, their fellow workers, the process of work, and the products of their labour. He also argued that resistance to this alienation was normally limited because the division of labour developed in individuals one-sided abilities which rendered them suited for repetitive work, and because the power of ruling ideologies meant that individuals tended to naturalize their conditions of existence (Marx, 1954: 342). Durkheim suggested that waged labour became anomic when there was a 'forcing' of individuals into jobs that did not match their natural talents, and a mismatch between the division of labour and the moral framework informing its organization. In this situation, the worker became harnessed to mechanized processes, becoming 'a lifeless cog, which an external force sets in motion' (Durkheim, 1984 [1893]: 306–8). Trapped in existentially meaningless work, the emotional state of individuals became increasingly conflicted, leading eventually not to active revolt but to a debilitating, melancholic resignation (Durkheim, 1952 [1897]). Simmel also wrote about how waged labour could eventually reduce the creative capacities of the embodied subject. He suggested that the long hours of mental labour typical of life in the money economy were associated with a 'nervous tension and sedentary mode of life' and a break-down in the relationship between our 'bodily constitution' and our means of nourishment (Simmel, 1990 [1907]: 420). Work frequently revolved around the intellectual apprehension of abstract calculations, failing to stimulate human passions, while the money economy's levelling of values promoted qualities such as a blasé attitude and a cynicism eminently suited to working in this milieu.

The writings of Marx, Durkheim and Simmel are characterized at times by bleak portrayals of human existence (in which the conditions of work within capitalism could damage human potentialities by exacerbating economic inequality, preventing the incorporation of individuals into moral collectivities, and stimulating personal characteristics that hindered the development of individuality). They did not view individuals as being defenceless against these conditions, however, and each identified the adoption of religious belief as entering into the job-related body work individuals undertook in order to make waged labour tolerable. The function of religion in this respect was explored most famously in Max Weber's (1991 [1904–5]) analysis of the Protestant ethic. Weber exemplifies how rationalized forms of work could be justified and made existentially bearable through a religious imperative. According to E.P. Thompson (1980), Methodism served this purpose during the English Industrial Revolution. Methodism emphasized that work 'must be undertaken as a *pure act of virtue* … inspired by the love of a transcendent Being, operating … on our will and affections', and sought to channel 'dangerous' or 'unproductive' emotions into harmless 'watch nights, band-meetings or revivalist campaigns' (Thompson, 1980: 398, 402). The idea that the Protestant ethic unwittingly provided industrialization with a disciplined workforce has become a common theme in historical sociology. Protestant values, it is suggested, 'regulated and organised the energies of the human body' in a manner suited to rationalized labour (Turner, 1992: 117). The promotion of religious belief had undoubted benefits for employers, but even Marx recognized that it was not just an instrument of the ruling class but was used by certain labourers to make tolerable the conditions of their existence. Furthermore, Marx, Durkheim and Simmel allow some space for the possibility that the creative capacities of embodied subjects could not only make work tolerable but may in future result in *social change*. For Marx, this involved a transcendence of oppression through revolution. For Durkheim, it involved the supersession of an anomic division of labour through the effervescent capacities of embodied subjects leading to the creation of a new moral framework informing work. For Simmel, it involved a continued thirst for the overcoming of forms that stunted the development of individuality.

A second view of the outcome of interaction between the body and structures of the workplace can be found in those studies which report overt and sustained resistance to the demands of waged labour. The discipline workers were subjected to in the early decades of industrialization was mostly of an external form (involving the physical, spatial, and temporal discipline described by E.P. Thompson and Foucault), and was rarely internalized completely in the form of personal dispositions. This was evidenced by the resistance of workers to the time constraints imposed on them, by the Luddite opposition to the introduction of new machinery, by a growth in political organizations dedicated to ameliorating the conditions of work, and by the levels of concern expressed by factory owners at workers who had not reconciled themselves to the regularities of industrial work (Thompson, 1980: 393).

In the early decades of industrialization, the management of appearance and the pretence of working hard were job-related forms of body work that could help individuals avoid physical punishment and dismissal, and provided at least a limited shield against the panopticon-like surveillance of workers instituted by certain factories (Foucault, 1979a). Sometimes resistance was much more overt. In Germany, for example, alcohol became a particular issue through which workers refused to comply with the patterns of factory work. As Roberts (1992: 104) explains, workers viewed alcohol as a thirst quencher, a dietary supplement, a stimulant and a vehicle of sociability, and insisted on their 'right to drink' even when employers sought to eliminate alcohol from the workplace. Such opposition to the demands of the workplace often drew on cultural customs within the community out-side of waged-work, and insisted on an affirmation of the sociable individ-ual within the structures of the economy.

If we look ahead to Fordist methods of factory organization, overt resist-ance and other ways of mediating the impact of work remained highly visi-ble. Numerous studies of factory work in the twentieth century have shown the continued significance of 'make work' and similar forms of job-related body work by highlighting how individuals manage the appearances they presented to supervisors while working in visually exposed 'front regions' (Goffman, 1969 [1956b]. Such studies have also illustrated how workers maximize the opportunities provided by 'back regions' in which they can relax, drop their guard and engage in 'profanity, open sexual remarks, elab-orate griping, smoking … "sloppy" sitting and standing posture' and so on (ibid.: 129). We have already mentioned Benyon's (1973) *Working for Ford* and this research illustrated how union meetings and industrial action pro-vided escape from the monotony at the Ford factory, while sabotage also became popular. Safety wires would be pulled at times of heightened dis-content. During the 1960s, some young men even made 'bostick bombs', placed into the steel dumpers, the explosive consequences of which would bring production to a halt (ibid.: 198, 139). If the body refused to be a pas-sive location for the effects of assembly-line work at Ford, studies of work-ers in other factories reveal a variety of other coping strategies. Many workers, indeed, decided to exit factory work altogether. Almost half of Chrysler's new workers in 1969 did not complete their first ninety days on the job (Braverman, 1974: 33).

The relative luxury of being able to leave a job one did not like was not available to everyone, of course, and became much more difficult with the growth of mass unemployment during the 1970s. The dull compulsions of work continued to exert a major influence on individuals who, quite simply, had to sell their labour in order to live, yet who also had to cope with the physical discomfort associated with manual labour. In these cases, job-related body work was, as in classical conceptions of the uses to which individuals put religion, often directed towards ameliorating the psychological effects of waged labour. Roy (1960) and Cavendish (1982), for example, provide clas-sic studies of how individuals rendered tolerable long hours of boring work by inventing imaginative ways of partitioning time. Boredom was not, how-ever, the only problem to be overcome in the workplace. Richard Sennett and Jonathan Cobb's (1972) analysis of the 'hidden injuries' incurred by blue-col-lar workers, who measured their own values against those lives and occupa-tions to which society gives a social premium, illustrates the deleterious effects waged work can have on people's sense of self.

The third view of how the embodied subject's interaction with eco-nomic structures ends up positioning people within waged labour is provided by writings which address some of the central characteristics of post-Fordism. There has been a major shift in the conditions of waged labour for many in the post-Fordist era which has involved an unprecedented overlap between the tasks required as a formal part of the job and the tasks that used to be associated with informal, job-related and other forms of body work. This is vividly illustrated by the growth of emotion work, a concept associated with Arlie Hochschild's (1983) pioneering study *The Managed Heart*. It can be supplemented by the more recent demands associated with the 'emotional intelligence' movement within the workplace, a concept associated with Daniel Goleman's (1996, 1998) influential writings.

Hochschild suggests that the tasks involved in managing one's feelings at work have become increasingly subject to the working contract, and that 'emotion work' is undertaken by employees required to manage their emotions in order to 'create a publicly observable facial and bodily display' and 'expressive behaviour' designed to encourage a particular emotional state in the customer (Hochschild, 1983: 7; Ashworth and Humphrey, 1993, 1995). This definition of emotion work incorporates the physical, physiological and psychological processes that are necessary to regulate one's emotions in line with the organizational demands of the workplace, but has been elaborated further into a multi-dimensional construct involving five elements. These are: (1) 'the requirement to display positive emotions'; (2) the requirement to display and handle a high variety of emotions, including negative emotions; (3) 'the requirement to sense the emotion of the interaction partner'; (4) the requirement to influence and control interaction; and (5) the requirement to cope with a dissonance between felt and displayed emotions (Zapf et al., 2001).

Emotion work is not an exclusive product of the post-Fordist era, having been carried out for generations by such professions as doctors, teachers and lawyers. Personnel departments became charged during the early twentieth century with the responsibility of avoiding displays of aggression in the workplace, white-collar staff have long been required to 'sell not only their time and energy but their personalities as well' (Streans and Streans, 1986: 118; Mills, 1953: xvii), while female sales and secretarial staff have also traditionally been required to draw directly on qualities of nurturing and sexuality considered natural to women (Streans and Streans, 1986: 117; Pringle, 1988). Emotion work has grown in significance during the post-Fordist era, however, with major increases in service sector work and a generally heightened emphasis on the display of the self within the work environment (Paoli, 1997). It has also been solidified in a number of cases by formalized 'feeling rules' or 'display rules' or emotional 'scripts' (rules which codify how employees should express emotion and manage their own experiences of typical on-the-job situations [Hochschild, 1983]) in certain airline companies and in organizations such as McDonald's and Disney (Leidner, 1993; van Maanen and Kunda, 1989). As such, there is now a much greater range of jobs which draw on displays once associated with job-related, cultural and reproductive body work.

Emotion work can assume the forms of surface acting (when employees pretend to feel an emotion), or deep acting (when they take over the levers of feeling production and actually experience an organizationally prescribed emotion) but it can also occur through *automatic* feelings which occur in response to the conditions or interactions employees encounter at work (Hochschild, 1983; Zapf, 2002). On the positive side, emotion work has been shown to have the potential of making social interaction more predictable and of helping to avoid embarrassing situations with clients (Ashforth and Humphrey, 1993). Emotional scripts have also provided some employees with a welcome resource through which interactions with clients can be controlled (Leidner, 1993). The employee management of automatic work-based emotions (as opposed to surface or deep acting) has more widely been associated with positive outcomes such as a greater sense of job satisfaction and personal accomplishment (Zapf, 2002). On the negative side, Hochschild (1983: 187) has suggested that when emotional workers begin to 'identify too wholeheartedly with the job' they risk burnout, that if they abandon emotional attachment to the job they can suffer from guilt, and that if they recognize the need for emotion work but feel cynical about engaging in such work, they can become 'remote and detached' from the people they serve. There is also a strong gendered dimension to these negative effects. There remain strong expectations that women are more 'naturally' suited to carrying out caring and nurturing types of emotion work, and this can increase their exposure to sexual harassment from customers (Fineman, 2000). Emotional dissonance (being required to experience an emotion that is not felt, as in being expected to feel sympathy at a complaints counter when dealing with rude customers) and situational overload (when a job's requirements are greater than the resources and opportunities individuals have for dealing with that situation) are particularly related to emotional exhaustion and a sense of 'depersonalisation' (Zapf et al., 1999, 2001). These conditions have also been associated with psycho-social stress which has itself been linked to detrimental effects on cardiovascular systems, on the endocrine systems, and on the immune system (Mills et al., 1989; Hodap et al., 1992; Elstad, 1998: 600–1).

The significance of emotion work to our concern with the positioning of embodied subjects is that it has the potential to tie people to their job in *productive* ways as well as in the predominantly negative ways associated with the compulsions of factory work. When employees engage in 'deep acting', by actually altering their feelings as well as their appearances in line with company expectations (Hochschild, 1983: 33–5), they are responding to a form of 'discipline' that exerts its effects by exhorting people to become *more* than they are in the workplace, rather than by allowing them to adhere passively to the demands of the job (Foucault, 1979a).[4] Now, managing our emotions is not something which is confined to the workplace. It is also part of the cultural, reproductive, and job-related body work we engage in. We may feign love for our husband, pretend we are sympathetic about our children's inability to reach a certain score on their Playstation, and bring ourselves to feel upset by Portsmouth losing another football match in order not to disturb the gloom surrounding one's colleagues. These are emotional displays that we possess some control over, however, and we could adapt or even withdraw them. In the world of waged labour, though, emotions have become commodities subject to the working contract, a development which involves 'a loss of autonomy at the level of everyday life' (Crossley, 2000: 293). In Habermasian terms, it has been argued that 'the capacity for regulation of emotion within the lifeworld is being lost to the system. Furthermore, this involves a demoralization of the lifeworld, as emotion is passed from the normatively regulated sphere of the lifeworld into the rather more anomic and instrumentally rational functioning of the system' (ibid.).

This conception of emotion work does not rule out the possibility of resistance. Hochschild argues that employees can engage in 'surface acting' by pretending to feel emotions, while others find ways to distance themselves from their working persona, ignore the demands of emotion work, or let off steam in their leisure time (see also Leidner, 1993). However, it is possible that Hochschild overstates these possibilities. As Barbalet (1998) argues, if we view most forms of emotion work as ongoing processes that inform who we are, rather than states that take us closer to or further away from our 'real' selves and that we can control voluntarily, we can see that this type of work draws on bodily capacities that can mould our individualities in line with the demands of the job. It is not just emotion work, moreover, that can tie people to waged labour in the post-Fordist era. Flexible working, home working, and combining jobs of various degrees of impermanence, mitigate against the development of stable front- and back-regions, and can also erode the relevance of 'make work' as a form of resistance. If networking and the presentation of self have become central to economic success, it is no longer just in certain 'front regions' that one has to be 'on duty'. Instead, like the sales staff in Oakes's (1989) study, every meeting provides the potential opportunity for extending our contacts. The logic of life in post-Fordism is that 'Everyone is a potential prospect, and every human encounter presents opportunities for prospecting' (Oakes, 1989: 240).

We can develop this discussion by looking briefly at development of 'emotional intelligence' in the workplace. Associated with research undertaken into brain functioning, emotional intelligence has become popularized (especially in the USA) by the writings of the corporate consultant Daniel Goleman. Referring to a set of core skills surrounding the intrapersonal competencies of knowing and managing one's emotions and motivating oneself, and the interpersonal capacities involved in recognizing and dealing with the emotions of others, emotional intelligence has been analysed as key to personal and corporate success (Goleman, 1996: 42). It can also be viewed as a further intensification of the management demand for emotional work (Hughes, 2003a). However, while the managerial demand to 'bring their emotions to work' can make employees 'more vulnerable, potentially more normatively incorporated, [and] more open to emotional surveillance', it also provides them with the potential to 'exercise control through subscribing to the very same managerial rationality to which they are subject' (Hughes, 2003b). Feelings can not only be a location for working structures but can provide employees with an opportunity for criticizing working conditions and their superiors.

These circumstances are associated with a breaking down of boundaries between waged labour and the cultural and reproductive spheres in which body work is undertaken. The joining of these areas of activity can, however, promote 'entrepreneurs of the self', constantly concerned with 'the preservation, reproduction and reconstruction of [their] own human capital' (Gordon, 1987: 44, 300). This is clear in Ehrenreich's (1990: 236) assessment of those middle-class Americans who structure their private lives in relation to the ascetic demands of their workplace, developing (through exercise, diet and an avoidance of smoking and heavy drinking) a form of physical capital which separates its bearers from the lower classes (see also Bourdieu, 1984). This apparent erosion of the boundary between waged labour and body work remains class-specific, however, and for every individual whose job appears to have absorbed their body whole, many others continue to be tied to the workplace through more mundane, traditional concerns such as the need to earn a living. For these subjects, the spheres in which cultural and reproductive body work occur may still provide a counter-balance to the demands and pressures they experience in the workplace.

These three visions of the interaction between the body and the structures of waged labour provide us with very different assessments of how embodied subjects are positioned within society. Classical and Fordist views hold out at least some possibilities for change, recognizing that the bodily capacities of subjects can ultimately resist, transform or transcend the formal structures of labour. Analyses of the significance of emotion work within the post-Fordist era, however, provide ammunition to those theorists who believe that the body has become robbed of its creativity and generative potential. Against this view, it is difficult to seriously suggest that the conditions of waged labour are more oppressive now than was the case during the period of industrialization examined by Marx, Durkheim and Simmel. Furthermore, rather than viewing emotion work as a colonization of the life world by the system, it is possible to view it as a manifestation of how bodily capacities continue to structure the parameters of waged labour. In this respect, it is interesting that Wharton (1993) suggests that individuals find jobs involving emotion work more satisfying than jobs that do not require it, while Hughes (2003b) points out that the validation of 'emotional intelligence' in the workplace may be used by employees to achieve a degree of control over their working lives. From the findings of research into emotion work covering such occupations as barristers, paediatricians, teachers and employees working in children's homes, care homes, call centres, restaurants, hotels, and banks, this satisfaction appears to be prominent in those jobs that allow individuals time and space to cope with the feelings that arise in their workplace (e.g. Leidner, 1993; Locke, 1996; Zapf et al., 2001). It may just be that the generative properties of the body have been at least as responsible for the erosion of the boundaries between waged labour and body work as the oppressive consequences of economic structures.

Conclusion

Work is not a social construction subject to termination. Our bodily needs mean that we have to establish a productive relationship with our environment while, phenomenologically, this need seems to contribute to the feeling held by many that work is a central part of their identity. The same can be said for body work. The 'openness', unpredictability and frailty of our bodies mean that we have to invest work and meaning into our physical selves if we are to survive and prosper as human beings, while the tasks associated with reproduction and caring have long been viewed as identity-giving activities across various cultures. Thus, it is again no surprise if people experience forms of body work as an essential part of their self-identity.

If our bodies constitute an inevitable source of work, however, the precise manner in which this work is undertaken is not genetically determined. As Marx demonstrated, the technological forces and social relations of production that humans have developed and entered into over the centuries have been enormously varied, distributing the ownership and types of labour power across societies in very different ways. People have also developed radically contrasting approaches towards body work, with social, cultural and religious norms encouraging people in different eras to view the body in widely different ways (Mellor and Shilling, 1997). It is this malleability that has meant that our bodies are not just a source of work but are a location for the effects of work.

Contemporary body theorists have expressed a concern that the body has become an increasingly passive location on which the designs of contemporary structures imprint themselves. Given the oppression and exploitation that people were subjected to during the early phase of industrialization, it would be difficult to argue that this 'passivity' has resulted in an increase in absolute exploitation since that time. In the affluent West, there has been a growth in occupational health legislation in an attempt to limit workplace accidents, and legal moves to limit children's involvement in the labour force. However, if Fordist, factory-based production methods provided plenty of reasons and opportunity to 'resist' some of the external constraints of formal work, the 'post-Fordist' economy relies less heavily on physical coercion and direct discipline. While the need to earn enough to survive remains a strong incentive for people to remain engaged with the labour market, the weakening boundary between waged labour and body work has promoted for some more productive ways in which people's jobs and identities have merged. Tasks traditionally associated with job-related, cultural and reproductive forms of body work have increasingly become incorporated into the structural parameters of waged labour.

These changes may indicate the body's continuing efficacy as a source of waged labour, involving the individual's capacities for emotional expression and experience. At the very least, it is only the human capacity for emotional display that enables jobs to trade on emotion work, while the expansion of emotion is associated in part with consumer demand. However, these and other changes wrought by the post-Fordist world of work also have consequences for social inequalities, communities and individuality that are of direct relevance to the concerns of Marx, Durkheim and Simmel. Financial inequalities in earnings have frequently been exacerbated, while the psycho-social sources of stress experienced by those involved in certain forms of emotion work have been seen as a new source of social inequalities (Williams, 2000). The flexible, changeable character of work and industry in the current era has further undermined traditional, *Gemeinschaft*-type communities, and has for many reduced the time they can devote to cultivating social relationships outside of their waged working lives. The effects on personality and individuality have been ambivalent. While the character of the contemporary labour market would appear to penalize those who display cynicism and the blasé attitude (outside of those limited spheres in which these attitudes are valued), the manipulation of appearance and feeling within waged work provides perhaps more reason than ever before to adopt these approaches towards working life. The creative and varied responses that embodied individuals adopt towards these conditions, however, demonstrate that people are not simply passive receptors of the structural parts of society.

Notes

1 The boundaries between types of body work are also permeable. Foucault's (1988a, 1988b) analysis of techniques of caring for the self, for example, illustrates how reproductive and cultural body work can be combined within philosophically and religiously informed regimes often associated with community status.

2 Sociologists often resist reference to evolution because of their understandable opposition to sociobiological analyses which draw spurious comparisons with animal life and, more recently, to evolutionary psychologists who reduce the complexity of our bodily being to the demands of hunter–gatherer societies. As Hirst and Woolley (1982: 66) point out, while evolutionary processes may have given us a significant degree of biological continuity with the primates, they have also produced 'massive' differences which 'undercut any attempt to treat contemporary man as merely a "naked ape" or a territorial and aggressive baboon in clothes'. These differences do not, however, downgrade the importance of the physical development of human embodiment over the millennia.

3 It should be noted that in their early years Ford's factories relied on physical coercion as well as the rationalized organization of production. Prior to unionization in the 1930s, for example, Ford's Detroit plant enforced discipline by physical attacks on those seeking to organize the workforce, and by employing private detectives who monitored the home lives of employees (Benyon, 1973). Efficiency in the workplace, it was assumed, required complementary types of body work in the private sphere.

4 I am reading Hochschild's work against itself. Hochschild associated deep emotional act-ing with alienation from the self, yet the findings of Wharton (1993) and others suggest emo-tional labourers are more likely to be satisfied with their jobs, and are less likely to experience their emotions as unauthentic than those engaged in other jobs. A problem here is that neither Hochschild nor any other of the case studies into emotional labour control for other aspects of work which may be responsible for negative emotional outcomes (Barbalet, 1998: 179).

5

Sporting Bodies

Introduction

The activities associated with sport, leisure and play are popularly viewed as providing an escape from the compulsions and disciplines of waged labour, and this chapter examines this 'antidote' to work by focusing in particular on the cultural sphere of *sport*. The definition of 'sport' has shifted historically, but now generally refers to those activities and games that have developed into, and are most highly prized as, competitive contests between teams or individuals. While sport is often treated as marginal to the core subject-matter of sociology, it has become a phenomenon of enormous importance to millions of participants and spectators world-wide (Dunning, 1999). It is also significant to the concerns of this book as sport constitutes an activity that has been viewed as emerging from basic human needs, yet whose development has come to structure and, some would argue, limit, the creativity of physical expression. Johan Huizinga (1970 [1938]), for example, identifies humans through the term *homo ludens* ('man as player'), in an analysis which suggests that sporting activities may be interpreted as a manifestation of human nature, but identifies a rationalization of the sporting field that has ossified the play impulse by objectifying the athletic body (see also Guttmann, 1978; Hoberman, 1992; Overman, 1997; Eichberg, 1998).

The idea that sport has turned the body into a physical instrument of rationalizing processes – making it closer to, rather than further away from, work – has become increasingly prominent within sociology. This contention should not, however, be accepted uncritically. Motor racing may exemplify how the flesh has become a location for commodification processes (with the driver encased in one of the fastest moving adverts on earth, shrouded in a helmet and suit littered with expensively placed signs; Blake, 1996), but sport is also spoken of as a *religion* for an apparently secular age. If sport really can provide a quasi-religious vehicle of understanding and transcendence from the mundane realities of daily life (Bellah, 1967: 12; Hoffman, 1992), it cannot reasonably be reduced entirely to the rationalized environs of the modern world, but deserves consideration in its own right and from a variety of perspectives. A recognition of the importance and diverse issues associated with sport has, indeed, made the subject of interest not just to those concerned with the over-trained bodies of elite athletes (constantly verging on the edge of a physical breakdown), or the beer-drinking, cholesterol-feasting bodies of armchair spectators (constantly verging on the edge of indigestion), but with colonialism and self-identity, masculinity and femininity, biomechanics and psychology.

In what follows, I seek to reflect something of the diversity of writings relevant to the sporting body within the general theoretical framework of this study. The next section examines the work of analysts who suggest that the body is a productive and creative *source* of sport, and contests the arguments of those who view sport as a disembodied *social* construction. I then examine how the sporting body's exposure to rationalization, nationalism, corporate advertising, injury and chemical experimentation, appears to have made it, at least in part, a *location* for sporting structures. The penultimate section examines certain of the outcomes resulting from the interaction of bodies and contemporary sporting structures by examining how various groups of people *position* themselves and others within and outside of the sporting sphere of society. It focuses on the emotional attractions of sport, and analyses how 'racial' and gender divisions have historically included and excluded different groups from organized sports. Finally, I look at whether recent trends towards non-sporting and 'Easternized' forms of physical exercise are posing any significant challenge to the archetypal sporting body.

The Body as a Source of the Sporting Sphere

Despite the popularity of those arguments which view sport as a social construction, it is not difficult to appreciate how the body has constituted a source of sporting activities and institutions. This becomes clear when we recognize that those evolutionary developments associated with the human struggle to survive, which resulted in the corporeal basis for characteristically human forms of work examined in the previous chapter, have also been implicated in the emergence of sport.

Sport developed historically, it has been suggested, because it helped people invent, rehearse and re-enact skills involved in securing and defending their means of subsistence. The origin of a number of sports involving running and throwing have been accounted for on the basis that they provided practice for hunting, or constituted a mimetic activity which lived on after the need for tracking prey disappeared. Lukas (1969) has argued that the first sport was spear throwing, for example, while Cashmore (2000: 59) suggests that biological evolution predisposes humans to revisit the hunting and gathering lifestyle that dominated their lives for over two million years before agricultural activities provided food. This is why sports often 'imitate the chase, mimic the prey, copy the struggle, [and] simulate the kill' (ibid.: 59). The historical need for human communities to defend themselves against attack has also been used to explain the rise of sports. Birley (1993: 2) identifies the playful basis of sport as helping humans 'master their own bodies by pitting themselves against obstacles or against other youngsters' in readiness for more serious encounters, while Brasch (1990: 4) uses the term 'natural sports' to refer to those 'games' which emerged from violent confrontation between social groups.

These arguments may be speculative but they usefully highlight possible relationships between sporting activity and basic human needs – even if the evidence available to support them is sometimes 'oblique and indirect' (Golden, 1998) – yet sport cannot be accounted for exclusively on the basis of its role in helping people secure their means of subsistence and defend themselves. As the provision of food, shelter and protection became more predictable, and the threat of attack regulated, those physical capacities and skeletal and muscular systems that made the body 'a serviceable locomotive machine for walking, running, and, to a lesser degree, swimming, climbing and jumping' no longer had to be employed exclusively in helping humans secure basic needs (Cashmore, 2000: 35). There emerged an increasing 'excess' or 'surplus' of human potentiality and energy that was no longer exhausted in the search for, and defence of, life's necessities (Bataille, 1991 [1967]). In these circumstances, it can be argued that while sporting activities came to transcend the requirements of material necessity, they remained important to communities as forms of *play* involving the ritual sacrifice of physical energies left over from securing the means of subsistence (Brasch, 1990; Sansone, 1988). From helping humans secure life's material necessities, sports assumed a vital role in establishing and maintaining the social relations and cultural identity of a collectivity.

Huizinga's (1970 [1938]) classic study *Homo Ludens* allows us to develop this argument in its suggestion that our embodied potentiality for play constitutes a source of sport, and a creative generator of wider societal forms, because it involves the creation of norms and rules. Play provides a vision of how life can be lived when not constantly dominated by necessity, and allows people to forge relationships that can mirror, sustain and antici- pate changes in sports and social life. Thus, when Huizinga argues that Roman society 'could not live without games', and that the fabric of medieval life was 'brimful of play', he is insisting on the importance of the body as a source of sporting and social structures (Huizinga, 1970 [1938]: 115, 203, 205). Norbert Elias's (1983) analysis of Court society also pro- vides support for this argument. From the fourteenth century, life in Court society was to all intents and purposes a serious game, a social sport in which individuals had to monitor their appearance and the impressions they pre- sented to those around them in an attempt to maximize their status. The stakes of this competition were high, but Courtly life was maintained by the body's creative implication in the symbolic struggle, and by the commit- ment of its participants to common (if shifting) rules of etiquette and the pursuit of distinction (Elias, 1983).

In summary, it is possible to identify two main ways in which the body can be seen as constituting a source for sport. First, there may have been a strong link between some people's attempts to secure their means of sub- sistence and the emergence of certain sporting activities: sport provided groups with practice in hunting and defending themselves, and in preparing new generations for these activities within a safe context. Second, once sur- vival became more predictable and regulated, and human energies liberated in part from the necessities involved in securing the basics of existence, the

subsequent progression of sport can be associated with the socially generative, playful capacities of the body and the development of individual and
collective identities.

This double association of sport with material necessity, on the one hand,
and with play and identity, on the other, should not be seen as referring to
two entirely incompatible factors. There is no recorded culture which has
spent every minute of its waking time seeking to secure its means of subsistence without engaging in non-instrumental activities (including ritualized
forms of play), and these activities could themselves shape the pursuit of
material necessities. However, it is also important to recognize that the
demands of material necessity and the activities involved in play could lead
to conflict between the perceived purpose and organization of sport within
a community. It is this tension that Huizinga (1970 [1938]) goes on to
explore in his argument that playful sporting activities historically became
ossified into structures shaped by the demands of utilitarianism and the
workplace. If it is possible that the body has lost much of its creative capacities in relation to sport, as Huizinga suggests, we need to examine the main
factors that appear to have turned the sporting body into a location for societal processes and structures.

The Body as a Location for Sport

Those factors which seem to have exerted most influence on the sporting
body in modern times are associated with the rationalization of the sporting
sphere, and with the structural vulnerability of the sporting body to politi-
cization, commodification, injury, and chemical invasion. The massive
process of rationalization that has transformed the spatial and temporal context in which sport occurs is of particular importance here as it has made
the sporting sphere more readily available for the expression of nationalism,
for demonstrating the economic, cultural and moral superiority of particular political regimes, for widespread commercialism, and for the limitless
demands of performativity (Goodger, 1985).

The rationalization of sport

The sporting sphere has been subjected to a process of spatial and temporal
rationalization in the modern era which contrasts dramatically with how
sport was organized and played in earlier times. In medieval Europe, for
example, ball games could encompass entire villages and were played over
roads, tracks and fields, while running, dancing and carnival occurred in
irregular and changing sites (Bale and Philo, 1998: 12). A similarly expansive
use of space is found later in North America. Among Native Indians, what
we now know as lacrosse approximated to a 'roving battle' with up to five
hundred warriors on each side (Brasch, 1990: 248). In contrast, the
Protestant association of games with sin, and its organization of leisure into
activities designed to promote moral fitness, brought about significant

changes to the sporting field in seventeenth-century Europe (Birley, 1993; Overman, 1997: 200). Events in the eighteenth and nineteenth centuries further increased the regulation of sport in comparison with the medieval era. This was the time that Michel Foucault refers to as the 'great confinement' of the body within schools, hospitals, prisons, and sports, and was associated with growing state power, an increase in workplace discipline as a result of factory production, and a series of 'moral panics' concerning the working-class threat to social order (Walvin, 1975; Stedmen-Jones, 1983). In this context, political movements joined their religious counterparts in seeking to instil through regulated sports a new moral ethic among the working classes. One prominent example of this was the promotion of 'rational recreation' in England (see Horne et al., 1999), and the associated attempt by the industrial middle classes to compact the length of sports events and matches into time periods which would fit the constraints of work (Eisenberg, 1990).

These developments had an enormous impact on sports. In place of the cyclical, season-informed sporting metric of the medieval era arose a performance-driven experience in which the ordering of space enabled time and speed to assume heightened importance. While the 'noble' exercises of Court Society (e.g. dance, rapier fencing, court tennis) were characterized by the 'dominance of spatial order over temporal dynamic', space was increasingly rationalized, becoming what Eichberg (1998: 152) refers to as an 'effaced panorama, a blurred horizon, a standardised channel for the streamlined body projectile'. This argument resonates with Virilio's (1986) suggestion that people have become fascinated with speed in a society whose multiple demands appear to have collapsed space into time. It can be illustrated by the development of cycling which was associated even in the 1890s with the projection of speed through space and a public desire to witness 'the accelerating pursuit of new record performances' (Hoberman, 1992: 9). Even boxing and football have been transformed into 'quick and dynamic exercises', suggests Eichberg (1998: 143), while the streamlined body is now generally valued over the massive mesomorph that used to be prized within most sports space (Park, 1987: 29). The valuation of speed over space is best exemplified, however, by the 'quintessential' modern sport of track and field, with its valuation of linear motion, timekeeping and the breaking of records, and by the 'gold standard' event of the Olympic Games, the 100 metres sprint (Brownwell, 1998).

This rationalization of the sporting sphere does much to support Huizinga's (1970 [1938]: 219) thesis about the subjugation of play. As sporting activities became more systematized, Huizinga argues, there was a diminution in the spontaneity and play-quality of sport. Sports increasingly removed the body from 'the peculiarities of the natural environment', suited to creativity and the expression of difference, and relocated it to 'the uniform geometries' of the gymnasium and the running track, and the 'straightened, right-angled, sealed up and segmented' blocks of the sports stadium (Bale and Philo, 1998: 12; Eichberg, 1998: 71). Sporting activities, which had once been expressions of cultural creativity, were now subject to reorganization along the principles of work (Mumford, 1967). There were exceptions to these developments (Eichberg, 1998: 52), yet the dominant form of sports in industrial society was characterized by the 'dictates of function, achievement and bureaucratic standardization' (Eichberg, 1998: 52; Sage, 1973; Guttman, 1978). As Hoberman (1992: 5) explains, this reflected 'a mania for measurement that continues unabated to this day' and which saw the development of the dynamometer (for measuring muscle strength), the sphygmograph (for recording the pulse), the pneumatometer (for measuring exhaled air), and the ergograph (for measuring muscular work). These changes reflected in sport the principles of scientific management examined in Chapter 4, principles which sought to transform the subject by timing every movement in order to maximize efficiency (Brohm, 1978).

These rationalization processes not only altered the relationship of the body to space and time, but were of particular importance in preparing the ground for sports to become a vehicle for the political, commercial and performative demands of society.

Nationalism

Political regimes have long embraced sports, and embarked on programmes designed to achieve success in international competitions as a symbol of their efficiency and superiority. The political use of athletes can be traced back to Ancient Greece. More recently, Britain placed team sports at the centre of its colonial domination in the nineteenth and early twentieth centuries. Sports such as cricket were seen as a means of building character and leadership skills within those who would become the future managers of the empire, and as an export which could help 'civilize the natives' (Mangan and Walvin, 1987; Brownfoot, 1992; Mangan, 1992). Subsequent political regimes were quick to recognize the value of sporting achievement. Adolf Hitler used the 1936 Olympic Games as an exemplar of German superiority and, in the same year, hailed Max Schmelling's victory over Joe Louis as evidence of racial superiority (when Louis won the return bout in just over two minutes, the German authorities edited the footage of the fight for their own newsreels in an attempt to support a claim that victory had been aided by a foul punch). Other fascist regimes of the 1930s also recognized the propaganda value of sport. In Franco's Spain, for example, soccer players displayed the fascist salute before games. Politically suspect players and referees were barred, and the press used a new political discourse to report games (Gilroy, 2000: 187).

Prior to the collapse of the communist block, however, the Soviet and East German athletic triumphs at the Olympic Games and World Championships were the most dramatic example of national sporting efficiency. These regimes invested massive amounts into sporting facilitates and training, and made huge efforts to identify sporting talent at a young age. In an attempt to maximize their chances of victory, the bodies of young sportsmen and women were closely managed and monitored. Often removed from their home environment, every detail of their training and diet was prescribed in order to produce the ideal sporting body. From 1960, East Germany inducted about 10,000 young people into sports academies where they were trained and given drugs designed to improve their performance. As Cashmore (2000: 193) explains, 'State Program 1425, as it was known, was responsible for some of the world's outstanding track achievements, including Marita Koch's 47.6 second 400 metres record set in 1985.' While Western governments criticized these sporting regimes as inhuman, they were only too eager to learn from them (Hoberman, 1992). Multi-million dollar sports centres are now commonplace in America, while the American university sports scholarship system subsidizes elite athletes and forms a key component in the development of sporting talent. Australia has established sporting academies which are widely accredited with enhancing their success in athletics, cricket and rugby, while other countries such as England have followed this example in. an attempt to improve their sporting achievements.

Developments such as these indicate just how serious a matter sport is in the political sphere, with the Olympic Games and the Soccer World Cup providing the pre-eminent examples of how much significance nations place on sporting success (with failure to do well in either competition portrayed by the tabloid press in England as an indisputable marker of national decline). Political conflict has been reflected in frequent boycotts of, and exclusions from, the Olympic Games, while the sporting isolation of South Africa was viewed as a central weapon in ending apartheid. It appears, in short, that it is no longer play that the individual participates in when engaging in sport, but a form of political activity in which the agenda of the social body envelopes the physical body (Wilson, 1994: 37). One direct manifestation of this is the moral censure so often placed by the media on sports competitors who are seen as 'letting down' their country. As Elspeth Probyn (2000) notes, to lose is to bring shame on the nation and the self (see also Ye, 1997).

If sport has been instrumental in constructing the 'imagined community' of nationhood (Anderson, 1991), the most prominent examples of this process suggest that it has not been used to facilitate the integration of individuals into what Durkheim (1961) referred to as a general moral collectivity compatible with the development of humanity *as a whole*. Sport has more usually been placed at the service of a 'centrifugal' nationalism involved in the stimulation of sectarian emotions and sentiments (ibid.: 77). However, while the national organization and uses of sport remain important, one must not underestimate the increasingly *global* dimensions of sporting participation and representation (Maguire, 1994). The international tennis circuit, the Kerry Packer inspired revolution in world cricket, and the migration of the world's soccer stars to the most successful and financially remunerative leagues in the world, provide examples of how national structures are not the only ones to affect sporting bodies (Blake,

1996). Multinational capital exerted an increasing effect on the development of sport during the late twentieth century, and this is particularly evident in the sphere of advertising and corporate sponsorship. With international finance having become so influential, global structures seem to have taken increasing (though far from exclusive) hold of the sporting sphere in recent years.

Advertising

If political agendas continue to imprint themselves on the bodies of athletes, commodification processes have also come to be located on the sporting body. The extent of corporate sponsorship in this area is now such that most major sporting events simply would not exist without it. Similarly, the training and success of elite athletes is frequently built on the subsidies provided by sponsors, while much of the wealth of sporting superstars is gained through this medium. Michael Jordan accumulated millions of dollars when he was the public body of Nike, for example, while the agent of the soccer player David Beckham argued in 2002 that his client's image alone warranted adding an extra £50,000 a week onto his wages.

The pervasiveness of advertising in contemporary sports has reached the stage where it sometimes appears as if commercial products are the only things represented in sports space. Advertising fills sporting stadia with commercial products, while the sporting body is itself increasingly 'sealed in signs', enveloped by the 'second skin' of the sponsor's choosing (Baudrillard, 1993: 105–7). From the professional soccer player's kit, to the work-out gear of the gym enthusiast, it has become commonplace for the body to act as a site for the advertising of multinational companies and sports brands. We have even reached the stage when a three-year-old can be signed up by a sportswear company (Reebok) in order for it to be associated with such a young basketball talent (Ayres, 2003). Companies like Nike, furthermore, monitor closely the space they have purchased on people's bodies. Goldman and Papson (1998: 18–19) report that the Nike 'swoosh logo police' were at the 1996 Summer Olympics and 'prowl the sidelines' in the National Football League 'protecting a $3 billion licensing business'. Players caught wearing the wrong logo stand to be fined a staggering $100,000 if this happens in the SuperBowl.

The value and significance of the sporting body to advertisers are inextricably linked with the power of television as a media (Maguire, 1993). Rupert Murdoch has been particularly influential here, building much of his vast media empire on the advertising opportunities associated with prime sporting events (Maney, 1995). Televised sports have the potential to attract significant audience share, and prime slots in major events attract huge advertising revenues. While the quantity and velocity of images we are surrounded by may dilute the impact of any *particular* advertiser, it is worth noting that in 1991 Nike was inducted into the American Marketing Association's Hall of Fame because of the impact its messages of global citizenship exerted over American lifestyles. Goldman and Papson (1998: 184) go so far as to argue that Nike managed to project onto their 'swoosh' sign the impression of a sturdy moral centre, and conclude that this imagery does not just adorn sporting bodies everywhere, but comes attached to a form of 'pop morality' that uses in its advertising the language of equal opportunities and humanism while relying on cheap outsourced labour in developing countries.

The use of sports as a location for advertisers is not, however, new. Discussing the growth of sport in Britain, Birley (1993) refers to the eighteenth century as heralding 'a new age of pleasure and profit' in which soccer and boxing promoters took advantage of the new advertising media, the press, and individual sportsmen began earning money and celebrity status. Later, promoters of foot races in the USA offered purses of up to $1,000 in the 1830s, while cycling tours became popular events for sponsorship in the late nineteenth century (Overman, 1997; Cashmore, 2000). The close relationship between profit, advertising and sport became increasingly influential and, by the twentieth century, provided impetus for the development of sport for women. For example, the growth of industrial league sport, which began in earnest during the 1920s, capitalized on the publicity value of the sexualized female body. Uniforms changed to 'brief shorts and tight fitting shirts emblazoned with the sponsor's name' (Emery, 1994: 114) and, as Lenskyj (1986) points out, the sexualized sporting women's body remains an object of value for companies, radiating a glamour and sexual attraction with proven market value.

If the body's location as a prime site for advertisers is not new, it has become increasingly important and pervasive in the current era. Those sporting stars who find themselves offered lucrative advertising contracts not only stand to have their image moulded, but their *behaviour* tightly constructed and controlled. Sponsors do not hesitate to disassociate themselves from athletes whose identities or actions they find unacceptable, and promotional contracts frequently include clauses about 'unacceptable behaviour' which will lead to contract termination. When elite sports performers often appear to be corporeal billboards, and when even a child's gym kit comes complete with the sign of the Nike swoosh, the place of play within these sporting structures seem at the very least to have been marginalised by other considerations. The archetypal sporting body has become a commodified body. Economic values are associated with its performance and profile, and the promise of economic profit is a prime determinant of the opportunities and rewards it receives.

The damaged sporting body

If the body has become a prime location for expressions of nationalism and advertising, it has not survived this development unscathed. John Hoberman (1992: 25) argues that the 'charisma of sport' for political regimes and advertisers alike 'grows out of its promise of limitless performances'. Capitalist and communist states both embraced a 'performance principle' in which productivity and efficiency were central political goals, while advertising enables corporations to associate their goods with images of functional utility and pleasure. In this context, the sporting body can represent for these authorities the essence of performativity, but only if it can be portrayed as embodying *success*. The physical costs of seeking to achieve this success, of attempting to live the promise of 'limitless performances', have proved considerable. Success in sport may involve 'subordinating the body completely to the will of the rational mind' (Cashmore, 1998: 84), but attempts to instrumentalize the flesh rarely leave it unmarked.

In attempting to push the body to its limits and elicit positive adaptational responses, the elite athlete is operating on the borders of physical breakdown. The training programmes an endurance runner needs for success, for example, often lead to injuries that hasten their demise (Toole, 1998). It is not uncommon for sportsmen and women who push their bodies beyond what they can stand to suffer from mood disturbances, sleeplessness, greater vulnerability to infection, generalized lethargy, and endocrine dysfunction, and these injuries are not confined to professionals (Flynn, 1998; Sparkes, 1999). Injuries aside, training regimes can take over an elite athlete's life. Diet, rest, sleep and practice, are all carefully specified in an attempt to maximize the individual's performance. As one 'iron man' triathlete commented, 'You're up at 4:30 to go training ... most of the day. And you are too tired to go out anyway and you've got to get your rest. It is a pretty disciplined sort of life. It's like being in jail' (Connell, 1990: 85). Max Weber described mechanized capitalism as an 'iron cage', and sport has a longstanding and growing tradition of attempting to incarcerate participants in a similarly restrictive regime. In the 1880s, for example, the manager of the Chicago Cubs baseball team hired detectives to spy on the 'extra-curricular activities' of his entire team (Overman, 1977: 199), while Sir Alex Ferguson's regime at Manchester United from the 1990s became well known for having a variety of informers who would report on any players who appeared in, or drank at, the city's nightclubs.

If the sporting body has become a location on which the effects of an increasingly rationalized, performance-oriented society are evident, children as well as adults are vulnerable (Evans et al., 2003). It is not unusual for children to be pushed into the sports training system at the age of three or four; a situation which contributes to what Devereux (1976) has referred to as the 'impoverishment of play' in American culture. Children are subjected to testing to assess which sport they have most aptitude for, and are sometimes encouraged to concentrate on it to the detriment of other activities (Devereux, 1976: 123–4). Compared to their previous physical pursuits, this can result in them participating in exercise requiring more repetitions of fewer movements: a tendency that has contributed to an increase in overuse injuries which can disrupt growth processes and result in life-long physical damage (Russell, 1986). The extent of this problem is such that the term 'battered child athlete' has been used in the USA to describe children who are physically and psychologically damaged as a result of such training (Hargreaves, 1994: 225).

Dreams of 'limitless performance' may underpin political and economic investments in sport, but despite the view that modernity has 'colonised nature' (Giddens, 1991), the body remains a mortal, limited phenomenon. There is a tension here which reveals the contradictory space inhabited by the modern sporting body. Increasingly treated like a machine, by institutions and individuals alike, the body simply cannot stand up in the long run to the stresses and workloads borne by machines. Professional athletes regularly train despite minor injuries, often making them worse, while marketing concerns lead teams to play at times and in places which add to the fatigue of their players (the alleged pressures placed on an ill Ronaldo to play in the 1998 World Cup final by the Brazilian team's sponsors, Nike, provide just one example of this phenomenon). The sporting structures that contribute to such events are not conducive to exercise being used for the development of the all-round individual, or the creation of unique personalities, but are possessed of a logic that subordinates action and values to the imperatives of performance. In this context, it is not surprising that there have been attempts to transform the body so that it can cope with the demands of the modern sporting environment.

The chemically enhanced body

In 1952, the US coach Bob Hoffman returned from the Olympics convinced that the successful Soviet weight lifting team had been using hormones. Hoffman subsequently obtained Dianabol, an anabolic steroid, for his own squad. Gains in strength and weight were impressive and, as there were no rules prohibiting the use of such drugs during the 1950s and 1960s, dianabol quickly spread among those involved in strength-oriented sports and events (Cashmore, 2000: 192). This practice has been banned for over three decades, but is still maintained by an estimated $1 billion dollar international unofficial market (Hoberman and Yesalis, 1995: 61).

The use of drugs and supplements in sports has become much more prominent since the 1950s, when political and sporting authorities sought to systematically manipulate the bodies of their sporting representatives, and examples are not hard to come by. Commenting on the East German situation from the 1960s, Hoberman (1992: 222) argues that the state possessed a 'secret and centrally administered [drug] program unlike that of any other society on earth'. Large numbers of athletes were administered drugs without their consent or knowledge, and there have been many other institutionalized examples of drug and supplement use. During the 1986 World Cup in Mexico City, the West German soccer squad were reported to have been given 3,000 injections, which included calf blood extract designed to reduce the effects of altitude (Hoberman, 1992). An entire cycling team was disqualified for drug use during the 1998 Tour de France, while the 2000

Olympic Games witnessed its usual conveyor belt of competitors expelled for drugs use. The recent 'crisis' over the discovery of a new, previously undetectable 'designer anabolic steroid' is just the latest in a very long line of drug episodes (Mackay, 2003a).

The use of performance-enhancing drugs and supplements has a long history, stretching back to Ancient Greece and continuing within contemporary sports (Hoberman and Yesalis 1995; George, 1996; Fotheringham, 2003), but the body continues to reveal its limits and has yet to be moulded into a completely suitable location for chemical attempts to fulfil the performance principle. Opinions about the first modern drug-related death in sport vary (e.g. Verroken, 1996: 18; cf. Cashmore, 2000: 103) but it appears to have been in cycling and to have occurred during the late 1960s. More recently, the German heptathlete Birgit Dressel died in 1987 having allowed her sports physician to inject her at least 400 times with dozens of substances. The damage that drug taking and intensive training (often through injuries) had done to her body were such that she had suffered from 'intervertebral disc injuries, fusion of the vertebrae, a pelvic dislocation, pathological degeneration of both kneecaps, and inflamed joints' (Hoberman, 1992: 2–3). The degree to which individual athletes agree voluntarily to consume drugs is difficult to determine precisely, and there are undoubtedly large numbers of non-competitive bodybuilders and others who take muscle building drugs without financial incentive (e.g. Bloor et al., 1998). Nevertheless, in those cases where the individual has been pressurized to take drugs, or has unknowingly had them administered, the athlete exemplifies how the body can become objectified into location for the designs of the state or other authority.

Official attitudes to performance-enhancing drugs have hardened over the years. By the 1968 Winter Olympics, drug testing had been introduced. Since that time there has been a cat and mouse game based on attempts to hide and detect drugs and techniques such as anabolic-androgenic steroids (versions of the male sex hormone testosterone), diuretics (which expel water from the body), and blood doping (injecting extra blood into the body to increase its uptake of oxygen). The moral outrage directed towards those caught 'cheating' by using drugs is illustrated by the furore surrounding Ben Johnson's disqualification from his record-breaking 100 metres in the Seoul Olympics (although the far less spectacular reaction that greeted the news in 2003 that Carl Lewis and other participants in that race had failed drugs tests, admittedly for less serious offences, in the run-up to competition suggests that a degree of cynicism may now surround the process; Mackay, 2003b).

Despite continued doubts about their efficacy, and the dangerous side-effects associated with them, most commentators believe that the use of performance-enhancing drugs remains widespread. The sporting body has, it has been suggested, become a 'chemical experiment' (Bloor et al., 1998) designed to maximize the capacity of every blood cell and muscle in order to push forward the boundaries of athletic achievement. This experiment does not appear to have stopped with adults. Reports suggest that parents in the USA have asked paediatricians to administer human growth hormones to their children in order that they should become better athletes (Hoberman, 1992).

There is a paradox associated with the official view of drugs in sports. We live in a society in which the body is routinely changed in order to transcend its natural limits. Furthermore, the 'pharmacological revolution' of the 1960s made available a wide range of potent and cheap drugs which were less toxic than their antecedents (Hoberman, 1992). Stimulants, tranquillizers, painkillers, beta blockers, sleeping pills, antidepressants and a range of other drugs are now taken for granted. Given the wider social pharmacological context in which sporting drug use occurs, why is drug use in sports still frowned upon and why are strenuous attempts made to identify and exclude offenders from competition? One possible reason for this can be found in the suggestion that in an image-saturated world in which appearances have become 'unreliable', there exists a demand to see evidence of the *authentic* body (Hoberman, 1992: 111). Machines may have overtaken humans in terms of their capacity for performance, but the natural body-in-motion provides evidence of our humanity. This may explain a part of the public disapproval towards drug taking, but I think there is another political reason for attempting to maintain the idea of natural athletes. The existence of highly trained, highly paid, drug-free, record-breaking bodies provides a basis on which rationalization in society can be *naturalized*; viewed as the fulfilment of human destiny rather than as a technologically directed process imposed on humans. 'Natural' athletes show what performances can be achieved by an individual who submits their body to a regimented and productive lifestyle. They are a model of success and a sign of the social mobility that can be acquired by anyone prepared to work hard enough (though it is worth here remembering Dunning's [1999] estimate that the actual chances of economic mobility through sport are as low as 1 in 250,000). Ideologically, such naturally acquired success may do something to obfuscate wider social inequalities. Despite their prevalence in wider society, then, it seems that the taking of (performance-enhancing) drugs in sports represents at best an example of 'positive deviance'. Drug taking is an unacceptable action that is carried out in order to cope with a regime which 'demands that athletes strive to achieve success amidst pain and injuries, and in spite of deteriorating bodies' (Overman, 1997: 208). Even when the athlete has sought out drugs using their own initiative, however, such behaviour shows that sport clearly provides the conditions in which human potentiality can be damaged in a search for competitive perfection.

This section has identified a number of structural factors concerned with the rationalization of the sporting sphere, with nationalism, commercialism, injury and drugs that have threatened to make the sporting body a pure location for societal forces. Having provided examples of sporting bodies that illustrate the efficacy of these forces, however, I am *not* suggesting that these structures *determine* the bodily actions and identities of *all* individuals. To stop here, with a structural analysis that portrays human physicality as a passive, objectified site on which society inscribes its effects, would be to present a partial picture of the relationship between the body, sport and society. This is because it fails to address the varied ways in which interaction between people's generative capacities and sporting structures position people within and outside of the sporting sphere. While the bodies of many athletes in the world of elite sport may be shaped by the structural pressures outlined in this section, other embodied subjects respond to the sporting sphere in quite different ways.

The Positioning of Sporting Bodies

The rationalization of the sporting sphere may help prepare the body to be a location for the ambitions of political regimes and corporate advertisers, but we have already noted the limits and frailties of the body, and its ultimate inability to act as a completely calculable and reliable bearer of any performance principle. While injury and wear and tear have been portrayed in this chapter as a structural corollary of the organization of sport, they also point to the limitations of the sporting body as a bearer of wider social forces. If sporting bodies are subject to chemical invasion, stress, and punishing training schedules, though, why is there such competition to succeed in the world of sports? Furthermore, if sports have become hyper-rationalized and devoid of an aesthetically pleasing spatial geometry, as Eichberg (1998) argues, why are they still so popular with spectators? In exploring the reasons for such phenomena, we can see that bodies are not usually passive locations for sporting structures. Instead, the creative interactions of embodied subjects with the sporting 'social facts' they confront serve to attach certain people to, and distance others from, this sphere. This becomes clear when we consider the role of emotions in sports, and the significance of 'race' and gender in the construction of sporting inequalities.

Emotions and sports

Despite its rationalized structures, large numbers of people express a commitment and attachment to at least some part of the sporting sphere. As Dunning (1999: 1) observes, 'No activities have ever served so regularly as foci of simultaneous common interest and concern to so many people all over the world.' The financial rewards earned by elite sports people may explain something of the pull of sports to participants, although this should be seen in the context of the tiny chances of actually achieving social mobility through this route, but cannot account for most people's interest in sport. Far from making money out of sport, indeed, it is more usual for people to *spend* money on their sporting interests. Many soccer fans spend hundreds and even thousands of pounds a year following their team around the country, for example, by buying gear from club shops and other outlets, and paying to see games on subscription or pay-per-view television.

In seeking to explain the non-economic attraction of sports, Elias (1986b: 114) and Dunning (1999: 41) point to the growing gap that has emerged in the modern world between the evolutionarily given capacities of the human body and the restricted opportunities embodied subjects have for exercising their emotional capacities. This argument engages with some of the themes contained in Huizinga's (1970 [1938]) analysis of the rationalized subjugation of play that we explored above. However, while Huizinga views sport as having lost its vitalism through rationalization, Elias and Dunning suggest that sport continues to provide people with much needed opportunities to experience the emotional satisfactions associated with exercising these capacities. They express this by arguing that sport provides a space in which people can engage in a 'quest for excitement' (Elias and Dunning, 1986: 3), the results of which can commit them to participating in, or watching, certain activities. Specifically, sports are well suited to this quest because they are associated with *motility, sociability* and *mimesis*(Dunning, 1999). Motility involves the pleasure and loss of self that can sometimes result from being immersed in movement. This mobility may itself be rationalized but, if so, the suggestion is that it provides a rationalized escape from a rationalized society, affording a subjective immersion in an activity that individuals rarely experience in most contemporary jobs. Sociability brings satisfactions derived from playful interaction that occurs for its own sake, outside the rationalized environs of work (Simmel, 1971 [1910]). Finally, mimesis involves the enjoyable arousal of strong affects in safe contexts; affects that are not usually prized in the contemporary workplace (Dunning, 1999: 26–7). The result of such experiences involves a building and release of emotional tension; a controlled de-controlling of emotional controls which humans may both want and *need* on a regular basis.

Elias and Dunning suggest that this quest for excitement serves two wider social purposes. First, it can make tolerable a highly rationalized society, facilitating a liberating transcendence from mundane routine. Andrew Blake (1996), for example, discusses the intrinsically pleasurable sense of 'loss of self' that can be experienced by spectators and participants. The 'runner's high' that joggers talk of has been described as a sense of euphoria involving a 'breaking free of the mind from the body which allows persons to reach a meditative state similar to that attained by Eastern mystics' (Higdon, 1992: 80). Surfing has similarly been described as a 'spiritual experience', involving transcendence of the self (Sheehan, 1992). Other related experiences are associated with what Lyng (1990) calls 'edgework'; the excitement, pleasure and 'rush' involved in pushing oneself to the limits in extreme, dangerous sports. These can become examples of what Csikszentmihalyi (1975) refers to as 'flow'; the holistic sensation experienced when immersion and performance in a demanding challenge reach a stage when the participant is perfectly attuned to the task. Flow is 'a

harmonious experience where mind and body are working together effort-
lessly, leaving the person feeling that something special has just occurred'
(Jackson and Csikszentmihalyi, 1999: 5). In contrast, David Le Breton
(2000: 1) analyses participants in extreme sports as undergoing a self-
imposed ordeal that provides them with a sense of self in a world 'where reference points are both countless and contradictory and where values are in
crisis'. Rather than 'flow', Le Breton (2000: 2) prefers to talk in terms of 'a
personally generated spirituality achieved through the ordeal of or activity'
of extreme sport. In each of these cases, though, individuals gain a refreshment and a release from the rationalized structures of work. In contrast to
the assessments of Huizinga and others, this analysis suggests that sport
appears to be regaining (or has never lost) some of its potential to be an antidote to work.

Second, in an argument that mirrors Durkheim's views on the enhancement of identity that results from being incorporated into a community,
Dunning (1999: 6) holds that 'membership of, or identification with, a
sports team can provide people with an important identity prop, a source of
"we-feelings" and a sense of belonging.' This ability of sport to morally attach
individuals to the society in which they live is absolutely central, for
Dunning, to why sport has become so significant in modern society: it is
sport that 'has come to perform some of the functions performed earlier by
religion' (Dunning, 1999: 7). Again, this argument is supported by other
studies. Zurcher and Meadow's (1967) account of the national sports of
Mexico (bullfighting) and the USA (baseball), for example, links the emotional characteristics of sport to the tensions generated by the family forms
of these countries (Goodger and Goodger, 1989). Zurcher and Meadow
(1967) suggest that national sports allow individuals to mimetically experience and discharge the emotional tensions they experience in the family,
and thus help reattach them to the basic unit of society. In a related vein,
Goodger (1985) points out that 'the team' may be a totem for its players
and fans, and cites studies which argue that jockeys, boxers and judo players are concerned with 'the celebration of moral virtue' which reflects and
develops moral codes in the wider society (Weinberg and Arond, 1952;
Scott, 1968; Goodger, 1982). Alternatively, the views expressed by many
writers on soccer culture and hooliganism suggest that the intense attachment of individuals to a team is part of a sectarian commitment often associated with racism (e.g. Back et al., 2001).

These concerns with transcendence and emotional attachment stand in
strong contrast to the arguments put forward by those like Eichberg who
view sport as a symbol and extension of rationality. However, both views
may be significant. The emotional release Elias and Dunning refer to
involves a *controlled* decontrolling of affects, and it is no accident that
moves have been made to regulate the behaviour of sports stars and fans
(the imposition of all-seater stadia in elite British soccer illustrates one
reform that has been made in relation to the latter). Furthermore, it is also
important to recognize that sport can be seen as a differentiated field that

both rationalizes and provides escape for *different* groups of participants and spectators. It is also possible to see particular sports such as boxing as providing an escape *into* rationalized life for many of their participants; an escape in which the body gains a certain vitality from its involvement in this punishing discipline. As Loic Waquant's (1995) phenomenologically informed study of pugilists suggests, boxers must reject the drink and drugs that might otherwise have characterized their lifestyle and embrace the rigid physical regime of the gym. We may also want to recognize, however, that there exists for some people a genuine tension and even irreconcilable conflict between the rationalized and transcendent potentialities of sport. This clash is illustrated by Hoffman's (1992a) fascinating study of those athletes who seek to make sense of their experiences in the context of their 'orthodox Christianity'. Hoffman details how these athletes are pulled between their religion and the ethical demands of organized sport; a tension they seek to manage by emphasizing the ascetic demands of training and romanticizing pain in a manner which turns sport into a 'spiritual offering' (ibid.: 276). The highly rationalized demands of modern sport, however, make this an almost impossible conflict to manage. While their Christian religion teaches them that the human body is made in the image of divine creation, sports like American football appropriate the athlete's body as an 'instrument of destruction' while the organization of other sports treats the bodies of their participants as 'expendable machinery' by subjecting them to over-training, drugs, and operations that condemn their participants to short careers and future problems such as arthritis. In short, it is difficult to view such sports as a simple preparation for leading a moral life. The sporting ethics discussed by Hoffman appear instead to represent a voluntary embrace of this-worldly control in which 'the individual demonstrates he/she is willing to sacrifice his/her body for the good of society or the corporation that sponsors the team' (Goldman and Papson, 1998: 161). If sport really does represent an extension of the Weberian 'iron cage', then studies like Hoffman's may lead us to conclude that many athletes are ready to embrace life in this cage in exchange for material reward rather than spiritual transcendence.

The suggestion that there exists some link between sports and group or societal attachment may not be universally valid, but it undoubtedly speaks to many people's experiences. If there exists an effervescent attraction of individuals into sporting communities, however, there is a related process of alienation and exclusion. Sports teams can be described as 'totems' for their fans (Goodger, 1985), for example, but it is important to remember that totems are inflected with cultural meanings which define who can and cannot belong in the community. Despite the multiracial, multicultural character of professional soccer, for example, there exists a strong 'grammar of race' around the sport through which groups of white fans articulate their racial hatred (Hall, 1981; Back et al., 2001). In Britain, one consequence of this can be seen in the small number of black and Asian people who attend live professional matches.

Having recognized that the emotional attachment of some to sports is related to the exclusion of others, it is important to trace how people came to occupy these contrasting positions in relation to the sporting field. I shall do this by focusing on the links between social inequalities and 'race' and gender. This cannot be done without outlining, if only briefly, the emergence of racialized and gendered sporting structures, but I then move to a consideration of how these became used and challenged by people in order to either reinforce or alter their positioning within the sporting field.

Masculinity and racial otherness

Despite its potential to mobilize people, sport in the West has a long history of perpetuating inequalities by excluding or marginalizing from its spaces those considered 'others' on the basis of their racialized or gendered bodily identities. This can be illustrated through the 'cult of manliness' that became a pervasive feature of middle-class life in Britain and America from the latter half of the nineteenth century, and was used by the white male establishment in these societies to confirm its dominance over the expanding field of sports. As Roberta Park (1987) explains, this cult maintained that a man of muscular 'character' was one who stamped his personality on the world. Ostensibly a gendered code which, among other things, designated the male body as the archetypal sporting body, this cult was also racialized: the sporting body was a *white* body, the physical prowess of which was associated with keen judgement and a free, strong will, demarcated from the 'brute' black bodies whose passions were viewed as overriding any capacities they had for free action (Mangan, 1986: 113–14; Park, 1987: 29; Hoberman, 1992).

In Victorian Britain, this cult of manliness was manifest through the influence of 'muscular Christianity', an ethic which combined moral ideals of the good life and the righteous, vigorous body. Muscular Christianity informed the education of the public school elite who were viewed as the future leaders of Britain's empire (Mangan and Walvin, 1987: 2–3). In America, the cult of masculinity peaked during the late nineteenth century in response to fears that the domestication of space (represented by the closing of the frontier) was 'feminising society' (Hantover, 1980: 293; Messner, 1987; Kimmel, 1990). In this context, only aggressive sports could provide a space in which masculine supremacy could flourish (Dubbert, 1979; Vetinsky, 1994). Once again, however, the notion of masculine supremacy was not racially neutral. It was white men who were the exemplars of this character, in contrast to the animalistic brute strength associated with blacks suited to a small range of 'unsophisticated' sports, such as boxing, that could be traced to slavery (Wiggins, 1977; Sammons, 1994).

The cult of manliness manifested itself in distinctive ways in Britain and America yet developed by the end of the nineteenth century into a pervasive normative ideal used by the white sporting establishment to exclude black people from sporting space. Indeed, the trend towards racially segregated sports was accentuated in America as society became increasingly racially intolerant (Dunning, 1999). Wiggins (1979) notes how the 1890s saw whites forming 'anti-coloured unions' to monopolize the career of jockey, for example, even though it had been stigmatized as 'nigger work' in the decades immediately following the Civil War. Exclusionary tactics were often reinforced by the use of violence in sports such as baseball (Captain, 1991), and Wiggins (1986: 110) concludes that black athletes had been virtually eliminated from white organized sport by the 1890s.

The twentieth century witnessed great changes in the sporting participation of black peoples. As Eichberg (1998) states, the rationalization of sports space reduced the importance that had been attributed to an individual's ascribed status, and increased that placed on achieved sporting *performance*. This enhanced the opportunities for upward mobility through sports to the black bourgeoisie (Dunning, 1999), and was readily seized upon by black individuals whose abilities at various sports could now be deployed and eventually rewarded by corporate sponsors keen to widen their market appeal. By the end of the twentieth century, indeed, black success in sports was even associated with a change in colour of the archetypal sporting body. In the world of advertising, racial cosmopolitanism now sells. As Goldman and Papson (1998: 100) argue, during the heyday of Michael Jordan and Bo Jackson, Nike advertisements drew their value from black athletes. The apparent value placed on the black body, however, obfuscates other racialized issues which continue to surround sport. Hoberman (1997) argues that black sports stars use their bodies to entertain audiences, the majority of whom are white. If the surface of sporting stars can now legitimately be black, furthermore, the sporting spaces in which they perform are usually managed by white owners. It is also important to note that 'blackness' and 'exotic primitivism' are often framed within sporting images to encompass 'immediacy and pleasure', and have come to signify 'the ability to be in touch with one's natural and essential mode of being' (Goldman and Papson, 1998: 107). Such images resurrect colonial views of the black body as less civilized and more primitive than the white colonizer, albeit within a less derogatory discourse (Gilroy, 2000: 258), and suggest that the identities available for black people within the sporting sphere remain constrained around normative conceptions of racial character.

The increased prominence of black sports stars has had other negative effects. Research has long suggested that schools tend to push those with an Afro-Caribbean background into sports to the detriment of their academic work (Carrington, 1982), while the increased prominence of high-earning black sports people may have encouraged economically disadvantaged black youth to neglect education in favour of sport as *the* means of upward mobility (Hoberman, 1997). Figures suggest that around 75 per cent of black men who are awarded athletic scholarships never graduate, (McKay, 1995), while many of those who are successful graduate with either physical education degrees or majors especially created for athletes that have a low exchange value in the labour market (Majors,

1990: 114). While this may mean that a number of black athletes are grad-
uating who may not have otherwise done so, it seems that 'whilst sporting
prowess and success may be an individual power resource, they are not
necessarily always a collective one' (Dunning, 1999: 217). For Cashmore
(2000: 131), indeed, 'sports' vilest function is in persuading whites that,
as long as blacks continue to succeed athletically, the American dream is
still alive, and race poses no barrier to achievement'.

Women and sports

The archetypal sporting body may have altered its colour in recent years,
but the cult of manliness that informed its construction exerted a continuing influence throughout the nineteenth and twentieth centuries. It was *men*
who were instructed by sport in the uses of power and technique (Connell,
1983: 18). Exercise for women was not absent, but was subject to constant
ideological scrutiny and women in Britain and America were placed in a typically contradictory situation. The social Darwinist 'national efficiency' and
'racial health' movements prominent in the nineteenth century insisted that
women had a responsibility to meet their 'destiny' by being fit for birth and
motherhood, yet would be breaching their biological destiny by developing
vigorous sporting bodies (Searle, 1971; Dyhouse, 1976; Mangan, 1986;
Russett, 1989; Hargreaves, 1994: 47). In this context, the systems of exercise developed for women were restrictive, designed mainly to increase their
vitality and 'to correct the female form and provide appropriate physical
discipline to fit women better for their work in the home' (Vetinsky, 1994:
65–6). Similar norms have long been used to remove women from the
boundaries of elite sport. The founder of the modern Olympics, for example, proclaimed that women's sport was against the 'laws of nature' and
excluded women from the first modern Olympics in 1896 (Simri, 1979),
while any woman engaging in activities suggestive of competitiveness and
muscularity stood to be viewed as deviant.

Women did not, however, simply accept these gendered sporting structures. Hockey, lacrosse, rounders, basketball, netball and cricket were all
played by women before the close of the nineteenth century, while bicycling
has been assessed as highly significant in relation to women's physical emancipation (Vetinsky, 1994: 70), and became popular towards the end of this
century. Cycling provided women with unprecedented spatial mobility, and
helped stimulate dress reforms as well as a series of moral panics about
women's reproductive health and the dangers of them venturing into 'dangerous spaces' (Mrozek, 1983; Hargreaves, 1994: 92; Vetinsky, 1994). The
progress that women made within the sporting sphere was reinforced by
developments in education. While competitive activities were often
excluded from the curriculum because they were 'unladylike', by the end of
the nineteenth century middle-class girls were participating in forms of
exercise which would have been unimaginable a few decades earlier
(Hargreaves, 1994).

Women's participation in the sporting sphere was facilitated by the active roles they played during war. As Cashmore (2000: 169) observes, women's filling of previously male roles in the factory helped erode the illusion that they were 'delicate creatures in need of men's protection'. Women working in British wartime munitions factories formed soccer teams, and by 1921 there were about 150 such clubs in England (Hargreaves, 1994: 141). In the USA, industrial-sponsored women sports were common in the 1920s – including bowling leagues, baseball and basketball – and a professional women's baseball league existed during the Second World War (Emery, 1994). Moving forward to the last decades of the century, equal opportunities legislation also made a difference to the position of women. The 1971 passage of Title IX in the USA, for example, did much to address unfair inequalities in the distribution of sports-related resources (although it led to a big decrease in the percentage of women coaches) and was followed by a large increase in girls' participation in high school sport (Weinberg and Gould, 1995).

The importance of these breakthroughs should not be under-estimated. Powerful stereotypes and ideologies about the limitations of women's bodies may remain, while the widespread segregation of women's from men's sport continued (Boslooper and Hayes, 1973; Snyder and Spreitzer, 1983). Nevertheless, as Therberge (1986: 202) argues, sport can act as a liberatory space in which women can experience their bodies as 'strong and powerful and free from male domination'. Furthermore, women now compete in sports previously deemed 'categorically unacceptable'. Women's boxing is increasingly popular and marketable, there are thousands of martial arts clubs catering for women in Britain and the USA, while the first women's rugby world cup took place in 1991. Certain inequalities remain, however, and it has been suggested that the differences that characterize women's and men's sports extend to their use of space (Costa and Guthrie, 1994: 141; Brownwell and Fairburn, 1995; Cashmore, 2000: 154). Aerobics classes, 'hips and thighs' classes, 'legs and bums' classes, and other exercise sessions that dominate the timetables of health clubs present 'fitness' for women as the pursuit of a toned, shapely and trim body. Being 'healthy' has now been eclipsed by an emphasis on *looking* healthy; a look which seems to have become embodied within 'anorectic females ... whose bodies suggest hard work, discipline and abstinence' (Overman, 1997: 207). If instrumentalism now dominates sports space, as Eichberg suggests, it often takes different forms for non-elite male and female participants. While the relative emphasis for men continues to be on competition against others within an *external* social space which has to be conquered, the relevant space for many women often involves a somewhat greater emphasis on altering the contours of their own bodies. While the aesthetic demands of the 'perfect' body – the body free of excess fat and flesh, and sexualized in keeping with selected norms – may be directed at men almost as much as women these days, it appears to be having a greater *effect* on the forms of exercise women engage in.

These distinctions suggest that while gender inequalities have diminished in the sporting sphere, they have not disappeared. Above all, the sphere of sport and exercise continues to be used as a means of classifying women and men as *different*. Media coverage renders women who play sports perceived as classically male, such as rugby, invisible, and generally gives less coverage to women's events than to men's. Furthermore, while the media may have largely (but not completely) discarded anachronistic images of women as frail, it still represents women's sporting bodies in a sexualized manner, often in passive poses.[1] In an era when the distance between women's and men's sporting achievements is narrowing (Dyer, 1982), sex difference also continues to preoccupy the authorities and provides a means whereby women's and men's sporting space is still separated. Since 1966 sex testing has become a major means of ensuring that individuals are segregated into two sexes at such events as the Olympic Games. At a national level, various sporting authorities have sought to keep girls out of the authorized youth leagues for their major sports. The Ontario Hockey Association, for example, went to court several times in an ultimately unsuccessful attempt to prevent a 13-year-old girl from playing in one of its teams (Kane, 1995). Sporting authorities seem ably supported in this task of sex segregation by groups of men who play sports and remain determined to exclude women from their particular space. Sheard and Dunning (1973), for example, argue that the efforts made by rugby players to discourage women's presence in the 'male world' of rugby stems from their determination to maintain an all-male sporting space, while Curry's study of fraternal bonding in the locker room examines how 'jock talk' promotes a similarly aggressive male space (cited in Costa and Guthrie, 1994; see also Kane and Disch, 1993). For Birrell and Therberge (1994), preserving the sanctity of such spaces assumes a greater significance when women have moved into traditionally male areas of activity in the workplace, and tends to intensify when changes in relations between the sexes do most to threaten male privilege (see also Lenskyj, 1986; Peiss, 1986; Birrell, 1987; Messner, 1987; Hargreaves, 1994; Dunning, 1999). Finally, the apparently liberal attempts by sports psychologists to talk in terms of 'male' and 'female' characteristics (rather than in terms of men and women) has not necessarily helped this bipartite division. While emphasizing that individuals usually possess masculine *and* feminine personality characteristics, such analysis continues to operate on the basis of binary oppositions. Furthermore, by concluding that 'females in competitive sports possess more masculine or instrumental personality characteristics than female nonparticipants' (Gill, 1986), it risks the danger of unintentionally revisiting the nineteenth century view that sporting women are somehow sexually unnatural.

Despite the continued existence of inequalities, however, the importance attributed in our rationalized world to goal-oriented motion continues to provide women with opportunities for entering and advancing within the increasingly quantifiable milieu that is sports space. Women are playing team games such as soccer and basketball in increasing numbers, outnumber men in aerobics, fitness walking, swimming, exercising with equipment and cycling, and women constitute the fastest-growing category of sporting-good consumers (Goldman and Papson, 1998: 118).

Conclusion

Bodies are not just a source of sporting activities, but their interaction with sporting structures created by previous generations has served historically to position embodied subjects differentially within this societal sphere. As we have seen, sport has reflected and sometimes extended broader patterns of social inclusion and exclusion. While these have not disappeared, and continue to affect the opportunities that different groups of people have for participating in the sporting arena, they have been vigorously contested and reduced over the last couple of centuries. This relative equalization of sporting opportunity is not, however, solely the result of action on the part of the disadvantaged. Instead, it has much to do with the increased pervasiveness and dominance of rationalized, goal-oriented activity within the sporting sphere that has been associated with an increased valuation of performativity by governments and corporate sponsors.

This rationalized goal-orientation has done much to shape the opportunities available for developing identity and personality within the sporting sphere. While there are plenty of opportunities for people to become involved in sport of one kind or another, the identities of elite performers have become tied increasingly to the demands of a highly disciplined corporeal rationality. Connell (1990: 91), for example, notes the huge discrepancy between the norms of masculinity and the disciplined life of the endurance sports star in which drinking, clubbing and womanizing are all rejected as incompatible with training (see also Wacquant, 1995). Similarly, elite sportswomen must cope with a major gap between the norms of femininity and the highly rational requirements of being a successful female within the sporting sphere. The identity of the sporting body is increasingly being defined according to quantifiable measurements, inputs and outputs. This is clearly a tendency and we should take care not to over-generalize. Nevertheless, if the performative demands of sport are gradually turning the body into a producer of quantifiable performance, albeit an unreliable producer, then perhaps the boundaries of sporting identity are moving away from traditional conceptions of masculinity, femininity, class or race, and towards the cellular and molecular factors that sports scientists associate with sporting capacity (Gilroy, 2000: 36, 47). Analysing the possible future effects of genetic technology, Blake (1996) looks forward to a time when gender may cease to have fixed bodily or sporting boundaries. This vision of sports populated by scientifically programmed humans may not promise much for the future of human creativity and spontaneity. However, there is another way of interpreting such tendencies within the field of sports. In a rationalized world associated with the search to colonize nature, attempts by athletes to exceed the limits of the body could be viewed as heroic. Nike advertising, for example, has used images which focused on the psychological and physical casualties resulting from the pushing of competition to its outer limits (Goldman and Papson, 1998: 157). While the deaths and injuries occurring as a result of American Football matches in 1905 prompted President Theodore Roosevelt to seek reform of the game (Mechikoff and Estes, 1993: 256), and fatal injuries from boxing continue to provoke calls to ban the sport, less spectacular and more routine examples of athletes pushing their bodies to the limits of endurance tend to be portrayed as illustrations of heroism. Despite this, sport does appear to have placed some restrictions on the human capacity for play and creativity. Thus, Sheehan (1992: 85) argues that 'on our way to becoming adults', sports-oriented 'physical education' turns 'what was joy into boredom, fun into drudgery, pleasure into work'. As Novak (1976) puts it, if play involves living for a time in the 'Kingdom of Ends', then the spirit of play is antithetical to that of goal-oriented sport which requires athletes to live a mind/body dualism by treating their bodies as objects to be managed by the regimes they must internalize (Overman, 1997: 193). The effects of this rationalization certainly appear to have seeped down the age scale. Devereux (1976) refers to the gradual 'impoverishment' of play in children's games, while research has suggested that youth sport programmes are typically run by adults who propagate achievement-oriented values (Brower, 1979).

Does this mean that the body has become a location for sporting structures that have subjugated its powers of creativity and generativity? This does not appear to be the case for everyone as many find something in sports activities that enables them to transcend their daily lives. As we have seen, writings abound on those groups of spectators and participants who forge real or imagined communities that provide emotional stimulation and outlets for those involved (e.g. Maffesoli, 1996). Sport has even been viewed as a religion for the modern age, fulfilling many of the functions that used to be carried out by religious belief systems in earlier times.[2] Furthermore, it is important to take account of those diverse forms of exercise outside of high status Western sports. Thus, Yoga, Tai Chi Chuan, and other East Asian exercises (often mixed with elements of Oriental spirituality such as Zen, Taoism or Tantra) have become increasingly popular among those disillusioned with rationalized uses of leisure time (Eichberg, 1998: 105). Disassociating exercise and health from 'work', such forms of exercise focus on internal energy, posture, and the slow, carefully controlled movement of the body and breathing through routines which can sometimes be traced back hundreds of years. They have proved popular with young and old alike and can be practised outside of rationalized sporting environments at home, in the park, or by the beach. As Eichberg (1998: 153–4) argues, these exercises 'are following older movement patterns to create a new slowness, contrasting sharply with the configuration of modern speed and acceleration'. Commenting on what he sees as an associated trend of opposition to organized sports, Eichberg (1998: 146) also suggests that 'joggers, skate boarders, roller skaters and carnivalistic festivals are reconquering the road as a space of body culture and games'.

Suggestions that these alternative exercises may herald a new and non-rationalized form of Western 'body culture', however, need critical scrutiny. The impact 'new wave' exercises have had on elite sports is marginal. Multinational corporations continue to focus their funding and exploitation of sports on long-standing elite areas such as soccer, basketball, American Football and baseball. The form these Eastern exercises take in the West, moreover, often involves a process of translation in which they become higher velocity and/or competitive activities. For example, we have seen instances of the aerobicization of Tai Chi and Yoga. Even individualized forms of exercise, such as jogging, can involve a form of 'conspicuous exertion' (Krauthammer, 1984) in which exercise is made visible to others as a form of physical capital and cultural distinction (Bourdieu, 1984). Finally, if there has been any 'reconquering of the road', there is precious little sign of this in most of the highways and byways that continue to promote the dominance of the car over the health, safety and expressiveness of the human body.

Cashmore (1998: 88) has quite reasonably suggested that 'Sport can both humanize and dehumanize depending on historical circumstances and who controls them.' The sporting sphere (especially the elite sporting sphere) does appear to have become ever more rationalized in its treatment of the body, yet there remains the potential for individuals to develop their identities within this sphere, and for participants and spectators to find within it opportunities for transcending the mundane conditions of their working lives and attaching themselves to a collectivity. Furthermore, the fact that there has in recent years been a proliferation and growing popularity of those forms of exercise and games that exist outside of the formal sporting sphere demonstrates that there remain alternative avenues for physical activity.

Notes

1 Men's health magazines, for example, have run 'Sexiest sportswomen in the world' competitions replete with contenders pictured in underwear and poses suggestive of sexual availability (e.g. *Men's Fitness*, 2002). These images often incorporate aesthetic ideals of almost unattainable shape for most women (Leath and Lumpkin, 1992; Gill, 1994; Costa and Guthrie, 1994). It has been suggested by some commentators that such representations may have contributed to the vast growth in eating disorders to have afflicted young women in recent years, disorders which are more prevalent in certain sports than in the general population (Grogan, 1999).

2 The idea that sport is a religion has proven popular, but it is important to ask whether sport can be described accurately in these terms. Religion, for Durkheim (1995 [1912]: 44), constituted a 'unified system of beliefs and practices relative to sacred things ... which unite into one single moral community called a Church all those who adhere to them'. Despite the

flexibility of Durkheim's analysis, it is difficult to argue that most sports are associated with a 'unified system of beliefs and practices' (see the debates in Hoffman, 1992b). This does not mean that sport does not share certain characteristics and functions with religion. It does make it important to stipulate whether analysts are arguing that sport attaches individuals to a whole society, a sect, a team, or simply to the existence of a self possessed of a tolerably coherent identity, and to be able to distinguish between the joy of the spectator when their team scores, and the experience of the medieval Christian who believes they have eaten the flesh and blood of Christ during communion.

6

Musical Bodies

Introduction

The significance of work and sport to our consideration of the body–society relationship is self-evident – each has historically exerted a profound effect on the exteriors and organic/emotional interiors of people's bodily selves – yet the inclusion of music within this study warrants justification. This need to explain my decision to devote a chapter to this subject is reinforced by characterizations of modern culture as an essentially visual phenomenon (Jenks, 1995), yet such depictions underestimate the importance of sound to the environments in which we live and completely ignore the significance of music to social action. Music, in particular, has been identified by classical social theorists as central to those rituals which have historically forged embodied subjects into moral collectivities (Durkheim, 1995 [1912]), and has become a prominent and pervasive part of the structural contexts in which we move. It helps lure us into shops and can shape our purchasing decisions, 'narrates' the films we watch and sporting events we attend, and has been shown to increase productivity among manual labourers (Hargreaves and North, 1997). Music does not just shape people's actions, however, but plays an important part in how individuals form and sustain their identities (e.g. Finnegan, 1989). People can be moved emotionally by specific songs that remind them of key people or events in their lives, and many imaginatively 'play' music in their heads for significant parts of the day in order to create or reflect a mood. The importance of music to individual identities appears to be increasing, at least for certain age groups: the amount of time teenagers spend listening to music (and watching music videos on the television) has grown enormously over the last few decades (Sagi and Vitanyi, 1988; Zillman and Gan, 1997; Reynolds, 1998). Since the advent of radio, the mass production of cheap records, tapes, CDs, and personal stereos, the proliferation of music television, the commercial use of songs, and the development of digital technology which allows music to be more or less created as well as stored on and downloaded from computers, we now live in an age in which it is said that music is 'practically a permanent part of most people's every day mental activity' (Storr, 1997: 123).

If more people now have more means to listen to more music than ever before, aural culture has historically been considered an important issue. Classical philosophers such as Plato viewed music as central to the shaping of the soul and the education of citizens. While contemporary social theorists too often follow the example of Enlightenment rationalists in marginalizing the significance of music to embodied life, cultural critics have done much to elevate the academic significance of the subject over the last few decades. These analysts emphasize the importance of the subject, yet agree about little else and have suggested variously that music has the power to 'punctuate the core of our physical being' and 'temporarily transform our whole existence' (Storr, 1997: 4), that it enables oppressed subjects and sub-cultural groups to resist dominant norms and values (Frith, 1983, 1988), and that it stimulates actions and attitudes implicated in the decline of civiliza-tion and the end of liberal education (Bloom, 1987). Thus, depending upon whom we choose to believe, the significance of music is demonstrated by its association with religious epiphanies, with its centrality to the counter-cul-tural movements of the 1960s and early 1970s, and with the 'Free Nelson Mandela' campaign and 'Live Aid' concerts, or with the commodified banal-ities of popular music that reduce the attraction of art and thought, and turn life into a non-stop, musically narrated and 'commercially prepacked mas-turbational fantasy' (Bloom, 1987: 68, 75). The issue of whether music is associated predominantly with physical creativity or passivity is clearly important and contentious.

Music may be all around us, constituting an essential part of the aural culture in which we live, but there is disagreement not only about its sig-nificance but about what constitutes music. Some cultures recognize bird song as music. Opposing this view, Western analysts of classical music tend to follow the composer Stravinsky in arguing that natural sounds may *sug-gest* music to us, but are not themselves music. From this perspective, the definition of music is confined to those 'tonal elements' organized as a result of a conscious human act (Storr, 1997: 6). If the precise definition of music remains contested, societal views of what constitutes music have changed radically over the centuries. Beethoven's work was at one point rejected as substandard, for example, while every new generation seems to engage in a struggle over what constitutes acceptable and legitimate criteria against which music may be judged. The boundaries of taste that have historically surrounded devotees of classical, folk, rhythm and blues, rock, punk and rap, for example, have at various times been linked to a pursuit for distinction in which certain social groups seek to separate and elevate themselves as 'supe-rior' in relation to their predecessors (Bourdieu, 1984; Grossberg, 1990).

It is already clear from this introduction that questions of social status and inequalities, of identity, and of the relationship between music, individ-ual transcendence and group membership abound in the study of music. As such, music is obviously important to the concerns of this book. The next section focuses on how the body can be seen as an essential source of, and as being deeply attuned to, music. Various theories address these issues, but there is no doubt that evolution has equipped humans with the potential to develop the body techniques and postures essential for the production of musical sounds, and with the ability to 'tune into' and be deeply affected by musical processes. Music has the capacity to take the body 'beyond' itself, to facilitate a form of experience and communication which transcends that associated with the spoken or written word. If the body is deeply attuned to the rhythms and beats of music, however, this also provides a basis which can serve as a location for music, and that has been exploited for commercial and political purposes. The chapter then examines this issue with the assistance of two major theories concerned with how music locates itself on the bodies of listeners. It examines the commercialization of music, the ways in which music can shape people's actions in the spheres of production and consumption, and the social status of the musician. In these cases, concern is as much with how music has been utilized by structures as it is with music as a structure in its own right. The following section focuses on some of the outcomes of the interaction between people's agentically creative and structurally receptive capacities by analysing how music contributes towards the positioning of people within their social environment. Finally, the conclusion assesses whether it is still realistic to associate 'musical bodies' with a significant degree of creativity, given the pervasiveness of commercially produced music in the contemporary Western world.

The Body as a Source of Music

Music is a cultural universal that is universally dependent upon the body. Certain physical attitudes and postures must be assumed in order for music to be produced, our senses of hearing and touch are vital to the consumption as well as the production of music, while fingers need flexing and coordinating into complex patterns of movement if sound is to be made on a variety of musical instruments. Singing also requires a palpable bodily discipline: particular stances tend to accompany the shaping of the lips and the tensing of the vocal chords and diaphragm that are integral to this activity. If making music is associated with the development of body capacities, however, the organization of these capacities within particular body techniques varies enormously through time and across cultures. Classical opera singing is characterized by an upright and 'open' standing posture, for example, and is associated with facial expressiveness. Men's evening singing in Polynesia, in contrast, involved participants sitting in small circles, with their heads held closely together, displaying inexpressive faces (Burrows, 1936; Merriam, 1964).

These cultural variations illustrate that the body is not simply an unchanging source of music, but is possessed of the capacity to develop itself and music through the acquisition of new competencies. In this respect, David Sudnow's (1978) account of how he learnt to perform jazz improvisation provides a good illustration of what is involved in the development of a musical body. From gradually assimilating the keyboard to his body schema, Sudnow struggled through hundreds of hours of practice with stiff, non-synchronized hands, undertaking procedures that seemed to have no results. Initially, the music he produced 'was literally out of hand', but Sudnow eventually reached the point at which he could finally see his hands 'for the first time now as "jazz piano player's hands"' equipped with the practical knowledge which makes it seem as if 'the fingers are making the music all by themselves' (Sudnow, 1978: xiii, 33). Comparing his past incompetence with his newly acquired skill, Sudnow (ibid.: 85) likens the difference to that between a student's first attempt to put together a smooth sentence in a foreign language, and a native speaker's speech. All manner of cultural norms and procedures informed Sudnow's apprenticeship to jazz, but underpinning them all were the capacities of his body; a physical organism equipped with the potentiality to transcend its previous achievements in order to become a musical body equipped with new skills. Music is not, and cannot be analysed adequately as, a pure social construction, but is deeply connected to the generative powers of the body.

If the body is an irreducible source of music, there is no absolute agreement about the precise evolutionary development of music. What we find instead (similar to the case of sports) is a variety of 'origin narratives'. Darwin argued that music preceded speech, and links its rise with the elaboration of mating calls. Rousseau viewed the origin of language as melodic and poetic, with musically informed communication between humans being driven by passion rather than utilitarian considerations. A distinctive, more cognitive origin narrative is the Chomskyian view that the structures of the mind determine the human capacity to generate music (Lerdahl and Jackendoff, 1983). In contrast, Ellen Dissanayake (1990) looks to the early interactions that characterize a child's development, holding that music develops from the ritualized verbal exchanges which take place between mothers and babies during the first year of life (cited in Storr, 1997: 8). According to Gregory (1997: 124), these exchanges are stimulated by the cross-cultural need to calm babies which has resulted in lullabies becoming 'one of the most universal forms of music'. It is 'emotional expressiveness' rather than the simple conducting of 'factual information' that informs this origin narrative (Storr, 1997: 8).

There may be disagreement about how music began, but much philosophical argument suggests that the body is possessed of a strong *affinity* with music; an affinity enabling humans to transcend the world of appearances and become connected to a deeper level of reality. This suggestion is associated most famously with Schopenhauer and Nietzsche. Schopenhauer's (1966) writings are based on the metaphysical assumption that 'the will' underpinning the essence of objects, (or what Kant called the 'thing-in-itself') is normally unavailable to us, and that we can usually only perceive its external representations in the world. Schopenhauer does, however, identify two ways in which we can gain intimations of 'the will'. These are the experience we have of our bodily being, and our experience of *music*. As Storr (1997) elaborates, these constitute closely related aspects of an aesthetic mode of knowing that seeks neither to represent nor to evaluate the external world, but to transcend appearances and connect with 'the true nature of all things' (Schopenhauer, 1966: vol. 1, 262). Music, in other words, does not speak to objectifications of the will, but to 'the *will itself*' (Schopenhauer, 1966: vol. 2, 448). It expresses the 'inner-being, the in itself of the world' (Schopenhauer, 1966: vol. 1, 264). Nietzsche endorsed much, though by no means all, of Schopenhauer's approach. He associated music with the Dionysian flow of the life force, rather than the Apolline sphere of appearance and organization, and suggested it connected us to the essence of reality (Nietzsche, 1993 [1872]), yet viewed music as a way of experiencing human sensuality to its fullest rather than as a way of achieving an inner calm away from the disturbances of the emotions.

These arguments could be dismissed as groundless metaphysical speculations by the sociological empiricist, but this would be unfortunate as the link between the body and music is one that has been made by a number of disparate writers on the subject. Blacking (1976: vi), for example, argues that music's essential processes derive from 'the constitution of the human body and in patterns of interactions of bodies in society', while Schutz (1964) argues that embodied interaction requires an ability to 'tune into' the other which is analogous to musical processes. In a slightly different vein, DeNora (2000: 123) suggests that music can 'profile' and offer to individuals 'ways of moving, being and feeling' through the way its materials are organized into such 'sonic parameters as pace, rhythm, [and] the vertical and horizontal "distances" between tones'.

Physiological evidence on our early introduction to beat and rhythm lends some support to these views. The unborn child hears the 'intrauterine symphony' of its mother's voice, heartbeat, and the 'rhythmic swooshing' of the blood rushing through the placental vessels (Collins and Kuck, 1990: 24; DeNora, 2000: 77). As the use of music in neonatal intensive care facilities suggests, this is associated with the rapid development of a strong affinity between the body and music. Music is used in these environments to help the body achieve an equilibrium in terms of its heart beat, colour, blood pressure, movement, crying and ability to sleep (DeNora, 2000: 81). The bodies of adults continue to reflect this attunement. Music has been shown to possess the capacity to affect blood pressure, respiration, muscular energy, and receptivity to sensory stimuli. Furthermore, despite the learned passivity and silence of the concert audience (a relatively recent development), hearing music often prompts people to move. Foot tapping or finger drumming may be minor manifestations of this phenomenon, but hearing music can make individuals feel compelled to dance, or engage in other vigorous physical activity (e.g. Frith, 1983). This is illustrated by Willis's (1978) study of bikers who felt that loud music 'demanded' that they immerse their bodies in the experience of speed. If we want to understand the affinities and attunements that exist between the body and music, then we need to acknowledge that there is a phenomenology of musical experience in which individuals can become connected to the rhythms and beats of music. Music can penetrate deeply into the body, and may vibrantly activate the tastes and dispositions of the listener.

There are a variety of philosophical, physiological, evolutionary and psychological narratives about the evolutionary origins of music. Nevertheless, it is clear that the human body is both a source of music (even in these electronic days when it is possible to 'summon' recordings via the click of a mouse attached to a computer), and is deeply attuned to musical rhythms (to the extent that music can affect physiological processes). In this context, it seems reasonable to follow Storr (1997: 149) in concluding that if we accept that music is rooted in the body, and closely connected with our lived experience of physical movement, then the philosophical view that 'both our experience of the body and our experience of music possess a depth, an immediacy, and an intensity which cannot be obtained in other ways, becomes comprehensible and persuasive.' If the body is deeply attuned to music, however, we must also recognize that this presents clear opportunities for social groups to manipulate music in ways which seek to make a specific impact on the behaviour and identities of individuals.

The Body as a Location for Music

In examining how music can inscribe itself on bodily character and behaviour, it is useful to turn to two of the major theories in this area. These are classical philosophical views of music as a stimulant that can have dangerous effects on citizens, and critical theories of the sedative effects of music in a mass, capitalist society. Having looked at these highly general views of the relationship between music and the structures of society, I shall turn to more substantive considerations of the use of music within waged labour and consumption, and the structural location of musicians in society.

Music and the political and economic shaping of the embodied subject

Among the classical Greek philosophers, it was Plato who developed a clear view of the effects that music could have on the citizen. Plato (1981 [1888]) argued that the structures of music directly shaped the embodied character of citizens, and was convinced that simplicity in music 'makes for moderation in the soul', while excess led to physical corruption and immorality. His concern over the potentially deleterious effects of music on character was such that in the third book of the *Republic* he is keen to ban 'the harmonies expressive of sorrow' as well as those 'suitable for drinking', and is only prepared to legitimate music for use in such occasions as battle or to encourage prudent and temperate behaviour in daily life.

This view that particular styles of music constituted a structurally dangerous stimulant has been a repeated concern of authorities through the ages. It was thought that music could signify social situations, scenes and relationships that conjured up alternatives to the status quo. In the sixteenth century, Calvinists banned the use of the organ in church services and, even today, tightly regulate the use of music for religious purposes. Among religious authorities, it was not just the Calvinists who recognized the power of music. As DeNora (2000: 46) elaborates, Johan Sebastian Bach was reprimanded in 1730 by the church authorities for including new and unsanctioned hymns in the liturgical service. Music was seen in these cases as a potent force which had to be guarded and licensed if order was to be maintained.

The idea that music is a structural cultural resource that inscribes its effects on the dispositions and desires of those subject to its sounds is not confined to 'elite' philosophers such as Plato. The critical cultural theorist Theodore Adorno argued that music acts not as a stimulant, but as a *sedative* in subduing the masses within capitalist society. Adorno was a key member of the Frankfurt School which developed in Germany during the 1920s and 1930s before going into exile during the Nazi era. He analysed the structures of the culture industry in general, and the growth of popular music in particular, as *the* central resource through which capitalism was able to create and satisfy false needs. These needs underpinned the spheres of production and consumption, and helped entrench an exploitative economic system. Adorno's views are worth exploring in more detail as they remain so pertinent to contemporary concerns about the commercialization of music.

Adorno's (1978 [1932]) analysis proceeds on the basis of a fundamental distinction between two structurally different forms of music. On the one hand, there is music which has been commodified, produced simply for sale in the marketplace, and which is passive and does not engage actively with the totality in which it was formed. On the other hand, there are types of music which engage seriously with a tradition, legacy and context, and reflect the contradictions of the social totality. In the twentieth century, Adorno argues, music became increasingly market oriented and was characterized by 'the imposition of a standard formula, endlessly repeated' (Martin, 1995: 94). Its distinctive parts were so bland as to be interchangeable. Repeated listening to such music, Adorno suggested, encourages an 'infantalization' of embodied subjects. This is because they are exposed to and affected by a musical form in which tensions are resolved in the most comfortable and fluent manner possible (Adorno, 1991 [1938]). Popular music, in short, helps to reify capitalism, misrepresenting its exploitative nature by portraying the world within a structural form that eschews uncomfortable developments or conclusions.

Adorno's analysis constitutes a powerful critique of a popular musical industry which, since the time of his writing, appears to many to have become even more bland and devoid of critical content. The 1960s witnessed the rise of civil rights and anti-Vietnam war protest songs, whereas the records and stars of today are manufactured by corporate employees (lately, in Britain and America, in conjunction with television popularity contests such as *Pop Idol*), with the behaviour of singers being subject to tight contractual regulation. A common criticism made against Adorno's work, however, is that it fails to explore the specific ways in which music actually affects embodied subjects. How does listening to popular music alter bodily dispositions in ways which render individuals the passive dupes of capitalism? For Adorno, it is as if individuals were blank tapes, waiting to have recorded on them the rhythms of work, consumption and the habits of compliancy and passivity supposedly necessary for the structural reproduction of the system. If Adorno's work presents us with an over-socialized conception of the individual, however, it would be premature to dismiss his writings entirely. This is because contemporary research into the commercial effects of music has come up with some fascinating findings about the uses and effects of music which remain relevant to the concerns raised by Adorno.

Work, consumption and the effects of music

Music may no longer be seen by many as an important part of the education of citizens, as Plato suggested it should be, but it is certainly very big business. Billions of dollars a year are spent world-wide on the commercial and industrial uses of music, and this has major implications for the aural culture in which we live (Bruner, 1990; Gardner, 1985).

Research into the commercial uses of music was developed during the Second World War through a series of occupational studies designed to assess the effects of music on economic productivity and morale. As Hargreaves and North (1997: 11) summarize, these generally indicated that appropriate types of music could 'decrease boredom, conversation and absenteeism whilst improving morale, particularly on repetitive tasks' (e.g. Kaplan and Nettel, 1948; Kirkpatrick, 1943; McGehee and Gardner, 1949). The effects of music on productivity were less conclusive, but studies by Humes (1941) and Smith (1947) suggested it could increase the speed at which repetitive work was undertaken and decrease wastage rates (Hargreaves and North, 1997: 11; Merriam, 1964: 112). If music could be used to 'oil the wheels' of capitalist productivity, it has also been associated with previous modes of production. Slaves in the American South developed a rich musical culture, while music has had a role of long-standing importance in traditional societies. There is a long history of music being used to accompany work among sailors, for example, and to facilitate the rhythm of work in fields and in various indoor activities, such as grinding and pounding corn, in African societies (Hugill, 1961; Gregory, 1997).

If music has for centuries accompanied certain types of work, and cannot be associated exclusively with the 'manipulation' of workers within capitalism, its specific uses within advertising do appear to have been significant in encouraging the growth, or at least the consolidation, of a historically unique system of modern consumerism. Theorists have argued that advertised images contain within them a 'surplus' which promises to enhance the bodily identity of the individual and which provides an impetus to consume (Falk, 1994). The role that music has in depicting and conveying that surplus in television and radio advertising has been generally neglected, yet music has long been analysed as something that, when combined with an appropriate narrative, can stimulate, intensify and associate an emotion with a particular (set of) idea(s) (Davis, 1947; Merriam, 1964: 240). The commercial potential of these associations is substantial. Gorn's (1982) experiments, for example, have suggested that liked music can condition a preference for a product associated with it (North and Hargreaves, 1997).

This conditioning appears particularly effective when individuals are not consciously paying attention to the advertised product (Gorn, 1982; Tom, 1995), and less so when consumers are overtly interested in the product and are motivated to evaluate product-related information (Gorn, 1982). Brannon and Brock (1994) have suggested that a further variable in determining the persuasiveness of music in advertising is the extent to which it is assessed as being appropriate for the relevant products (North and Hargreaves, 1997). In an attempt to ensure this appropriateness, it is interesting to note that advertising clearly holds little respect for an Adorno-type distinction between popular and serious music. As Martin (1995: 65) points out, it is not just pop music that is used to sell products. Parts of Dvorak's New World Symphony have been used on British television to sell bread and cat food, for example, while engine oil is sold to the public with the aid of an extract from Mahler's Seventh. It is now possible to buy compilation CDs made up exclusively of music used in advertising.

Research into advertising may show how music can play a role in shaping people's tastes and dispositions towards particular brands and products, but some of the most striking studies into its commercial effects have been done into the actual purchases made by shoppers. With the growth of large shopping malls and superstores, marketing experts have begun to talk of 'selection stress' and have employed a range of technologies to ease the purchasing experience for consumers (Straw, 1998: 41). Structuring the emotional dimensions of the shopping environment is vital to retailers, not least because it has been suggested that up to 60 per cent of all purchase decisions arise as a result of in store browsing (Yelanjian, 1991; DeNora, 2000: 134–5), and music has become a key resource employed in enhancing the profitability of this environment. DeNora's (2000) study of clothes outlets found that the choice of music played in shops was taken very seriously, with head office often making decisions about what should be played. The music in these stores was seen as affecting who would be attracted to the store and in determining how much time individuals would spend in the store. More generally, music has been shown to affect the amount of time it takes to eat and drink (Milliman, 1986; Roballey et al., 1985), the average length of stay in a shop (Milliman, 1982), the choice of one brand or style over another (North and Hargreaves, 1997) and the amount of money spent on purchases (Areni and Kim, 1993; DeNora, 2000: 18). The playing of classical music in wine stores prompted people to make more expensive purchases, for example, while the alternative playing of French and German music enhanced sales of wine from these respective countries (North and Hargreaves, 1997).

The pervasiveness of music in commercial environments is such that it is easy to forget just how frequently music accompanies our consumption decisions and actions. Introducing and punctuating the action at baseball games, welcoming the teams onto the pitch at football games, music sets the atmosphere for sports and film as well as for consuming in shops and advertising on television or radio. Music is used to rouse a crowd to support the

135

home team, yet also to calm people about to embark on a flight. Background music in airports is carefully assessed for its capacity to reassure travellers (Lanza, 1994), and the relaxing music that greets passengers newly boarded onto a plane has been analysed as an attempt by the airline to instil faith into the safety of its products and systems (DeNora, 2000: 13). As North and Hargreaves (1997: 268) argue, the use of music to sell things has become so widespread that such commercial uses now 'constitute one of the principal sources of our everyday exposure to music in the western world'.

Adorno may have a simplistic view about the effects of music on listeners, and its efficacy in helping to reinforce the ideological climate in which capitalism has been able to expand and flourish, but this evidence suggests that his concerns are not completely anachronistic. The deep affinity that exists between bodily and musical processes does not just help individuals transcend (in part) their biological being, but can be utilized for all manner of commercial ends which posit the body as a location for structures. What is particularly revealing in this respect is the fact that some of the research noted above suggests that music can inscribe its effects on the preferences of the individual *without* their knowledge. Indeed, recent research undertaken into 'infrasound' (which occurs when an instrument produces resonance of inaudible frequency) suggests that such influence may be even more insidious. Infrasound has been linked to bodily changes and unusual experiences that embodied subjects are unable to link with sound (Radford, 2003a). The uses of music in commerce cited above may be as close as we will come to a 'hailing' of individuals to assume particular subject behaviours (Althusser, 1971); a hailing that operates via its effects on our hearing at a preconscious or non-conscious level by shaping the senses of those involved. It seems that the ear, and not just the eye, is a profound mediator of contemporary structures.

The social status of the musician

If the bodies of listeners can serve as a location for the effects of commercially deployed music, what significance do musicians, the producers of music, have in this process? The importance of music to commercial business is not generally reflected in the social status of the musician. It is true that at the very top end of their profession, fame and fortune awaits the professional rock or pop singer. The likes of Frank Sinatra, Elvis Presley, the Beatles, and Michael Jackson, for example, transcended their status as performers to become general cultural celebrities and iconic role models to their followers (Rojek, 2001). The world of classical music and opera has its own stars. The opera singer Luciano Pavarotti, for example, has done much to try to popularize the medium and his rendition of *Nessun Dorma* was used as the theme music for television coverage of the soccer World Cup finals. Music can be a lucrative business for the talented, enterprising, and lucky few. These examples are very much the exception, however, and it is, and has long been, extremely difficult for the vast majority of musicians to earn anything like a comfortable or stable existence on the basis of their music alone. As Merriam (1964: 125) notes, it is not enough to be a skilled specialist if one wants to become a professional musician: social *recognition* and *reward* are required for someone to assume this position. Thus, while the efforts, interests and priorities of those engaged in artistic pursuits are often contrasted with the crude logic of profit and loss that dominates the market place, this contrast is not replicated in the structural position of musicians. Musicians are particularly exposed to commercial and social pressures and frequently have to compromise their artistic priorities. In this context, as Martin (1995: 212) explains, a musician's career is frequently supplemented, or even dominated, by casual work. This may involve private tuition and playing at weddings, dances, clubs and other events. While Becker's (1963) study of jazz musicians shows that this does not rule out the possibility that close and highly supportive subcultures may develop in which musicians celebrate their own values against those of the wider society, they still have to work within the structural constraints laid down by others. The bodies of musicians can only become the creators and practitioners of music to the extent that they can earn a living from these or other activities that allow them to sustain their musical activities. Those who stray too far outside of the musical norms of society, furthermore, risk accusations of incompetence and publicity-seeking and ultimately risk complete obscurity (Martin, 1995: 176). It is also worth noting here the heavy toll that long hours of playing and practising on a musical instrument can have on the body. As Hoberman (1992) reports, orchestral musicians tend to suffer from a disproportionate range of ailments and injuries (including tendonitis, muscle cramps, pinched nerves, and a high incidence of heart attacks) which can have a marked, detrimental effect on their life expectancies.

The marginal position of most musicians in modern industrial societies represents a certain continuity with their origins as a distinct occupational group in the 'travelling players of medieval Europe' (Martin, 1995: 206). Furthermore, if musicians find themselves on the economic margins of society, women are especially disadvantaged within this group. As Sophie Fuller (1995) explains, while learning a musical instrument has for centuries been seen as part of the proper education of ladies, playing in public would have brought shame and disgrace. Women from the working and artisan classes may have worked as professional musicians from the earliest days of the medieval musical guilds, and there were successful women soloists working in Britain in the late eighteenth century, but women were long excluded from most of the 'education, networking and job opportunities through which male musicians and composers established successful careers' (Fuller, 1995: 24). This is despite the fact that many famous hymns were written by women in the nineteenth century. Prior to the 1850s, indeed, the large majority of orchestras simply refused to employ women.

The situation of women has improved over time, but they still only constitute about ten per cent of British composers and the most powerful positions in the music business remain male-dominated. Women conductors are a rarity, and works by women composers make up a small fraction of contemporary music concerts, broadcasting, publishing or recording (ibid.: 34). This is despite the fact that in Britain, at least, more girls than boys are learning to play musical instruments, while girls have generally achieved a higher percentage of passes than boys in school music exams.

If musicians as a group occupy an economically marginal position, they enjoy a more ambivalent cultural status. Musicians tend to be seen as both 'irresponsible' (partly no doubt because of their precarious economic position), but also as key to the cultural heritage of a collectivity. This ambivalence is especially clear in societies that are more traditionally oriented than our own. In Basongye, for example, musicians were seen as irresponsible and untrustworthy (being the object of jokes about them being lazy, heavy drinkers, debtors, hemp smokers, and weaklings), yet life without them was considered inconceivable and allowances were made for their behaviour. A visiting professional musician who committed adultery with the wife of a high village notable, for example, was forgiven and allowed to continue his journeying (Merriam, 1964). As Merriam (1964: 137) argues, this pattern of low status and high importance, coupled with 'deviant behaviour allowed by the society and capitalised upon by the musician' appears to be common across a range of societies (e.g. Malinowski, 1925), and extends into various forms of contemporary music. There are, however, limits to the behaviour that musicians can get away with. As the recent prosecution and imprisonment for drugs and firearms offences of various rap artists illustrates, the public may grant musicians a certain licence in relation to 'bad behaviour', but their bodily actions do not cease to be a location for the legal structures of society.

The status of musicians has arguably been eroded further in recent decades as a result of technological developments in the production and reproduction of music. Computer programs, sampling and other techniques of modern musical production have arguably made possible the extension of the designation 'musician' to anyone wanting the term (Longhurst, 1995). One manifestation of this decline in the status of musician is the rise of the disc jockey in the past couple of decades. From being a simple player of the music of others, disc jockeys are now seen as taste makers and, by sampling and combining excerpts from records, as producers of dance music. They have enjoyed a 'burgeoning profile in the media and record industry' and have risen to become some of the most highly paid people in the entertainment business (Haslem, 1998). Paul Oakenfold (at the time of writing, reportedly the highest earning DJ in the world) earned an estimated £4.5 million in 2002, while Pete Tong earned approximately £1.75 million during the same year.

Professional musicians may never have been unconstrained authors of their own artistic projects, but current social developments seem to be restricting further their artistic prominence at the same time that they open up and democratize the potential for creating and playing music to historically unprecedented numbers of people. More generally, if the commercial uses of music do indeed shape the behaviour and purchasing decisions of consumers, these same consumers are themselves enjoying unparalleled access to the means of creating music and also enjoy at least a degree of choice concerning the types of aural environments they expose themselves to in their leisure time. Embodied subjects are not completely passive recipients of musical structures and it is important to examine what results from the active interactions that occur between individuals and the existing uses of music within society. Music may facilitate the location of certain structures on the bodies of individuals, but this does not always happen and is by no means the only social significance of music.

The Positioning of Musical Bodies

Music can be used by some groups in society (e.g. business interests) to shape the behaviour of others (e.g. consumers), yet no consensus exists yet about the precise mechanisms through which this 'persuasion' occurs. Semiotic approaches assume that responses can be structurally derived from music, but fail to attribute due weight to the variety of reactions that different individuals may have to the same stimulus. 'Correspondence' theories, such as that expounded by Plato, have attempted to associate particular sounds with specific emotions, but these explanations rarely stand up to cross-cultural or historical analysis. Specific music–emotion correspondences, it would seem, are learnt and variable rather than having a more foundational link with human embodiment.

A more minimal, but potentially more workable, approach to musical experience can be found in Storr's (1997) suggestion that music has the potentiality to cause a general heightening or lowering of arousal (which can be associated with a range of behaviours), rather than directly determining the emergence of specific emotions (or of causing particular actions). This approach has two great advantages over its competitors. First, it recognizes that music has been shown to exert physiological effects on the body, and can be used to examine responses to music which are as diverse as the 'peak experiences' described by musicians, and the more prosaic tapping of feet, humming, or beating out of a rhythm on the steering wheel of a car. This allows us to accept that the physiological stimulation occasioned by music can be associated with epiphanies and the recovery of religious faith, but may also merely make time appear to pass more quickly (North and Hargreaves, 1997: 44–5; Storr, 1997: 22, 96). Second, the space afforded to cultural difference and individual design in Storr's approach accepts that the individual response to, interpretation of, and emotional label attached to, the physical stimulation occasioned by music, is socially variable. Social, political and economic structures that incorporate music within them may be able to produce a physiological response in people, a response which may make certain sets of actions more likely than others, but cannot *determine* the precise meanings or behaviours that result from this process.

Storr's approach avoids the problem of positing a deterministic relationship between listener, stimulus and specific outcome, and allows us to take into account a variety of other social and cultural factors in analysing how music can be associated with, and give rise to, particular feelings and actions. Crucially, in relation to the concerns of this section, music may affect the body in certain ways, through the heightening or lowering of physical affect, but it is also possible that individuals may creatively utilize this stimulation in order to achieve a variety of social outcomes. This can help us to understand how individuals and groups can attempt to use music as a resource in order to position themselves, and other people, within a social environment in quite different ways. It can be illustrated by looking at how music has been employed in various ways by individuals to attach themselves and others to groups, to cultivate and express individuality, and to pursue distinction within, and exercise resistance against, society.

Music in ritual, therapy, and technologies of the self

Collective rituals and social therapies are two ways in which music is implicated in some of the interactions that occur between individuals and structures, while music's association with more individualized 'technologies of the self' provides us with a different example of how it can be involved in the positioning of people within society. Dealing with collective rituals first, song, music and dance have historically been important elements of those practices that have been analysed as stimulating people's emotions in a manner which enables them to transcend their individual selves and join together as a group possessed of an identifiable moral order (Durkheim, 1995 [1912]). Ritualized possession by spirits is facilitated by drums among the Siberian or Eskimo shaman (Gregory, 1997), for example, while music has also been used as an important resource in the development and resolution of conflict. Bohannan (1957) recounts a legal case among the Tiv in which insulting songs and drum beats were exchanged between complainants, and in which a lengthy musical performance from both sides preceded the judging and settlement of the case (Merriam, 1964: 142–4). Music has not only entered into ritual ceremonies, but has itself become a ritualized means through which activity is initiated or consolidated. The Tutsi of Rwanda, for example, sang ritualized songs to prepare for war, for greeting others, when reminiscing about absent friends, when initiating relationships, and when dealing with cattle (Merriam, 1959). Meek (1926) makes a similar point in his research among the Jukun. Recognized tunes summon people to war or work, and to a range of other activities.

Ethnomusicologists (who study the structures and uses of music within their cultural context) have suggested that while music had a pervasive ritual significance in traditional societies, and especially within non-literate cultures, this is no longer the case in modern western society (Merriam, 1964). As Crozier (1997: 67) points out, however, music continues to play a key role in 'many of the ceremonies that mark the significant events in people's lives – weddings, funerals, bar mitzvahs, parties, dances, church services, thanksgiving, and state ceremonies of commemoration, coronations'. These rituals have evolved over time in response to people's changing views and needs, while music also serves to consolidate contemporary identities by binding people within groups and demarcating the boundaries between groups. In Northern Ireland, for example, the parades by Protestant Orangemen with fife and drum bands seek to define their local identity as linked with British rule, while traditional Irish music is commonly played in the pubs and clubs situated within Catholic areas (Stokes, 1994). National anthems continue to perform a similar role on a wider scale, while the politically integrative importance of music was perhaps never more clearly illustrated than at the Nuremberg Rally of 1936. Here, massed bands were used to heighten emotion and prepare the way for Hitler's appearance (Storr, 1997).

The above examples represent uses of music which result from various interactions between people's agentic preferences and existing structures. Even the use of music within National Socialism can be seen as utilizing the deep bodily and psychological insecurity, resentment and anger that characterized portions of the German population (Scheff, 1994). In contemporary as well as traditional cultures, it is clear that music has been used in ritualized form to increase or release tension, to consolidate group identity, to mark stages in ceremonial events, and to signify or accompany work and leisure activities. By helping to physiologically arouse people, music can heighten the effects of symbols and ritual practices directed towards attaching people to a social group. Within these contexts, people become more than themselves, being attached to a collectivity which heightens their sense of identity and belonging, and which can make them capable of acts of 'superhuman heroism' or 'bloody barbarism' (Durkheim, 1995 [1912]: 213).

If rituals constitute the first means in which music intervenes in the relationship between individuals and structures, the second involves its deployment within therapeutic culture. Music therapy has been defined as 'the use of sounds and music within an evolving relationship between child or adult and therapist to support and encourage physical, mental, social and emotional well-being' (Bunt, 1997: 251). While music has long been used to alleviate illness and distress (Moreno, 1988), modern music therapy began after the Second World War when musicians were employed to help with the rehabilitation of returning war veterans (Bunt, 1997). By the mid-1990s, there were over 70 degree courses in music therapy and over 3,000 music therapists practising in the USA alone (Bunt, 1997: 250). The scope of music therapy is considerable: it covers the medical use of music as an analgesic in the reduction of pain, as a resource employed to increase general sensory responses in the case of brain-damaged patients, stroke victims or premature neonates, and as a means of helping patients control certain physiological functions such as blood pressure (Standley, 1995; Bunt, 1997). However, there is often a much stronger normative element to the employment of music therapy than simply achieving 'well-being'. This is because it is often used as a means of promoting those habits and skills that are central to the smooth continuation of what Goffman (1983) refers to as the 'interaction order', the mechanisms central to social interaction which enable individuals to develop and maintain a self accepted as morally worthy within society. Bunt (1997: 257), for example, shows how music therapy is used to help enable children to learn and respond to the 'rules' of social intercourse such as 'listening, watching, vocalising, cause and effect, turntaking, and all the subtleties of reciprocal interaction'. Depending on one's point of view, music therapy can be seen as helping to expand the powers of the individual (by helping them function within a social milieu), and/or a means of reinforcing social norms.

The uses of music not only result in the attachment of individuals to preexisting norms, however, but have in recent years been associated with a contrasting, and unprecedented, *individualization* of the self. Far from being incompatible with social integration, this can be associated with a societal commitment to what Durkheim referred to as the 'cult of the individual', a collective valuation of individual difference. DeNora (2000) has talked about the role of music in this process of self-structuration by using the Foucauldian notion 'technologies of the self'. Foucault (1988b: 18) employed this term in order to refer to the process whereby individuals utilize resources which permit them

> to effect by their own means or with the help of others a certain number of operations on their own bodies and souls, thoughts, conduct and way of being, so as to transform themselves in order to attain a certain state of happiness, wisdom, perfection, or immortality.

DeNora's suggestion is that individuals use music as a resource which helps them to shape their relationship with the immediate *environments* they occupy, and assists them in carrying out certain *self-directed tasks* and activities.

In terms of structuring the *environment*, music appears to perform two major functions. First, the use of radios, Walkmans and personal stereos can be used to seal off and regularize an environment 'by predetermining the types of sonic stimuli it contains' (DeNora, 2000: 60–1). External noises can be avoided and music can be listened to which the individual associates with the type of activity, or thought, they wish to engage in. Second, individuals use music to help structure 'open' social environments in which they wish to express or develop themselves. Thus, music is used to set a particular mood at a party (Zillman and Gan, 1997), and to create a particular ambience during romantic encounters. Within football crowds, singing and chanting are used to soundtrack a game, to set a mood depending on the quality of play and the fortunes of a team, and to facilitate the type of engagement fans seek to establish with teams. In her study of music and 'erotic agency', DeNora (1997) examines how the choice of music in intimate surroundings can facilitate a 'tuning into' or a tuning out of an erotic encounter. Ravel's *Bolero* has been used as a way of pacing sexual intercourse, for example, while Bach's *Saint Matthew Passion* was adjudged by one respondent to be 'inappropriately pious' for a romantic liaison (DeNora, 1997: 57–9).

In terms of individuals using music to facilitate certain tasks or activities, North and Hargreaves's (1997) review of research suggests that individuals chose music to moderate their level of arousal in line with the needs of a particular task or situation. Pop music was considered desirable in situations like 'being at a nightclub, while jogging, when doing the dishes, and when ironing', for example, while classical music was preferred for more formal dining (Zillman and Gan, 1997: 180). In the case of exercise, Gimlin's (2002: 66) study of aerobics classes reports on how the women she observed yelled, clapped their hands and sang along with the music as a means of helping them achieve strong, independent bodies that complemented their desired sense of self and which contrasted with dominant media images of 'model women'. In such classes, women were using music to facilitate their own goals. As one woman interviewee in DeNora's (2000: 91) study explains, '[music] can make me work harder ... if it's just a simple beat then it's easier to work with ... and if it very slowly gets faster ... I don't sort of realize it.' As DeNora (ibid.: 95) notes, what is crucial to this music is that it provides a mnemonic rhythm for movement; a rhythm which affords participants the opportunity to 'latch' their movements onto the music and in line with the progression of the class.

Music, distinction and resistance

If music has been used to attach people to certain social milieu and physical activities, it has also been used as a resource by those seeking to distance themselves from the 'mass', through the pursuit of distinction, and to express political protest and alienation from the status quo.

Music has long been used by individuals as a means of expressing their elite status and their distance from all that is common or ordinary. Historically, the aristocracy in the eighteenth century maintained their own private orchestras as a mark of distinction (DeNora, 1991, 1997). While the status attached to such actions decreased by the end of that century, music still serves to differentiate between people. As Bourdieu (1984: 18) elaborates, there is no more clearly demarcated act of distinction 'than concert-going or playing a "noble" instrument', while 'nothing more clearly affirms one's "class", nothing more infallibly classifies, than tastes in music.' The taste for socially prestigious musical 'works of art' is strongest among those fractions of the dominant class richest in educational capital, for example, while 'popular' taste for 'songs totally devoid of artistic ambition or pretension' tends to predominate among those with lowest levels of educational capital (Bourdieu, 1984: 16).

Such classifications are not, of course, uncontested, and nor are they maintained without a struggle between social groups. The 'popular' music Bourdieu associates with low levels of educational capital, for example, has long assumed a 'monumental significance during adolescence' for teenagers across the social class spectrum (Cooper, 1995: 4). Chosen as the music with which to 'soundtrack' many 'rites of passage', allegiances to various 'groups and artists can take on almost tribal significance' (ibid.). Similarly, many other musical styles that ultimately achieve mass popularity – such as jazz, rock 'n' roll, punk and rap – have their roots in the activities and tastes of minority age, class and ethnic groups, and are linked with 'challenging styles of dress, rebellious behaviour, and delinquency' (Crozier, 1997: 73). This illustrates how music can be used by individuals and groups to facilitate their opposition to dominant norms and values, and to distance themselves from the status quo.

The association of music with particular counter-cultures and minority groups has prompted various fears about its effects on people's bodily identities and actions. During the 1920s, jazz was not only associated with crime and national degradation, but with individual physical collapse. As Merriam reports, one 'Coach Know' of Harvard reported that 'jazz parties' give boys 'spindle legs and hollow chests' (Anon, 1924: 18, cited in Merriam, 1964: 242). Jazz, indeed, became something of a 'symbol of evil': it was denounced as an enemy of civilization within Ireland and was banned from Russia (Merriam, 1964: 243).

In the 1950s, it was the turn of 'Rock 'n' Roll' to be portrayed as a threat to the values of civilized society, while 'progressive' rock came in for particular vilification during the 1960s when it was seen as a 'unifying strand' in the civil rights and anti-Vietnam war protest movements (Martin, 1995). The 'anti-social' effects of punk rock became the targets of the British tabloid press in the 1970s, while the political impact of rock music is such, it has been suggested, that it contributed to the fall of East Germany in 1989. Rock groups, having long been derided by the state, helped mobilize opposition to the totalitarian regime (Wicke, 1992). More recently, since its development in the 1980s and 1990s, rap music has become a major target of moral disapproval in the USA. As Perkins (1996: 1) notes, 'Rap music has been the subject of lawsuits and arguments before the Supreme Court, the target of hell-fire-and-brimstone sermons by preachers, and even political ammunition for presidents and presidential candidates.' Judged to be 'one of the principal vehicles by which young African Americans express their views of the world' rap music is seen as a way of attempting to create 'a sense of order out of the mayhem and disorder of contemporary urban life' (Allen, Jr., 1996: 159–60). As Allen Jr. (ibid.: 16) points out, however, the lyrics of rap music are also often characterized by 'misogyny, homophobia [and] … a moral relativism that repudiates any responsibility for one's own actions'. As a resource used to express alienation and distance from a social order, music clearly does not always play a progressive role.

In this section I have examined how music can help position people within their social environment, attaching them to or distancing them from this milieu. Music may be used in formal rituals to attach people to collectivities, but contemporary studies of the everyday use of music also demonstrate that people are still concerned to create an appropriate sonic environment for undertaking various tasks and achieving particular goals that can help develop an individual's identity. Music may be used commercially in a way which sometimes renders the body as a relatively passive object on which the designs of multinational companies are recorded, but the uses of music for political and personal projects suggest that the concerns of theorists who portray the body as a defenceless location for social structures are, at the very least, exaggerated. Instead, the implication of music in the interaction between embodied individuals and structures helps to position people within society in very different ways.

Conclusion

Music provides us with an excellent example of how the body is a source of a cultural product which has subsequently developed an important association with social and economic structures. As a source of music, the body possesses a deep capacity for, and affinity with, this phenomenon, which allows it to transcend its existing capacities. Thus, with sufficient practice, the body can develop physically into an organic entity possessed of the postures, dexterities and skills enabling it to produce music, and embodied subjects can also experience a feeling of transcendence by listening to and being involved in music which immerses them in something new and profound. The production and organization of music are not there to be invented by each new generation, of course, and the human affinity for music also provides a basis on which societal structures have been able to locate themselves on embodied subjects. Research into the commercial uses of music, for example, has shown that externally imposed aural environments can shape people's consumption decisions and preferences in ways that they are not even aware of. This shows that our bodily affinity with music is not only associated with generative and transcendent capacities, but with the potential for us to be made an object of, or immanent in relation to, our structural environment.

It would be a mistake to assume that embodied subjects automatically lose their generative powers in this context, however, and this chapter has also been concerned to identify some of the ways in which music has mediated the outcomes of the interactions between creative individuals and social structures. One result of this interaction is anticipated in Durkheim's (1995 [1912]) analysis of the body's capacity to be enhanced through integration into a social group. Music clearly sometimes serves to help 'knit together' individuals into a social group by stimulating a physiological response which can be directed through ritual action towards a support for collectively defined symbols, values and actions. The occasions on which music serves such a purpose may have declined in the contemporary era, but as its importance to religious groups in Northern Ireland shows, they certainly have not disappeared.

If music still constitutes a resource through which collectivities can be reinforced, it also remains a means by which individuals can facilitate their own actions, express their emotions and develop their personalities. In J.J. Gibson's (1979) terms, music can provide 'affordances' to individuals (it provides them with opportunities for action) enabling them to create a range of personally structured micro-environments and develop particular orientations to the social environment (DeNora, 2000). Music is clearly not, however, a neutral medium in the collective or individualized uses to which it is put. If it offers to groups and individuals particular 'ways of moving, being and feeling' through the manner in which its materials are organized (DeNora, 2000: 123), it also tends to aurally obstruct other ways of being. Loud music, for example, tends to occupy significant portions of cognitive and emotional attention. This can be distracting and undesirable for those engaged in complex procedures requiring functional expertise, yet can help individuals 'psyche' themselves up to do a particular task (Konecni and Sargent-Pollack, 1976; Konecni, 1982). More specifically, the idea that music can foreground certain ways of thinking and being and devalue others helps to explain why there has been so much controversy about the relationship between Wagner's compositions and Nazi Germany. On a more mundane level, the music used to accompany exercise classes must be appropriate. Without an adequate and varied rhythm which profiled the movement of aerobics routines, for example, DeNora (2000: 97) found that for women in aerobics classes 'not only was co-ordination difficult' but 'movement was laboured, [and] uninteresting because it was not lodged in any devices of musical-aerobic arousal.'

The research which has been conducted into how people use music to express and develop their identity, suggests that individuals are aware of the suitability of particular types of music for their purposes. Nevertheless, Adorno's concerns about the dominance of 'popular' music remain pertinent to the contemporary era. As we have seen, people may use pop music to help them engage in all manner of tasks. Nevertheless, if we accept the argument that music is not a neutral resource, then the pervasiveness of unsophisticated, commercially produced songs must in some way limit the aural affordances on offer to individuals. Individuals may be able to engage in semiotic practices of decoding songs and their meanings, and be highly creative in putting music to purposive or expressive ends, but the fact that many people are exposed to a relatively restricted range of music is likely to limit the extent to which music can be used as a creative resource. This does not mean that the body is a completely passive location for social structures, but it does suggest that the contemporary music scene is not allowing individuals to become all that they could be.

The ways in which individuals utilize music to facilitate their own agendas is not only related to personal development, but is also relevant to the issue of social inequalities and oppression. As Bourdieu (1984) notes, the capacity to play a musical instrument and the preference for 'classical' over 'popular' music are one of the surest signs of cultural capital, while music has historically entered into inter-generational struggles to define legitimate taste, and political attempts to ban subversive influences on youth. Music has also historically provided a medium in which class, gender and 'racial' relations are expressed and reformulated at an aural level through rhythm and lyrics. More generally, despite the existence of groups protesting against piped background music in shops, hotels and offices, music is integral to the expansion of virtual environments into the everyday world (DeNora, 2000). Given the influence which music can exert on us physiologically, the control of such environments should be an important political issue. If music serves to calm one's bodily responses to oppressive social relations or material conditions, it is time we recognized its deployment as an important dimension of the structures that characterize society. It has been suggested that a 'world without elevator music would be much grimmer than its detractors (and those who take it for granted) could ever realize' (Lanza, 1994: 233; DeNora, 2000: 162). The assumption here is that we have grown used to living in socially structured, 'Disneyfied', environments which shield us from unpredictable stimuli, but it is important not to become deaf to the political dimensions of this situation. If the case of music suggests that the concern of body theorists about the subjugation of human creativity and generativity are exaggerated, it also provides us with enough evidence to confirm that they are reflecting very real developments in the contemporary era.

7

Sociable Bodies

Introduction

Sociology sometimes treats the body as an absent-presence. As I have tried to emphasize throughout this study, however, its central analytical concerns can provide us with extremely useful resources with which to interrogate the body–society relationship. Of particular importance to this chapter is the traditional distinction sociology has made between the roles and relationships internal to economic and political *structures*, and the more localized, non-instrumental relations of bodily *sociability* or sociality. These relations of sociability may occur within a wider structural environment, but they are irreducible to that environment and influence its development and sustainability. Both Durkheim and Simmel, for example, are concerned with the 'structural' features of society, but also identify the roots or source of human sociability in the needs and propensities of the embodied subject, and examine how this sociability develops through rituals or forms that are consequential for society as a whole. More recently, Erving Goffman (1983) developed this distinction between structures and sociability in his analysis of the 'interaction order'. The order of sociability contained within the interaction order is based on people's management of 'encounters', and cannot be reduced to the wider structures that develop from social action. This is because it is based on our 'intrinsic' need to maintain a *social self*, a self that validates individuals as morally worthy participants in interaction *wherever* this occurs. Furthermore, Goffman's interaction order is not only relatively autonomous from wider societal structures, but is responsible for the emergence of collective meanings and practices which make demands on, and even persist within, 'total institutions' such as asylums (Rawls, 1987; Shilling, 1999). While classical writers often viewed sociable bodies as an energizing source of collective life, however, contemporary body theories imply that the creative vitalism or effervescence central to such interaction has gone. In its place, they suggest, this realm of bodily interaction has lost its autonomy and has been transformed into a *location for* the structures of government, class or patriarchy, or the processes of rationalization. The question of whether or not there still exists the space for sociable bodies within the contemporary era is, then, of considerable importance for body theories.

Sociability or sociality (I use the terms interchangeably) has been analysed as occurring in a wide variety of social milieux. The arenas of work, sport, leisure and music, for example, have all been identified as possible 'containers' for such relationships. In what follows, however, I explore sociality by focusing on *food*, *eating* and the *meal* in the affluent West.[1] Food has historically been key to the generation of social relationships. The consumption of food constitutes a universal human need, while the organization and flow of food between people have been analysed as helping to create 'the conditions for social life' (Douglas, 1984: 12). The automatic and unquestioned sharing of food has been viewed as key to the maintenance of kinship systems, while the Latin etymology of the word 'companion' is 'one who takes bread with someone' (Visser, 1991; Falk, 1994). From the Eucharistic meal which joins the body of the individual to the body of the Church through the eating of the body of Christ, to the traditional potlatch and the medieval feast, the human need to eat has been associated with socially generative rituals. This link between food and sociality is not arbitrary, but is bound up with the physical process of eating. Eating both opens the body up to the material and social world (involving the *incorporation* of food frequently invested with symbolic significance), and can stimulate feelings of satiety and even mild euphoria conducive to the establishment of 'positive social relations' (Freud, 1918; Siskind, 1973; Fischler, 1988; Counihan, 1999: 6, 67). Indeed, this openness of the body during eating also helps explain why this act has historically been surrounded by rituals which promote certain social relationships while also guarding against the physical, social and supernatural 'dangers' associated with food (e.g. Iossifides, 1992).

Food is 'good to think with' not simply because it helps illustrate how the body is a *source* of sociality, but because it demonstrates how the sociable body can be a *location* for wider structural forces (Lévi-Strauss, 1963, 1969). Recent writings on the subject argue that there has been a decline in those communal occasions in which the human need for food has been organized into feasts that create social alliances or actively reproduce a society, and a rise in structurally determined individualizing acts of consumption in which the meal (associated with rituals and rules) has been reduced to a snack (eating ungoverned by communal structure). 'Fast food', it is argued, reflects the triumph of rationalization in the modern world and illustrates how embodied subjects have been transformed into 'bearers' of economic efficiency: 'refuelling' may replenish the energy of the worker, but its socially creative impact is minimal (Ritzer, 1996).

In what follows, I explore these issues by drawing on the contrasting writings of Bataille and Simmel in order to explore the bodily foundations of sociality and to establish the significance of food to these foundations. I then explore the potential for the eating body to become a location for wider structures by drawing on Pasi Falk's (1994) thesis. Falk argues that the shift from *Gemeinschaft*/community to *Gesellschaft*/society was accompanied by a decline in 'eating communities', and a change in the structure of the embodied subject from an 'open body/closed self' to a 'closed body/open self'. Falk's periodization glosses a number of changes in 'food regimes' (Atkins and Bowler, 2001), but captures an essential bodily shift that occurred within the modern world. According to Falk, modern society has forced our selves to be 'open' and in need of individual development. In this context, food no longer serves primarily as a vehicle of sociality, but is consumed for its symbolic value as a resource that enables individuals to maintain the project of the self. The chapter then moves away from this general thesis, and examines a collection of empirically informed writings which focus on how food has actually been used by people as a means of positioning themselves and others within and outside of specific forms of sociality. As the growth in demand for organic food, the rise of 'real food' movements, and the protests at the influence of fast food outlets illustrates, people have not reacted passively to the massification and instrumentalization of food. Fast food and convenience foods have altered how eating is associated with sociality, but food remains of immense creative significance in maintaining non-rational personal relationships. In conclusion, I discuss briefly the implications of these developments for the concerns of contemporary body theories.

The Body as a Source of Sociable Eating

Georges Bataille and Georg Simmel come from different philosophical traditions, but there are certain similarities between their writings which make them useful commentators on the subject of how the body is a source of sociality. Both argue that the generation of, and participation in, sociable relations constitute a realization of what it means to be a human being. Sociality enables individuals to experience their bodily being as a positive resource rather than a constraint, and is a domain of sovereignty in which people feel themselves to be acting freely, away from the burdens and inequalities that confront them in the rest of their lives (Simmel, 1971 [1910]: 133; Bataille, 1993 [1976]: 168). This bodily engagement in sociality, a 'negation of withdrawal into self', can also generate a 'gratitude' and 'good will' that helps establish wider collectivities (Simmel, 1950; Bataille, 1993 [1976]: 43).

Bataille's theory (grounded firmly in the Durkheimian tradition) is based on his view that the body is possessed of an *excess* of energy and resources (an excess that is essential for the growth and reproduction of all animal and plant life) and he argues that it is how embodied subjects use this excess (rather than produce it) that provides the key to understanding the societies they inhabit (Bataille, 1991 [1967]: 21, 27). This is because distributions and offerings of food, of goods, and of services, establish a 'life beyond utility' in which contacts are established between people and relations of sociality energized and revitalized (Bataille, 1993 [1976]: 43). For Bataille, in short, it is how we order our bodily consumption, rather than the productive relations we engage in, that creates sociality.

Simmel's (1971 [1910]) starting point, in contrast, involves the argument that humans are possessed of a basic bodily drive to socialize, a drive linked to the intrinsic satisfaction gained from merging into 'a union with others'. Interaction is prized because it constitutes a realization of the social capacities of the embodied subject (the particular purpose of interaction is frequently of secondary importance), and reaches its purest manifestation in the form of 'sociability'. Like the impulses associated with art and play, sociability is distanced from utilitarian concerns, yet constitutes for Simmel 'an ideal sociological world' (ibid.: 131). This is because sociability can only be successful if *all* participants are involved. Social inequalities and power differentials have to be put to one side, as do any deeply personal consider- ations, as these would prejudice the free play of interaction in which 'the pleasure of the individual is always contingent upon the joy of others; here, by definition, no one can have his satisfaction at the cost of contrary expe- riences on the part of others' (ibid.: 132). Sociability may be 'artificial' but Simmel insists that even though it maintains a distance from the business of ordinary life, it contains within itself the essence of society, allowing partic- ipants to 'experience the meaning and the forces of its deepest reality' (ibid.: 140). By satisfying the drive embodied subjects have to associate with each other, sociability provides a key to, and also helps energize, social relation- ships.

Simmel and Bataille provide us with contrasting ways of viewing the body as a source of sociality, but the importance of these bodily powers in their work is beyond doubt. Furthermore, both writers appreciate the importance of the materials used by individuals to forge relations of social- ity and, in this respect, see food or, more precisely, *the meal*, as a prime facil- itator of these non-rational relationships.

From the need to eat, to the social meal

The need to eat is a human universal, and feeding constitutes the immedi- ate and most important physical basis of the relationship between mothers and children. Various theories also suggest that food has, since the beginning of time, been implicated in the creation and consolidation of wider social relationships. One popular view, for example, suggests that the evolutionary development of a relatively large brain among our species (together with the high metabolic demands of this brain) necessitated the maintenance of a nutrient-rich diet which was instrumental in the formation of social rela- tions based on a hunter–gatherer lifestyle (Leonard and Robertson, 1994; Washburn and Lancaster, 1968; Beardsworth and Keil, 1997: 202). Other theorists suggest that eating and intimate sociality are physically and even causally related in that the instinctual drives for food and sex are similar, while both acts promote a social merging (Freud, 1962).

If food has long been implicated in the creation and consolidation of social relationships, Simmel's writings on the sociology of the meal seek to demonstrate how the act of eating has also been harnessed to, and collec- tivized by, the specific human need for *sociability*. Sociability is linked to the free-play of conversation in Simmel's writing, but he also suggests that the drive for association is so fundamental to human existence that it marshals to its service other human needs such as hunger. As Simmel (1997c: 135) elaborates, by linking food to sociality through the meal, embodied subjects accomplish a 'triumph over naturalism' in which the depths of our biologi- cal make-up lead to more 'meaningful and spiritual things'. This 'triumph' (which marks a shift from the relatively 'asocial' to the more 'social' pole of the *homo duplex* character of humans) facilitates the bringing together in sociality of people who may share no common instrumental interests. Thus, far from being a subject that resides on the outer fringes of sociology, Simmel suggests that eating is possessed of an 'immeasurable sociological significance' and that this can be illustrated through the history of the meal (ibid.: 130).

The history of the meal is exemplified by the rituals that surrounded sacrifice in traditional societies, rituals that brought together members of a community with strangers and even enemies, yet involved the offering and consumption of food. This sharing of food unleashed an enormous 'socializing power' that bound participants together, and demonstrated how 'an event of physiological primitiveness' could be elevated into 'the sphere of social interaction' (Simmel, 1997c: 131). The social ordering of meals was evident subsequently in what Simmel refers to as the 'commandments of the communal table' (ibid.). The medieval Guild system and later Trade Clubs, for example, placed great significance on ritualized patterns of consumption in order to consolidate group identity. This subordination of the potentially individualizing act of eating through the social organization of the meal is also used by Simmel to explain the advance of table manners and the development of utensils, plates and other 'technologies of consumption'. These developments have reached the stage in modern times when 'a dinner in educated circles appears to be completely schematized and regulated on a supra-individual level with regard to the participants' movements' (ibid.: 132).

Throughout his discussion of the harnessing of the human need to eat to the human desire for sociality, Simmel insists that sociality can never totally dominate eating. As he puts it, 'the aesthetics of the meal must never forget *what* it is actually supposed to stylize: the satisfaction of a need located in the depths of organic life and therefore absolutely universal' (ibid.: 133). Ideally, a balance is reached between these two deeply embodied aspects of what it is to be human so that the 'refinement of the table' facilitates sociality, yet also invites those assembled to satisfy their hunger and thirst (ibid.:133).

If Simmel's analysis revolves around an 'ideal type' vision of sociality in which external factors of domination/subordination and inequality are minimized within the intrinsic democracy of the meal, Bataille focuses on the distribution and consumption of food in ritual contexts as a prime means through which 'separate beings communicate' (Bataille, 1991 [1967]: 58–9, 67). Bataille's (1991 [1967]) analysis of sacrifice among the Aztecs exemplifies this perspective as it illustrates how a link between food and social relationships was continued even in cannibalism; a form of consumption which joined warrior with victim, priest and deity. Like Simmel, Bataille is concerned to demonstrate that collective acts of eating can effect a joining of individuals within non-instrumental and non-rational relations of community. However, his analysis of sacrifice also shows that food circulates and is consumed in a manner which is often generative of status differences. This is again evident in his analysis of the potlatch, an analysis dependent upon Mauss's (1990 [1950]) writings on the subject, which shows how food not only facilitates relations of sociality but can also stimulate wider *structural* relationships. At its broadest, the potlatch system ('the most ancient system of economy and law that we find') met the human need to generate social relationships by placing people under a sacred obligation to give and receive food and other gifts to other groups (Mauss, 1990 [1950]: 90). Gifts were never exchanged without obligation, but carried with them a morally binding system of rules tying people together. However, the offering of gifts by a chief to a rival was often done 'for the purpose of humiliating, challenging and obligating him' (Bataille, 1991 [1967]: 67). Thus, the potlatch illustrates how the implication of food (as well as other goods and services) in relations of sociality can be part of a competitive system generative of social inequalities.

The consumption of food is connected to one of the most basic needs of human being, the need to eat, yet it is also a major *source* of sociality. As Counihan (1999: 13) argues, eating is crucial to 'the very definition of community, the relationships between people, interactions between humans and their gods, and communication between the living and the dead', while the collapse of food sharing is associated with 'the breakdown of social solidarity'. The sociality engendered by eating bodies, however, can also become a *location* for wider structures that confront subjects as 'social facts'; relations of domination and subordination that seem to constrain people's social relationships within pre-existing patterns. Thus, Bataille's and Mauss's discussions of potlatch place as much emphasis on the damaging obligations necessitated by this system as they do on the creative and enabling relations of sociality generated by it. More generally, this focus on the *structural determination* of food and social relationships is evident in those writings which suggest that differently ordered societies *impose* different patterns of eating on people.

The Eating Body as a Location for Structures

If the eating body constitutes a source of sociality, it is also a location for wider structures. This is evident in terms of the meanings associated with food, the preparation of food, and the types and quantities of food eaten. The structuralist writings of Claude Lévi-Strauss (1969) and Mary Douglas (1980 [1966]; Douglas and Gross, 1981) provide us with one method of examining this situation. They view food as part of a rule-bound system of binary oppositions imposed on individuals by the societies in which they live. Rather than using these structuralist theories as an exclusive guide to the discussions in this section, however, I want to begin instead with some basic, but important, physiological factors that illustrate how the eating body is *itself* possessed of physiological characteristics, and a malleability, that make it suited for being a location for wider structural forces.

First, there is an enormous range of foods that can be digested by, and provide nutrition for, the human organism. This variety means that social institutions can shape diet, without necessarily harming the basic nutritional needs of its members. Indeed, humans consume a quite incredible variety of foodstuffs and this malleability means that food selection has as much to do with *social* taboos and *cultural* preferences as it does with the need to satisfy hunger (Douglas, 1984). Thus, societies have variously sanctioned diets high in hot, spicy foods, diets high in meat or in which the consumption of certain meats is taboo, and diets dominated by vegetables and grain. This variability is often shaped by climactic and other environmental conditions surrounding the production of food, but also attests to the influence that society has on food consumption.

Second, in addition to the types of food consumed, societal norms can shape *levels* of individual consumption. The sense of being sated by food is associated with a number of mechanisms involving stomach distension, the release of hormones from the duodenum, and the stimulation of receptors along the intestine (Conner and Armitage, 2000). As Mennell (1985: 21) points out, however, there is no unmediated biological link between hunger and appetite. Instead, the indirect linkage between them is provided by what is sometimes referred to as the 'appetstat'. The appetstat is a psychological control mechanism implicated in the regulation of food intake and helps explain why some people continue eating despite no longer being hungry while others do not eat sufficient to meet their biological needs. The appetstat can, like a thermostat, be set too high or too low and this is manifest in cases of obesity and anorexia. The feminist writings of Susie Orbach (1988 [1978]) and Kate Chernin (1983), for example, as well as a host of more recent works on the 'epidemic' of eating disorders affecting girls and young women (e.g. Gordon, 2001), are based on the implicit assumption that the appetstat can be affected so deeply by societal norms of body image that it can override *any* link between hunger and appetite.

Third, it is worth mentioning the obvious but important point that there are no biological restrictions on *who* food is eaten with and very few on *when* and *where* it is eaten (humans need to eat before starvation occurs and in an environment that does not immediately threaten life). Within these extremely broad limits, societies can sanction large feasts, for example, in which consumption is ordered by elaborate rituals designed to make fine distinctions in social status, or can organize eating through rationalized modes of consumption which interfere as little as possible with the instrumental routines of work.

These three features of the eating body's physiological malleability make it relatively open to the influence of structural forces, and these forces are illustrated in recent writings on the demise of 'eating communities', on the irrationalities of modern rationalized food, and on the persistence of patriarchal relations surrounding food preparation and eating.

Eating communities and their modern demise

Much of the historically informed theoretical writing on the relationship between food and societal forms suggests that a fundamental shift occurred in the transition from traditional *Gemeinschaft*/communities to modern *Gesellschaft*/associations. It also suggests that, once established, *Gesellschaft*/associations took precedence over, and devitalized, localized relations of sociality, and installed a structural relationship between eating and social relationships that individuals were powerless to alter. This is exemplified by Falk's (1994) analysis of the character and demise of 'eating communities'.

Falk defines an eating community as a social system which 'ate into' and 'filled up' the bodily identities of its members via its organization of food, ritual and other cultural activities. The individual's body was 'open' to collective determination while individual identities were relatively 'closed', being undifferentiated and underdeveloped. In medieval Catholicism, for example, the bodies of members were incorporated into the body of the Church through sacred and symbolically sacrificial rituals which had as their main cultic act the Eucharist (Mellor and Shilling, 1997: 67–8). Individuals were not passive within such eating communities – their active participation in collective rituals was crucial to the continuation of the collectivity – but this social form promoted a 'group self' in which identities were relatively homogeneous. As Elias (2000 [1939]: 58) suggests, this undifferentiated self was reflected in the standard eating techniques prevalent in medieval Europe. People helped themselves from communal dishes, meat was taken and eaten by hand, there were no special implements for different foods, and plates and dishes were lifted to the mouth. Judgements concerning what should be eaten and how things should be eaten remained communally determined, existing 'in the "mouth" of the community, as it were' (Falk, 1994: 13). Food and bodies merged into the preset community: the collective act of eating involved being 'eaten by' the collectivity.

If traditional societies were characterized by (sacred) eating communities, Falk (1994) argues that modern *Gesellschaft*/associations have instituted a far greater degree of individualization in the relationship between eating and bodily identity. Judgements of taste have been transferred from the collectivity to the individual, even though they are conditioned by cultural representations, while food and drink become markers of *individual* identity. From the 'open body/closed self' of the medieval era, individuals developed a 'closed body/open self': the organism is shut off from *collective* determination while the self is freed up as an empty space to be filled by the *individual* (Falk, 1994: 29, 144). The role of food in this project of the self is evident in the marginalization of the meal and in the rising consumption of fast food, snacks and other foods *symbolically* associated with enjoyment, contentment and a meaningful lifestyle (ibid.: 29). A sign of just how far this individualization has progressed is that it has been suggested that every mouthful of food is evidence of someone's political and moral responsibility (Heldke, 1992). While holy communion once involved the 'digestion' of the individual into the sacred community, the consumption of chocolate bars or the chewing of sugar-free gum are now individualized acts of rewarding the self or maintaining oral hygiene (James, 1990). This individualization is also apparent during meals: utensils and plates are differentiated and allocated separately to each participant. As Elias (2000 [1939]: 60) notes, this 'separateness' is illustrated by the fact that while medieval bodies were relatively untroubled by other people's bodily fluids and functions, disgust and embarrassment now accompany 'the mere approach of something that has been in contact with the mouth or hands of someone else'. In contrast to the 'eating communities' of old, there is now no undifferentiated merging with others or with food, but a set of prohibitions which seek to suppress everything we have in common and subordinate eating to the display of finesse and the loose association of individuals through communicative speech acts.

This transformation from the traditional to the modern relationship between food and social structure was a long-term process, but the Church and the State were highly influential in effecting this change. In medieval Europe, the Catholic Church imparted the pleasures of the flesh with positive religious meaning, and had a relatively relaxed approach towards food and drink in comparison with later Protestant Reformers.[2] Religious rituals had eating at their centre. In early modern Europe, however, the rise of Protestantism and the development of increasingly extensive economic markets signalled a trend away from eating communities. Calvin and later reformers elevated the individual over the worldly collectivity, and made a strong link between the pleasures of eating/drinking and sin (rejecting anything not explicitly *approved* by the Bible). Later, Protestantism was also central to the reception of new medical writings on diet. George Cheyne's influential system of 'diaetic management', for example, was intended to control melancholy, disease, and to promote longevity by returning people to a more 'natural' life of moderation, sobriety and exercise. However, Cheyne's work only became popularized as a result of the efforts of John Wesley, who promulgated Cheyne's views on the importance of diet and exercise to the middle classes through the Wesleyan chapels (Turner, 1991c).

It would be wrong to think that the influence of religion has disappeared in the contemporary West. Puritan values of bodily abstinence and purity continue to inform the attitude, increasingly common among the urban middle classes in the USA and in Europe, that the consumption of 'healthy food' is a marker of ethical worth and that 'only the consumption of sugar-free food that is non-fattening and non-toxic' can permit the individual 'to occupy the moral high ground' (Stein and Nemeroff, 1995; Rozin, 1982: 100). However, Protestantism was not alone in being responsible for the decline of eating communities.

From the nineteenth century, the State became increasingly influential – via debates about nutrition, efficiency and urban management – in changing the status of food from a reproducer of communal identity to 'an expedient fuel (healthy and economic) for the body-machine turned instrument' (Falk, 1994: 66). Research into the poor health of military recruits, the minimum nutritional requirements of prisoners, and the extent of malnourishment among local communities reflected this change and shaped government policy (Schwarz, 1986; Turner, 1991c: 167). In Britain, worries about the maintenance of Empire and military recruitment, for example, contributed to an interest in the health of schoolchildren, regular medical inspections and the establishment of school meals. In Australia, concerns about the health and 'virility' of the population from the 1890s led to a growing focus on the diet of children (Lupton, 1996: 72). As the twentieth century progressed, the state's role in equating food with health and efficiency increased. In Britain, the establishment of the Nutrition Task Force in the 1990s promised an 'ambitious and far-reaching programme of nutritional intervention and persuasion ... with a view to improving overall health standards' (Beardsworth and Keil, 1997). More widely, there has been a general tendency for governments to draw up guidelines intended to promote health through eating (Conner and Armitage, 2000: 47), while contemporary debates about health care commonly equate illness and premature death with individual decisions about diet. Instead of being a collective generator of sociality, eating now constitutes a crucial link between individual responsibility and state health care. The British Government has even recently considered placing a 'fat tax' on unhealthy foods as a way of pressuring people to take more responsibility for their own health.

Theoretically informed writings on the role of food in *Gemeinschaft*/communities and *Gesellschaft*/associations are highly suggestive, yet tend to portray individuals as caught up in changes they are powerless to stop. From being 'consumed' by eating communities, individuals are turned into 'bearers' of processes that individualize and discipline them so completely that they find it difficult to engage in the convivial sociability discussed by Simmel, at least when it involves food. Food becomes an instrumental vehicle for the delivery of nutrition which can enable the individual to live a long and *productive* life, while the embarrassment potential of eating is so great that it is best done in private (Elias, 2000 [1939]). This sense that the eating body has become a location for social structures, rather than an active source of sociality, is strengthened when we examine analyses which focus explicitly on the *rationalization* of food within the modern era.

The irrationality of rationalized food

The demise of eating communities is associated with a major *rationalization* of the links between food and social relationships. This involves the substitution of an instrumental concern with 'eating for productivity' for previous non-instrumental relations of 'feasting for sociality'. Such a process has reached its height within contemporary 'fast food culture', a culture which prizes efficiency, calculability and standardization in the production of food, and convenience and individualization in the consumption of food (Ritzer, 1996). This rationalization is not, however, devoid of contradictions or perverse outcomes. As Weber (1991 [1904–5]; 1948 [1919]) pointed out, rationalized systems can result in an *irrational* social environment which damages human development, and this can be seen in the direct effects food is having on eating bodies in the modern world.

There may be no absolute 'point zero' in the rationalization of food and eating. As Deborah Lupton (1996: 68–9) points out, however, the rational explication of dietary regimens appeared to be crystallized within Hippocratic injunctions which associated food and hygiene with maintaining corporeal equilibrium. More recently, as summarized above, the state and church provide some of the 'deep background' to a rationalized view of diet. In terms of the direct rationalization of food production, however, the development of industrialization was associated with a number of techniques (e.g. canning, freezing, mechanized distribution, and large-scale retailing) which accelerated efficiency, durability and standardization (Beardsworth and Keil, 1997: 66). This has been complemented by a major intensification of production (farm machinery, chemicals, etc., resulting in large increases in output per hectare and rising average yields of most crops and livestock) and a growth in substitutionism (the reduction of agricultural products in favour of purely industrially produced foodstuffs) (Atkins and Bowler, 2001: 65, 74). Processes of globalization have also sometimes had a homogenizing impact on food production. In seeking to ensure a steady supply of genetically standard potatoes, for example, the corporate empire MacCain foods has had a major impact in reorganizing of agriculture in parts of North America (ibid.: 45). This massification and rationalization of food production have also been reflected in the sphere of food marketing. In western Europe, 'supermarkets now account for over seventy per cent of purchases of packaged food, soft drinks and cheese, and over forty per cent of fresh fruit, vegetables and wine', while the demise of small, independent food retailers has been marked (Atkins and Bowler, 2001: 91–2). In the UK, for example, there was a loss of 120,000 food shops between 1971 and 1991 (ibid.: 92).

These trends are mirrored in the sphere of consumption. The increasing personal domestic ownership of fridges, freezers and microwaves in the twentieth century made possible a huge growth in the market for, and use of, such rationalized foods. The taste for quick, convenient, prepackaged, frozen foods and 'TV dinners' was further complemented by the growth of the fast food restaurant (the 'drive-in' restaurant concept was developed in the 1920s, while the first fast food restaurant was opened by the McDonald brothers in 1937 in Pasadena, California, and franchised in 1955 [Beardsworth and Keil, 1997: 111; Atkins and Bowler, 2001]). By the mid-twentieth century, the emphasis on speed and convenience in the preparation and consumption of food had been firmly established.

The impact and scope of the fast food industry have been enormous.

McDonald's, still the most visible example of a fast food outlet, has about 30,000 restaurants world-wide and annually hires about one million people (more than any other public or private organization) (Schlosser, 2002: 4). While Americans spent about $6 billion on fast food in 1970s, this had risen to a staggering $110 billion in the year 2001 and informs Schlosser's (ibid.: 3, 7) argument that what we eat 'has changed more in the last 40 years than in the previous 40,000' (see also Prevost et al., 1997). The growth of fast food outlets has also been a catalyst in the 'malling and sprawling of the West' (Schlosser, 2002: 9), and in helping to turn efficiency into a key value of Western society. As Ritzer (1993: 35) puts it, 'Many sectors of society have had to change or develop in order to operate in the efficient manner demanded by those accustomed to life in the fast-lane of the fast food restaurant.'

The attractions of fast food have been well documented. By paying careful attention to the sourcing of supplies, and by utilizing a Taylorist process which has automated jobs and increased control over the production of food by minimizing worker discretion, fast food offers to the consumer speed and predictability (Ritzer, 1993: 10, 38). It also appears to be implicated in an unprecedented individualization of a society in which eating has become a means of refuelling rather than feasting; a refuelling which facilitates hectic work and leisure schedules, which fits in with pressured lives of growing numbers of single-parent families, and which might be seen as allowing little room for non-purposeful interaction over the meal table. The growth of fast food restaurants, the frequency with which people eat at work (in seemingly ever shorter lunch breaks), and the increase in functional food outlets in shopping malls, railway buffets and airport lounges, testifies to this trend. If fast food has helped accelerate the rationalization and individualization of society, however, its location within the bodies of subjects has resulted in some very irrational consequences.

First, it has been suggested that the act of producing and consuming fast food has become a highly *alienating* experience. In terms of production, the power of supermarkets to place stringent conditions on suppliers may have regularized the quality of food they are able to sell to Western consumers, but they also frequently ensure low rates of pay and unregulated conditions of work for farm and factory workers in countries where poverty is already commonplace (Atkins and Bowler, 2001: 284–5). The conditions in Western processing plants have also been exposed as highly dangerous (Schlosser, 2002). In terms of consumption, Finkelson (1989) argues that restaurants in general are characterized by structural features that serve to alienate social interaction as a result of the emphasis placed on throughput, money, and the surveillance and control that diners are subjected to by staff and surroundings (see also Wood, 1995). Fast food restaurants, or drive-bys, accentuate this alienation by serving to minimize, or even eliminate, visual contact between people. When people do take a few minutes to eat their meal while resting, they can come up against the problem that some outlets have installed chairs designed to become uncomfortable after a short stay (Ritzer, 1993: 110).

Second, the type of efficiently packaged and delivered food that dominates the fast food business is characterized by high levels of saturated fat and salt, and has been linked with health concerns including obesity, high cholesterol levels, hypertension and diabetes. The USA now has the highest obesity rate in the world, running at around one in every three adults, with more than half of American adults and about one-quarter of American children classified as over-weight (Schlosser, 2002: 240; Atkins and Bowler, 2001: 305). This obesity rate has roughly doubled since the late 1970s and can be correlated with the increased consumption of fast food during that period (Schlosser, 2002: 240).[3] Such an increase is not surprising. Children are bombarded by adverts for food products such as burgers, crisps, sweets, and snack foods designed for school lunch boxes, yet nearly all of these adverts are for foods 'that are high in fat, salt or sugar' (Lewis and Hill, 1998; Conner and Armitage, 2000: 120).[4] In Britain, people receive between 70 and 80 per cent of their salt intake from processed foods, yet this has led to a situation where many individuals are consuming ten times recommended levels of salt (something that has been linked with high blood pressure and heart disease) (Atkins and Bowler, 2001: 214). The need to eat is a natural, universal feature of being human, but our fast food culture seems to exploit that need in its pursuit of profit by offering products which do little to meet our nutritional requirements.

Third, the production and marketing of this high salt, high fat food have occurred at the same time as increasing social cachet is attached to the slim body, and growing prejudice aimed at those who do not achieve this body type. While fast food does much to produce fat bodies, there is a considerable amount of social psychological research that has demonstrated bias against those considered over-weight. This is summarized by Conner and Armitage:

> [This prejudice] begins in childhood, with children preferring not to play with overweight peers and assigning negative adjectives to drawings of overweight individuals. In adulthood, overweight individuals tend to be rated as less active and athletic, but also less intelligent, hardworking, successful and popular ... They also experience prejudice in relation to getting places in good colleges and getting good jobs ... Such negative views of the overweight individual appear to be particularly common in individualistic cultures where individuals are held to be responsible for their own fates. (2000: 77–8)

Both food and body images have become highly rationalized. The problem for the consumer is that the forms of rationalization they are predicated on are contradictory. Convenience, speed and immediate gratification govern the former, in line with the principles informing consumer culture, while effort, denial and asceticism govern the latter, in line with the emphasis on hard work in the sphere of production.

Fourth, if the nutritional content of fast food is associated with health problems that build up over time, and with the social consequences of having to conform to an increasingly normative body image, its mass production poses more immediately dangers. Studies suggest that the conditions in which cows are slaughtered are conducive to the spreading of microbes that are found mostly in faecal matter, a situation which helps account for the one-quarter of the American population that suffers from food poisoning each year (Schlosser, 2002: 195). From salmonella in eggs, to unacceptably high levels of pesticide residues and additives being found on supermarket fruit and vegetables, to E coli outbreaks, to BSE and the discovery of its cross-over into the human form of CJD, people have periodically to confront the news that mass-produced food is unsafe for human consumption. While specific food 'scares' or 'panics' may come and go, the cumulative effect of such events may leave people with 'chronic low level anxiety' about food or even a state of *gastro-anomy* (Fischler, 1980, 1988; Beardsworth and Keil, 1997: 163). Fischler (1980) suggests that this has resulted in the 'omnivore's paradox', with us becoming increasingly anxious about food at the same time that our food options are greater than ever before. As our food preferences are no longer shaped communally by 'eating communities', the potential objects of human appetite are left to 'turn in' on us, 'eating away' at our contentment and identity.

Patriarchy and food

The identification of general shifts involving the decline of traditional eating communities and the advance of rationalization can do much to illuminate the argument that the body is a location for wider structural forces, but it is also important to recognize forms of stratification that occur *within* these general shifts. In this respect, feminists have done much to illustrate the *gendered* character of the relationships surrounding food (e.g. Bordo, 1993).

Problems of obesity and over-consumption may preoccupy nutritionists and other western health experts concerned with our current fast food culture, but women have historically had less access to food than men. From Hellenistic Rome to medieval France, girls and women were allocated less food than boys and men (Pomeroy, 1975), while contemporary UN reports testify to the higher rates of infant death and malnutrition that occur as a result of the continuation of gender inequality (Wolf, 1990: 190–1). If women have had less access to nutritious food, they also continue to have more responsibility for preparing food than do men. Men may take charge of 'luxury' consumption (barbecue cooking, carving a roasted joint, collecting take-away meals, and making decisions about wine and beer purchases, e.g. Whitehead, 1984: 123–4), but it is women who are usually responsible for routine food purchasing and preparation (Murcott, 1983; Charles and Kerr, 1988; DeVault, 1991; Warde and Hetherington, 1994; Warde and Marteens, 2000; cf. Kemmer, 2000). For many women with restricted budgets, this involves worrying about spending, shopping frequently in order that food is eaten only when it can be afforded, and struggling to provide their children with conventional snacks to take to school in order to avoid the stigma of poverty (Beardsworth and Keil, 1993; Dobson et al., 1994). It also involves having to plan meals in relation to husbands' preferences (Goode et al., 1984: 199; Charles and Kerr, 1988; McKie et al., 1993). The price for failing in their 'duties' to the family can be high: male dissatisfaction over cooking and mealtimes is a frequent trigger of domestic violence against women (Ellis, 1983).

Women's relationship to food appears to have a highly damaging impact on their self-identities and their ability to engage in the generation of intrinsically satisfying relations of sociality. In the affluent West, pressures on women to be slim and sexually attractive appear to condemn them to a highly ambivalent relationship with food (Mori et al., 1987). These pressures of body image have grown enormously over the last century. The 'ideal' women's body size has grown generally smaller through the generations. From Mae West to Marilyn Monroe to Twiggy, to Kate Moss, to 'supermodels' who are both slim and muscular, conceptions of what is a desirable female size have become increasingly difficult to attain for the vast majority of women (see also Fallon, 1990). Weight loss is now a multi-billion dollar industry and a plethora of diet drugs, diet books, exercise tapes, classes, 'fat farms', and diet foods are utilized by the 60 per cent of women in the USA who are estimated to be dieting at some point in any single year (Meadow and Weiss, 1992; see also Germov and Williams, 1996). As noted above, severe consequences await those unable to become slim or achieve a 'reasonable' size. Thought of as morally suspect and lazy, rejected as sexually undesirable, one research project has even found that parents were less likely to financially support their daughters through college if they regarded them as overweight (Crandall, 1995). Men are also subjected to increasing pressures concerning their bodily size and appearance, but ideal visions of masculinity tend to incorporate within them size and power, rather than lightness and slimness, and sometimes involve men eating more in order to 'bulk up' rather than dieting to lose weight.

It is against this background that we should view Charles and Kerr's argument that

> the precarious balancing act continually being performed by women to retain control over their food intake and, through that, over their bodies ... points to the fact that eating disorders, such as anorexia nervosa or compulsive eating, are not so far removed from women's so-called normal relationship to food. (1988: 142)

Other feminists agree that 'chronic, restrained eating' can lead directly to eating disorders by disrupting the body's equilibrium and by contributing towards a malnourishment which leaves women psychologically vulnerable (Wolf, 1990: 196). In these circumstances, a woman's body image can become seriously distorted, providing them with no realistic sense of their size and with an inability to re-establish a healthy relationship with food.

These conditions take us some considerable distance from the creative and beneficial social eating described by the likes of Simmel and Bataille. There is no sense here of an energetic 'excess' that women can expend on the creation of new social relations (Bataille, 1993 [1976]). Instead, women's relationship with food is more likely to remind us of government attempts to calculate the minimum possible number of calories compatible with the sustenance of life. Illustrating how these rationalized concerns are often internalized by women, one of Counihan's (1999: 118) respondents admits that 'I always think of food in terms of calories ... I don't seem to think in terms of nutrition, just calories.'

Writings on the rationalization of food, and on patriarchy and food, provide us with distinctive visions of how the body has become a location for wider structures. As the above example of calorie counting illustrates, however, they can usefully complement each other. Elias (2000 [1939]: 375), for example, analysed how the rationalization and individualization of consuming bodies was associated with pressures of self-management in which 'drive-satisfaction and drive-control' could be subject to 'major or minor disturbances', and 'revolts of one part of the person against the other'. Although Elias's observations were not directed specifically towards gendered relations, they resonate strongly with the writings of those concerned with women's relationship with food. Expected to cater for *other people's* hunger, to make decisions about their own consumption based on how *slim* they look rather than on how *hungry* they feel, and to engage in highly rationalistic calculations about the number of calories they consume, it is no wonder that eating can become psychologically and physiologically problematic.

The increasingly rationalized and individualized organization of modern society does not uniformly reinforce oppressive gender relations, however, and the increasing involvement of women in the labour market at all levels is having a significant effect on consumption and sociality. In England, the increase in women's full-time employment appears to be the most significant factor affecting men's preparedness to cook family meals or to engage in related 'ancillary feeding tasks' (Warde and Hetherington, 1994; Warde and Marteens, 2000: 99), for example, while the increase in single person households has meant that more people are living in dwellings where they do not cater for others or have others cater for them (Hall et al., 1999; see also Kemmer, 2000). Coupled with the spread of convenience foods, these type of factors have led some commentators to suggest that the future might be characterized by more cooperative and less gendered patterns of cooking and eating in which family members make their own food choices and time their eating to coordinate with their own personal schedules (Beardsworth and Keil, 1997). Such a prospect can, of course, be interpreted in various ways, and Counihan's (1999: 60) study suggests that the absorption of women into the labour market and their reduced involvement in the preparation of food are likely to entail the loss of 'their traditional prestige and influence'.

The Social Positioning of Eating Bodies

The material examined above suggests that the decline of community and the forces of rationalization, and patriarchy have severed the link between eating and sociality, yet other writings on the subject argue that there exists the space for eating bodies to *actively* position themselves (as well as being positioned by others) in relation to their wider social environment. Douglas (1984), for example, argues that there is a wide range of social intercourse based on food and its reciprocity which cannot be reduced to the rationalized environs of the modern economy. Gifts of food (and drink) continue to help provide the conditions for social life: 'More effective than flags or red carpets which merely say welcome, food actually delivers good fellowship' (ibid.: 12). Such edible flows of sociality go beyond small-scale examples of hospitality in the current era, and are evidenced in a range of behaviours concerning how people relate to the production, organization, preparation and consumption of food. One of the most visible of these in recent years involve public protests, as well as less visible forms of action, against the rationalization of food and the continuing spread of a fast food culture. I shall also examine people's creative relationship with food by looking at how individuals continue to adhere to enduring cultural values, and at the continuing significance of food as a vehicle for the pursuit of distinction.

Resisting rationalization, resisting patriarchy

Fast food culture has firmly established itself in the contemporary era, but there exist a range of responses to it. As Ritzer (1993) argues, while some have become comfortable with the 'McDonaldized' organization of food and the rationalized social relationships it reflects, and others see it as a cage from which there is no escape, many people use convenience food to enhance other areas of their lives. Indeed, Fantasia's (1995) analysis of French teenagers and food suggested that they valued the informality and freedom provided by McDonald's in contrast to the formality governing most other restaurants. Fast food can enable one to meet up with friends engaged in sports or other activities with the minimum of 'lost time'. Furthermore, while fast food may have replaced home cooking in many instances, evidence still suggests family meals remain a norm in parts of Europe (Murcott, 1997; Warde and Marteens, 2000: 107): convenience food may enable families to eat together (even if this is often in front of the television) despite growing constraints on the time available to prepare meals. In terms of its effects on 'eating bodies', consumer groups have also managed to ameliorate some of the excesses of the fast food industry. In response to the complaints of vegetarians and nutritionists, Burger King, Wendy's and McDonald's announced in July 1991 that they were switching to the use of vegetable oils in the cooking of french fries (Ritzer, 1993: 164). McDonald's has also been pressurized into adapting the appearance of their outlets, so that they do a better job of blending into the surrounding architecture of the communities in which they are located, and into eliminating some of the environmentally destructive containers they used (ibid.: 165). Finally, while the thrust of our discussion has been on how fast food helps rationalize social relations, the long opening hours that typify these outlets enables people to meet for breakfast and chat prior to starting work, and makes the likes of McDonald's a popular meeting place for teenagers wishing to integrate eating into weekend shopping trips. In this respect, contemporary fast food chains can be seen as fulfilling the social functions of their antecedents. In Britain, for example, fish and chip shops have traditionally been places for sociality (welcoming women and children in contrast to many of their higher status equivalents). In the period between the First and Second World Wars, they also became a place for courting adolescents to go after an evening out together (Walton, 1992).

There have also been a number of spectacular protests at the spread of fast food. In 1996, Indian farmers ransacked a Kentucky Fried Chicken restaurant in Bangalore, convinced that the chain threatened their traditional agricultural practices, while France has recently been at the centre of protests against the poor quality of fast food (Schlosser, 2002: 244). The sheep farmer and political activist Jose Bove was prominent in a group that destroyed a McDonald's under construction in his hometown of Millau. Bove's defiant attitude, imprisonment, and impassioned speeches against 'lousy food' have made him a cultural hero in France. An estimated 30,000 demonstrators gathered in Millau when Jose Bove went on trial in 2000, some carrying signs that said 'Non à McMerde' (ibid.). Fast food chains and products have also been targeted as symbols of multinational capital's prioritization of profits over people and of American imperialism. In 1995, for example, a crowd of four hundred Danish anarchists looted a McDonald's in Copenhagen and burnt the restaurant to the ground. At least a dozen McDonald's and four Kentucky Fried Chicken restaurants were damaged by Chinese protests against the bombing of Chinese Embassy in Belgrade in 1999. In recent years, other attacks on and protests against McDonald's have taken place in Russia, Athens, Cape Town, Belgium, and London (Schlosser, 2002: 243), while marchers protesting against the war against Iraq in London used McDonald's symbolism as a way of expressing their opposition to American and British action (Chrisafis, 2003).

If fast food remains a prominent part of the contemporary landscape, dissatisfaction with many of its effects and symbolic associations has informed the development and popularity of a variety of alternative food 'movements'. Organic food production and consumption have soared in the past two decades, while 'farmers' markets' and 'veggie boxes' sourced by local produce have sprung up in response to fears about the health risks of massproduced food. Organic farming is labour-intensive (supporting more jobs per hectare of farmland) and, as such, 'contributes to the social stability of the farm population and rural society' (Atkins and Bowler, 2001: 69). The massive popularity in Britain and elsewhere of food, drink and cookery programmes on the television and radio reflects an interest in food and cooking which goes beyond the needs of energy refuelling. For some, the significance of these developments is reduced because they are seen as occurring within patriarchal relations, with women assuming the primary mundane responsibilities for preparing and cooking food within the household. However, Elias and Dunning (1969: 57) and Mennell (1985: 265) argue that this is an oversimplification of the matter. While cooking, eating and drinking usually are routinized up to a point, they also play a central part in 'the pleasures of sociability', being amenable to de-routinization and the facilitation and affirmation of close personal relationships for men *and* women. Furthermore, eating out continues to grow in popularity and it is important to note the 'great sense of pleasure and satisfaction' that people often express when asked about their experience of this activity (Warde and Marteens, 2000).

If there has been resistance to the rationalized, mass-produced and de-personalized organization of food in the modern era, writers have also identified opposition to the patriarchal social relations surrounding food. Vegetarianism has been interpreted by Adams (1990) as a feminist response to the supposedly patriarchally inspired slaughter and eating of animals, but it is the more radical abstinence from food that has been seen as the deepest bodily refusal of patriarchal norms surrounding food and sex. Systematic fasting was viewed above as a possible consequence of the location of patriarchal norms on the bodies of women. However, Bell (1985), Bynum (1987) and Brumberg (1988) each examine the possibility that such action might be seen as a manifestation of active *opposition* to male-dominated society. In the medieval era, women used food (and the refusal of food) as a means of transcending their earthly roles, avoiding marriage and the perils of childbirth, and gaining status and a degree of power (Bynum, 1987). Some 'holy fasters' ate only the Eucharist, received godly visions in the process and, in a challenge to the authority of the priest, would vomit a host that they deemed to be unconsecrated. Other women pursued their edible pilgrimage by consuming dirt and disease as an act of self-abnegation. Vomit, scabs, leprous water, pus, rotten food and lice were all eaten by the likes of Catherine of Siena, Saint Veronica and Catherine of Genoa (Bell, 1985; Bynum, 1987).

The systematic fasting that was undertaken by women in the medieval era gradually lost its spiritual dimensions (Brumberg, 1988), but it still appears to involve a bodily repudiation of gendered norms. As Counihan (1999: 104–5) notes, 'Across time a shared characteristic of Western women who fast excessively is the denial of their reproductive potential and their sexuality … All starving women … stop menstruating and their feminine curves disappear.' In many respects this represents a radical rejection of patriarchal norms of feminine beauty and sexuality, but it is a highly problematic challenge which, for modern women, results in a loss of control over, rather than a transcendence of, the self, physical damage, and even death. Nevertheless, systematic fasting provides us with another illustration of how the body does not serve as a passive location for external structures but can reject these structures, even to the point of death. As Counihan

(1999: 95) argues, food refusal is a meaningful cultural statement which signifies the denial of dominant social relationships.

Eating cultural values

This resistance to, and space that has developed around, fast food culture is not just based on a refusal to eat but, more commonly, is associated with long-standing values forged around food and health beliefs that have endured for decades and, sometimes, centuries. Trusted cultural values about 'good' and 'appropriate' foods continue to inform people's general orientation towards eating. Roland Barthes (1972), for example, has identified national foods and drinks (such as wine for the French and tea for the British) which have remained popular in recent decades (see also Lupton, 1996: 26), while food avoidance behaviour is also linked to values that have proven resistant to rationalization (Rozin and Fallon, 1987). More widely, Jelliffe's (1967) identification of culturally prestigious 'super foods' associated with energy, health, particular age-groups, etc., retain a relevance in the contemporary era, as does the notion of equilibrium in diet. Snow's (1993) analysis of African-American folk beliefs concerning health, for example, illustrates the enduring importance of 'balance and moderation' regarding food intake. In Malaya, folk beliefs concerning health suggest that the right balance has to be struck between 'hot' and 'cold' foods. The former tend to include 'foods which are spicy or which are higher in fats, calories or protein (e.g. animal products)' with the latter including 'foods higher in water content (fruits, vegetables, etc.)' (Beardsworth and Keil, 1997). The notion of a balanced diet also continues to hold significant sway in Europe, with government campaigns in Britain promoting the importance of 'five portions of fruit and veg' a day to a healthy diet. Vegetarianism, traditionally encoded into particular religious practices, has become increasingly popular in the past few decades in the affluent West, while long-standing religious prescriptions of food include pork in Judaism and Islam and beef in Hinduism. These prescriptions have persisted in the face of a massive rationalization of food organization and consumption, and illustrate the enduring significance of cultural values to what we eat. In Japan, for example, rice continues to be seen as a spiritual food possessed of transcendental properties.

Such comments are not meant to suggest that cultural values have been unaffected by rationalization. The fast food revolution has not just focused on the promotion of meat in easily consumable forms but has sought to regularize, package, and sell in high volume *all* types of food and drink. As Weber argued, there is little that remains unaffected in the modern world in the tendency to substitute instrumentalism for tradition. Ritzer (1993) is realistic in this respect: the 'alternatives' to McDonaldization he identifies and supports are *less* rationalized (rather than non-rationalized) alternatives which, if successful, become vulnerable to the same processes that have governed the expansion of fast food outlets. In this respect, it is noteworthy that small-scale business has not been able to cope with the demand for organic produce, and it is the supermarkets that have assumed the dominant position in this market.

The persistence of cultural values which retain some distance from rationalized views of fast food reinforces the point that the *Gemeinschaft/Gesellschaft* opposition employed by sociologists to describe the shift into modernity hides some important continuities in practice. Eating is such a basic need that it would become ontologically intolerable to constantly doubt or re-evaluate the desirability, safety or nutritional value of every foodstuff (Sellerberg, 1991). Is it possible that the endurance of these values is also associated with the maintenance of small-scale eating communities?

Eating communities do not exist on the scale they used to, but evidence suggests that people have made efforts to maintain elements of these communal affairs. The organization and consumption of food as a means of creating and consolidating sociality are especially evident in relation to faith and non-faith-based weddings. Despite the fact that it is possible to get married in a few minutes in a drive-by wedding parlour in Las Vegas or, more commonly, in a simple civil ceremony, lavish formal meals remain a central component of many weddings. The wedding remains, within many communities, 'the highest level feast' (Goode et al., 1984). In such occasions, family members and, sometimes, close friends perform traditional roles which are integrally related to the consumption of food and drink. More generally, food is still a central component of numerous religious rituals designed to mark the acceptance of the individual, and the continued integration of the individual, into the faith, while offerings of food to the dead on All Souls' day in parts of Europe remain a common cultural means of ensuring good relations with them (Counihan, 1999: 15). In the West, other religious rituals, like Christmas, continue to thrive despite their increasingly secular character. As a time for sharing food and gifts, Christmas continues to be seen as an occasion in which families reconfirm their identity and significance.

These festive occasions are not the only times at which food and sociality still play a key role in people's lives. Counihan (1999) explores the continuing significance of food for Florentines who remain 'passionate about their own cooking', 'establish their cultural identity through attachment to it', and 'mitigate the effects of gendered body norms by defining femininity through *doing* relationships' rather than *being* a perfectly sculpted body. Goode et al.'s (1984: 184–5) research into the Italian American community notes how a household will not ordinarily eat Sunday dinner alone 'but will either have extended family present or attend the meal at another household linked by kinship, fictive kinship, or intimate friendship'. This implication of food in sociality involves a transcendence of immediate household patriarchal relations. While the husband's preferences are influential in filtering decisions about basic menu structure, considerations involving guests on occasions such as these 'supersede all household members in influencing food items' (ibid.: 200). This is not an isolated example of the continued implication of food in modern forms of sociality. Collectively prepared church meals in Bakersfield, North Carolina, serve to include all within a particular territory, demonstrating and actualizing 'community solidarity'; a solidarity which continues to be displayed through gifts of food when a family has suffered a disaster (Douglas, 1984: 33).

Cultural, as well as religious, prohibitions and sanctionings of particular foodstuffs promote specialist (e.g. vegetarian, halal meat) food outlets that serve and help to integrate communities of people. Ideologically compatible events and meetings are sometimes advertised in such outlets, and the people that work there will often be a source of valuable local information to those for whom diet is integral to their social identity. It is, of course, possible to argue that food has been and will continue to be rationalized within religious and cultural contexts such as these. Evidence does not always support this conclusion, however, and it is interesting to note research that suggests food consumption can actually become *more* important as outward markers of ethnic distinctiveness decline in the face of wider processes of rationalization and integration (Powers and Powers, 1984). Perhaps people's intrinsic need for sociality means that eating remains central to patterns of interaction through time and across cultures (Goffman, 1983).

Food and the pursuit of distinction

The pursuit of distinction is becoming a recurring theme in our analysis of how people position themselves and others in relation to the wider social environment, and it is as prominent in the field of food as it is in the area of music or sport. The potlatch ceremonies of traditional societies were implicated in status competition, as well as in the establishment of social relationships, while the wealthy in medieval society confirmed their status through extravagant feasts that promoted gluttonous consumption. Contemporarily, the beef-eating orgies of the Gurage Men's Societies in Ethiopia, and the close association of certain cooking styles with the cultural elite in Europe, show that eating remains implicated in the search for status (Douglas, 1984). As Conner and Armitage (2000: 124) point out, food is not 'socially inert' as it possesses a communicative function. Individuals readily make status judgements about others depending on what they eat, and seek to communicate messages about themselves via the food they consume.

The traditional potlatch system and medieval feasts illustrate how *quantities* of food were implicated in status considerations. However, the break from medieval cookery in Europe (originating in the city-courts of Renaissance Italy) involved 'a shift in emphasis from quantitative display to *qualitative celebration*' which spread from courtly circles to the bourgeoisie during the eighteenth century (Mennell, 1985: 33, emphasis added). This shift remained confined to the elite, and it is important to remember that survival was the principal concern of the working classes, while country dwellers continued to live principally on a diet of soup, black bread and dairy produce (ibid.: 62). Nevertheless, as the eighteenth century progressed, the inclusion of people within an elite group, and their distance from others outside of these parameters, was expressed by styles of cooking and serving as well as through quantity and variety. Food had become a means of what Robert Merton (1968 [1949]) referred to as 'anticipatory socialization', involving the adoption of the tastes and manners of the social group to which one aspired (Mennell, 1985: 75).

The type, variety and preparation of food eaten remain a marker of difference and distinction in the current era – being seen as a demarcator of 'race', class and other social classifications including that of nationhood (e.g. Symons, 1984). Whitehead's (1984: 116) research into a southern community in the USA also shows how these distinctions are partly a matter of perception. Whitehead notes that certain pork products, chicken necks, black-eyed peas and dried beans are seen as poor people's food by middle-class black and white people, while working-class whites consider them to be black people's food. The association of food and status is particularly evident in the case of working-class whites. For them, not to eat such foods is a marker of superiority (Whitehead, 1984: 116). The status implications of food are also evident in the actions of recipients of food stamp benefits in the USA. While food benefits are based on assumptions about nutritional requirements, and on the idea that their recipients eat differently from the rest of American society, the poor actually try to eat like others in society in order to avoid the stigma associated with their economic plight (Fitchen, 1997; Counihan, 1999). If food and status are inextricably related, it is Bourdieu (1984) who has done most to illustrate the centrality of food in the search for distinction within contemporary relations of sociality. Despite the determinist elements of his analysis, its suggestiveness makes it worth revisiting here.

For Bourdieu (1984: 79, 177), taste in food constitutes 'the strongest and most indelible mark' of class background and learning. In contemporary French society, such status differences are organized on the basis of a 'fundamental opposition' between 'quantity and quality, belly and palate, matter and manners, substance and form'. Material necessity remains an important factor in the formation and maintenance of these tastes – and this is evident in the propensity of the working classes to buy foods which are cheap and filling – but the 'art of eating and drinking' is also one of the areas in which the working classes explicitly challenge elite norms of 'sobriety' and 'slimness' via 'a conviviality which sweeps away restraints and reticence' (ibid.: 177–9). Among working-class men, the consumption of large quantities of meat and the enjoyment of strong alcohol constitutes the production of social relationships and provides the basis for the 'solid', 'strong' and visually masculine body (ibid.: 192). We do not have to agree with Bourdieu that such actions represent the near inevitable corollary of a working-class *habitus*, but can view these as a creative generation of sociability among eating bodies and a rejection of the 'over-concern' with appearance characteristic of the new middle classes. As we ascend the social hierarchy, in contrast, we find that the reduction of economic constraints on food consumption is accompanied by a very different attitude towards eating and sociality. For the petite bourgeoisie, food and sociality become things to be approached with caution: social contacts must be strategically selective, and coarseness and fatness avoided if upward mobility is to be realized for this group. As Bourdieu (1984: 183) puts it, 'the sobriety' of the petit bourgeois is experienced as a break: 'in abstaining from having a good time and from having it with others, the would-be petit bourgeois betrays his ambition of escaping from the common present'. Sociality re-enters into eating and drinking for the established bourgeoisie, but social relations are here mediated and consolidated by following a 'strict sequence', a 'restraint and propriety' at mealtimes which is associated with their approach towards the body and interaction (ibid.: 196).

As Norbert Elias (2000 [1939]) explains, what underlies these modern distinctions is a fundamentally different relationship to animal nature than existed in the medieval era. The animalistic elements of eating have been obscured, but they have been obscured for some groups more than for others, while the standards associated with eating that still separate social groups betray fundamentally different moral orientations to the body and sociality. As Bourdieu (1984: 199) concludes, in matters of sociable eating 'what for some is shameless and slovenly, for others is straightforward, unpretentious; familiarity is for some the most absolute form of recognition, the abdication of all distance, a trusting openness, a relation of equal to equal; for others, who shun familiarity, it is an unseemly liberty.'

Conclusion

By focusing on eating bodies, this chapter has examined how the embodied subject can be seen as constituting an enduring source of sociality. However, it has also taken seriously the concerns of contemporary body theorists by exploring how this aspect of human life has become a location for social structures. While Bataille (1993 [1976]) discusses the excess energy that provides humans with a physiological basis for the creative development of social relationships, for example, there have in modern times been a number of state-centred initiatives which seek to match the nutritional intake of individuals to the efficient operation of capitalism and the market place. Coupled with the pervasive spread of fast food culture, and the associated rationalization of social relationships, it might appear as if individuals have been subject to a variety of (sometimes contradictory) structural developments that they are powerless to alter.

Falk's (1994) notion of the 'open self', however, provides us with a different perspective on this situation. His thesis suggests that individuals have been subjected to a bodily re-formation that has emerged as a result of the decline in eating communities, but its suggestion that individuals are now forced to make their own decisions about food unhampered by collective relationships implies that there exists space for personal creativity. In this context, while many may indeed be attracted to fast food as a convenient solution to living in a pressurized world, individuals are free not only to choose to consume such products, but to *re-evaluate* such a decision in the light of their experience of the effects of such food. People have made changes to their diet in response to food scares and have demanded foods that are more suited to the needs of their families and friendships, and to their continuing valuation of sociability (e.g. Wheelock, 1990; Buckland, 1994; Schlosser, 2002). Food continues to be used as a way of cementing and maintaining social relationships, and of demarcating certain relationships and identities as distinct and worthy of recognition and others as being low status and morally suspect.

If eating continues to provide opportunities for the generation of intrinsically satisfying relations of sociality, feminists have argued that this creativity is gender-specific and that women's relationship with food continues to be over-determined by oppressive gendered relations. Food has even been viewed as key to the 'continued existence of the patriarchal family, in both its nuclear and extended form, throughout the class structure' (Charles and Kerr, 1988: 288). This argument underplays the enormously positive and empowering links that exist between food preparation, eating and women's sociality in certain southern European cultures (Counihan, 1999: 75). There is no doubt, though, that the relationship between food and wider social relations has provoked many women to retreat into their own bodies and to eschew that partial transcendence which connects eating bodies in relations of sociability. Here, structural relationships can indeed be viewed as having broken the link between food and sociality. In contrast to contemporary body theories, however, it would be a mistake to interpret such a situation as a manifestation of the body's passivity. As feminists themselves argue, even the enormously damaging effects of eating disorders such as anorexia seem to manifest a refusal of dominant structures, and constitute a sign that the body is capable of carrying out its own protest against society.

Notes

1 There is not the space to pursue the wider role of food in the international community, but issues of starvation, malnutrition and under-nutrition are enormously potent bodily indicators of inequality, conflict and war. For a useful summary of these issues, see Atkins and Bowler (2001).

2 This did not prevent the church and civil governments acting in concert to combat excessive displays of consumption and drunkenness (Sekora, 1977).

3 It is also worth noting that since Japanese diets became westernized after the Second World War, there has been an increase in heart disease there alongside an increased consumption of red meat (Atkins and Bowler, 2001: 205). More generally, the World Health Organization estimates that one-third of the ten million annual global cases of cancer could be avoided by 'feasible and appropriate diets and by physical exercise' (ibid.: 207).

4 There has been widespread concern about advertising campaigns aimed at children. In Britain, it was announced in October 2003 that the Commons Health Select Committee has asked the big fast food chains and Coca-Cola to answer charges that they have targeted children to make profits from products that damage health.

8

Technological Bodies

Introduction

'Technology' is conventionally understood as referring to the practical application of techniques and knowledge to productive processes and, as Chapter 4 suggested, is one of the major forces to have threatened the generative significance of the body in the contemporary era. Technology has long been viewed as significant to the formation of social relationships, and has sometimes been analysed as determining the very structure of society. Karl Marx adopted this position briefly in his argument that 'the hand mill will give you a society with the feudal lord, the steam mill a society with the industrial capitalist', even though he also insisted that the technological forces of production always operated in conjunction with the social relations of production. The idea of 'technological bodies', however, suggests not only that the work-based and other *contexts* in which we live have become more technologically dominated than ever before, but that productive techniques and knowledge have moved *inwards*, to invade, reconstruct and increasingly dominate the very contents of the body. This raises the possibility that the spatial and functional arrangements of the organic properties of our bodies have been altered in line with the structures of society, and to an extent which challenges conventional notions of what it is to be and have a body. As such, the subject of 'technologized' bodies provides fertile grounds on which to examine the concerns of those theorists who view modern life as having robbed embodied subjects (at least as they have been traditionally conceived) of their significance and creativity. In contrast to those issues associated with sociality examined in the previous chapter (which illustrate the human capacity to transcend, albeit briefly, the material necessities of society), technology appears, at least initially, to be illustrative of how the body can be made immanent in relation to its environment.

This chapter focuses on two interrelated developments that have become significant to the rise of technologized bodies in the contemporary era. These are, first, the widespread proliferation (especially in the affluent West and in parts of Asia) of 'cyberspace'. Cyberspace is a broad, umbrella term that refers to computer- or electrically-mediated communications which generate 'information space' or 'technospace' (Munt, 2001: 11), virtual places in which people can interact or access information without having to be physically co-present with others. Technologies which produce such virtual spaces include interactive and multimedia communications, the Internet together with the World Wide Web, video conferencing, computer-aided design, digital television, mobile phones, and electronic surveillance. The second major development concerns the myriad ways in which the flesh and internal contents of the body have been supplemented and altered in recent years. This includes the incorporation of non-human material into the body in order to monitor, repair, or replace damaged organs, and to enhance appearance via plastic surgery, but is also concerned with the more spectacular combinations of human and machine conjured up by the term *cyborgs*. As Donna Haraway (1994 [1985]: 83) puts it in her oft-quoted article on technology and feminism, a cyborg is 'a hybrid of machine and organism', a 'creature' that may be most visible in science fiction but that is making its presence increasingly felt in the real world. Film series such as *The Terminator* and performance artists such as Stelarc (1998) provide us with fantastic images of 'cyborgs', images which seem to be extended in contemporary developments in nanotechnology (Radford, 2003b), but the term has also been applied to the more prosaic 'mergings' of humans and computers which occur every time we work on our computers or 'log on' to the Internet. It is here, so we are told, that our 'virtual selves' come to life 'through keyboards, screens, wires and computers' (Jordan, 1999: 180). Ultimately, however, cyborgs have been viewed as possessing the potential to constitute 'a self-regulating human-machine system', a 'hybrid in which the machine parts become replacements … to enhance the body's power potential' (Featherstone and Burrows, 1995).

Developments within cyberspace and cyborgs can be referred to collectively as 'cyber-technologies'. These developments combine in the views of those such as Jordan (1999) who imply that the computer age has turned us all into cyborgs of one type or another, while their potential to shape human life has been discussed most extensively in a literary tradition known as 'cyberpunk'. Associated primarily with the novels of William Gibson, cyberpunk draws on the science of cybernetics (Weiner, 1948a, 1948b) in order to argue that our enfleshed being is becoming increasingly irrelevant and that we will soon be able to leave our bodies behind and 'download' ourselves onto the Internet as pure information and 'disembodied consciousness' (Jordan, 1999).

It is easy to dismiss such fiction on the basis that it is ungrounded in social reality. Nevertheless, the writings of Gibson and others envisage future scenarios concerning the interaction between individuals and structures which apply to the mundane uses of technology, as well as to the more spectacular human–machine couplings envisaged by cyberpunk, and which are central to the concerns of this book. On the one hand, their writings suggest that this expansion of cyberspace can provide individuals with unprecedented opportunities to pursue their projects and develop their identities without having to worry about the traditional constraints associated with being possessed of frail bodies subject to governmental controls. On the other hand, their visions of the future also raise the possibility that such space could become colonized by existing social, cultural and economic structures, and could be used to reconstruct and reconfigure the malleable bodily identities of subjects in line with societal norms. While cyber-technologies clearly acquire meaning from the narratives of those who invent and use them, the suggestion here is that they also possess a material presence which can 'fix' social relationships and people's identities in place, effectively structuring human networks and the individual sense of self around key material artefacts (Pels et al., 2002: 11).

These alternative scenarios cannot be analysed with any degree of sociological adequacy while they remain purely speculative, however, and it is necessary to contextualize future possibilities within a view which takes account of existing developments and the past realities of technology. This can help caution us against attributing an unjustifiable novelty to the social significance of recent developments. Winston (1998), for example, challenges the concept of a revolution in common technology by exploring the history of these developments. Thus, the fax was introduced in 1847, the idea of television patented in 1884, digitalization demonstrated in 1983, and even the concept of the Web dates from 1945. Similarly, Strum and Latour (1999) argue that technological artifacts have made society possible from its very beginnings and are nothing new. Looking back into the distant past, Heim (1995: 69) makes the point that while the virtual environments of cyberspace may appear to possess an unprecedented power to imprint themselves on humans, harnessing the technological force of *fire* was historically at least as spectacular in its effects.[1] Similarly, the development of prostheses provides us with another example of how technology has long been significant for human embodiment. There has been a tendency in recent social theory to use such terms as 'prosthetic memory' or 'prosthetic identity' to refer to the body being supplemented by *any* mechanistic device (e.g. Landsberg, 1995; Lury, 1998), but prostheses have historically referred to artificial body parts intended to *restore* the body's functioning. Prostheses, simply, are 'something created to replace a part of the body that has been removed' (Haiken, 2002: 172). From wooden peg legs, to the Jaipur foot in India, to legs for athletes modelled on the biomechanics of animals, to the hundreds of thousands of people who walk successfully with the aid of artificial hips, prostheses have historically transformed the capacities of those seriously injured and should make us pause before attributing cyber-technologies with unique significance (Ott et al., 2002a).

In this chapter, I use these examples of fire and prostheses in order to provide a comparative dimension to my consideration of cyber-technologies. The next section analyses how the needs of the flesh-and-guts body constituted a productive impetus for the elaboration of cyber-technologies. The power that 'informational elites' appear to possess over these technologies can make it easy to assume that cyberspace and cyborgs stand like 'social facts' above, out of reach, and disconnected from the needs of those subject to them. However, if the desire of embodied subjects for warmth, light and protection steered the uses of fire, and the concern for restoring physical mobility shaped the purpose and design of artificial limbs, we should be wary of dismissing the possibility that basic bodily needs continue to remain a *source* of technological innovation. The chapter then shifts focus by taking seriously those writings which suggest that the human body has, in recent decades, become a passive *location* for the technological designs of political and informational elites; designs which have served to exacerbate inequalities, obstruct individual development, and stifle community. If the body constituted a source for the initial formation of cyber-technologies, these writings suggest that the development and deployment of these technologies have become removed from the needs that set them in motion. I then draw on empirical as well as theoretical studies in order to ascertain how interactions between bodies and technology are actually positioning people within the contemporary social environment. Finally, the conclusion suggests that while present realities are nowhere as clear-cut or spectacular in their effects as suggested by many critics of cyber-technology, they do raise serious concerns about how people are seeking to deal with life in an increasingly technologically rationalized capitalist system.

The Body as a Source of Technology

Karl Marx and Frederich Engels (1977 [1846]) were two of the first modern social theorists to base their theory of humanity on a view of the body as a productive source of technological interventions into the environment. Humans were part of, yet were also set apart from, nature, and people's ability to objectify themselves and their surroundings enabled them to develop tools that could begin to change the natural world according to their own designs. As tool use did not just change the environment, but led to immediate and longer-term changes in the structure and evolution of the body, these developments also involved certain corporeal changes in what it meant to be a human being. The development of bipedalism and increases in the size and cognitive capacity of the brain, for example, were both related to the human invention and use of tools (Hirst and Woolley, 1982). Thus, the fact that the body is a source of technology (and, as analysed in previous chapters, a source of work, sport, music and sociability) does not make it an unchanging generator of these phenomenon.

Simmel's (1971 [1918b]) essay on the transcendent character of life provides us with a distinctive development of this approach to the relationship between the body, technology and the environment. Taking as his starting point the assumption that bodily life is characterized by boundaries and limitations, he argues that the human capacities of sensory imagination and calculation do not simply constrain what we can do, but allow us to extend technologically some of these corporeal limits. People have historically accomplished this by learning how to utilize organic and inorganic matter to enhance their mobility and sensory range. When humans learned to ride horses, for example, they managed to relearn balance and physical control through a mediated relationship with motion in order to overcome the limits of their foot-based speed and stamina. Simmel himself examines the telescope and microscope in order to show how humans have expanded vastly their sense of the world, and concludes by arguing that the body is the source of its own transcendence: 'the process of "reaching beyond itself"' is 'the primary phenomenon of life' (Simmel, 1971 [1918b]: 356, 364). Simmel does not view this physical transcendence as arbitrary or limitless, however, but grounds its scope and direction firmly in the aims of our 'practical conduct': the bodily boundaries that humans seek to reach beyond remain informed by their imagination of what is realistically conceivable and desirable (ibid.: 355). This is an important argument as it suggests that there tends to be a certain homology between people's existing bodily capacities and projects, and the types of physical development planned and achieved by humans. Technologies are not necessarily 'inhuman', being imposed on us externally without regard to the realities of our bodily being, but can be seen as integrally related to people's plans, purposes and capacities. The body, in short, remains an important source of technological development.

Simmel's consideration of how the body is a source of technology (which is in turn, as Marx and Engels also recognized, consequential for future physical development), can usefully be applied to the case of cyber-technologies. However, I first want to show how it can further aid our general understanding of technological forces by looking briefly at the cases of fire and prostheses. As Johan Goudsblom (1992) argues, the human capacity to start fires and control them by clearing ground and utilizing water to limit their spread and extinguish them made our bodies a source of the development of this technological resource. The control of fire, furthermore, is associated with humans changing from being an ecologically secondary to an ecologically dominant species. Fire was a vital resource in the human struggle for survival that enabled people to transcend the existing limits of their environment and physical energy. Through its ability to generate warmth and light, the human control of fire offered protection against cold and darkness, kept predators at bay, and aided hunting (ibid.: 37). Once its cooking and preservative properties were discovered, fire also took over some of the digestive work that had to be undertaken previously by the stomach, and allowed humans to consume a wider variety of fruits, vegetables and meats. This aided digestion, made the transportation of food easier, and helped humans hunt for long periods. Later developments in the use of fire continued to enable humans to break the currently encountered limits of their bodies and environment. Agrarianization and the employment of 'slash and burn' techniques of clearing land prior to planting, for example, would have been 'inconceivable' without the controlled use of fire, yet allowed people to settle in an area and plan ahead without having to worry about the source of every new meal (Goudsblom, 1992: 7–10, 49). Constraints, however, still existed. The use of fire did not involve a complete transcendence of the body. The internal parts of the body maintained their broad relationship with each other, while fire was domesticated with reference to the constraints of the built environment. Nevertheless, the control of fire was closely associated with a significant extension in people's bodily capacities.

The case of prosthetic limbs provides us with an insight into how some technologies *restore* rather than extend people's capacities. The body can be seen to constitute a source for prostheses not only because our capacities allow us to make these products, but in so far as the body's appearance and functioning set the standards for this technology: artificial limbs have traditionally been considered successful only if they mirror the function and/or aesthetics of what has been lost to the organism. So, while disability through war or accident has historically made reintegration into the social and working life of a community highly problematic, the acquisition of a suitable prostheses could help bring about an alignment between the capacities of the individual body and the environment offered to that individual by the social body (Featherstone, 1995; McDaid, 2002: 121, 131). Furthermore, while the fitting of artificial limbs does not offer the transcendence of the body dreamt of by writers of cyberpunk, their effects remain dramatic for the individuals concerned. In his account of being fitted for a new artificial leg, for example, Steven Kurzman (2002: 229) notes the point at which 'the prosthesis just felt right and I stopped thinking about walking because it no longer felt remarkable ... I cheered and raised my arms like a goal post. We got it right: the socket was comfortable and the prosthesis was aligned.' The missing limb had itself been functionally 'erased', and a disability minimized, through the imaginative deployment of a substitutive technology.

The analytical distinction between the restoration of human capacities accomplished by prostheses, and the enhancement of human capacities brought about by more radical human–machine combinations mentioned earlier in this chapter, is a useful way of separating sociological fact from science fiction. However, with the gradual weakening of the organic–inorganic boundary, it has become increasingly difficult to sustain. During the last century there has been an intensive search for 'the perfect biocompatible cosmetic prosthetic', and gore tex, teflon, glass balls, silk floss, celluloid, paraffin, ox cartilage and silicon, are just a few of the materials to have been incorporated into the body in an attempt to create 'physical perfection' (Haiken, 2002: 185, 171). Other developments with a robotic dimension to them have also weakened the boundary between humans and machines. Runners' legs made for competitive athletes, for example, imitate the flexion of the cheetah's leg and resemble 'the suspension band in a pickup truck more than a familiar articulated leg' (Ott, 2002a: 24). Even more dramatically, some researchers are using computer technology with micro-surgery to create neuronal prostheses designed to recreate vision for blind people, while others are working on a new generation of hand prostheses 'that will communicate with computers and bypass the keyboard hardware' (ibid.: 24–5). Such radically innovative prostheses seem to reveal a continued human desire to transcend the currently encountered limits of the body (Simmel, 1971 [1918b]), whatever these may be, and lead us back to the subject of cyber-technologies.

The most radical writings on cyberspace and cyborgs suggest that technology is making irrelevant the 'cloddishness', 'treachery' and 'mortality' of the physical body (Benedikt, 1991), yet it is worth looking at how cyber-technologies relate to people's *current* bodily identities. Far from transcending the individual material flesh altogether, we can see instead how these technologies remain grounded in, and constrained by, material bodily needs: the body continues to steer their development. Despite its technological determinism, McLuhan's (1962) *The Medium is the Message* pointed out several decades ago that the invention of technologies such as television can be seen as building on and enhancing the senses, displaying a strong affinity with rather than negating the conditions of human embodiment. The first moment in cyberspace is spent by nearly everyone in their own individualized area by the computer, for example, while a number of analysts have explored how our 'on-line' behaviour remains dependent on a material 'off-line' presence (Jordan, 1999; DiMaggio et al., 2001; Horner, 2001). There is no complete suspension of the body and 'behaviour in cyberspace is contingent upon, and a function of, the physical persons we happen to be' (Horner, 2001: 82).

This same point applies to the general human relationship with technology and can be illustrated with reference to some of the developments in 'telehealth' where robotics has extended the surgeon's body in order to operate on the patient's body. In microsurgery, for example, a computer helps mediate the surgeon's movements in order to achieve a degree of precision that is impossible for the human hand. There is an enhancement of bodily capacities here but no complete transcendence of the body: telehealth remains dependent on the skills, capacities and routines of the medical specialist (Lehoux et al., 2002). Thus, if everyone connected to computer-mediated communicative environments is indeed inhabiting a virtual space, and can be described as a cyborg, we should not think that this involves a letting go of their physical being. Nor, however, should we pretend that the body's relationship with cyber-technology is purely a one-sidedly productive and creative affair. Technology may allow us to overcome our currently encountered boundaries on the basis of our existing goals, as Simmel argued, but embodied subjects also feel removed from, and constrained by, technological developments.

The Body as a Location for Technology

The body may constitute a source of technology, yet history shows that technologies become embedded in customs, procedures and societal structures that seem to inscribe themselves on the actions and identities of embodied individuals and often appear fixed to new generations. There has even been talk of technologies creating sensory and information environments to which most people remain oblivious (McLuhan, 1969). These technical artefacts, environments, and technologically enhanced structures have been analysed as possessing the potential to restrict individual plans, reinforce social inequalities and oppress people, and damage communities. In this section, I begin by examining some of the ways in which the body

179

can be analysed as a location for this phenomenon by identifying how the development of technological bodies has long been steered by warfare and the economy.

War, production and inequality

The most overtly and immediately destructive consequences of technology can be seen in the case of warfare. The technological force of fire has long served as a military resource, and its devastating effects are well illustrated by the huge quantities of incendiaries dropped on Hamburg and Dresden in the Second World War, and by the extensive American use of napalm during the Vietnam War. The former created 'fire storms' that claimed the lives of tens of thousands of people (Goudsblom, 1992), while the latter obliterated crops, forests and whole communities. If the technological uses of fire accelerated during wartime, the development of prostheses was also linked directly to (the bodily damage wrought by) military conflict. The civil war in the USA and the Napoleonic Wars in Europe prompted the first large-scale concern with the design and use of prosthetics (Ott, 2002a: 26), while demand for artificial limbs grew during the twentieth century as a result of the widespread use of land-mines in civil wars across such countries as Angola, Cambodia, and Sierra Leone (Perry, 2002; Ott, 2002a).

Military considerations did much to govern the past use of technological forces, and remain highly pertinent to a consideration of cyber-technologies. This becomes clear if we consider how Weiner's (1948a, 1948b) cybernetics provided the background not only for cyberpunk, as already noted, but for the actual development of cyberspace and cyborgs. Drawing on the Greek word for 'steersman', Weiner (1948a) coined the term 'cybernetics' to refer to a unified science of communications and control theory which adopted a common approach to the mind, the body and automated machines (Featherstone and Burrows, 1995). Cybernetics was developed initially in Weiner's military research during the Second World War when he worked on an anti-aircraft predictor 'designed to characterise an enemy pilot's zigzagging flight, anticipate his future position, and launch an anti-aircraft shell to down his plane' (Galison, 1994: 229).[2] Weiner's vision of the body was such that the enemy pilot was effectively merged with the machinery of the aircraft.[3] He suggested that, when acting under stress, humans acted repetitively and, therefore, predictably, and that a refined anti-aircraft predictor based on electrical networks could use a pilot's characteristic flight pattern to calculate future moves and destroy the plane (Galison, 1994: 236). As David Tomas (1995: 27–8) puts it, human being is reduced in cybernetics to an informational pattern 'whose operational logic' is coextensive with 'types of machine systems'. Although Weiner's anti-aircraft predictor did not prove successful, the influence of cybernetics looms ever larger in modern warfare. Commenting upon the (first) Gulf War, for example, Balsamo (2000: 495) points out that despite the 'rhetorical disclaimers that this was not a Nintendo war', there were 'numerous examples' of the deployment of a 'technological gaze' which effectively combined human visual steering systems with weapons of mass destruction.

Despite its importance, military conflict has not been the only factor steering the development of technological bodies. Economic needs have long loomed large in their invention and deployment. The use of fire in ancient urban life, for example, illustrates how the economy required potters, smiths, bakers, cattle-branders, brick-makers and other crafts to extend their capacities for action via a specialized knowledge and use of fire (Goudsblom, 1992). Furthermore, while war stimulated the development of destructive technological forces, the physical damage it visited on combatants and civilians alike was turned into an economic demand for productive prostheses. The invention of the Siemens–Schuckart arm, for example, was designed to get disabled veterans back to work after the First World War. The 'arm' was strapped to the worker's body and shoulder, and had a metal joint at the end to which working 'hands' (ranging from tools like hammers, to brushes, to craft inserts designed to fit particular pieces of machinery) could be inserted and fastened (Perry, 2002). Well into the twentieth century the primary aim for the prosthetist remained that of making the worker as economically productive and efficient as possible. This 'quest for efficiency', which as we have already seen was to be accelerated by Taylorism, caused the body to be treated as a machine or motor. In this context, the managemental approach towards disabled workers was to restore 'missing functions' rather than 'missing limbs', and the role artificial limbs fulfilled in the workplace prompted commentators to suggest that the worker had become nothing more than a 'living appendage or human prosthesis' to the machine (Brown, 2002: 270; Perry, 2002: 89; Rabinbach, 1990; Serlin, 2002: 67).

If economic considerations were associated with the development of technological means of supplementing the human body, so too have they been linked with the expansion of cyberspace. Indeed, it has been the economically driven expansion of informational space that has been the biggest impact of this technology on most people's lives, and has done much to create the sense that we are living in a 'runaway world', riven with inequalities, that is beyond our control (Giddens, 1990). Cyberspace has, in particular, become of key importance for the circulation of capital in the contemporary era:

> The immense strength of finance capital and its emergence as global 24 hrs a day and always in real time occurred because it migrated to cyberspace. Banks and markets are connected via dedicated computer networks that transfer money, stocks or bonds and report prices. Money and information flow ceaselessly and at extraordinary speeds around the world, pushing trillions of dollars globally both in case and other forms such as stocks or bonds. All this frenetic activity occurs in cyberspace. (Jordan, 1999: 148)

These developments have accelerated the scope and importance of informational labour (concerned with cognitive and semiotic work) (Rabinbach,

1990: 298). As early as 1961, the classic French industrial sociological study *Traité de Sociologie du Travail* typified the extension of automation as presaging a transformation from '"work of the laborer to the work of communication", from work centring on the physiology of muscles and nerves, to work of a "cognitive or semiotic" nature' (cited in Rabinbach, 1990: 298). However, recent developments have massively accelerated this process. As Rabinbach (ibid.: 298) concludes, 'The appearance of the cerebral worker whose material and product is "information" is emblematic of the vast distance traversed between the worker who surveys complex technologies of communication and the "man-beef of Taylor".' Perhaps the most famous statement of these changes comes from Castells (1989: 17) who argues that we have entered a new informational mode of development, the main feature of which is 'the emergence of information processing as the core fundamental activity conditioning the effectiveness and productivity of all processes of production, distribution, consumption and management'.

These developments in the economy and work also lead us to a consideration of the relationship between technology and inequality. As Castells (1996) argues, technologically driven information generation, processing and transmission systems have not only become fundamental sources of productivity and power, but have altered the environment in which wealth, influence and inequality circulate. Informational labour is valued and rewarded higher than manual labour, to an extent that is perhaps unprecedented in human history (Rabinbach, 1990: 298), while the 'digital divide' became during the mid-1990s a new way of talking about the accentuation of social inequalities (and the creation of new opportunity structures) in relation to information technologies and their use across the financial, educational, medical and other sectors of society (Robinson and Flowers, 1999; Liff et al., 2002). Sean Cubitt (1998) argues that this digital divide has consolidated the class structures of contemporary societies and, in the context of arguments like these, it is no surprise that the typical user of the Internet throughout the 1990s was white, male, professional/managerial, earning above average income, and resident in the developed world (Wyatt et al., 2002). This is reinforced by the fact that American English is by far the most frequently used language on the Internet. For Castells (1996: 371), this digital divide is likely to result in an Internet characterized by two distinct populations of users, the 'interacting' and the 'interacted'. While the former have the skills and technology to make use of the full capacities of the medium, a capacity which may well become of growing importance given widespread cutbacks in governmental welfare provision (Burrows and Nettleton, 2002), the latter are confined to limited access and commercially pre-packaged options.

Aesthetics, identity and technological overload

Societal structures related to military conflict and the economy are not the only ones to have confronted the embodied subject with technologies that appear preset in their form and consequences. Class and gender norms have also inscribed themselves on the deployment of technological resources, and have constrained and contoured the space in which individuals are able to express themselves and develop their identities. If the control of fire was related to social status from ancient times (Goudsblom, 1992), social stratification is most obviously evident in the development of prostheses.

Class-based norms of physical decency were apparent in the use of artificial limbs. In the anonymous urban environments of the mid-nineteenth century, the influence of phrenologists and others contributed to a situation in which appearance was seen as an indicator of character and distinction. For those disabled members of the middle classes who earned their living through dealing with other people, the issue of an aesthetically passable prosthetic became vital (Mihm, 2002). As Holmes (1863) wrote of the problems facing the amputee, 'just at the period when personal graces are most valued, when a good presence is a blank check on the Bank of Fortune, with Nature's signature on the bottom, he found himself made hideous' (cited in Mihm, 2002: 288). Gender norms of appearance also permeated artificial limbs and other prosthetic developments. As Serlin (2002: 47) points out, social and political discussion of veterans returning home from the Second World War reflected anxieties associated with 'the public specter of the damaged male body', and the 'feminisation of social life' that had occurred with the absence of so many men during wartime. The amputated body was often treated as physical proof of emasculation or as 'a kind of monstrous defamiliarization of the "normal" male body' (Serlin, 2002: 48). Rehabilitation manuals routinely correlated physical disability with heterosexual anxieties regarding the pursuit of a 'normal' sex life and social life, and were infused with a concern that prostheses should assist individuals in securing an independence which would enable them to resist the potentially 'feminising' influences of family life (ibid.). Subsequent developments in prostheses – which cross the line between corporeal replacement and cyborgian enhancement – continue to reflect strong gender norms. The use of silicone gel implants in the second half of the twentieth century, for example, made it possible for a woman having undergone a mastectomy to restore her 'femininity', while *Cosmopolitan* magazine's 1970 proclamation that 'surgically enhanced breasts have a better contour than the real thing' seemed to reflect the mood of those women who used them to supplement rather than restore breast appearance (cited in Haiken, 2002). During 2001, for example, over 200,000 women underwent breast augmentation in the United States (Seager, 2003). Not even the penis was safe from the masculine norm that 'bigger is better'. During the 1990s, fat injections and grafts were used to increase the width of the penis, albeit with often disastrous effects.

Prosthetic enhancements may have made very real contributions to the restoration and enhancement of people's mobility and motility, but the extent to which they allowed individuals to pursue their own projects was overlaid by the pervasiveness of gendered norms which came increasingly via technological 'advances' to invade and, in the case of breast and penile implants, often damage, the body. The 'masks' of masculinity and femininity were clearly not confined to the exteriors of the flesh, but appeared to locate themselves in the interiors of the embodied subject (Tseelon, 1995).

If prevailing social norms have affected the development of prostheses, cyberspace also places constraints on the extent to which individuals are able to use technology to express and develop their identities. The vast expansion of electronic information that has characterized the development of contemporary society in general, and the Internet in particular, has contributed to a situation in which cultural analysts can suggest that there is nowhere outside of the 'information order' (Lash, 2002: vii). This situation places very real constraints on the ability of individuals to discriminate between, and utilize effectively, the data made available to them. Simmel (1971 [1918a]) talks about the 'cultural tragedy' of modernity residing in the proliferation of forms that could neither be ignored nor properly assimilated by the interested individual, yet these conditions point to a 'technological tragedy' of potentially far greater proportions. According to Shenk (1997), the sheer volume of information to which individuals are subjected places limits on their agentic capacities, and this 'information overload' has damaged people's health through its association with frustration and high blood pressure, and has also led to an increase in poor decision-making. Stone (1992) similarly identifies stress as a primary response to the quantity and speed of information in contemporary society, and suggests that it is a symptom of the growing gap that exists between human physical evolution and human cultural evolution. The increase in eye problems and repetitive strain syndrome associated with computer work (which persists despite design alterations such as adapted keyboards and mouses) and mobile phone texting are manifestations of this gap – bodies simply were not made to undertake such work. More radically, Heim (1995) suggests that this disjunction between physical and cultural evolution can result – when prolonged time is spent in virtual environments – in a fundamental disorientation of the senses and a disconnection from reality. Furthermore, as Lupton (1995) points out, the manner in which we have come to conceptualize our relationship with computers tells us much about how images of health have become tied to a general sense that we have lost control of ourselves and our environment. Computer users now have to worry about their communicational selves being 'infected' by viruses, and about 'cybercriminals' exploiting weak points in their systems, as they strive to cope with a new informational milieu in which data appears to circulate at a quantity and velocity without regard to any effective human controlling force (Baudrillard, 1993; Gonzalez, 2000: 542–3). Finally, in a departure from the overload thesis, Lash (2002) has argued that global information flows have become increasingly detached from *any* external referents and that we have become absorbed within informational space.

Community and technology

Technological forces have for centuries entered into the maintenance of communities. In the case of fire, Fustel de Coulanges's (1864) study of *The Ancient City* noted how it became a 'sacred obligation' for the master of every house to keep the household fire burning day and night. Fire was viewed as a form of, and a metaphor for, the life of the household and of the communal body, and its potential longevity made it conducive to this display of symbolism. Instead of reflecting positively the life of communities, however, many recent analyses of the effects of technology tend to suggest that it has *damaged* the cohesion of human collectivities. Drawing on Marx's argument about the rising technical composition of capital and unemployment, Cubitt (1998) suggests that computer-driven electronic communications have made a major contribution to the 'demolition' of jobs, communities and cultures that were not immediately translatable into rationalized forms of digital information. Cyberspace, it has been suggested, has also reinforced relations of dominance and subordination between Western and non-Western societies and *within* non-Western societies. For Dyrkton (1996), for example, the business and communicational possibilities provided by the Internet operate by linking individuals in countries such as Jamaica with the First World, thus creating a Western-oriented widening of social divisions within non-Western localities.

Cyberspace has not only damaged certain existing communities, according to some, but has reconstructed more generally how people relate to each other and build collective relationships. The mediated communications which have become the norm within cyberspace have been seen as disconnecting people from each other and from external physical environments (Virilio, 2000). For critics, this 'living-at-a-distance' has corroded the moral dimensions of human collectivities. Email, texting and other ways of sending virtual messages entail for some 'a refusal to recognise the substantial and independent reality of others and to be involved in relations of mutual dependence and responsibility' which open up the possibilities of collective action (Robins, 1995: 144; Nguyen and Alexander, 1996: 122). Cyberspace may have been constructed with reference to the ease of information flow, but this does not address the moral problem of 'arousing sympathy for those who are Other' in the modern world (Sennett, 1994). For Heim (1992: 75–6), the reduction in meetings involving bodily co-presence with others results in an increase of egoism, a possible amplification of 'an amoral indifference to human relationships' and a situation in which 'our ethics languish'. These diagnoses of the effects of the Internet on community are not uncommon. Others believe that the Internet poses a grave threat not only to day-to-day personal interaction, but even to democracy itself (Slouka, 1995; Brown, 1997).

Such scenarios may strike us as alarmist, but if cyberspace has for some contributed towards an erosion of moral communities, it has certainly been used to increase surveillance over those 'untrusted others' who fall outside of the boundaries of moral orders and who constitute an embodied source of risk (Beck, 1991). Thus, CCTV cameras have turned an increasing amount of the urban environment in the West into 'observational space', with a growing number of government authorities seeing this technology as 'providing the answer to institutional control over urban and social degeneration' (Ainley, 2001: 86). In London, for example, it has been estimated that a person in a public space is captured on camera at least once every five minutes (ibid.). Surveillance cameras also often pervade privately owned shopping malls, with continuous observation being seen by some as the 'price' shoppers and tourists have to pay to enter such 'sanitised' environments (Ostwald, 1997: 668). While commercial centres and affluent residential areas are replete with video cameras to monitor and keep away undesirables, those on the 'other side of the tracks' are located as the objects of surveillance (Hirsch, 1976). Indicators of privilege and poverty such as education and income can now clearly be supplemented with reference to the amount of surveillance to which oneself and one's community is subject, and whether this surveillance is undertaken in the interests of one's own security or the security of others. Even if moral communities continue to exist, against the predictions of certain critics of cyberspace, the use of surveillance may be a sign that these collectivities define themselves as increasingly threatened by people who exist outside of their morally regulated spaces.

In direct contrast to those who view the body as an agentic source of cyber-technologies, facilitating and extending the voluntary projects of individuals, the writings examined in this section suggest that many bodies have become an increasingly powerless location for the technological designs of informational elites. This determinism plays upon the recognition that it is not ordinary users who set the agenda for the development of this technology. Contemporary arguments over confidentiality and encryption procedures on the Internet are dominated instead, especially after the events of September 11th, by the political desire to monitor and the business concern to ensure a conduit through which safe commercial transactions can occur (Jordan, 1999: 1–2, 132). Similarly, for Cubitt (1998), the surge in electronic communication has been sponsored and steered by corporate designs which facilitate individual actions only to the extent that they fit into the plans of multinational companies. Military agendas have also done much to inform the contemporary character of cyber-technologies. As Galison (1994) argues, progressivist visions of cyborgs (e.g. Haraway, 1994 [1985]) neglect the fact that far from being 'always open to modification', the cyborgian 'blurring of human and non-human' has been intimately linked with battle simulations and military conflict. The cyborg, in short, is 'a creature of the battlefield' (Galison, 1994: 261). If Simmel conceptualized technology in terms of a human-driven transcendence of our current boundaries and limitations, perhaps cyber-technologies have broken that link and confront people as intransigent social forms that have become divorced from their founding desires.

Such pessimistic evaluations of cyber-technologies may, however, be based as much on speculation as they are on reliable research. As Jordan (1999) argues, there is a strong case for concluding that both 'doom slayer' and utopian commentators on cyborgs and cyberspace construct their speculations around 'the twin fantasies of heaven and hell', and rely for their speculations on the unrealistic belief that everything can be made of, harnessed to, or turned into, information, machines or communication systems. Those who focused exclusively on the body as a source of technology may provide a one-sidedly optimistic view of human agency, but those whose narratives are dominated by a view of the body as a location offer us an equally partial view of the present situation. There is now, indeed, a large amount of research suggesting that technologies such as the Internet tend to complement rather than transform social relationships, and result not in revolution but in opportunities for certain types of innovation and change (Mackenzie and Wajcman, 1999; DiMaggio et al., 2001). Doom and utopian narratives are both considered examples of naïve, anachronistic speculation. To get a more realistic assessment of how the developments we are concerned with in this chapter are affecting people at the present time, and to shift emphasis from the preference some have for the 'mythology' over the sociology of cyberspace (Robins, 1995: 153), it is worth turning to studies that are at least informed by research into the actual uses to which such technologies have been put.

The Positioning of Technologized Bodies

Far from being a passive location on which the technological designs of political and informational elites are imprinted, research suggests that embodied subjects engage with the parameters, opportunities and constraints associated with technologies in ways which actively attach them to, or distance them from, societal structures. This does not mean that technologies are infinitely flexible in the social uses to which they can be put, but it does imply that these forces and artefacts are usually possessed of at least a limited range of 'affordances' that provide users with options as to how they are applied to the social and natural world (Gibson, 1979; Pels et al., 2002: 9).

In this context it is worth returning to Simmel's argument that humans attempt to transcend the *current* boundaries of their flesh, but with one eye on their existing projects and concerns, as it remains highly relevant to an exploration of already existing developments in cyber-technology. We can identify three main ways in which people are using this technology in attempting to alter the current constraints associated with particular forms of physical being and of the social milieu in which they live. These involve *physical substitution* (and, as such, resonate strongly with previous restorative developments in prostheses), and *physical extension/enhancement* (oriented towards supplementing and increasing the capacities and opportunities afforded by our bodies and

environment), but I want to focus mostly in what follows on how technology has been used to effect *communal/political transformation* (concerned with constructing new forms of community which are sometimes
seen as radically transformative).

Substituting the body

The physically substitutive effects of technology have already been noted
in the case of artificial limbs – and apply equally to the increasing range
of organ transplants to have taken place in recent decades – but Mike
Featherstone (1995) has been one of the few to explore their potentially
widespread effects in the case of contemporary cyber-technologies. For
those with serious mobility problems, machines have already been developed to carry out chores (such as vacuuming), while remote control
devices enable the temperature and lighting of the domestic environment
to be altered. Email, chat rooms and other forms of electronically mediated communication can help reduce the social impact of physical disabilities, while also enabling individuals to avoid those social stigmas that
can damage an individual's chances of being treated as an equal in situations of physical co-presence. As Featherstone (1995: 612) notes, 'technological modes of interchange' can provide a substitutional corrective to
the body's limitations and 'open up new possibilities for intimacy and self-
expression'. In this respect, it is interesting that Chen and Person's (2002)
research suggests that older users of the Internet were more positive than
non-users concerning their psychological well-being and personality characteristics (though it should be added that this category of web users seem
to be least adequately catered for; Marwick, 1999). This argument about
the new possibilities opened up by the Internet is supported by Sherry
Turkle's (1995: 244) research in which she reports that many users report
that 'the rooms and mazes on MUDS [multi-user dungeons] are safer than
city streets, virtual sex is safer than sex anywhere, MUD friendships are
more intense than real ones, and when things don't work you can always
leave.'[4] Such conclusions suggest that the risks and vulnerabilities that
characterize physical space, and which are often felt keenly in situations
of physical co-presence (Goffman, 1983), can be reduced through the
substitutional use of this technology even in the areas of sex and eroticism
(Springer, 1996). People can use technology in such ways in order to enter
into, and feel part of, a version of the social fabric.

In using technology to restore previous bodily capacities and the options
that social environments may once have offered, but now no longer seem to,
there is a sense in which the substitutive effects of this resource also extend
and enhance the physical body and its environment. These supplementary
uses of technology have long been significant in terms of how people are
positioned within society, but they have become increasingly prominent in
recent decades with the development of cyber-technologies.

Extending/enhancing the body

Science fiction films and cyberpunk literature may revel in exploring how the body can be enhanced through spectacular human–machine combinations, but technology has long allowed people to extend their bodily capacities. Fire, for example, has not only allowed people to transcend the previously encountered limits of their diet, or imposed itself as a force to be harnessed in order for people to function in particular occupations, but has been used in an attempt to reinforce and enhance status inequalities. In sixteenth-century Western Europe, for example, the upper classes engaged in the expensive practice of burning wax candles in order to prolong the hours of light during which they could extend their activities. As Goudsblom (1992: 206) observes, 'Thanks to their lavish use of candles, the upper classes were able to distinguish themselves not only by what they did, but also by when they did it.' Prostheses also came to be developed as extensions to, rather than simply substitutions for, bodily actions. The progression of cyber-technologies, however, has massively accelerated these possibilities.

Cyberspace has often been analysed in terms of the opportunities it provides people for experimenting with their self-identity. Role-playing sites on the Internet, for example, allow people to program their appearance and project a version of the self which is 'inherently theatrical' (Nakamura, 1995: 712). Furthermore, technological and scientific advances in the realms of transplant and cosmetic surgery are also making the body more of a site of alternatives than it ever has previously been in human history. Social norms of beauty, thinness and fitness continue to inform many of these body changes, however, and the pursuit of an appearance indicative of youth, energy and effectiveness, and prized by corporations, continues to exert a powerful influence over the choices of individuals. At the same time, it is clear that individuals use the technological resources available to them to in order to develop their own esteem and sense of self, and to increase their physical capital. This is exemplified by Gayne and McGaughey's (2002) argument that women who change their bodies in line with dominant ideals of beauty frequently achieve a greater sense of power and control over their physical selves and social life, even though they may be reinforcing gendered norms that are disadvantageous to women as a group. The room that people have to develop their identities, despite the existence of strong social norms, is also emphasized by Celia Lury's (1998) argument that cyber-technologies afford to people an opportunity to experiment with various versions of individuality.

Communal/political transformation

One of the most contentious issues surrounding the development and use of cyber-technologies relates to their effect on communities. We have already noted some of the pessimistic diagnoses of those who believe that cyberspace signals the end of embodied moral orders, but research suggests a far more diverse and, in many ways, less certain outcome. Before analysing these findings, however, it is important to remember that technological forces have long been consequential for the development of human community. This is amply illustrated by the collective uses to which fire has been put.

Fire has historically been used as a focal point for human gatherings, during which communal priorities have been decided and chiefs elected (Goudsblom, 1992). It has additionally served as a conduit of interaction which can operate across the social classes. The safety match (invented in 1852) became the only human artefact so cheap that people would ask complete strangers for one, while the request 'Have you got a light?' continues to initiate interaction among 'communities' of cigarette smokers (Goudsblom, 1992; Hughes, 2003c). As well as creating solidarities, fire has been used by people as a way of distancing themselves from society, and in expressing political protest and alienation from the status quo. As Goudsblom (1992: 208) notes, 'During riots, public buildings – law courts, police stations, tax offices, headquarters of ruling political parties – form a favourite target for arsonists.' The actual damage inflicted during these occasions is usually relatively small, 'but the dramatic impact may be great, since the state's authority has been openly defied and flouted' (ibid.). In each of these cases, fire has been used by people to actively position themselves in relation to a community and, despite the technological distance that exists between them, embodied subjects continue to make creative use of the collective possibilities afforded to them by cyber-technologies.

In contrast to those doom-laden predictions of what mediated communications will do to democracy and morality outlined earlier in this chapter, the Internet has been used by some to positively attach themselves to 'virtual communities'. This notion of virtual community needs some explanation as it signifies a different understanding of a group than that offered by conventional sociological understandings of community. For Rheingold (1993: 5), virtual communities are 'social aggregations that emerge from the Net when enough people carry on those public discussions long enough, with sufficient human feeling, to form webs of personal relationships in cyberspace'. Their role is seen as vital to the maintenance and restoration of collectivities at a time when the 'lifeworld' appears to be under so much pressure from commercial enterprises (Rheingold, 1993; Wilbur, 1997). These communities have, since the 1980s, been constituted by the creation of 'virtual places' where people could 'meet' and see representations of themselves. 'Habitat', for example, was produced by Lucasfilm and Quantum Computer Services and became by 1987 'the world's first electronic urban environment' (Ostwald, 1997: 670). Habitat supported tens of thousands of users, yet various chat rooms and gaming rooms now provide basic and often much more sophisticated opportunities to interact and exchange views in cyberspace. These arenas have been celebrated as 'providing a space and form for a new experience of community' which is freed from the limitations of bodily co-presence 'multiple, liberating, equalising and thus providing a richer experience of together-ness' (Willson, 1997: 655; see also Jones, 1995; Baym, 1995).

Despite the utopian elements to such thinking, the possibility that cyberspace may possess the capacity to enhance individual life via incorpo-ration into a community is supported by a considerable amount of evidence. Research conducted into collective interactions on the Internet suggests that a sense of individual transcendence and strong group norms can develop within this environment. Multi-user Dungeons (MUDs), for example, pro-vide individuals with opportunities for dwelling in virtual communities, and participating in fantasy games in which some of the limitations associated with the physiognomic self are left behind. Heather Bromberg's (1996: 150) research into MUDs reported that ordinary bodily needs and responses were forgotten for a while as participants lost track of time, forgot to eat, became euphoric, and expanded their sense of self through immersion in a virtual community. Wyatt et al. (2002: 62, 68, 77) provide some possible reasons for this sense of transcendence in their findings that virtual interactions are experienced as being at least as real as face-to-face interactions, as regulated strongly by group norms, and as accentuating 'feelings of group belonging-ness and identification'. Bakardjieva (2003: 291–2) continues in this vein by referring to the 'immobile socialization' facilitated by the Internet, a social-ization of private experience leading to the 'invention of new forms of inter-subjectivity and social organization online'. The depth of feeling that can be associated with being part of a virtual community is further illustrated by the sense of pain, loss and grief that has been expressed by individuals on receiving news that someone attached to a group they participated in, but had never met in the flesh, had died (Argyle, 1996). In short, a certain form of group participation can sometimes be *enhanced* by computer-mediated communications (Sproull and Kiesler, 1986, 1993), a conclusion supported by Slater's (2002: 242) study of Internet groups which suggests that the maintenance of a normative order 'between anonymous and unregulated persons' took precedence over transactional concerns.

If cyberspace provides an arena in which people can attach themselves to communities, it has also been identified as a resource through which it is possible to achieve a degree of collective political transformation. This is clear in those writings associated with cyberfeminism, a movement which emerged initially in order to challenge the male domination of the new 'vir-tual' frontier of cyberspace (Kemper, 2002). Springer (1991), for example, associates cyberspace with the valuable female experience of omnipotence, an experience which may carry over into political activity on-line or off-line, while Plant (1993) focuses on its potential to provide women with a space in which their physicality will no longer be associated with inequality and oppression. Identities can be fluid, language can flow without constraint, and women's potentialities can be realized. These and other cyberfeminists have celebrated the potential afforded by the Internet, and other forms of virtual space, to liberate women from the binary oppositions that are incorporated within modern institutions and to enable them to think, communicate and act outside of the constraints of male-dominated physical space. Research into online learning experiences, for example, suggests that women develop a confidence in themselves and their interactions which is absent when they are subjected to the male visual scrutiny that usually accompanies the student environment (Sullivan, 2002). Email interaction has also been found to neutralize gender strategies that are found in face-to-face student situations (Michaelson and Pohl, 2001). Similarly, research on women's fat discussion groups suggests that electronic space can provide a communal 'comfort zone' in which women can meet similar others in an environment that is more free and welcoming than can be found elsewhere. These women experienced a sense of belonging that was often denied them in social contexts of physical co-presence (Munt, 2001: 176–8). As Gerard (2002) summarizes, women can and have used the web to influence political arenas, to support one another's careers, and to sabotage misogynist language and stereotypes.

Normative groups may emerge in cyberspace, and provide some individuals with genuine opportunities for discussion and for enhancing their identity and binding together with others through participation in fantasy games, a fans' web site, or a political organization. If nations can be analysed as 'imagined communities' (Anderson, 1991), then it does not seem unreasonable to conclude that cyberspace may bring into existence a differently imagined collectivity (Jordan, 1999: 6; Mitra, 2000). The normative basis of virtual groups has been illustrated further in cases of inter-group clashes in which individuals go to considerable lengths to defend their virtual spaces (e.g. Jordan, 1999: 87–99). That individuals are prepared not only to establish regular patterns of group-based communication, but to defend them against external incursion and threat, supports the idea that cyberspace can facilitate at least a partial emotional transcendence of the self.

These virtual groups clearly do not fulfil all the conditions of mutual responsibility and caring valued by communitarians, however, and there is something to be said for the criticism that genuine communities consist of more than a collection of individuals spread across different time zones tapping on their keyboards (Snyder, 1996; Mitra, 2000). It is also important to recognize some of the other limitations of these virtual groups. The design of the virtual spaces in which they meet sometimes incorporate within them 'gender scripts' which encourage male and discourage female participation (Rommes et al., 2001). Furthermore, these groups not only often focus on single issues – based on what one critic has referred to as 'purveyors of pornography, addicts of western pop music and culture, right-wing extremists, lunatics who go on about aliens, [and] paedophiles' (Sardar, 1996) – but involve a limited bodily involvement which can restrict the extent to which the individual is transformed through their involvement with a group. In this respect, participants in virtual chat, gaming, discussion and even cyber-sex have reported a heightened sense of loneliness when they switch off their computer and return to life off-line. This lack of physical co-presence and full sensory involvement also heightens the possibilities of fraud in on-line relationships. A frequently cited example involves the case of 'Julie', a middle-aged male psychiatrist who posed as a disabled woman offering 'life-transforming' advice to other women on the net. Julie was eventually tracked down by one of her admirers and the case of 'fraudulent' identity was greeted by responses ranging from 'humorous resignation' to 'blind rage'. Worst affected were those who had shared their innermost secrets with Julie, including one woman who said that she felt 'raped' by the experience (Stone, 1992). Far greater damage has been done to those children and teenagers lured into meeting paedophiles who passed themselves off as contemporaries in chat rooms. The cases of physical abuse following these meetings were implicated in the decision taken by Microsoft to close their chat rooms in 2003.

If individuals are able to attach themselves to virtual groups in cyber-space, individuals also deliberately disrupt interaction and disaffiliate themselves from communities within this milieu. Sproull and Kiesler (1986, 1993) found that participants in virtual interaction were more frequently and more openly angry with each other than they were in situations of physical presence. This is exemplified by Mitra's (2000) analysis of a news group based on Indian culture. Participants may have been well educated and professional, but the site was characterized by abusive and inflammatory remarks. The multiplicity of voices displayed by Indian participants ensured that no grand narrative could dominate – something celebrated by cyber-feminists and others who concentrate on the liberatory possibilities of cyberspace – but the site reflected a 'community' that was 'divisive' and characterized by 'internal contradictions' concerning issues of religion, gender and political affiliation (Mitra, 2000: 678–85). Examples of anti-social, non-normative 'behaviour' have also been reported as characterizing those MUDs specifically created to provide virtual communities. 'Theft', 'assault', 'rape' and 'murder' have all been simulated in virtual habitats such as LambdaMOO (Jordan, 1999). While the consequences of these 'crimes' should not be compared to their physical equivalents (a conflation which is all too common in writings on the subject), Ostwald (1997: 671) raises an interesting question about their status by asking how they would be seen if they provoked shock leading to a deadly heart attack in a real person sitting at their computer screen.

In the context of these examples, it is perhaps easy to discount the communal potentialities of cyberspace (though it is important to note that disrupting a virtual community in cyberspace requires that individuals take the trouble to enter and explore that community in the first place). Before taking that step, however, it is important to note Woolgar's (2002) argument that virtual activities not only sit alongside 'real' activities but can stimulate them. Involvement in virtual communities has been shown to lead to physically co-present meetings between participants (Slater, 2002). Similarly, teleworkers end up travelling more than they did previously because clients want to meet face-to-face (Woolgar, 1998), virtual support networks have been shown to complement and extend physical meetings rather than act as a substitute for them (Nettleton et al., 2002), while email contacts tend to enable people who have physically interacted to keep in touch (Koku et al., 2001). Finally, Internet dating sites provide a prime example of how virtual and physical space can be seen as a continuum. Here, virtual relationships were established with the intention that they may eventually lead to co-present meetings and physical relationships (Hardey, 2002).[5] More research is clearly needed, but it is possible that participation in virtual communities leads, for at least some individuals, to an increased participation in neighbourhood, regional, national and even international groups. Perhaps it is time to stop thinking about cyberspace and physical space as opposites and pay more attention to how they interact and constitute extensions of each other. From this perspective, we might begin to redefine cyberspace as a set of media technologies used by people within specific social contexts (Slater, 2002: 240; see also Burrows and Nettleton, 2002).

Conclusion

Technological forces have, at least since the domestication of fire, exerted a major impact on the bodies and environments of people. In using technology to transform their environment, humans began to change themselves and their physical capacities, accomplishing what Simmel has referred to as a practically grounded yet imaginative breaking of the currently encountered, specific limitations of their bodies and environment. The current status of cyber-technologies, however, has been viewed by many as exerting an unprecedented impact on the bodies of those subject to them, robbing them of their creativity and productive significance for society. In the case of cyborgs, plastic surgery and genetic engineering, together with the growing number of ways in which machines can be harnessed to the flesh, seem sometimes to be leading to an ever-deeper incorporation of social norms and economic imperatives into the bodies of those subject to them. In a related vein, cyberspace has been viewed as a new frontier ocer which political and economic elites have sought to extend their control, and this is reflected in the most prominent conflicts over its format and use. From the resources devoted to tracking down cyberhackers, to the free-flowing character of information on the Internet that makes censorship so difficult, to the concerns of the FBI that 'uncrackable encryption' will provide unprecedented opportunities for criminals and terrorists, contemporary debates about virtual communication illustrate the importance of this technology for the maintenance of contemporary social systems (Jordan, 1999). We should not be surprised by the degree of control that appears to be associated with this technology, especially in the wake of the security concerns that have dominated debate post-September 11th.

Some people spend unprecedented amounts of time in front of computer screens, or involved in other forms of cyberspace, but it would be inaccurate to describe the body as a passive location for this technology. Individuals and groups make their own uses of cyberspace, extending local communities into virtual spaces and constructing new networks of communication unhindered by the constraints of physical co-presence. Even the most apparently intrusive and imposed uses of cybertechnology – such as to be found in the case of CCTV surveillance cameras – are often stimulated by demand from those being observed keen to improve their safety (e.g. tenants on council estates) (McGrail, 2002). It is clear that people are using these technologies to respond and actively position themselves in relation to the social structures that surround them. Avoiding such technology completely, however, is an altogether different issue. The pervasiveness of computer-mediated communication at work and in the leisure sphere, for example, has led some to argue that the body 'must become a cyborg to retain its presence in the world, resituated in technological space and refigured in technological transfers' (Bukatman, 1993: 247).

It is the scope and future potential of such developments that lie behind the dreams and nightmares of cyberspace and cyberbodies that we have examined in this chapter. If the boundaries between the masculine and the feminine, and the human and animal, worried people in ages gone by (Laqueur, 1990; Yamamoto, 2000), it is that between people and machines which dominates the contemporary imagination. Such actions as talking to machines, reconstructing our bodies via prosthetic and genomic technologies, spending increased amounts of time speaking into mobile phones and exploring the Internet, mingle 'our humanity with not-so-mute, active, performative objects in a way which we find equally fascinating as disconcerting' (Pels et al., 2002: 1).

Despite the fact that cyber-technologies remain at a relatively early stage of their development, we can make several tentative conclusions which alert us to their current trajectory while also warning us against discounting the continued significance of the body. First, as the history of cybernetics shows us, these technologies are not politically neutral but are likely to be driven by military, economic and normative traditions that are sometimes of questionable value to flesh-and-blood humanity as a whole. Just as Taylorism sought to reduce social relations and the body itself to 'performance', so too is there the danger that the future development of cyberspace and cyberbodies will be subordinated to such imperatives (Rabinbach, 1990: 183; Galison, 1994). To take but one example, research findings suggest that workplace email is experienced 'as a formal space of communication where personal accountability is constantly at issue' rather than something that individuals have much control over (Brown and Lightfoot, 2002: 229). In the case of technological enhancements of the body, it is Western ideals of physical perfection and attractiveness which dominate the type of plastic surgery and cosmetic procedures available to, and requested by, people. The possibility of adopting an active orientation towards such technology is further limited by social inequalities. Even a simple operation such as laser surgery to restore 20/20 vision can cost as much as £1,000 per eye. As sociologists we should not, perhaps, be surprised by this situation. If we view specific technologies and material designs as incorporating within them particular choices, we can see how their very operation articulates a politics which can materially 'act back' on their users (Akrich, 1992; Pels et al., 2002).

Second, it is important to note that some of the most influential narratives associated with cyber-technologies indulge themselves in a very old Cartesian trick of 'forgetting about the body' (Burkitt, 1999; Horner, 2001: 79) As Stone (1992) argues, this has particularly oppressive consequences for those whose aims and desires are omitted from the design of these technologies. Technology may have extended enormously human potential, but we should not mistake the capacity for representing informational space, and storing and sorting through masses of information, with the human needs, emotions, and intentional actions that provide data with meaning (Nguyen and Alexander, 1996). As the values which inform these needs, emotions and actions vary between individuals and groups, it is important to ask whose interests are represented in the management and operation of such technology. In the case of virtual communities, it is important to remember that collectivity 'originates in, and must return to, the physical. No refigured virtual body, no matter how beautiful, will slow the death of a cyberpunk with AIDS. Even in the age of the technosocial subject, life is lived through bodies' (Stone, 1992: 525).

Third, and relatedly, despite all the talk about the transcendence of the human, the incorporation of machines *into* the body has actually proven incredibly difficult to accomplish successfully. Cyberspace may have altered the technological contexts in which millions of people work, while genetic and transplant surgery has made spectacular gains, but the body retains a tendency to reject foreign matter. In this respect, it is instructive to note that after nearly a century of searching unsuccessfully for the 'perfect biocompatible cosmetic prosthetic' practitioners have returned to the human body itself as the source as well as the object of reconstruction (Haiken, 2002). The boundaries between the human organism and machinery may have weakened, but the question of whether there will ever be a complete 'coupling' of the two remains unanswered.

The body may continue to exert its productive role not only in relation to the development of technology, but also in relation to its limitations. This emphasis on the facticity and consequentiality of the body is complemented by Winston's (1998) strong scepticism concerning the transformative potential of the Internet, and by a growing consensus that the Internet tends to complement rather than displace existing patterns of behaviour (DiMaggio et al., 2001).

Fourth, and finally, while not confusing the fiction of cybertechnology with the sociology of the subject, it is possible to say something about the fantasies and nightmare visions that all too frequently accompany writings on cybertechnology. In a capitalist system built on 'mechanical foundations' which seems increasingly to ignore considerations of human frailty (Weber, 1991 [1904–5]: 181–2), the futuristic promise of cyberbodies and cyberspace may be interpreted as providing some sort of ontological comfort to individuals confronting expectations of heightened performance and productivity. Stelarc (1998: 561), for example, argues that machines provide us with the opportunity to liberate ourselves from bodies which malfunction, fatigue, become diseased, degenerate and die. The need for us to 'shed' our 'skin' is made all the more urgent as the body 'cannot cope with the quantity, complexity and quality of information it has accumulated; it is intimidated by the precision, speed and power of technology and it is biologically ill-equipped to cope' with life in the computer age (ibid.). This may be comforting for some but, as Dr Richard Restak (a professor of neurology) argues, images of mind–machine hybrids can be viewed not only as unrealistic but as 'pathological', reflecting an extreme alienation from and self-hatred of the body (Dery, 1996: 582). In contrast to Simmel's view that technology could enable humans to transcend the specific boundaries posed by their bodies in order to enhance the environment available to them, Stelarc is concerned to jettison the body in order to *cope* with and *survive* within an increasingly alien informational milieu. Similarly, in contrast to those non-Western cultures which seek to enhance human embodiment by unifying the powers of the mind and body, Western culture has sought to manage these circumstances by seeking a transcendental liberation from the body through a corporeal dissolution into machinery (Sardar, 1996: 749). As Durkheim (1977 [1938]: 337) argued, the consequences of such attempts to remove people from an essential part of their bodily being involve a 'denaturing' and a 'truncating' of humanity that should deeply concern us; a concern that is justifiably reflected in recent body theories even if they portray the body as too passive in its relationship with the wider environment.

Notes

1 Interestingly, images of fire live on in computer technology through the use of such terms as 'firewires' (means of interlinking computers to other machines in order to facilitate high speed data transmission) and 'firewalls' (security systems).

2 In contrast to previous historical images of the body as clay, as a clockwork mechanism, and as an engine, Weiner (1948b, 1948a: 15) viewed the body as an electronic communications network. What united humans and automatic machines, and meant that they could be viewed in the same way, was that they operated on the basis of information feedback and possessed the capacity to adjust future conduct on the basis of past performance.

3 A merging which perhaps culminated with Japanese suicide bombers during the Second World War.

4 The pleasures of cybersex (presently conducted mostly via erotic exchanges in chat rooms) seem to have substantial appeal. An estimated 50,000 people a day engaged in cybersex in the early 1990s (Kane, 1994: 21), even though they faced the obvious problem of 'not being able to type quickly enough especially with one hand' (Nguyen and Alexander, 1996: 116–17).

5 In contrast to this emphasis on the socially stimulating effects of virtual communities, Putnam (2000) argues that Internet users are no different to non-users on measures of civic engagement. However, Puttnam also argues that this situation may change among future users.

9
Conclusion

Social studies of the body have made enormous strides since the 1980s, but there is a general sense that the subject has reached something of an impasse in recent years. In addressing itself to this situation, this book has focused on four major aims designed to provide a basis for theoretical and substantive advancement in the area. First, it examined the enigmatic nature of embodiment in social theory by analysing the contested character of the concept and detailing how the body came to be attached to diverse and incommensurate agendas. These agendas not only produced widely different definitions of 'the body', but tended ultimately to submerge any sense of the materiality of embodiment beneath other considerations. Instead of approaching the body as an independent variable, forged through the interrelation of social and natural processes in the course of evolution and that needed to be treated as a sociologically significant phenomenon in its own right, theorists of consumer culture, feminists, Foucauldian analysts of governmentality, and others, dealt with embodiment as a dependent issue which became meaningful only in relation to their pre-existing intellectual and political priorities. While any sociological treatment of the body may justifiably involve a focus on structures at the temporary expense of the body, these studies all too often failed to return to the materiality and socially generative properties of the body. In these circumstances, it is not surprising that the organic facticity of the body appeared only briefly in focus, before fading in relation to other issues.

These radically diverse agendas towards the body were associated with equally disparate theoretical approaches towards embodiment, and the second aim of this study has been to provide a critical overview of the most important of these contributions. Social constructionist theories of governmentality, action-oriented and phenomenologically informed writings on the 'lived body', and structuration theories of the body as simultaneously constituting and constituted, have been enormously influential and have done much to set the parameters of this area. They have also yielded key insights that have advanced our understanding of the body, highlighting respectively how the body has been treated as an object to be managed and distributed, how the body is our sensory vehicle of being-in and engaging with the world, and how the body is deeply implicated in, and moulded by, the reproduction of social and sexual structures. Each of these approaches, furthermore, has expressed deeply rooted concerns about the fate of the body's generative and creative capacities in the current era.

The accomplishments of these approaches have been considerable. To establish a new field of studies – which has not only produced a wealth of theoretical publications, and a growing number of empirical works, but has had an important general impact in the humanities and social sciences – is a major achievement. At the same time, it is necessary to recognize that the incompatibility of these structuralist, phenomenological and structuration theories (which view the body as an object, a subject, and as a medium and outcome of structures), and their inability to agree on even the most basic definitions of their subject matter, has contributed towards a field that may have a recognizable identity yet that is possessed of little coherence. Furthermore, the only aspect of analysis these approaches do seem to converge around, a sense that the contemporary age has subjugated our embodied potentialities, is associated with a view of the body bereft of capacities to create, resist or generate change in the contemporary era of rational capitalism.

In this context, the third aim of this study has been to consolidate the insights yielded by, but also to go beyond, these existing approaches, by explicating and developing a view of the body as a *multi-dimensional medium for the constitution of society*. The writings of Marx, Durkheim and Simmel differ on all manner of grounds, but they each contain within them and converge around a hitherto neglected appreciation of the body as a source of society, as a location for the structures of society, and as a means through which individuals interact with, and are positioned within, society. Marx, Durkheim and Simmel may focus respectively on the body's relationship with economic and technological structures, with cultural structures, and with social forms, but they each invest the body with properties possessed of the capacity to generate, and to be receptive to, structural aspects of society. They also view the body as a central means by which the outcomes of individual interaction with societal structures are mediated. Finally, they anticipate the concerns of recent theories about the subjugation of the body's creative capacities without, however, erasing embodied agency from their general conception of the individual.

This view of the body as a multi-dimensional medium for the constitution of society is based on a *homo duplex* model of the body and this assists us in stabilizing what we mean by the body. It also has the advantage of incorporating within it the key insights of existing dominant approaches in the field, while containing these within a framework which eschews the theoretical excesses and reductionisms of social contructionism, voluntaristic phenomenology and structuration theory. It is able to do this, I suggested, because it is predicated upon a form of corporeal realism. As presented in this study, the approach of Marx, Durkheim and Simmel is corporeal because it puts the body at the centre of its concern with social action and structures. Social action is embodied, and must be recognized as such, while the effects of social structures can be seen as a result of how they condition and shape embodied subjects. This approach remains realist, however, in that it recognizes a distinction between embodied action and social structures. It does this by attributing bodies with their own ontology, irreducible to the social, by treating 'society' as an emergent level of reality, and by acknowledging the importance of examining their interaction over time. It is this interaction that results in the body also being a *means* through which embodied subjects are positioned within and oriented towards their social milieu.

Another useful characteristic of the corporeal realism contained within this convergence is that Marx, Durkheim and Simmel each propose critical grounds on which to assess the outcomes of the interaction between embodied subjects and societal structures. These grounds are diverse. It is their concern to critically evaluate how the body positions people within society that they converge around, *not* the precise criteria employed to undertake this evaluation. Nevertheless, they collectively provide us with a suggestive basis on which to examine the effects that rationalized capitalist society is exerting on the embodied potentialities of humans. Marx's work is predominantly concerned with how the social inequalities and oppressions surrounding the economic system have stunted embodied human potential. Durkheim's writings are interested in how participation within a community could enable individuals to transcend the egoistic pole of their *homo duplex* nature, and become moral beings possessed of socially enhanced capacities. Simmel's analysis is of the development of individuality and he was acutely conscious of the ambivalent effects that social forms had on the flourishing of personality.

The point of outlining this classical convergence around a form of corporeal realism was not to engage in an exclusively theoretical exercise. Instead, it was related to the fourth aim of this study, to provide a framework in which it was possible to undertake a series of substantively informed analyses of the body. It has been a common complaint in the sociology of the body in recent years that the area is over-theorized and lacking in empirical studies. My diagnosis is different, as I would suggest that the field of body studies has been suffering *not* from a surfeit, but from a *lack of theories adequate to the task of facilitating substantive studies*. The basic parameters of corporeal realism can be employed to rectify this situation. They allow us to build on a view of the body as a simultaneously biological and social phenomena, that successively constructs and is partly constructed by society (Shilling, 1993, 2003), by encouraging analysis of the relationship between embodied subjects and social structures. It is in the context of this aim that the second half of this book was devoted to a series of substantive studies which examined the relationship between embodied subjects and the structural features of the economy, culture, sociability and technology. Coverage of issues was deliberately wide and my intent was to demonstrate the utility of the approach adopted in this study only in the most general of terms. There remains much work to be done in explicating the nature/society interface before we can understand fully the body's productive capacities. There is also a need for more specific case-studies which follow a *particular* event or bodily phenomena over time in order to trace precisely how the creative capacities of embodied subjects interact with societal structures in order to produce particular outcomes that set the scene for subsequent interactions (e.g. Williams, 1999). Nevertheless, these substantively informed chapters provide a background against which it is possible to demonstrate the utility of this corporeal realist view of the body as a multi-dimensional medium for the constitution of society. In particular, they enabled me to focus in the relevant section on *structural* forces without losing sight elsewhere in the chapter of the body's socially generative properties. They also allowed me to examine in more detail the concerns of those recent influential body theories which imply that modern rational society has subjugated and erased the creative and generative capacities of the embodied subject.

Subjugated Bodies?

My discussions of work, sport, music, sociability and technology raised a number of questions about the fate of embodied subjects in the current era. Social constructionist theories of the ordered body, Leder's phenomenological theory of the absent body, and Bourdieu's conception of *habitus* suggest that the creative capacities of embodied subjects have been deeply affected by the rationalized structures of modern society (concerns about this loss of creativity are expressed in slightly different ways by Giddens and Grosz). From this perspective, embodied action and experience are no longer under the control of the individual subject, but have been controlled and appropriated by structures of governmentality, the demands of the instrumentalist, goal-oriented activities associated with contemporary work and leisure, and the constraints of social class.

It is certainly possible to identify rationalization processes which have affected the bodies of many over recent decades. The increasing scope of emotion work has incorporated more bodily capacities into the rational structures of waged labour, and subjected them to the monitoring involved in the employer–employee relationship. The structures of work also continue to be associated with increasingly pressurized schedules designed to maximize productivity. These persist not only in traditional factory contexts, but in the new 'Fordist' workplaces of tele-sales and call centres, and also resonate outside of the conventional sphere of waged labour. The competitive character of the sporting sphere, for example, searches out athletic talent at ever younger ages in its search for maximum performativity, and subjects even children's bodies to rigorous training regimes designed to push forward the boundaries of achievement. The ubiquity of the sporting body to government, commerce and television has made the dominant practices associated with this sphere more prone to treat the body as a machine than any other sector of society (with the possible exception of medicine). Physical training and fitness focus on hard work (embodied, literally, within the gruelling 'work-out'), while contemporary discourses on health appear have taken to their heart exercise as *work* rather than exercise as well-being. In contrast to the Taoist principle of *Wu Wei* (acting in harmony with nature), incorporated into such activities as Tai Chi Chuan, dominant Western sports equate exercise with speed, with exhaustion, with competitive outcomes, and with the *conquering* of nature.

Music has also undergone a process of rationalization which can be illustrated in the sphere of exercise, with companies specializing in producing compact discs organized around a beats-per-minute formula designed to facilitate the repetitive routines that govern the aerobics and fitness studio. More generally, the production of popular musical 'stars' now follows a rationalized formula in which the age, sex appeal, and branding potential of the performer take precedence over their capacity to sing or play a musical instrument. It is particularly striking how music has become a key resource for business, helping to establish a certain pace of work, to attract certain demographic groups into shops, and to enhance sales. Given the effects of music on behaviour – effects which sometimes appear to operate at an unconscious level – it is not surprising that critics have expressed deep concern about this development.

These rationalizing developments in the spheres of work, sport and music have, not surprisingly, restricted the scope of and increased the pressures associated with non-rational spheres of life such as sociability. Fast food has replaced the feast, and 'refuelling' has replaced socializing, as a typical mode of consumption in the West. The 'family' meal may persist within substantial numbers of households, but even here it may be based around the television and snatched briefly before other, more time-demanding, activities take precedence. Advances in cyber-technologies also reflect the influence and increasing pervasiveness of rationalization on the embodied subject. Technological and medical interventions have subjected the body to an unprecedented level of invasion and have provided societal structures at least with the theoretical possibility of altering aspects of the body in line with wider governmental norms. The extended reach of societal structures is also illustrated in the case of those electronically mediated communications which have enabled billions of dollars to be transferred across the world in a split second. The global flow of capital has never happened so quickly.

These examples can be used to support the claims of those who believe that the body has become a location for the structural properties of society, or has become tied into a circuit of reproduction in which individuals draw on and reproduce the rationalized rules and resources made available to them in society. If the methodological implications of contemporary body theories do not allow us to account for interaction between embodied subjects and structures over time, the above summaries demonstrate that it is possible to garner significant evidence in support of their pessimistic conclusions. The substantively informed analyses of this study do not, however, bear out their concerns about a uniform subjugation and loss of the creative and generative capacities of the body. Instead, the outcomes of the interaction between embodied subjects and societal structures we have examined provide evidence of a considerably more varied picture.

To continue with the above examples, emotion work does not just represent a demand to manage rationally some of the sensual capacities of the body, it is also evidence of how the potentialities of embodied subjects have come to inform the contents of work. This is apparent in one of the more recent manifestations of emotion work to have become popularized within the corporate world, the demand for 'emotional intelligence' to be deployed within the workplace. Similarly, the institutional sphere of competitive sports may have exerted a constraining effect on physical creativity, but challenges to, changes within, and the proliferation of forms of exercise *outside* of this sphere continue to provide evidence of the creativity and vitality of the physically active human body. It also needs to be remembered that the levels of relative physical inactivity that characterize much human behaviour in the West continue to reveal the limited reach of organized sports. Many embodied subjects take the active decision to position themselves outside the realm of active sports and to eschew the option of treating the body like a project. The relationship between sociability and food also seems to have endured as a result of the agentic actions of embodied subjects. 'Eating communities' are not as significant as they were in the medieval era, but cultural values continue to inform people's eating preferences and are linked closely to the role food still has in generating and consolidating social relationships outside of the rationalized environs of the workplace. In the case of music, commercially packaged, formulaic records may dominate the mainstream popular music charts, but there is continued evidence of the ability of younger generations to produce and stimulate demand for sounds that challenge, and frequently offend, established tastes. Such developments influence established forms of music and provide a stimulus to creativity that outlasts its own lifespan. Technological advances have also been used by embodied subjects to pursue their own goals, helping individuals to minimize the functional consequences of physical disabilities, and have allowed many people to supplement and extend their capacities. Furthermore, the frailties and constraints of the body continue to steer and limit the development of cyber-technologies in the contemporary era. While the increased rationalization and scope of major economic, cultural and social structures may have shaped and constrained embodied subjects in all manner of ways, this has not prevented the body from continuing to exert a generative effect on society.

Critical Bodies

One of the biggest controversies in the field of body studies, and in social thought more generally, has concerned the issue of the criteria used to evaluate the effect of social relations and structures on human beings. Those who wish to make judgements about the damaging effects of particular economic or cultural structures face the issue of having to invest humans with a particular nature or character; a step which requires a willingness to make significantly trans-historical and cross-cultural statements about the bodily properties that people share and to admit that there might be something essential about human beings that has only changed very slowly over the *longue durée* of evolution. In contrast, those who insist upon the historical and cultural variability of the human condition face the problem of finding any firm grounds on which to criticize power relations or customs they perceive to be damaging to or limiting of people's capacities. This debate has a long philosophical heritage, but became crystallized for modern social science as a result of Marx's concern to recognize the socially collective and variable determination of human being, *and* to identify a human nature that gave rise to a bodily potentiality that could only be realized through economic transformation (Geras, 1983; McLellan, 1985).

The issue addressed by Marx goes to the centre of what is perhaps the most intractable problem facing body studies. This is manifest in the work of Judith Butler, for example, who portrays the 'heterosexual matrix' as damaging to the expressivity and capacities of women. In denying the material facticity of the human body, however, Butler is left without grounds (other than her own cultural preferences) on which to identify the damaging effects of this matrix and those practices with which it is associated. It is this very problem that has informed Bryan Turner's (1993, 2003) theory of human rights, based as it is upon a recognition of the universal frailty of the body (see also Turner and Rojek, 2001). An understanding that we are all subject to illness and pain, disease and ultimately death allows us to realize the inevitability of interdependency as a key part of the human condition and can provide a basis, he suggests, for evaluating the adequacy of political and institutional arrangements (Turner, 1993).

Instead of focusing exclusively and one-sidedly on the *frailties* of the body, however, we saw in Chapter 2 how Marx, Durkheim and Simmel each developed a stratified model of human embodiment which not only explored those biological needs or emotional dispositions that needed to be fulfilled and exercised for humans to survive, but also those productive capacities that enable people to *partly* transcend their biological nature and forge relationships and structures that help them become more than they are. It was this recognition that humans could transcend the biological conditions of their existence that informed the ethical criteria these classical theorists used to evaluate the relationship between embodied subjects and the structural properties of modern society. The substantive chapters in this study demonstrate that these criteria (concerned with inequality/oppression, community, and individuality) continue to be relevant to assessing the fate of the body in the current era.

Inequality, oppression and the body

Issues concerning inequality and oppression have long been integral to sociological discussions of waged labour, and are prominent in even the briefest comparison of 'Fordist' factory-based production methods, so-called 'post-Fordist' modes of work, and the various forms of body work examined in Chapter 4. Financial inequalities in earnings remain, and have frequently been exacerbated in an age when informational work is increasingly valued over manual work, while it also appears that there may have been an increase in health inequalities stemming from those whose work involves having to respond emotionally to the demands of others. As the boundaries between waged labour and body work have weakened for many, more of the embodied subject becomes vulnerable to the pressures, strains and inequalities of the workplace. These outcomes continue to highlight the stratified, difficult character of work in the contemporary era, yet it is also important to recognize the legislative, political and other improvements that have taken place since the early decades of industrialization and which have at least reduced the scope (for indigenous if not always for immigrant workers) in the affluent West of the ruthless exploitation and degradation chronicled by Marx and Engels.

Sport is a form of employment for many elite competitors (albeit one which is differentially available to participants as a result of forms of discrimination based on gender, ethnicity and other variables), and its training regimes and competitive forms frequently mirror the structures of work in other ways. Bodies are placed under huge strain in attempting to maximize their efficiency, and physical breakdown is a frequent result of training regimes. Indeed, the lists of injuries that athletes and others have suffered in recent decades would seem to warrant a study of 'The condition of the athletic class' in the twenty-first century that would complement at least certain aspects of Engels's investigations into the conditions of the working class in the nineteenth century.

The relationship between eating and sociability may not have been eradicated in the contemporary era, but gender inequalities continue to be evident in these activities. Women have traditionally had less access to food than men, but more responsibility when it comes to preparing it for consumption. Current changes in household and labour market structure may be in the process of altering this situation, but evidence suggests that the relationship between food and sociability continues to be more problematic for many women than it is for most men. Ideal body images have become increasingly difficult to attain for both sexes, but surveys still confirm while men are expected to develop a muscular, well-honed body, women are pressured to conform to standards of slimness. Within a consumer culture that emphasizes hedonistic enjoyment, yet is surrounded by norms that expect women to achieve a trim and taut body, it is no wonder that feminist analysts have drawn a link between eating disorders and women's *general* relationship with food.

Music has become an increasingly important resource for business and commerce, yet musicians usually struggle economically. However, the cultural meanings associated with music continue to provide a means through which social groups have sought to acquire and express distinction. As Bourdieu (1984) notes, the ability to play a musical instrument and the preference for 'classical' over 'popular' music is one of the surest signs of cultural capital, while music has historically entered into inter-generational struggles to define legitimate taste, and political attempts to ban subversive influences on youth. Music has also historically provided a medium in which class, gender and 'racial' relations are expressed and reformulated, at least at an aural level, through rhythm and lyrics in ways which challenge, as well as reflect, wider social inequalities (Shusterman, 1992).

Finally, cyber-technologies have been associated with all manner of literary imaginings of freedom from the body and transcendence from the inequalities and oppressions associated with being an enfleshed subject in society. However, the actual uses of technology have increased the efficiency with which capital circulates, and have increased the intensity of work for many. Fantasies of human–machine couplings may also say something about the thoroughly embodied alienation that people experience in the contemporary West. In the case of technological enhancements of the body, it is Western ideals of physical perfection and attractiveness which dominate the type of plastic surgery and cosmetic procedures available to, and requested by, people. Furthermore, the continuing existence of the 'digital divide' shows that technology remains implicated in the consolidation of social inequalities.

Collectivities and individual bodies

Community and the individual were not opposites for Durkheim, but essential elements in all human societies. Societies could not exist in the long term without the vitalism generated by people meeting together in the context of what they considered to be sacred, while individuals could only remain energized and healthily attached to life by being integrated into a collective group (Durkheim, 1995 [1912]). However, the flexible, changeable character of waged labour in the current era has for many commentators undermined further traditional, *Gemeinschaft*-type communities, reduced the time individuals can devote to cultivating social relationships outside of their waged working lives, and contributed to an increase in what Goffman has referred to as a 'bureaucratisation' of the spirit. At the same time, it is interesting that elements of 'eating communities' have persisted in modern societies and continue to provide a space for the creation of sociable relations and 'secular' and religious rituals that have yet to be absorbed fully into the 'performative logic' of contemporary society. It is also important to note that sporting and musical attachments appear to have become increasingly important for many. Much discussion in the sociology of sport, for example, is devoted to how following a team, or participating in sporting activities, can enable people to transcend the mundane conditions of their working lives by attaching themselves to a collectivity. Such communities may not share all of the characteristics associated with Durkheim's view of moral orders, but it would be a mistake to underestimate their significance in a contemporary era in which so many relationships and contacts with others take place for instrumental reasons. Similarly, despite its commercialized uses, music has also been associated with transcendental experiences. Immersion in inspirational music has long been viewed as a potentially quasi-religious experience which can sometimes help 'knit together' individuals into a social group by stimulating a physiological response which can be directed through ritual action towards support for collectively defined symbols, values and actions.

The most talked about influence on human communities in recent years, however, has been the Internet and other electronically-mediated forms of communication. Visions of the complete destruction of moral collectivities compete with the utopian belief that cyberspace has allowed people to create communities unbound by the constraints of time, space and body. What both these speculations ignore, though, is the increasing research that shows how virtual communications not only sit alongside co-present or traditionally imagined communities, but interact with them. Involvement in virtual communities sometimes increases physically co-present meetings between participants (Slater, 2002), virtual support networks have been shown to complement and extend physical meetings rather than act as a substitute for them (Nettleton et al., 2002), while Internet dating sites provide a prime example of how virtual and physical space can be seen as a continuum (Hardey, 2002).

Individuality, personality and the body

The effects of contemporary trends in the workplace on personality and individuality have been ambivalent. While the significance of emotion work in the contemporary labour market would appear to penalize those who display cynicism and the blasé attitude (outside of those limited spheres in which these attitudes are valued), the manipulation of appearance and feeling within waged-work provides perhaps more reason than ever before to adopt these approaches towards working life. At the same time, the weakening boundary between waged labour and body work has resulted in a situation where paid work frequently draws on an increasing number of human characteristics.

If the effects of work on individuality have been ambivalent, this is also the case when we consider the sphere of sport. While the sporting sphere (especially the elite sporting sphere) does appear to have become ever more rationalized in its treatment of the body, sporting identities are moving away from traditional conceptions of masculinity, femininity, class or race, and towards the cellular and molecular factors that sports scientists associate with sporting capacity (Gilroy, 2000: 36, 47). Analysing the possible future effects of genetic technology, Blake (1996) looks forward to a time when gender may cease to have fixed bodily or sporting boundaries. If ascribed cultural characteristics cease to have the influence they once did in the sporting sphere, however, the overriding emphasis placed on performance hardly seems conducive to the development of varied forms of individuality. These type of developments are not all-pervasive, however, and there has in recent years been a proliferation and growing popularity of those forms of exercise and games that exist outside of the formal sporting sphere, demonstrating that there remain alternative physical avenues for individual expression and activity.

If food used to provide a prime means by which the individual was 'eaten into' by the collectivity, it has now become an important resource through which individuals pursue the project of self-identity (Falk, 1994). The choices, alternatives, risks and sheer quantity of information with which we are now bombarded about the food we buy and eat means that what we place in our mouths, chew, and swallow has become a prime symbol of who we are. Every mouthful we eat, we are told, is a political statement about our preferences, our class, our attitude to the slaughter of animals, and our relationship to societal norms (Heldke, 1992). The food we eat is also likely to shape the forms of sociality we engage in, and is often linked closely to the particular body projects that individuals are involved in.

One of the uses to which music has been put involves the 'sound tracking' of significant events, rituals and activities in people's lives. The beats and rhythms of music provide affordances to individuals which enable them to create a range of personally structured micro-environments and develop particular orientations to the social environment (Gibson, 1979; DeNora, 2000). Modern technology has assisted these possibilities greatly in recent years, with developments such as the Walkman facilitating the individualization of aural environments. I have commented on the rationalization of the musical sphere and this overlaps with the field of sport and exercise in terms of those frenetic beats which are used to encourage people to engage in ostentatious displays of the body as productivity. Even with exercise, however, there is a diversity of music that provides real choices to the individual. The music that generally accompanies classes in eastern forms of exercise such as Yoga or Tai Chi Chuan (focusing as they do on posture, controlled breathing, the relationship between the mind and the body, and the slow, carefully controlled execution of precise movements), for example, is unhurried and often incorporates within its flows natural sounds that are designed to encourage the meditative aspects of exercise.

Cyber-technologies have also provided significant opportunities for people to develop their individualities. Technological and scientific advances in the realms of transplant and cosmetic surgery are making the body more of a site of alternatives than it ever has previously been in human history. The Internet has provided a resource through which people can experiment with and construct their identities. Role-playing sites, for example, allow individuals to program their appearance and project experimental versions of the self (Nakamura, 1995: 712), while personal web pages provide a prime example of how individuals construct their own autobiographies on the Net and narrate their personal pathways through illness and life crises.

Body Research

The field of body studies has become home to an increasingly diverse collection of work in the past two decades, and, more recently, to an increasingly rich assortment of empirical studies. The social study of embodiment will undoubtedly continue to expand in terms of its variety, but I have argued in this study that there is also a case for consolidation in the area. Social theories of the body and substantive studies on the subject need to enter into a sustained dialogue, to take stock of the advances made and the intransigent problems that still confront the area. In this book I have argued that one way of accomplishing this task is to recognize the advances that have already been made by classical writers in viewing the body as a multi-dimensional medium for the constitution of society. This view of how embodied subjects interact with the structural properties of society, which is underpinned by a form of corporeal realism, provides us with a way of maintaining the insights of contemporary body theories while avoiding their excesses and conflationary tendencies. Just as importantly, it provides us with a framework that can be used to steer substantive work on the subject, and to accumulate knowledge about the body–society relationship which can continue to enrich the humanities and social sciences.

Bibliography

Adams, C. (1990) *The Sexual Politics of Meat*. New York: Continuum.

Adkins, L. (1995) *Gendered Work: Sexuality, Family and the Labour Market*. Buckingham: Open University Press.

Adorno, T. (1978 [1932]) 'On the social situation of music', *Telos*, 35: 128–164.

Adorno, T. (1990 [1941]) 'On popular music', in S. Frith and A. Goodwin (eds), *On Record*. London: Routledge.

Adorno, T. (1991 [1938]) 'On the fetish character in music and the regression of listening', in *T. Adorno, The Culture Industry*, ed. J. Bernstein. London: Routledge.

Ahmed, S. (2000) *Strange Encounters: Embodied Others in Post-Coloniality*. London: Routledge.

Ahmed, S. and Stacey, J. (eds) (2001), *Thinking Through through the Skin*. London: Routledge.

Ainley, R. (2001) 'Keeping an eye on them', in Sally Munt (ed.), *Technospaces*. London: Continuum.

Ainsworth, M., Bell, S. and Stayton, D. (1974) 'Infant–mother attachment and social development: socialization as a product of reciprocal responsiveness to signals', in M. Richards (ed.), *The Integration of a Child Into a Social World*. Cambridge: Cambridge University Press.

Akrich, M. (1992) 'The de-scription of technical objects', in W. Bijker and J. Laws (eds), *Shaping Technology/Building Society*. Cambridge, MA: MIT Press.

Allen, Jr. (1996) 'Making the strong survive: the contours and contradictions of message rap', in W. Perkins (ed.), *Droppin' Science*. Philadelphia, PA: Temple University Press.

Althusser, L. (1969) *For Marx*. Harmondsworth: Penguin.

Althusser, L. (1971) 'Ideology and ideological state apparatuses', in L. Althusser (ed.), *Lenin and Philosophy and Other Essays*. London: New Left Books.

Amin, A. (1994) 'Post-fordism: models, fantasies and phantoms of transition', in A. Amin (ed.), *Post-fordism: A Reader*. Oxford: Blackwell.

Anderson, B. (1991 revised edition) *Imagined Communities*. London: Verso.

Archer, M. (1988) *Culture and Agency*. Cambridge: Cambridge University Press.

Archer, M. (1995) *Realist Social Theory*. Cambridge: Cambridge University Press.

Archer, M. (1998) 'Introduction: Realism realism in the social sciences', in M. Archer, R. Bhaskar, A. Collier, T. Lawson, and A. Norrie, (eds), (1998) *Critical Realism: Essential Readings*. London: Routledge.

Archer, M. (2000) *Being Human: The Problem of Agency*. Cambridge: Cambridge University Press.

Archer, M., Bhaskar, R., Collier, A., Lawson, T. and Norrie, A. (eds) (1998) *Critical Realism: Essential Readings*. London: Routledge.

Areni, C. and Kim, D. (1993) 'The influence of background music on shopping behaviour: Classical versus top-forty music in a wine store', *Advances in Consumer Research*, 20: 336–40.

Argyle, K. (1996) 'Life after death', in R. Shields (ed.), *Cultures of Internet*. London: Sage.

Argyle, K. and Shields, R. (1996) 'Is there a body in the Net?', in R. Shields (ed.), *Cultures of Internet*. London: Sage.

Arksey, H. (1998) *RSI and the Experts: The Construction of Medical Knowledge*. London: UCL.

Armstrong, D. (1983) *Political Economy of the Body: Medical Knowledge in Britain in the Twentieth Century*. Cambridge: Cambridge University Press.

Armstrong, D. (1995) 'The rise of surveillance medicine', *Sociology of Health and Illness*, 17 (3): 393–404.

Arthur, C. (1977) 'Introduction', in K. Marx. and F. Engels, (1846) *The German Ideology*. London: Lawrence and Wishart.

Ashworth, B. and Humphrey, R. (1993) 'Emotional labor in service roles', *Academy of Management Review*, 18: 88–115.

Ashworth, B. and Humphrey, R. (1995) 'Emotion in the workplace: a reappraisal', *Human Relations* , 48: 97–125.

Atkins, P. and Bowler, I. (2001) *Food in Society*. London: Arnold.

Ayres, C. (2003) 'Basketball prodigy aged 3 signed up by sportswear firm', *The Times*, 14th June, p. 17.

Back, L., Crabbe, T. and Solomos, J. (2001) *The Changing Face of Football*. Oxford: Berg.

Bain, P. and Taylor, P. (2000) 'Entrapped by the "electronic panopticon"? Worker resistance in the call centre', *New Technology, Work and Employment*, 15 (2): 2–18.

Bakardjieva, M. (2003) 'Virtual togetherness: an everyday-life perspective', *Media, Culture and Society*, 25: 291–313.

Bale, J. and Philo, C. (1998) 'Introduction', to H. Eichberg, *Body Cultures: Essays on Sport, Space and Identity*. London: Routledge.

Balsamo, A. (2000) 'The virtual body in cyberspace', in D. Bell and B. Kennedy (eds), *The Cybercultures Reader*. London: Routledge.

Barbalet, J. (1988) *Emotion, Social Structure and Social Theory*. Cambridge: Cambridge University Press.

Barley, S. and Kunda, G. (2000) 'Design and devotion: surges of rational and normative ideologies of control in managerial discourse', reprinted in K. Grint (ed.), *Work and Society: A Reader*. Cambridge: Polity.

Barnharrt, R. (ed.) (1988) *The Barnhart Dictionary of Etymology*. New York: Wilson.

Barthes, R. (1972) *Mythologies*. London: Paladin.

Bartky, S. (1988) 'Foucault, femininity and the modernization of patriarchal power', in I. Diamond and L. Quinby (eds), *Femininity and Foucault: Reflections of Resistance*. Boston: Northeastern University Press.

Bataille, G. (1962) *Eroticism*. London: John Calder.

Bataille, G. (1991 [1967]) *The Accursed Share*, Vol. 1. New York: Zone.

Bataille, G. (1993 [1976]) *The Accursed Share*, Vols .2 and 3. New York: Zone.

Baudrillard, J. (1993) *Symbolic Exchange and Death*. London: Sage.

Baym, N. (1995) 'The emergence of community in computer-mediated communication', in S. Jones (ed.), *Cybersociety*. London: Sage.

Beardsworth, A. and Keil, T. (1993) 'Hungry for knowledge? The sociology of food and eating', *Sociology Review*, November: 11–15.

Beardsworth, A. and Keil, T. (1997) *Sociology on the Menu*. London: Routledge.

Beck, U. (1991) *Risk Society*. London: Sage.

Beck, U. (2000) *The Brave New World of Work*. Cambridge: Polity.

Becker, H. (1963) *Outsiders*. New York: The Free Press.

Beechey, V. (1987) *Unequal Work*. London: Verso.

Bell, R. (1985) *Holy Anorexia*. Chicago: University of Chicago Press.

Bellah, R. (1967) 'Civil religion in America', *Daedalus*, 96: 1–21.

Bendelow, G. and Williams, S. (eds) (1998) *Emotions in Social Life*. London: Routledge.

Benedikt, M. (1991) 'Cyberspace: Some proposals', in M. Benedikt (ed.), *Cyberspace: First Steps*. London: MIT Press.

Benton, T. (1991) 'Biology and social science: why the return of the repressed should be given a (cautious) welcome', *Sociology*, 25 (1): 1–29.

Benyon, H. (1973) *Working for Ford*. London: Allen Lane.

Berg, M. and Medrich, E. (1980) 'Children in four neighbourhoods', *Environment and Behaviour*, 12 (3): 320–48.

Berger, P. (1990 [1967]) *The Sacred Canopy*. New York: Anchor Books.

Bhaskar, R. (1986) *Scientific Realism and Human Emancipation*. London: Verso.

Bhaskar, R. (1989) *The Possibility of Naturalism*. Hemel Hempstead: Harvester Wheatsheaf.

Bhaskar, R. (1998) 'General introduction', in M. Archer, R. Bhaskar, A. Collier, T. Lawson and A. Norrie (eds) *Critical Realism: Essential Readings*. London: Routledge.

Biermann, J.S., Golladay, G., Greenfield, M., and Baker, L. (1989) 'Evaluation of cancer information on the internet', *Cancer*, 86 (3): 381–90.

Birke, L. (1999) *Feminism and the Biological Body*. Edinburgh: Edinburgh University Press.

Birley, D. (1993) *Sport and the Making of Britain*. Manchester: Manchester University Press.

Birrell, S. (1987) 'Women and the myth of sport', cited in S. Birrell and N. Theberge, (1994) 'Ideological control of women in sport', in D.M. Costa and S.R. Guthhrie (eds), *Women and Sport: Interdisciplinary Perspectives*. (1994). Champaign, Il: Human Kinetics.

Birrell, S. and Therberge, N. (1994) 'Ideological control of women in sport', in D.M. Costa and S.R. Guthrie (eds), *Women and Sport: Interdisciplinary Perspectives*. Champaign, Il: Human Kinetics.

Blacking, J. (1976) *How Musical is Man?* London: Faber and Faber.

Blake, A. (1996) *The Body Language: The Meaning of Modern Sport*. London: Lawrence and Wishart.

Bloom, A. (1987) *The Closing of the American Mind*. London: Penguin.

Bloor, M., Monaghan, L., Dobash, R.P. and Dobase, R.E. (1998) 'The body as a chemistry experiment: Steroid use among South Wales bodybuilders', in S. Nettleton and J. Watson (eds), *The Body in Everyday Life*. London: Routledge.

Bohannan, O. (1957) *Justice and Judgement among the Tiv*. London: Oxford University Press.

Bordo, S. (1989) 'Reading the slender body', in M. Jacubus, E. Fox Keller and S. Shuttleworth (eds), *Women, Science and the Body Politic*. New York: Methuen.

Bordo, S. (1993) *Unbearable Weight: Feminism, Western Culture and the Body*. Berkeley: University of California Press.

Bordo, S. (1998) '"Material girl": The effacements of postmodern culture', in D. Welton (ed.), *Body and Flesh: A Philosophical Reader*. Oxford: Blackwell.

Boslooper, T. and Hayes, M. (1973) *The Femininity Game*. New York: Skein and Day.

Bourdieu, P. (1977) *Outline of a Theory of Practice*. Cambridge: Cambridge University Press.

Bourdieu, P. (1978) 'Sport and social class', *Social Science Information*, 17: 819–40.

Bourdieu, P. (1981) 'Men and machines', in K. Knorr-Cetina and A. Cicourel (eds), *Advances in Social Theory and Methodology*. London: Routledge and Kegan Paul.

Bourdieu, P. (1984) *Distinction: A Social Critique of the Judgement of Taste*. London: Routledge.

Bourdieu, P. (1986) 'The forms of capital', in J. Richardson (ed.), *Handbook of Theory and Research for the Sociology of Education*. New York: Greenwood Press.

Bourdieu, P. (1990a) *In Other Words: Essays Towards towards a Reflexive Sociology*. Cambridge: Polity Press.

Bourdieu, P. (1990b) 'Droit et passe-droit. : Le le champ des pouvoirs territoriaux et la mise en oeuvre des règlements', *Actes de la Recherche en Sciences Sociales*, 81/2: 86–96.

Bourdieu, P. (1990c [1980]) *The Logic of Practice*. Cambridge: Polity.

Bourdieu, P. (1992) 'The purpose of reflexive sociology', in P. Bourdieu and L. Wacquant, *An Invitation to Reflexive Sociology*. Chicago: University of Chicago Press.

Bourdieu, P. (1998) *Acts of Resistance*. Cambridge: Polity.

Bourdieu, P. (1999) *The Weight of the World: Social Suffering in Contemporary Society*. Cambridge: Polity.

Bourdieu, P. and Wacquant, L. (1992) *An Invitation to Reflexive Sociology*. Chicago: University of Chicago Press.

Brannon, L. and Rock, T. (1994) 'Test of schema correspondence theory of persuasion', in E. Clark., T. Brock and D. Stewart (eds), *Attention, Attitude and Affect in Responses to Advertising*. Hillsdale, NJ: Lawrence Erlbaum Associates.

Brasch, R. (ed.) (1990) *How did Did Sports Begin?* Thornhill: Tynron Press.

Braudel, F. (1973) *Capitalism and Material Life 1400–1800*. London: Weidenfeld and Nicolson.

Braverman, H. (1974) *Labor and Monopoly Capital*. New York: Monthly Review Press.

Breton, D. Le (2000) 'Playing symbolically with death in extreme sports', *Body and Society*, 6 (1): 1–11.

Brohm, J.-M. (1978) *Sport: A Prison of Measured Time*. London: Ink Links.

Bromberg, H. (1996) 'Are MUDs communities?', in R. Shields (ed.), *Cultures of Internet*.

London: Sage.

Brower, J. (1979) 'The professionalisation of organised youth sport', *Annals of the American Academy of Political and Social Science*, Vol. 445: 39–46.

Brown, D. (1997) *Cybertrends: Chaos, Power and Accountability in the Information Age*. London: Viking.

Brown, E. (2002) 'The prosthetics of management', in K. Ott., D. Serlin and S. Mihm (eds), *Artificial Parts, Practical Lives*. New York: New York University Press.

Brown, P. (1988) *The Body and Society*. London: Faber and Faber.

Brown, S. and Lightfoot, G. (2002) 'Presence, absence and accountability: email and the mediation of organisational memory', in S. Woolgar (ed.), *Virtual Society? Technology, Cyberbole, Reality*. Oxford: Oxford University Press.

Brownfoot, J. (1992) 'Emancipation, exercise and imperialism: girls and the games ethic in colonial Malaya', in J. Mangan (ed.), *The Cultural Bond: Sport, Empire, Society*. London: Frank Cass.

Brownwell,, K. and Fairburn, C. (eds) (1995) *Eating Disorders and Obesity: A Comprehensive Handbook*. New York: The Guildford Press.

Brownwell, S. (1998) 'Thinking dangerously: The person and his ideas', in H. Eichberg, *Body Cultures: Essays on Sport, Space and Identity*. London: Routledge.

Brumberg, J. (1988) *Fasting Girls*. Cambridge, MA: Harvard University Press.

Bruner, G. (1990) 'Music, mood and marketing', *Journal of Marketing*, 54 (4): 94–104.

Buckland, R. (1994) 'Food old and new: What limitations?', in B. Harris-White and R. Hoffenberg (eds), *Food: Multi-disciplinary Perspectives*. Oxford: Basil Blackwell.

Bukatman, S. (1993) *Terminal Identity*. Durham, NC: Duke University Press.

Bunt, L. (1997) 'Clinical and therapeutic uses of music', in D. Hargreaves and A. North (eds), *The Social Psychology of Music*. Oxford: Oxford University Press.

Burkitt, I. (1991) *Social Selves*. London: Sage.

Burkitt, I. (1992) 'Beyond the "iron cage": Anthony Giddens on modernity and the self', *History of the Human Sciences*, 5: 71–9.

Burkitt, I. (1999) *Bodies of Thought*. London: Sage.

Burkitt, I. (2002) 'Technologies of the self: habitus and capacities', *Journal for the Theory of Social Behaviour*, 32 (2): 219–37.

Burrows, E. (1936) *Ethnology of Futuna*. (Honolulu: Bernice P. Bishop Museum Bulletin 109), cited in A. Merriam (1964) *The Anthropology of Music*. Evanston, IL: Northwestern University Press.

Burrows, R. and Nettleton, S. (2002) 'Reflexive modernisation and the emergence of wired self help', in K. Ann Renninger and W. Shumar (eds), *Building Virtual Communities*. New York: Cambridge University Press.

Butler, J. (1990) *Gender Trouble*. London: Routledge.

Butler, J. (1993) *Bodies that Matter*. London: Routledge.

Butler, J. (1994) 'Gender as performance: An an interview with Judith Butler', *Radical Philosophy*, 67: 32–39.

Butler, J. (1997) 'Imitation and gender subordination', in L. Nicholson (ed.), *The Second Wave: A Reader in Feminist Theory*. New York: Routledge.

Buytendijk, F. (1974) *Prolegomena to an Anthropological Physiology*. Pittsburgh, PA: Duquesne University Press.

Bynum, C.W. (1987) *Holy Feast and Holy Fast*. Berkeley, CA: University of California Press.

Capra, F. (2002) *The Hidden Connections*. New York: Doubleday.

Captain, G. (1991) 'Enter ladies and gentlemen of color', *Journal of Sport History*, 18 (1): 81–102.

Carlson, A. (1991) 'When is a woman not a woman?', *Women's Sport and Fitness*, March, pp. 24–29.

Carrington, B. (1982) 'Sport as a sidetrack', in L. Barton and S. Walker (eds), *Race, Class and Education*. London: Croom Helm.

Case, S.-E., Brett, P., and Foster, S.L. (1995) *Cruising the Performative*. Bloomington: Indiana

University Press.

Cashmore, E. (1998) 'Between mind and muscle' (review article), in *Body and Society*, 4 (2): 83–90.

Cashmore, E. (2000) *Making Sense of Sports* (3rd edition). London: Routledge.

Cassirer, E. (1951) *The Philosophy of the Enlightenment*. Princeton, NJ: Princeton University Press.

Castells, M. (1989) *The Informational City*. Oxford: Blackwell.

Castells, M. (1996) *The Rise of the Network Society: The Information Age*, Vol. 1. Oxford: Blackwells.

Cavendish, R. (1982) *Women on the Line*. London: Routledge and Kegan Paul.

Charles, N. and Kerr, M. (1988) *Women, Food and Families*. Manchester: Manchester University Press.

Chen, Y. and Person, A. (2002) 'Internet use among young and older adults: relation to psychological well-being', *Educational Gerontology*, 28 (9): 731–744.

Chernin, K. (1983) *Womansize: The Tyranny of Slenderness*. London: The Women's Press.

Chrisafis, A. (2003) 'Anti-war protesters vent their frustration', The *Guardian*, 29 September, p. 9.

Classen, C. (1993) *Worlds of Sense*. London: Routledge.

Coakley, S. (ed.) (1997) *Religion and the Body*. Cambridge: Cambridge University Press.

Cockburn, C. (1983) *Brothers: Male Dominance and Technological Change*. London: Pluto Press.

Colletti, L. (1975) 'Introduction and commentary', in *Karl Marx: Early Writings*. Harmondsworth: Pelican.

Collier, A. (1998) 'Stratified explanation and Marx's conception of history', in M. Archer., R. Bhaskar., A. Collier., T. Lawson and A. Norrrie (eds), *Critical Realism: Essential Readings*. London: Routledge.

Collins, S. and Kuck, K. (1990) 'Music therapy in the neonatal intensive care unit', *Neonatal Network*, 9 (6): 23–6.

Connell, R.W. (1983) *Which Way is Up?* Sydney: George Allen and Unwin.

Connell, R.W. (1990) 'An iron man: The body and some contradictions of hegemonic masculinity', in M. Messner and D. Sabo (eds), *Sport, Men and the Gender Order*. Champaign, IL: Human Kinetics.

Connell, R.W. (1995) *Masculinities*. Oxford: Polity Press.

Conner, M. and Armitage, C. (2000) *The Social Psychology of Food*. Buckingham: Open University Press.

Connerton, P. (1980) *How Societies Remember*. Cambridge: Cambridge University Press.

Cooper, S. (ed.) (1995) *Girls! Girls! Girls! Essays on Women and Music*. London: Cassell.

Coser, L. (1971) *Masters of Sociological Thought: Ideas in Historical and Social Context*. New York: Harcourt Brace Jovanovich.

Coser, L. (1977) 'Georg Simmel's neglected contribution to the sociology of women', reprinted in D. Frisby (ed.), *Georg Simmel: Critical Assessments*, Vol. 2. London: Routledge.

Costa, D.M. and Guthrie, S.R. (eds) (1994) *Women and Sport: Interdisciplinary Perspectives*. Champaign, Il: Human Kinetics.

Counihan, C. (1999) *The Anthropology of Food and Body*. New York: Routledge.

Craib, I. (1997) 'Social constructionism as social psychosis', *Sociology*, 31 (1): 1–15.

Crandall, C. (1995) 'Do parents discriminate against their heavy-weight daughters?', *Personality and Social Psychology Bulletin*, 21: 724–35.

Crawford, R. (1994) 'The boundaries of the self and the unhealthy other: reflections on health, culture and AIDS', *Social Science and Medicine*, 38: 1347–65.

Crawford, R. (2000) 'The ritual of health promotion', in S. Williams, J. Gabe and M. Calnan (eds), *Health, Medicine and Society*. London: Routledge.

Creaven, S. (2000) *Marxism and Realism*. London: Routledge.

Crompton, R. and Mann, M. (1986) *Gender and Stratification*. Oxford: Polity.

Crossley, N. (1995), 'Merleau-Ponty, the elusive body and carnal sociology', *Body and Society*, 1 (1): 43–63.

Crossley, N. (1996), 'Body-subject/body-power: agency, inscription and control in Foucault and Merleau-Ponty', *Body and Society*, 2 (2): 91–116.

Crossley, N. (1998) 'Emotion and communicative action', in G. Bendelow and S. Williams (eds), *Emotions in Social Life*. London: Routledge.

Crossley, N. (2000) 'Emotions, psychiatry and social order', in S. Williams, Gabe, J. and M. Cananan (2000) *Health, Medicine and Society*. London: Routledge.

Crossley, N. (2001) *The Social Body: Habit, Identity and Desire*. London: Sage.

Crozier, W. (1997) 'Music and social influence', in D. Hargreaves and A. North (eds), *The Social Psychology of Music*. Oxford: Oxford University Press.

Csikszentmihalyi, M. (1975) *Beyond Boredom and Anxiety*. San Francisco: Jossey-Bass.

Csordas T. (ed.) (1994) *Embodiment and Experience: The Existential Ground of Culture and Self*. Cambridge: Cambridge University Press.

Cubitt, S. (1998) *Digital Aesthetics*. London: Sage.

Davis, G. (1947) *Music-Cueing for Radio Drama*. London: Boosey and Hawkes.

Davis, K. (1995) *Reshaping the Female Body*. London: Routledge.

Dawe, A. (1970) 'The two sociologies', *The British Journal of Sociology*, 21 (2): 207–218.

Dawe, A. (1979), 'Theories of Social Action', in T. Bottomore and R. Nisbet (eds), *A History of Sociological Analysis*. London: Heinemann.

Dawkins, R. (1976) *The Selfish Gene*. London: Paladin.

de Castro, J. (1997) 'Socio-cultural determinants of meal size and frequency', *British Journal of Nutrition*, 77: Supplement 1, 539–554. Discussion S54–S55.

DeNora, T. (1991) 'Musical patronage and social change in Beethoven's Vienna', American *Journal of Sociology*, 92: 310–346.

DeNora, T. (1997) 'Music and erotic agency: Sonic resources and socio-sexual action', *Body and Society*, 3 (2): 43–65.

DeNora, T. (2000) *Music in Everyday Life*. Cambridge: Cambridge University Press.

Dery, M. (2000) 'Ritual mechanics: cybernetic body art', in D. Bell and B. Kennedy (eds), *The Cybercultures Reader*. London: Routledge.

Descartes, R. (1974) *The Philosophical Works of René Descartes*, Vol. 1. Cambridge: Cambridge University Press.

DeVault, M. (1991) *Feeding the Family*. Chicago, IL: University of Chicago Press.

Devereux, E. (1976) 'Backyard versus little league baseball', in A. Yiannakis (ed.), *Sport Sociology: Contemporary Themes*, 2nd edn. Kendall: Dubuque, IA.

Dex, S. (1985) *The Sexual Division of Work*. Brighton: Wheatsheaf Books.

Diamond, I. and Quinby, L. (eds) (1988) *Feminism and Foucault*. Boston, MA: Northeastern University Press.

DiMaggio, P., Hargttai, E., Neuman, W.R. and Robinson, J. (2001) 'Some implications of the Internet', *Annual Review of Sociology*, 27: 307–336.

Diprose, R. (1994) *The Bodies of Women*. London: Routledge.

Dissanayake, E. (1990) 'Music as a human behaviour: an hypothesis of evolutionary origin and function', unpublished paper presented at the Human Behaviour and Evolution Society Meeting, Los Angeles, August.

Ditton, J. (1979) 'Baking time', *Sociological Review*, 27: 156–67.

Dobson, B., Beardsworth, A., Keil, T., and Walker, R. (1994) *Diet, Choice and Poverty*. London: Family Policy Studies Centre / Joseph Rowntree Foundation.

Douglas, M. (1980 [1966]) *Purity and Danger: An Analysis of the Concepts of Pollution and Taboo*. London: Routledge and Kegan Paul.

Douglas, M. (1984) 'Standard social uses of food', in M. Douglas (ed.), *Food in the Social Order*. New York: Russell Sage Foundation.

Douglas, M. (ed.) (1987) *Constructive Drinking*. Cambridge: Cambridge University Press.

Douglas, M. and Gross, J. (1981) 'Food and culture', *Social Science Information*, 20 (1): 1–35.

Doyal, L. and Gough, I, (1991) *A Theory of Human Need*. London: Macmillan.

Du Gay, P. and Salaman, G. (2000) 'The cult[ure] of the customer', in K. Grint (ed.), *Work and Society: A Reader*. Cambridge: Polity.

Dubbert, J. (1979) *A Man's Place: Masculinity in Transition*. Englewood Cliffs, NJ: Prentice-Hall.

Dubin, C. (1990) *Commission of Inquiry into the Use of Drugs and Banned Practices Intended to Increase Athletic Performance*. Ottawa: Canadian Government Publicity Centre.

Dunning, E. (1999) *Sport Matters*. London: Routledge.

Dunning, E., Murphy, P. and Williams, J. (1986) 'Spectator violence at football matches: Towards a sociological explanation', in N. Elias and E. Dunning, E. (1986), *Quest for Excitement: Sport and Leisure in the Civilizing Process*. Oxford: Blackwell.

Dunning, E. and Sheard, K. (1979) *Barbarians, Gentlemen and Players: A Sociological Study of the Development of Rugby Football*. New York: New York University Press.

Durkheim, E. (1952 [1897]) *Suicide*. London: Routledge.

Durkheim, E. (1961) *Moral Education*. New York: The Free Press.

Durkheim, E. (1973a [1898]) 'Individualism and the intellectuals', in R.N. Bellah (ed.), *Emile Durkheim on Morality and Society*. Chicago: University of Chicago Press.

Durkheim, E. (1973c [1925]) *Moral Education*. New York: Free Press.

Durkheim, E. (1974 [1914]), 'The dualism of human nature and its social conditions', in R. N. Bellah (ed.), *Emile Durkheim on Morality and Society*. Chicago: University of Chicago Press.

Durkheim, E. (1977 [1938]) *The Evolution of Educational Thought: Lectures on the Formation and Development of Secondary Education in France*. London: Routledge.

Durkheim, E. (1984 [1893]) *The Division of Labour in Society*. London: Macmillan.

Durkheim, E. (1995 [1912]) *The Elementary Forms of Religious Life*, trans. Karen E. Fields. New York: Free Press.

Dyer, K. (1982) *Challenging the Men*. New York: University of Queensland.

Dyhouse, C. (1976) 'Social Darwinist ideas about the development of women's education in England, 1880–1920', *History of Education*, 5 (1): 41–58.

Dyrkton, J. (1996) 'Cool runnings: the contradictions of cyberreality in Jamaica', in R. Shields (ed.), *Cultures of Internet*. London: Sage.

Edie, J.M. (1963) 'Introduction', in M. Merleau-Ponty, *The Primacy of Perception*. Evanston, IL: Northwestern University Press.

Ehrenreich, B. (1990) *The Fear of Falling: The Inner Life of the Middle Class*. New York: Harper Perennial.

Ehrenreich, B. (2001) *Nickel and Dimed: Undercover in Low Wage USA*. London: Granta.

Eichberg, H. (1998) *Body Cultures: Essays on Sport, Space and Identity*. London: Routledge.

Eisenberg, C. (1990) 'The middle class and competition: Some considerations of the beginnings of modern sport in England and Germany', *The International Journal of the History of Sport*, 7 (2): 265–282.

Eisenstein, Z. (1988) *The Female Body and the Law*. Berkeley, CA: University of California Press.

Elias, N. (1983) *Court Society*. Oxford: Blackwell.

Elias, N. (1986) 'Introduction', in N. Elias and E. Dunning, *Quest for Excitement: Sport and Leisure in the Civilizing Process*. Oxford: Blackwell.

Elias, N. (1986b) 'The genesis of sport as a sociological problem', in N. Elias and E. Dunning (eds), *Quest for Excitement: Sport and Leisure in the Civilizing Process*. Oxford: Blackwell.

Elias, N. (19991a) 'On human beings and their emotions: a process-sociological essay', in M. Featherstone and B.S. Turner (eds), *The Body: Social Process and Cultural Theory*. London: Sage.

Elias, N. (1991b) *The Symbol Theory*. London: Sage.

Elias, N. (1994) 'A theoretical essay on established and outsider relations', in N. Elias and J. Scotson (eds), *The Established and the Outsiders*, 2nd Edition. London: Sage.

Elias, N. (2000 [1939]) *The Civilizing Process*, 2 Vols. Oxford: Blackwell.

Elias, N. and Dunning, E. (1969) 'The quest for excitement in leisure', *Society and Leisure*, 2: 50–85.

Elias, N. and Dunning, E. (1986) *Quest for Excitement: Sport and Leisure in the Civilizing Process*. Oxford: Blackwell.

Elias, N. and Scotson, J. (1965) *The Established and the Outsiders*. London: Frank Cass.

Ellis, R. (1983) 'The way to a man's heart: food in the violent home', in A. Murcott (ed.), *The Sociology of Food and Eating*. Aldershot: Gower.

Elstad, J. (1998) 'The psycho-social perspective on social inequalities in health', *Sociology of Health and Illness*, 12 (4): 452–77.

Emery, L. (1994) 'From Lowell to Mills to the Hall of Fame: Industrial league sport for women', in D.M. Costa and S.R. Guthrie (eds), *Women and Sport: Interdisciplinary Perspectives*. Champaign, IL: Human Kinetics.

Engels, F. (1958 [1845]) *The Condition of the Working Class in England*. Oxford: Blackwell.

Engels, F. (1968 [1925]) 'The part played by labour in the transition from ape to man', in *Marx/Engels: Selected Works in One Volume*. London: Lawrence and Wishart.

Ettorre, E. (2002) *Reproductive Genetics, Gender and the Body*. London: Routledge.

Evans, J., Davies, B. and Wright, J. (2003) *Bodies of Knowledge*. London: Routledge.

Falk, P. (1994) *The Consuming Body*. London: Sage.

Fallon, A. (1990) 'Culture in the mirror: sociocultural determinants of body image', in T. Cash and T. Prusinsky (eds), *Body Images: Development, Deviance and Change*. New York: Guilford Press.

Fanon, F. (1984 [1952]) *Black Skin, White Masks*. London: Pluto Press.

Fantasia, R. (1995) 'Fast food in France', *Theory and Society*, 24: 201–43.

Featherstone, M. (1982) 'The body in consumer culture', *Theory, Culture and Society*, 1: 18–33.

Featherstone, M. (1995) 'Post-bodies, aging and virtual reality', reprinted in D. Bell and B. Kennedy (eds) (2000) *The Cybercultures Reader*. London: Routledge.

Featherstone, M. and Burrows, R. (1995) 'Cultures of technological embodiment: An introduction', *Body and Society*, 1 (3-/4): 1–20.

Featherstone, M. and Hepworth, M. (1991) 'The mask of ageing and the postmodern life course', in M. Featherstone, M., Hepworth and B.S. Turner (eds), *The Body: Social Process and Cultural Theory*. London: Sage.

Featherstone, M. and Wernick, A. (eds) (1995) *Images of Ageing*. London: Routledge.

Feher, M., Nadaff, R. and Tazi, N. (1989) *Fragments for a History of the Human Body*, 3 Vols. New York: Zone.

Fernie, S. and Metcalf, D. (1998) *(Not) Hanging on the Telephone: Payments Systems in the New Sweatshops*. London: London School of Economics Centre for Economic Performance.

Fineman, S. (2000) *Emotion in Organizations*. 2nd edn. London: Sage.

Finkelson, J. (1989) *Dining Out*. Cambridge: Polity.

Finlay, M. and Plecket, H. (1976) *The Olympic Games: The First 100 Years*. London: Chatto and Windus.

Finnegan, R. (1989) *The Hidden Musicians*. Cambridge: Cambridge University Press.

Fischler, C. (1980) 'Food habits, social change and the nature/culture dilemma', *Social Science Information*, 19: 937–53.

Fischler, C. (1988) 'Food, self and identity', *Social Science Information*, 27 (2): 275–92.

Fitchen, J. (1997) 'Hunger, malnutrition and poverty in the contemporary United States', in C. Counihan and P. V. Esterik (eds), *Food and Culture: A Reader*. New York: Routledge.

Flynn, M. (1998) 'Future research needs and directions', in R. Kreider., A. Fry and M. L. O'Toole (eds), *Overtraining in Sport*. Champaign, Il: Human Kinetics.

Fotheringham, W. (2003) 'EPO spectre back to haunt Tour', *The Guardian*, 28th July.

Foucault, M. (1970) *The Order of Things*. London: Tavistock.

Foucault, M. (1977) *Language, Counter-Memory, Practice: Selected Essays and Interviews*. Oxford: Blackwell.

Foucault, M. (1979a) *Discipline and Punish*. Harmondsworth: Penguin.

Foucault, M. (1979b) 'Governmentality', *Ideology and Consciousness*, 6: 5–22.

Foucault, M. (1980) 'Body/power', in C. Gordon (ed.), *Michel Foucault: Power/Knowledge*. Brighton: Harvester.

Foucault, M. (1981) *The History of Sexuality, Vol. 1, An Introduction*. Harmondsworth: Penguin.

Foucault, M. (1988a) *The Care of the Self: The History of Sexuality*, Vol. 3. Harmondsworth:

Penguin.

Foucault, M. (1988b) 'Technologies of the self', in L. Martin, H. Gutman and P. Hutton (eds), *Technologies of the Self: A Seminar with Michel Foucault*. London: Tavistock.

Frank, A. (1991) 'For a sociology of the body: an analytical review', in M. Featherstone, M. Hepworth and B.S. Turner (eds), *The Body: Social Process and Cultural Theory*. London: Sage.

Frank, A. (1995) *The Wounded Storyteller*. Chicago: University of Chicago Press.

Freud, S. (1918) *Totem and Taboo*. New York: Vintage.

Freud, S. (1923) 'The ego and the id', in *Standard Edition of the Complete Psychological Works of Sigmund Freud*, Vol. XIV. London: Hogarth Press.

Freud, S. (1930) 'Civilization and its Discontents', in *Standard Edition of the Complete Psychological Works of Sigmund Freud*, Vol. XXI. London: Hogarth Press.

Freud, S. (1962) *Three Contributions to the Theory of Sex*. New York: Dutton.

Freund, P. (1982) *The Civilized Body: Social Domination, Control and Health*. Philadelphia, PA: Temple University Press.

Freund, P. and McGuire, M. (1991) *Health, Illness and the Social Body*. Engelwood Cliffs, NJ: Prentice-Hall.

Frith, S. (1983) *Sound Effects*. London: Constable.

Frith, S. (1988) *Music for Pleasure*. Cambridge: Polity.

Fuller, S. (1995) 'Dead white men in wigs: Women and classical music', in S. Cooper (ed.), *Girls! Girls! Girls! Essays on Women and Music*. London: Cassell.

Fustel de Coulanges, N. (1956 [1864]) *The Ancient City*. New York: Doubleday Anchor.

Galison, P. (1994) 'The ontology of the enemy: Norbert Weiner and the cybernetic vision', *Critical Inquiry*, Autumn: pp. 228–273.

Gardiner, H., Metcalf, R., Beebe-Center, J. (1937) *Feeling and Emotion: A History of Theories*. New York: American Book Company.

Gardner, , M. (1985) 'Mood states and critical behaviour', *Journal of Consumer Research*, 12: 281–300.

Gatens, M. (1996) *Imaginary Bodies: Ethics, Power and Corporeality*. London: Routledge.

Gayne, P. and McGaughey, D. (2002) 'Designing Women', *Gender and Society*, 16 (6): 814–838.

George, A. (1996) 'The anabolic steroids and peptide hormones', in D. Mottram (ed.), *Drugs in Sport*. London: E. and F.N. Spon.

Gerard. L. (2002) 'Beyond "scribbling women": women writing (on) the Web', *Computers and Composition*, 19 (3): 297–314.

Geras, N. (1983) *Marx and Human Nature: Refutation of a Legend*. London: Verso.

Geras, N. (1995) 'Human nature and progress', *New Left Review*, 213: 151–160.

Germov, J. and Williams, L. (1996) 'The epidemic of dieting women', *Appetite*, 27: 97–108.

Gibson, J. (1979) *The Ecological Approach to Human Perception*. Boston: Houghton Mifflin.

Giddens, A. (1979) *Central Problems in Social Theory*. Houndmills: Macmillan.

Giddens, A. (1984) *The Constitution of Society*. Cambridge: Polity.

Giddens, A. (1988) 'Goffman as a systematic social theorist', in P. Drew and A. Wootton (eds), *Erving Goffman: Exploring the Interaction Order*. Cambridge: Polity.

Giddens, A. (1990) *The Consequences of Modernity*. Cambridge: Polity.

Giddens, A. (1991) *Modernity and Self-Identity*. Cambridge: Polity.

Giddens, A. (1992) *The Transformation of Intimacy*. Cambridge: Polity.

Giddens, A. (1994) *Beyond Left and Right*. Cambridge: Polity.

Giddens, A. (1998) *The Third Way: The Renewal of Social Democracy*. Cambridge: Polity.

Gilbert, N., Burrows, R. and Pollert, A. (1992) *Fordism and Flexibility*. Houndmills: Macmillan.

Gill, D. (1986) *Psychological Dynamics of Sport*. Champaign, Il: Human Kinetics Publishing.

Gill, D. (1994) 'Psychological perspectives on women in sport and exercise', in M. Costa and S. Guthrie (eds), *Women and Sport: Interdisciplinary Perspectives*. Champaign, IL: Human Kinetics.

Gilroy, P. (2000) *Between Camps*. London: Penguin.

Gimlin, D. (2002) *BodyWork*. Berkeley, CA: University of California Press.

Goffman, E. (1956) 'Embarrassment and social organisation', *American Journal of Sociology*, LXII (3): 264–271.

Goffman, E. (1961) *Asylums*. Doubleday: Anchor Books.

Goffman, E. (1963) *Behaviour in Public Places: Notes on the Social Organisation of Gatherings*. New York: The Free Press.

Goffman, E., (1968) *Stigma: Notes on the Management of Spoiled Identity*. Harmondsworth: Penguin.

Goffman, E. (1969 [1956]) *The Presentation of Self in Everyday Life*. London: Penguin.

Goffman, E. (1983) 'The interaction order', *American Sociological Review*, 48: 1–17.

Golden, M. (1998) *Sport and Society in Ancient Greece*. Cambridge: Cambridge University Press.

Goldman, R. and Papson, S. (1998) *Nike Culture*. London: Sage.

Goleman, D. (1996) *Emotional Intelligence: Why It Can Matter More than IQ*. London: Bloomsbury.

Goleman, D. (1998) *Working With Emotional Intelligence*. New York: Bantam Books.

Gonzalez, J. (2000) 'Envisioning cyborg bodies', in D. Bell and B. Kennedy (eds), *The Cybercultures Reader*. London: Routledge.

Goodchild, P. (1996) *Deleuze and Guattari: An Introduction to the Politics of Desire*. London: Sage.

Goode, J., Curtis, K. and Theophanon, J. (1984) 'Meal formats, meal cycles and menu negotiation in the maintenance of an Italian-American community', in M. Douglas (ed.), *Food in the Social Order*. New York: Russell Sage Foundation.

Goodger, J. (1982) 'Judo players as a gnostic set', *Religion*, 12: 333–334.

Goodger, J. (1985) 'Collective representations and the sacred in sport', *International Review for the Sociology of Sport*, 20 (3): 179–186.

Goodger, J. and Goodger, B. (1989) 'Excitement and representation: toward a sociological explanation of the significance of sport in modern society', *Quest*, 41: 257–272.

Gordon, C. (1987) 'The soul of the citizen: Max Weber and Michel Foucault on rationality and government', in S. Whimster and S. Lasch (eds), *Max Weber: Rationality and Modernity*. London: Allen and Unwin.

Gordon, R. (2001) 'Eating disorders East and West: a culture bound system unbound', in M. Naser, M. Katzman and R. Gordon (eds), *Eating Disorders and Cultures in Transition*. Hove: Brunner-Routledge.

Gorn, G. (1982) 'The effect of music in advertising on choice behaviour', *Journal of Marketing*, 46: 94–101.

Goudsblom, J. (1992) *Fire and Civilization*. London: Penguin.

Green, E. and Adam, A. (2001) *Virtual Gender*. (2001) London: Routledge.

Gregory, A. (1997) 'The roles of music in society: the ethnomusicological perspective', in D. Hargreaves and A. North (eds), *The Social Psychology of Music*. Oxford: Oxford University Press.

Grint, K. (ed.) (2000) (ed.), *Work and Society: A Reader*. Cambridge: Polity.

Grogan, S. (1999) *Body Image*. London: Routledge.

Grossberg, L. (1990) 'Is there rock after punk?', in S. Frith and A. Goodwin (eds), *On Record*. New York: Pantheon.

Grosz, E. (1994) *Volatile Bodies*. London: Routledge.

Guttman, A. (1978) *From Ritual to Record: The Nature of Modern Sports*. New York: Columbia University Press.

Haiken, E. (2002) 'Modern miracles: The the development of cosmetic prosthetics', in K. Ott., D. Serlin and S. Mihm (eds), *Artificial Parts, Practical Lives*. New York: New York University Press.

Hakim, C. (1989) 'New recruits to self employment in the 1980s', *Employment Gazette*, June.

Hall, R., Ogden, P.E. and Hill, C. (1999) 'Living alone: evidence from England and Wales and France for the last two decades', in S. McRae (ed.), *Changing Britain: Families and Households in the 1990s*. Oxford: Oxford University Press.

Hall, S. (1981) 'The whites of their eyes: racist ideologies and the media', in G. Bridges and R.

Brunt (eds), *Silver Linings: Some Strategies for the Eighties*. London: Lawrence and Wishart.

Hamilton, P. (1992) 'The Enlightenment and the birth of social science', in S. Hall and B. Gieben (eds), *Formations of Modernity*. Cambridge: Polity.

Hancock, P. et al. (2000) *The Body, Culture and Society*. Buckingham: Open University Press.

Hantover, J. (1980) 'The Boy Scouts and the validation of masculinity', in E. Pleck and J. Pleck (eds), *The American Man*. Englewood Cliffs, NJ: Prentice-Hall.

Haraway, D. (1994 [1985]) 'A manifesto for cyborgs: Science, technology and socialist feminism in the 1980s', in S. Seidman (ed.), *The Postmodern Turn*. Cambridge: Cambridge University Press.

Hardey, M. (2002) 'Life beyond the screen: embodiment and identity through the Internet', *Sociological Review*, 50 (4): 570–585.

Hargreaves, D. and North, A. (eds) (1997) *The Social Psychology of Music*. Oxford: Oxford University Press.

Hargreaves, Jennifer. (1994) *Sporting Females*. London: Routledge.

Hargreaves, John. (1986) *Sport, Power and Culture*. Cambridge: Polity Press.

Harré, R. (1983) *Personal Being*. Oxford: Blackwell.

Harris, L. (2002) 'The emotional labour of barristers', *Journal of Management Studies*, 39 (4): 553–584.

Hartmann, H. (1976) 'Capitalism, patriarchy and job segregation by sex', *Signs*, 1 (3): 137–69.

Hartmann, H. (1979) 'The unhappy marriage of Marxism and feminism: Towards a more progressive union', in L. Sargent (ed.), *The Unhappy Marriage of Marxism and Feminism*. London: Pluto Press.

Haslem, D. (1998) 'DJ culture', in S. Redhead (ed.), *The Clubcultures Reader*. Oxford: Blackwell.

Hassard, J. (1996) 'Images of time in work and organisation', reprinted in K. Grint (ed.) *Work and Society: A Reader* (2000). Cambridge: Polity.

Hassard, J., Holliday, R. and Willmott, H. (2000) *Body and Organization*. London: Sage.

Heim, M. (1992) 'The erotic ontology of cyberspace', in M. Heim (ed.), *Cyberspace: First Steps*. Cambridge, MA: MIT Press.

Heim, N. (1995) 'The design of virtual reality', *Body and Society*, 1 (3/4): 65–77.

Hekman, S. (1998) 'Material bodies', in D. Welton (ed.), *Body and Flesh: A Philosophical Reader*. Oxford: Blackwell.

Heldke, L. (1992) 'Food politics, political food', in D. Curtin and L. Heldke (eds), *Cooking, Eating, Thinking*. Bloomington, IN: Indiana University Press.

Heller, A. (1974) *The Theory of Need in Marx*. London: Allison and Busby.

Hendry, L. (1996) 'Puberty and the psychosocial changes of adolescence', in C. Niven and A. Walker (eds), *Reproductive Potential and Fertility Control*. Oxford: Butterworth-Heinemann.

Hepworth, M. and Featherstone, M. (1982) *Surviving Middle Age*. Oxford: Basil Blackwell.

Higdon, H. (1992) 'Is running a religious experience?', in S.J. Hoffman (ed.), *Sport and Religion*. Champaign, Il: Human Kinetics.

Hillman, C. and Mazzio, D. (1997) *The Body in Parts*. London: Routledge.

Hirsch, F. (1976) *Social Limits to Growth*. Cambridge, MA: Harvard University Press.

Hirst, P. and Woolley, P. (1982) *Social Relations and Human Attributes*. London: Tavistock.

Hobbes, T. (1914 [1651]) *Leviathan*, Introduction by A. Lindsay. London: J.M. Dent and Sons.

Hobbes, T. (1962 [1650]) 'Human nature or the fundamental elements of policy', in T. Hobbes, *Body, Man and Citizen*, (ed.) and with an introduction by R.S. Peters. New York: Collier Books.

Hobbes, T. (1972 [1658]) 'De Homine', in B. Gert (ed.), *Man and Citizen*. New York: Doubleday.

Hoberman, J. (1992) *Mortal Engines*. New York: The Free Press.

Hoberman, J. (1997) *Darwin's Athletes*. New York: Houghton Mifflin.

Hoberman, J. and Yesalis, C. (1995) 'The history of synthetic testosterone', *Scientific American*, February: pp. 60–65.

Hochschild, A. (1983) *The Managed Heart: Commercialisation of Human Feeling*. Berkeley:

University of California Press.

Hochschild, A. (1989) *The Second Shift*. New York: Viking.

Hodap, V., Bongard, S. and Heiligentag, U. (1992) 'Active coping, expression of anger and cardiovascular reactivity', *Personality and Individual Differences*, 13: 1069–1076.

Hoffman, S.J. (1992a) 'Nimrod, mephilism, and the athletae dei', in S.J. Hoffman (ed.), *Sport and Religion*. Champaign, Il: Human Kinetics Books.

Hoffman, S.J. (ed.) (1992b) *Sport and Religion*. Champaign, IL: Human Kinetics.

Holliday, R. and Hassard, J. (2001) *Contested Bodies*. London: Routledge.

Homans, G. (1958) 'Social behaviour as exchange', *American Journal of Sociology*, 63: 597–606.

Honneth, A. and Joas, H. (1988) *Social Action and Human Nature*. Cambridge: Cambridge University Press.

Horne, H., Tomlinson, A. and Whannel, G. (1999) *Understanding Sport*. London: E. and F.N. Spon.

Horner, D. (2001) 'Cyborgs and cyberspace', in S. Munt (ed.), *Technospaces*. London: Continuum.

Howes, D. (ed.) (1991) *The Varieties of Sensory Experience*. Toronto: University of Toronto Press.

Howson, A. and Inglis, D. (2001) 'The body in sociology: tensions inside and outside sociological thought', *Sociological Review*, 49 (3): 297–317.

Hughes, J. (2003a) '"Intelligent hearts": Emotional intelligence, emotional labour and informalization', Centre for Labour Market Studies (Working Paper 43), Leicester: University of Leicester.

Hughes, J. (2003b) 'Bringing emotion to work: Emotional intelligence, employee resistance and the reinvention of character', unpublished paper.

Hughes, J. (2003c) *Learning to Smoke*. Chicago: University of Chicago Press.

Hugill, S. (1961) *Shanties from the Seven Seas*. London: Routledge.

Huizinga, J. (1970 [1938]) *Homo Ludens: A Study of the Play Element in Culture*. London: Temple Smith.

Humes, J. (1941) 'The effects of occupational music on scrappage in the manufacturing of radio tubes', *Journal of Applied Psychology*, 25: 573–87.

Hunter, D. (1975, 5th edition) *The Diseases of Occupations*, 5th edn. London: Hodder and Stoughton.

Husserl, E. (1989 [1929]) *Ideas Pertaining to a Pure Phenomenology and to a Phenomenological Philosophy*. London: Kluwer.

Iossifides, A. (1992) 'Wine: Life's blood and spiritual essence in a Greek Orthodox convent', in D. Gefou-Madianou (ed.), *Alcohol, Gender and Culture*. London: Routledge and Kegan Paul.

Irigaray, L. (1986 [1977]) *This Sex Which Is Not One*. New York: Cornell University Press.

Jackson, S. and Csikszentmihalyi, M. (1999) *Flow in Sports*. Champaign, IL: Human Kinetics.

James, A. (1990) 'The good, the bad and the delicious: the role of confectionery in British society', *The Sociological Review*, 38 (4): 666–668.

Jameson, F. (1972) *The Prison-House of Language*. Princeton, NJ: Princeton University Press.

Janssen, J. and Verheggen, T. (1997) 'The double center of gravity in Durkheim's symbol theory: Bringing the symbolism of the body back in', *Sociological Theory*, 15 (3): 294–306.

Jelliffe, D. (1967) 'Parallel food classification in developing and industrialised countries', *American Journal of Clinical Nutrition*, 20: 279–81.

Jenks, C. (ed.) (1995) *Visual Culture*. London: Routledge.

Joas, H. (1996) *The Creativity of Action*. Cambridge: Polity.

Johnson, D. (1983) *Body*. Boston: Beacon Press.

Jones, S. (1995) 'Understanding community in the information age', in S. Jones (ed.), *Cybersociety*. London: Sage.

Jordan, T. (1999) *Cyberpower: The Culture and Politics of Cyberspace and the Internet*. London: Routledge.

Jung, H.Y. (1996) 'Phenomenology and body politics', *Body and Society*, 2 (2): 1–22.

Kane, M.J. (1995) 'Resistance/transformation of the oppositional binary: Exposing sport as a continuum', *Journal of Sport and Social Issues*, 19 (2): 191–218.

Kane, M.J. and Disch, L.J. (1993) 'Sexual violence and the reproduction of male power in the locker room: The "Lisa Olson incident"', *Sociology of Sport Journal*, 10: 331–352.

Kane, P. (1994) *Hitchhiker's Guide to the Electronic Highway*. New York: MIS Press.

Kant, I. (1964 [1785]) *Groundwork of the Metaphysics of Morals*. New York: Harper and Row.

Kant, I. (1985 [1797]) *Foundations of the Physics of Morals*. London: Macmillan.

Kaplan, L. and Nettel, R. (1948) 'Music in industry', *Biology and Human Affairs*, 13: 129–135.

Katz, C. (1993) 'Growing girls/closing circles', in C. Katz and J. Monk (eds), *Full Circles: Geographies of Women over the Life Course*. London: Routledge.

Keat, R. and Urry, J. (1982) *Social Theory as Science*. London: Routledge.

Kelly, K. (1994) *Out of Control: The New Biology of Machines*. London: Fourth Estate.

Kemmer, D. (2000) 'Tradition and change in domestic roles and food preparation', *Sociology*, 34 (2): 323–333.

Kimbrell, K. (1993) *The Human Body Shop*. London: Harper Collins.

Kimmel, M. (1990) 'Baseball and the reconstitution of American masculinity 1880–1920', in M. Messner and D. Sabo (eds), *Sport, Men and the Gender Order*. Champaign, IL: Human Kinetics.

Kirby, V. (1997) *Telling Flesh*. London: Routledge.

Kirkpatrick, F. (1943) 'Music in industry', *Journal of Applied Psychology*, 27: 268–274.

Koku, E. Nazer, N. and Wellman, B. (2001) 'Netting scholars: online and offline', *American Behavioural Scientist*, 44 (10): 1752–1774.

Kolder, V., Gallagher, J., and Parsons, M. (1987) 'Court-ordered obstetrical interventions', *New England Journal of Medicine*, 316 (19): 1192–1196.

Konecni, V. J. (1982) 'Social interaction and musical preference', in D. Deutsch (ed.), *The Psychology of Music*. New York: Academic Press.

Konecni, V.J. and Sargent-Pollack, D. (1976) 'Choice between melodies differing in complexity under divided-attention conditions', *Scientific Aesthetics/Sciences de l'Art*, 1: 47–55.

Krauthammer, C. (1984) 'The appeal of ordeal', *Time*, 14 May: pp. 93–4.

Kristeva, J. (1986) *The Kristeva Reader* (edited by. T. Moi). New York: Columbia University Press.

Kroker, A. and Kroker, M. (1988) *Body Invaders*. New Haven, Conn: Yale University Press.

Kurzman, S. (2002) "There's no language for this": Communication and alignment in contemporary prosthetics', in K. Ott, D. Serlin and S. Mihm (eds), *Artificial Parts, Practical Lives*. New York: New York University Press.

Lakoff, G. (1987) *Women, Fire and Dangerous Things*. Chicago: University of Chicago Press.

Lakoff, G. and Johnson, M. (1999) *Philosophy in the Flesh*. New York: Basic Books.

Landsberg, A. (1995) 'Prosthetic memory', *Body and Society*, 1 (3-/4): 175–189.

Lanier, J. (1990) 'Riding in the giant worm to Saturn: post-symbolic communication in virtual reality', in G. Hattinger et al. (eds), *Arts Electronica*, Vol. 2. Virtuelle Welten Linz: Veritas-Verlag.

Lanza, J. (1994) *Elevator Music*. London: Quartet Books.

Laqueur, T. (1990) *Making Sex*. Cambridge, MA: Harvard University Press.

Larrain, J. (1979) *The Concept of Ideology*. London: Hutchinson.

Lash, S. (2002) *Critique of Information*. London: Sage.

Laws, J. (2002) 'Objects and spaces', *Theory, Culture and Society*, 19 (5-/6): 91–105.

Laws, S. (1990) *Issues of Blood: The Politics of Menstruation*. Houndmills: Macmillan.

Leath, V.M. and Lumpkin, A. (1992) 'An analysis of sportswomen on the covers and in the feature articles of Women's Sports and Fitness Magazine, 1975–89', *Journal of Sport and Social Issues*, 16 (2): 121–6.

Leder, D. (1990) *The Absent Body*. Chicago: University of Chicago Press.

Lehoux, O., Sicotte, C., Denis, J.-L., Berg, M. and Lacroix, A. (2002) 'The theory of use behind telemedicine: how compatible with physicians' clinical routines?', *Social Science and Medicine*, 54: 889–904.

Leidner, R. (1993) *McDonalds*. Berkeley: University of California Press.

Lenskyj, H. (1986) *Out of Bounds: Women, Sport and Sexuality*. Toronto: Women's Press.

Leonard, W. and Robertson, M. (1994) 'Evolutionary perspectives on human nutrition: the influence of brain and body size on diet and metabolism', *American Journal of Human Biology*, 6: 77–88.

Lerdahl, F. and Jackendoff, R. (1983) *A Generative Theory of Tonal Music*. Cambridge, MA: MIT Press.

Levine, D. (1971) 'Introduction', in *Georg Simmel on Individuality and Social Forms*. Chicago: University of Chicago Press.

Levine, D. (1991b) 'Simmel and Parsons reconsidered', in R. Robertson and B.S. Turner (eds), *Talcott Parsons: Theorist of Modernity*. London: Sage.

Levine, D. (1995) *Visions of the Sociological Tradition*. Chicago: The University of Chicago Press.

Levine, D. (2000) 'On the critique of "utilitarian" theories of action: Newly identified convergences among Simmel, Weber and Parsons', *Theory, Culture and Society*, 17 (1): 63–78.

Lévi-Strauss, C. (1963) *Totemism*. Boston: Beacon Press.

Lévi-Strauss, C. (1969) *The Raw and the Cooked*. New York: Harper and Row.

Lewis, M. and Hill, A. (1998) 'Food advertising on British children's television', *International Journal of Obesity*, 22: 206–14.

Liff, S., Steward, F. and Watts, P. (2002) 'New public places for Internet access', in S. Woolgar (ed.), *Virtual Society? Technology, Cyberbole, Reality*. Oxford: Oxford University Press.

Locke, K. (1996) 'A funny thing happened! The management of consumer emotions in service encounters', *Organizational Science*, 7: 40–59.

Longhurst, B. (1995) *Popular Music and Society*. Cambridge: Polity.

Lukas, G. (1969) *Die Köorperkultur in frühen Epochen der Menscehentwicklung*. East Berlin: Sportverlagp.

Lukes, S. (1973) *Emile Durkheim*. London: Penguin.

Lupton, D. (1995) 'The embodied computer/user', *Body and Society*, 1 (3/4): 97–112.

Lupton, D. (1996) *Food, the Body and the Self*. London: Sage.

Lury, C. (1998) *Prosthetic Culture*. London: Routledge.

Lyng, S. (1990) 'Edgework: a social psychological analysis of voluntary risk taking', *American Journal of Sociology*, 95: 887–921.

McBride, T. (1992) 'Women's work and industrialisation', in L. Berlanstein (ed.), *The Industrial Revolution and Work in Nineteenth Century Europe*. London: Routledge.

McDaid, J. (2002) '"How a one-legged rebel lives": Confederate veterans and artificial limbs in Virginia', in K. Ott, D. Serlin and S. Mihm (eds), *Artificial Parts, Practical Lives*. New York: New York University Press.

McFarland, D. (2001) 'Student resistance: how the formal and informal organisation of classrooms facilitate everyday forms of student defiance', *American Journal of Sociology*, 107 (3): 612–78.

McGehee, W. and Gardner, J. (1949) 'Music in a complex industrial job', *Personnel Psychology*, 2: 405–417.

McGrail, B. (2002) 'Confronting electronic surveillance', in S. Woolgar (ed.), *Virtual Society? Technology, Cyberbole, Reality*. Oxford: Oxford University Press.

McKay, J. (1995) '"Just do it": corporate sports slogans and the political economy of "enlightened racism"', *Discourse*, 16 (2): 191–201.

McKie, L., Wood, R. and Gregory, S. (1993) 'Women defining health', *Health Education Research: Theory and Practice*, 8 (1): 35–41.

McLellan, D. (1980 second edition) *The Thought of Karl Marx*. London: Macmillan.

McLellan, G. (1985) 'Marx's concept of human nature', *New Left Review*, 149: 121–4.

McLuhan, M. (1969) *Counterblast*. London: Rapp and Whiting.

McLuhan, M. and Fiore, Q. (1962) *The Medium is the Message*. Harmondsworth: Penguin.

McNay, L. (1992) *Foucault and Feminism*. Cambridge: Cambridge University Press.

Mackay, D. (2003a) 'Drugs crisis deepens as yet another American athlete tests positive', The *Observer*, 26 October.

Mackay, D. (2003b) 'Lewis: "Who cares I failed drug test?"', The *Guardian*, 24 April.

Mackenzie, D. and Wajcman, J. (eds) (1999) *The Social Shaping of Technology*, 2nd edn. Buckingham: Open University Press.

Mackinnon, C. (1989) *Towards a Feminist Theory of the State*. Cambridge, MA: Harvard University Press.

Maffesoli, M. (1996) *The Time of the Tribes*. London: Sage.

Maguire, J. (1993) 'Globalisation, sport development and the media/sport production complex', *Sports Science Review*, 2 (1): 29–47.

Maguire, J. (1994) 'Preliminary observations on globalisation and the migration of sport labour', *The Sociological Review*, 42 (3): 452–80.

Majors, R. (1990) 'Cool pose: black masculinity and sports', in M. Messner and D. Sabo (eds), *Sport, Men and the Gender Order*. Champaign, IL: Human Kinetics.

Malcolmson, R. (1973) *Popular Recreations in English Society 1700–1850*. Cambridge: Cambridge University Press.

Malinowskiy, B. (1925) 'Complex and myth in mother-right', *Psyche*, 5: 194–216.

Maney, K. (1995) *Megamedia Shakeout*. London: Wiley.

Mangan, J. (1986) *The Games Ethic and Imperialism*. New York: Viking.

Mangan, J. (1992) 'Britain's chief spiritual export: imperial sport as moral metaphor, political symbol and cultural bond', in J. Mangan (ed.), *The Cultural Bond: Sport, Empire, Society*. London: Frank Cass.

Mangan, J. and Park, R. (eds) (1987) *From 'Fair Sex' to Feminism: Sport and the Socialization of Women in the Industrial and Post-Industrial Eras*. London: Frank Cass.

Mangan, J. and Walvin, J. (1987) *Manliness and Morality: Middle-Class Masculinity in Britain and America, 1800–1940*. Manchester: Manchester University Press.

Marcel, G. (1951) *Le Mystère de l'Etre*. Paris: 'Philosophie de l'esprit' series.

Marcuse, H. (1955) *Eros and Civilization*. Boston: Beacon Press.

Marcuse, H. (1964) *One-Dimensional Man*. London: Abacus.

Martin, E. (1987) *The Woman in the Body*. Milton Keynes: Open University Press.

Martin, E. (1994) *Flexible Bodies*. Boston: Beacon Press.

Martin, P. (1995) *Sounds and Society*. Manchester: Manchester University Press.

Martin, P. (2003) 'We'll mate again', *The Sunday Times Magazine*, 27 April, pp. 21–28.

Marwick, C. (1999) 'Cyberinformation for seniors', *JAMA*, 281 (16): 1–3.

Marx, K. (1954 [1867]) *Capital*, Vol. 1. London: Lawrence and Wishart.

Marx, K. (1968 [1849]) 'Wage, labour and capital', in *Marx/Engels: Selected Works in One Volume*. London: Lawrence and Wishart.

Marx, K. (1968 [1852]) 'The Eighteenth Brumaire of Louis Bonaparte', in *Marx/Engels: Selected Works in One Volume*. London: Lawrence and Wishart.

Marx, K. (1968 [1859]) 'Preface to a contribution to the critique of political economy', in *Marx/Engels: Selected Works in One Volume*. London: Lawrence and Wishart.

Marx, K. (1973 [1939]) *Grundrisse*. Harmondsworth: Penguin books/New Left Review.

Marx, K. (1975 [1844]) 'The Economic and Philosophic Manuscripts of 1844', in *Karl Marx: Early Writings*. Harmondsworth: Pelican.

Marx, K. and Engels, F. (1968 [1848]) 'Manifesto of the Communist Party', in *Marx/Engels: Selected Works in One Volume*. London: Lawrence and Wishart.

Marx, K. and Engels, F. (1977 [1846]) *The German Ideology*, ed. and with an introduction by C. Arthur. London: Lawrence and Wishart.

Mauss, M. (1973 [1934]) 'Techniques of the body', *Economy and Society*, 2: 70–88.

Mauss, M. (1989) 'A category of the human mind: the notion of person; the notion of self', in M. Carrithers, S. Collins and S. Lukes (eds), *The Category of the Person*. Cambridge: Cambridge University Press.

Mauss, M. (1990 [1950]) *The Gift*. London: Routledge.

Mead, G.H. (1938) *The Philosophy of the Act*. Chicago: University of Chicago Press.

Meadow, R. and Weiss, L. (1992) *Women's Conflicts about Eating and Sexuality*. New York: The Howarth Press.

Mechikoff, R. and Estes, S. (1993) *A History and Philosophy of Sport*. Madison, WI: Brown and

Benchmark.

Meek, C. (1926) *A Sudanese Kingdom*. London: Kegan Paul.

Mellor, P.A. and Shilling, C. (1994) 'Reflexive modernity and the religious body', *Religion*, 24: 23–42.

Mellor, P.A. and Shilling, C. (1997) *Re-forming the Body: Religion, Community and Modernity*. London: Sage.

Mennell, S. (1985) *All Manners of Food*. Oxford: Blackwell.

Men's Fitness (2002) January/February. London: Dennis Publishing.

Merleau-Ponty, M. (1962) *The Phenomenology of Perception*. London: Routledge.

Merleau-Ponty, M. (1963) *The Primacy of Perception*, ed. and with an introduction by J.M. Edie. Evanston, IL: Northwestern University Press.

Merleau-Ponty, M. (1968) *The Visible and the Invisible*. Evanston, Il: Northwestern University Press.

Merriam, A. (1959) 'African music', in W. Bascom and M. Herskovits (eds), *Continuity and Change in African Cultures*. Chicago: University of Chicago Press.

Merriam, A. (1964) *The Anthropology of Music*. Evanston, Il: Northwestern University Press.

Merton, R. (1968 [1949]) *Social Theory and Social Structure*, 3rd edn. New York: Free Press.

Messner, M. (1987) 'The life of a man's seasons: Male identity in the life-course of the jock', in M. Kimmel (ed.), *Changing Men*. London: Sage.

Michaelson, G. and Pohl, M. (2001) 'Gender in email-based co-operative problem-solving', in E. Green and A. Adam (eds), *Virtual Gender*. London: Routledge.

Mihm, S. (2002) '"A limb which shall be presentable in polite society", prosthetic technologies in the nineteenth century', in K. Ott, D. Serlin and S. Mihm (eds), *Artificial Parts, Practical Lives*. New York: New York University Press.

Milliman, R. (1982) 'Using background music to affect the behaviour of supermarket shoppers', *Journal of Marketing*, 46: 86–91.

Milliman, R. (1986) 'The influence of background music on the behaviour of restaurant patrons', *Journal of Consumer Research*, 13: 286–9.

Mills, C. W. (1953) *White Collar*. New York: Oxford University Press.

Mills, P., Schneider, R. and Dimsdale, J. (1989) 'Anger assessment and reactivity to stress', *Journal of Psychosomatic Research*, 33: 379–382.

Mitra, A. (2000) 'Virtual community', in D. Bell and B. Kennedy (eds), *The Cybercultures Reader*. London: Routledge.

Monaghan, L. (2002) 'Hard men, shop boys and others: embodying competence in a masculinist occupation', *The Sociological Review*, 50 (3): 334–355.

Moreno, J. (1988) 'The music therapist: creative arts therapist and contemporary shaman', *The Arts in Psychotherapy*, 15: 271–80.

Mori, D., Chaiken, S. and Pliner, P. (1987) '"Eating lightly" and the self-presentation of femininity', *Journal of Personality and Social Psychology*, 53: 672–693.

Mottram, D. (1996a) 'What is a drug?', in D. Mottram (ed.), *Drugs in Sport*. London: E. and F.N. Spon.

Mottram, D. (ed.) (1996b) *Drugs in Sport*, 2nd edn. London: E. and F.N. Spon.

Mrozek, D. (1983) *Sport and American Mentality, 1880–1910*. Knoxville: University of Tennessee Press.

Mumford, L. (1967) *The Myth of the Machine*. London: Secker and Warburg.

Munt, S. (2001) 'Introduction', in S. Munt (ed.), *Technospaces*. London: Continuum.

Murcott, A. (1983) 'It's a pleasure to cook for him: food, mealtimes and gender in some South Wales households', in E. Gamarnikow, D. Morgan, J. Purvis and D. Taylorson (eds), *The Public and the Private*. London: Heinemann.

Murcott, A. (1997) 'Family meals: a thing of the past?', in P. Caplan (ed.), *Food, Identity and Health*. London: Routledge.

Nakamura, L. (1995) 'Race in/for cyberspace', reprinted in D. Bell and B. Kennedy (2000) (eds), *The Cybercultures Reader* (2000). London: Routledge.

Nast, H. and Pile, S. (1998) *Places Through the Body*. London: Routledge.

Nettleton, S., Pleace, N., Burrows, R., Muncer, S. and Loader, B. (2002) 'The reality of virtual social support', in S. Woolgar (ed.), *Virtual Society? Technology, Cyberbole, Reality*. Oxford: Oxford University Press.

Nettleton, S. and Watson, J. (eds) (1998) *The Body in Everyday Life*. London: Routledge.

New, C. (2003) 'Feminism, critical realism and the linguistic turn', in J. Cruickshank (ed.), *Critical Realism: The Difference It Makes*. London: Routledge.

Newton, T. (2003a) 'Truly embodied sociology: marrying the social and the biological?', *The Sociological Review*, 51 (1): 20–42.

Newton, T. (2003b) 'Crossing the great divide: time, nature and the social', *Sociology*, 37 (3): 433–47.

Nguyen, D. and Alexander, J. (1996) 'The coming of cyberspacetime and the end of the polity', in R. Shields (ed.), *Cultures of Internet*. London: Sage.

Nicholson, L. (ed.) (1990) *Feminism/Postmodernism*. London: Routledge.

Nietzsche, F. (1993 [1872]) *The Birth of Tragedy*. Harmondsworth: Penguin.

Nisbet, R. (1993 [1966]) *The Sociological Tradition*. New Brunswick, New Jersey: Transaction.

North, A. and Hargreaves, D. (1997) 'Music and consumer behaviour', in D. Hargreaves and A. North (eds), *The Social Psychology of Music*. Oxford: Oxford University Press.

Novak, M. (1976) *The Joy of Sport*. New York: Basic Books.

Oakes, G. (1984) 'Introduction', in *Georg Simmel: On Women, Sexuality and Love*. New Haven, CT: Yale University Press.

Oakes, G. (1989) 'Sales as a vocation: the moral ethos of personal sales', *International Journal of Politics, Culture and Society*, 3 (2): 237–253.

Oakley, A. (1972) *Sex, Gender and Society*. London: Temple Smith.

Oakley, A. (1974a) *The Sociology of Housework*. Oxford: Blackwell.

Oakley, A. (1974b) *Housewife*. London: Allen Lane.

Obi, M. (2003) 'When night is right', The *Guardian* (Office Hours Supplement) 14 April, pp. 2–3.

O'Connor, J. (1973) *The Fiscal Crisis of the State*. London: St. Martin's Press.

O'Neill, J. (1972) *Sociology as Skin Trade*. London: Heinemann.

O'Neill, J. (1985) *Five Bodies: The Human Shape of Modern Society*. Ithaca, NY: Cornell University Press.

O'Neill, S. (1997) 'Gender and music', in D. Hargreaves and A. North (eds), *The Social Psychology of Music*. Oxford: Oxford University Press.

Orbach, S. (1988 [1978]) *Fat is a Feminist Issue*. London: Arrow Books.

Ostwald, M. (1997) 'Virtual urban futures', reprinted in D. Bell and B. Kennedy (eds), *The Cybercultures Reader* (2000). London: Routledge.

O'Toole, M. (1998) 'Overreaching and overtraining in endurance athletes', in R. Kreider, A. Fry and M.L. O'Toole (eds), *Overtraining in Sport*. Champaign, IL: Human Kinetics.

Ott, K. (2002a) 'The sum of its parts: An introduction to modern histories of prostheses', in K. Ott, D. Serlin and S. Mihm (eds), *Artificial Parts, Practical Lives*. New York: New York University Press.

Ott, K. (2002b) 'Hard wear and soft tissue: Craft and commerce in artificial eyes', in K. Ott, D. Serlin and S. Mihm (eds), *Artificial Parts, Practical Lives*. New York: New York University Press.

Ott, K., Serlin, D. and Mihm, S. (eds) (2002) *Artificial Parts, Practical Lives*. New York: New York University Press.

Overman, S. (1997) *The Influence of the Protestant Ethic on Sport and Recreation*. London: Avebury.

Paoli, P. (1997) 'Second European survey on the work environment 1995 European Foundation for the Improvement of Living and Working Conditions, Dublin. Cited in Zapf, 2002.

Park, R. (1987) 'Biological thought, athletics and the formation of a "man of character", 1830–1900', in J. Mangan and J. Walvin (eds), *Manliness and Morality: Middle-Class Masculinity in Britain and America, 1800–1940*. Manchester: Manchester University Press.

Parsons, T. (1968 [1937]) *The Structure of Social Action*, 2 vols. New York: The Free Press.

Parsons, T. (1991 [1951]) *The Social System*. London: Routledge.

Peiss, K. (1986) *Cheap Amusements*. Philadelphia, PA: Temple University Press.

Pels, D., Hetherington, K. and Vandenberghe, F. (2002) 'The status of the object: performances, mediations and techniques', *Theory, Culture and Society*, 19 (5/6): 1–21.

Perkins, W. (1996) 'The rap attach: an introduction', in W. Perkins (ed.), *Droppin' Science*. Philadelphia, PA: Temple University Press.

Perry, H. (2002) 'Re-arming the disabled veteran', in K. Ott., D. Serlin and S. Mihm (eds), *Artificial Parts, Practical Lives*. New York: New York University Press.

Peterson, A. (1997) 'Risk, governance and the new public health', in A. Peterson and R. Bunton (eds), *Foucault, Health and Medicine*. London: Routledge.

Peterson, A. and Bunton, R. (2001) *The New Genetics and the Public's Health*. London: Routledge.

Phelan, P. (1997) *Mourning Sex*. London: Routledge.

Piore, M. and Sabel, C. (1984) *The Second Industrial Divide*. New York: Basic Books.

Plant, S. (1993) 'Beyond the screens: film, cyberpunk and cyberfeminism', *Variant*.

Plato (1981) *The Republic*, trans. by G. Grube. London: Pan.

Poliakoff, M. (1987) *Combat Sports in the Ancient World*. New Haven, CT: Yale University Press.

Pollard, S. (1965) *The Genesis of Modern Management: A Study of the Industrial Revolution in Great Britain*. Cambridge, MA: Harvard University Press.

Pomeroy, S. (1975) *Goddesses, Whores, Wives and Slaves*. New York: Schocken Books.

Powers, W. and Powers, M. (1984) 'Metaphysical aspects of an Oglala food system', in M. Douglas (ed.), *Food in the Social Order*. New York: Russell Sage Foundation.

Prevost, A., Whichlow, M. and Cox, B. (1997) 'Longitudinal dietary changes between 1984–5 and 1991–2 in British adults: associations with socio-demographics, lifestyle and health factors', *British Journal of Nutrition*, 78: 873–88.

Pringle, K. (1998) *Children and Social Welfare in Europe*. Buckingham: Open University Press.

Pringle, R. (1988) *Secretaries at Work*. Cambridge: Polity.

Probyn, E. (2000) 'Sporting bodies: Dynamics of shame and pride', *Body and Society*, 6 (1): 13–28.

Puttnam, R. (2000) *Bowling Alone: The Collapse and Revival of American Community*. New York: Simon and Schuster.

Rabinbach, A. (1990) *The Human Motor: Energy, Fatigue and the Origins of Modernity*. New York: Basic Books.

Radford, T. (2003a) 'Silent sounds hit emotional chords', The *Guardian*, 8 September, p. 11.

Radford, T. (2003b) 'Nanotech moves the future to a new level', The *Guardian*, 28 July, p. 5.

Rawls, A. (1987) 'The interaction order *sui generis*: Goffman's contribution to social theory', *Sociological Theory*, 5: 136–49.

Reisman, D. (1959) *The Lonely Crowd: A Study of the Changing American Character*. New Haven, CT: Yale University Press.

Reskin, B. and Roos, P. (1990) *Job Queues, Gender Queues*. Philadelphia, PA: Temple University Press.

Reynolds, S. (1998) 'Rave culture', in S. Redhead (ed.), *The Clubcultures Reader*. Oxford: Blackwell.

Rheingold, H. (1993) *The Virtual Community*. Reading, MA: Addison-Wesley.

Richardson, J. (2000) 'What can a body do? Sexual harassment and legal procedure', in J. Hassard, R. Holliday, and H. Willmott (eds), *Body and Organisation*. London: Macmillan.

Ritzer, G. (1993) *The McDonaldization of Society*. Thousand Oaks, CA: Pine Forge.

Ritzer, G. (1996 rev. edition) *The McDonaldization of Society*. Thousand Oaks, CA: Pine Forge.

Roballey, T. et al. (1985) 'The effect of music on eating behaviour', *Bulletin of the Psychonomic Society*, 23: 221–2.

Roberts, J. (1992) 'Drink and industrial discipline in nineteenth century Germany', in L. Berlanstein (ed.), *The Industrial Revolution and Work in Nineteenth Century Europe*. London: Routledge.

Robins, K. (1995) 'Cyberspace and the world we live in', *Body and Society*, 1 (3/4): 135–155.

Robinson, C., and Flowers, C. (1999) 'Internet access and use among disadvantaged inner-city patients', *JAMA*, 281 (11): 1–2.

Rodaway, P. (1994) *Sensuous Geographies*. London: Routledge.

Rojek, C. (2000) *Leisure and Culture*. Houndmills: Palgrave.

Rojek, C. (2001) *Celebrity*. London: Reaktion Books.

Rommes, E., Van Oost, E. and Oudshoorn, N. (2001) 'Gender in the design of the digital city of Amsterdam', in E. Green and A. Adam, *Virtual Gender*. London: Routledge.

Rose, H. (1987) 'Victorian values in the test tube', in M. Stanworth (ed.), *Reproductive Technologies*. Cambridge: Polity.

Rose, H. and Rose, S. (eds) (2000) *Alas Poor Darwin: Arguments Against Evolutionary Psychology*. London: Jonathan Cape.

Rose, N. (1985) *The Psychological Complex*. London: Routledge.

Rose, N. (1989) *Governing the Soul*. London: Routledge.

Rosenbaum, M. (1993) *Children and the Environment*. London: National Children's Bureau.

Roy, D. (1960) 'Banana time: job satisfaction and informal interaction', *Human Organization*, 18: 156–68.

Rozin, P. (1982) 'Human food selection', in L. Barker (ed.), *The Psychobiology of Human Food Selection*. Chichester: Ellis Horwood.

Rozin, P. and Fallon, A. (1987) 'A perspective on disgust', *Psychological Review*, 94: 23–41.

Rubin, G. (1975) 'The traffic in women', in R. Reiter (ed.), *Toward an Anthology of Women*. New York: Monthly Review Press.

Russell, H. (1986) 'Competition and the growing child', in G. Gleeson (ed.), *The Growing Child in Competitive Sport*. London: Hodder and Stoughton.

Russett, C. (1989) *Sexual Science: The Victorian Construction of Womanhood*. Cambridge, MA: Harvard University Press.

Sage, G. (1973) 'The coach as management', *Quest*, XIX: 35–40.

Sagi, M. and Vitanyi, I. (1988) 'Experimental research into musical generative ability', in J. Sloboda (ed.), *Generative Processes in Music*. Oxford: Clarendon Press.

Sammons, J. (1994) '"Race" and sport: a critical historical examination', *Journal of Sport History*, 21 (3): 203–278.

Sansone, S. (1988) *Greek Athletics and the Genesis of Sport*. Berkeley, University of California Press.

Sardar, Z. (1996) 'ALT.CIVILIZATIONS.FAQ Cyberspace as the darker side of the west', reprinted in D. Bell and B. Kennedy (2000) (eds), *The Cybercultures Reader*. London: Routledge.

Sawday, J. (1995) *The Body Emblazoned*. Oxford: Blackwell.

Sawicki, J. (1991) *Disciplining Foucault*. New York: Routledge.

Sawyer, R.K. (2001) 'Emergence in sociology: Contemporary philosophy of mind and some implications for sociological theory', *American Journal of Sociology*, 107 (3): 551–585.

Sawyer, R.K. (2002) 'Durkheim's dilemma: Toward toward a sociology of emergence', *Sociological Theory*, 20 (2): 227–247.

Sayer, A. (2000) *Realism and Social Science*. London: Sage.

Sayers, S. (1994) 'Moral values and progress', *New Left Review*, 204, pp. 67–85.

Scambler, G. (2002) *Health and Social Change*. Buckingham: Open University Press.

Scambler, G. and Scambler, S. (2003) 'Realist agendas on biology, health and medicine', in S. Williams, L. Birke and G. Bendelow (eds), *Debating Biology*. London: Routledge.

Scarry, E. (1985) *The Body in Pain*. Oxford: Oxford University Press.

Scarry, E. (1994) *Resisting Representation*. Oxford: Oxford University Press.

Scheff, T.J. (1994) *Bloody Revenge: Emotions, Nationalism and War*. Boulder, CO: Westview Press.

Scheff, T.J. (1997) *Emotions: The Social Bond and Human Reality*. Cambridge: Cambridge University Press.

Schilder, P. (1978) *The Image and Appearance of the Human Body*. New York: International Universities Press.

Schlosser, E. (2002) *Fast Food Nation*. Harmondsworth: Penguin.

Schopenhauer, A. (1966) *The World as Will and Representation*, 2 vols. New York: Dover.

Schutz, A. (1964) 'Making music together', in *Collected Papers*, Vol. 2. The Hague: Martinus Nijhoff.

Schwarz, H. (1986) *Never Satisfied*. New York: Free Press.

Scott, J. (1995.) *Sociological Theory: Contemporary Debates*. Aldershot: Edward Elgar.

Scott, M. (1968) *The Racing Game*. Chicago: Aldine.

Seager, J. (2003) *The Atlas of Women*. London: Women's Press.

Searle, G. (1971) *The Quest for National Efficiency*. Oxford: Basil Blackwell.

Segerstrale, U. (2000) *Defenders of the Truth: The Battle for Science in the Sociology Debate and Beyond*. Oxford: Oxford University Press.

Sekora, J. (1977) *Luxury: The Concept in Western Thought*. Baltimore, MD: Johns Hopkins University Press.

Select Committee on Science and Technology (2000). Sixth Report: Complementary and Alternative Medicine. London: Stationery Office.

Sellerberg, A. (1991) 'In food we trust?', in E. Furst, R. Prattala, M. Ekstrom, L. Holm and U. Kjaernes (eds), *Palatable Worlds*. Oslo: Solum Forlag.

Sennett, R. (1994) *Flesh and Stone*. London: Faber and Faber.

Sennett, R. (1998) *The Corrosion of Character*. New York: Norton.

Sennett, R. and Cobb, J. (1972) *The Hidden Injuries of Class*. New York: W. Norton & Co.

Serlin, D. (2002) 'Engineering masculinity: Veterans and prosthetics after WW2', in K. Ott., D. Serlin and S. Mihm (eds), *Artificial Parts, Practical Lives*. New York: New York University Press.

Seymour, W. (1998) *Remaking the Body*. London: Allen Lane.

Shapiro, M. and McDonald, D. (1992) 'I'm not a real doctor but I play one in virtual reality', *Journal of Communication*, 42 (4): 94–114.

Sheard, K. and Dunning, E. (1973) 'The rugby football club as a type of male preserve', *International Review of Sport Sociology*, 5 (3): 5–24.

Sheehan, G. (1992) 'Playing', in S.J. Hoffman (ed.), *Sport and Religion*. Champaign, IL: Human Kinetic Books.

Shenk, D. (1997) *Data Smog: Surviving the Information Age*. San Francisco: Harperedge.

Shildrick, M. (2002) *Embodying the Monster: Encounters with the Vulnerable Self*. London: Sage.

Shilling, C. (1993) *The Body and Social Theory*. London: Sage.

Shilling, C. (1997) 'The undersocialized conception of the embodied agent in modern sociology', *Sociology*, 31 (4): 737–754.

Shilling, C. (1999) 'Towards an embodied understanding of the structure/agency relationship', *The British Journal of Sociology*, 50 (4): 543–562.

Shilling, C. (2001a) 'The embodied foundations of social theory', in G. Ritzer and B. Smart (eds), *Handbook of Social Theory*. London: Sage.

Shilling, C. (2001b) 'Embodiment, experience and theory: In defence of the sociological tradition', *The Sociological Review*, 49 (3): 327–344.

Shilling, C. (2002) 'The two traditions in the sociology of emotions', in J. Barbalet (ed.), *Emotions and Sociology*. Oxford: Blackwell.

Shilling, C. (2003) *The Body and Social Theory*, 2nd edn. London: Sage.

Shilling, C. (2004a) 'Embodiment, emotions and the foundations of social order: Durkheim's enduring contribution', in J. Alexander and P. Smith (eds), *The Cambridge Companion to Durkheim*. Cambridge: Cambridge University Press.

Shilling, C. (2004b) 'Physical capital and situated action: a new direction for corporeal sociology', *British Journal of Sociology of Education*, 25.

Shilling, C. and Mellor, P.A. (1996) 'Embodiment, structuration theory and modernity: Mind/body dualism and the repression of sensuality', *Body and Society*, 2 (4): 1–15.

Shilling, C. and Mellor, P.A. (2001) *The Sociological Ambition: Elementary Forms of Social and Moral Life*. London: Sage.

Shusterman, R. (1992) *Pragmatist Aesthetics*. Oxford: Blackwell.

Simmel, G. (1950) *The Sociology of Georg Simmel*. Glencoe, IL: Free Press.

Simmel, G. (1969 [1908]) 'Sociology of the senses: visual interaction', in R.E. Park and E.W. Burgess (eds), *Introduction to the Science of Sociology*. Chicago: University of Chicago Press.

Simmel, G. (1971 [1903]) 'The Metropolis', in D. Levine (ed.), *Georg Simmel on Individuality and Social Forms*. Chicago: University of Chicago Press.

Simmel, G. (1971 [1908a]) 'How is society possible?', in D. Levine (ed.), *Georg Simmel on Individuality and Social Forms*. Chicago: University of Chicago Press.

Simmel, G. (1971 [1908b]) 'The stranger', in D. Levine (ed.), *Georg Simmel On Individuality and Social Forms*. Chicago: University of Chicago Press.

Simmel, G. (1971 [1908c]) 'Subjective culture', in D. Levine (ed.), *Georg Simmel On Individuality and Social Forms*. Chicago: University of Chicago Press.

Simmel, G. (1971 [1908d]) 'Social forms and inner needs', in D. Levine (ed.), *Georg Simmel on Individuality and Social Forms*. Chicago: University of Chicago Press.

Simmel, G. (1971 [1910]) 'Sociability', in D. Levine (ed.), *Georg Simmel On Individuality and Social Forms*. Chicago: University of Chicago Press.

Simmel, G. (1971 [1918a]), 'The conflict in modern culture', in D. Levine (ed.), *Georg Simmel On Individuality and Social Forms*. Chicago: University of Chicago Press.

Simmel, G. (1971 [1918b]) 'The transcendent character of life', in D. Levine (ed.), *Georg Simmel On Individuality and Social Forms*. Chicago: University of Chicago Press.

Simmel, G. (1990 [1907]) *The Philosophy of Money*, edited and with an introduction by T. Bottomore and D. Frisby. London: Routledge.

Simmel, G. (1997) 'Sociology of the meal', in D. Frisby and M. Featherstone (eds), *Simmel on Culture*. London: Sage.

Simmel, G. (1997 [1904]) 'Religion and the contradictions of life', in H.J. Helle (ed.), *Essays on Religion*. New Haven, CT: Yale University Press.

Simmel, G. (1997 [1912]) 'Religion', in H.J. Helle (ed.), *Essays on Religion*. New Haven, CT: Yale University Press.

Simri, U. (1979) *Women at the Olympic Games* (Wingate Monograph Series No. 7). Netanya, Israel: Wingate Institute for Physical Education and Sport.

Siskind, J. (1973) *To Hunt in the Morning*. New York: Oxford.

Slater, D. (2002) 'Making things real: ethics and order on the Internet', *Theory, Culture and Society*, 19 (5/6): 227–245.

Slouka, M. (1995) *War of the Worlds: The Assault on Reality*. London: Abacus.

Smith, H. (1947) 'Music in Relation to Employee Attitudes, Piece-work Production, and Industrial Accidents' (Applied Psychology Monographs, No. 14).

Smith, T.S. (1992) *Strong Interaction*. Chicago: The University of Chicago Press.

Snell, B. (1960 [1948]) *Discovery of the Mind: The Greek Origins of European Thought*. Oxford: Basil Blackwell.

Snow, C., de Blauw, A. and van Roosmalen, G. (1979) 'Talking and playing with babies: the role of ideologies of childrearing', in M. Bullowa (ed.), *Before Speech*. Cambridge: Cambridge University Press.

Snow, L. (1993) *Walkin' Over Medicine*. Boulder, CO: Westview.

Snyder, E.E. and Spreitzer, E..A. (1983) *Social Aspects of Sport*, 2nd edition. Englewood Cliffs, NJ: Prentice-Hall.

Snyder, J. (1996) 'Get real', *Internet World*, 7 (2) 92–4.

Soper, K. (1995) *What is Nature?* Oxford: Blackwell.

Spallone, P. (1989) *Beyond Conception*. London: Macmillan.

Sparkes, A. (1999) 'The fragile body-self', in A. Sparkes and M. Silvennoinen (eds), *Talking Bodies: Men's Narratives of the Body and Sport*. Jyvaskyla: SoPhi.

Sparkes, A. and Silvennoinen, M. (eds) (1999) *Talking Bodies: Men's Narratives of the Body and Sport*. Jyvaskyla: SoPhi.

Springer, C. (1991) 'The pleasure of the interface', *Screen*, 32 (3) Autumn: 303–323.

Springer, C. (1996) *Electronic Eros: Bodies and Desire in the Post-Industrial Age*. London: Athlone.

Sproull, L. and Kiesler, S. (1986) 'Reducing social context cues: electronic mail in organizational communication', *Management Science*, 32: 1492–1512.

Sproull, L. and Kiesler, S. (1993) 'Computers, networks and work', in L. Harasim (ed.), *Global Networks: Computers and International Communication*. Cambridge, MA: MIT Press.

Standley, J. (1995) 'Music as a therapeutic intervention in medical and dental treatment: research and clinical applications', in T. Wigram, B. Saperston and R. West (eds), *The Art and Science of Music Therapy: A Handbook*. Langhorne: Harwood Academic.

Stanworth, J. and Stanworth, C. (1991) *Work 2000*. London: Paul Chapman.

Stedman-Jones, G. (1983) 'Working class culture and working class politics in London, 1870–1900: Notes on the remaking of the working class', in G. Stedman-Jones, *Languages of Class*. Cambridge: Cambridge University Press.

Stein, R. and Nemeroff, C. (1995) 'Moral overtones of food', *Personality and Social Psychology Bulletin*, 21: 480–90.

Stelarc (1998) 'From psycho-body to cybersystems', reprinted in D. Bell and B. Kennedy (eds) *The Cybercultures Reader* (2000). London: Routledge.

Stewart, J. (1999) 'Georg Simmel at the lectern: The lecture as embodiment of text', *Body and Society*, 5 (4): 1–16.

Stokes, M. (ed.) (1994), *Ethnicity, Identity and Music*. Oxford: Berg.

Stoller, P. (1997) *Sensuous Scholarship*. Philadelphia, PA: University of Pennsylvania Press.

Stoller, R. and Levine, I. (1993) *Coming Attractions: The Making of an X-Rated Video*. New Haven, CT: Yale University Press.

Stone, A. (1992) 'Will the real body please stand up? Boundary stories about virtual cultures', reprinted in D. Bell and B. Kennedy (2000) (eds), *The Cybercultures Reader*. (2000). London: Routledge.

Storr, A. (1997) *Music and the Mind*. London: Harper Collins.

Straw, W. (1998) '"Organised disorder": the changing space of the record shop', in S. Redhead (ed.), *The Clubcultures Reader*. Oxford: Blackwell.

Streans, C. and Streans, P. (1986) *Anger: The Struggle for Emotional Control in America's History*. Chicago: University of Chicago Press.

Strum, S. and Latour, B. (1999) 'Redefining the social link: from baboons to humans', in D. Mackenzie and J. Wajcman (eds), *The Social Shaping of Technology*, 2nd edition. Buckingham: Open University Press.

Sudnow, D. (1978) *Ways of the Hand: The Organization of Improvised Conduct*. London: Routledge and Kegan Paul.

Sullivan, P. (2002) '"It's easier to be yourself when you are invisible": Female college students discuss their online classroom experiences', *Innovative Higher Education*, 27 (2).

Super, C. and Harkness, S. (1982) 'The development of affect in infancy and early childhood', reprinted in M. Woodhead, D. Faulkner and K. Littleton (eds), *Cultural Worlds of Early Childhood* (1998). London: Routledge.

Symons, M. (1984) *One Continuous Picnic: A History of Eating in Australia*. Ringwood, Victoria: Penguin.

Synnott, A. (1991) 'Puzzling over the senses: From Plato to Marx', in David Howes (ed.), *The Varieties of Sensory Experience: A Sourcebook in the Anthropology of the Senses*. Toronto: University of Toronto Press.

Synnott, A. (1993) *The Body Social*. London: Routledge.

Taylor, F.W. (1947 [1911]) *Shop Management*. London: Harper and Row.

Taylor, S. and Tyler, M. (2000) 'Emotional labour and sexual difference in the airline industry', *Work, Employment and Society*, 14 (1): 77–95.

Tester, K. (1998a) 'Aura, armour and the body', *Body and Society*, 4 (1): 17–34.

Tester, K. (1998b) '"Bored and blasé": television, the emotions and Georg Simmel', in G. Bendelow and S. Williams (eds), *Emotions in Social Life: Critical Themes and Contemporary Issues* (1998). London: Routledge.

Therberge, N. (1986) 'Towards a feminist alternative to sport as a male preserve', *Sociology of Sport Journal*, 3: 193–202.

Therberge, N. (1991) 'Reflections on the body in the sociology of sport', *Quest*, 43: 123–134.

Theweleit, K. (1989) *Male Fantasies, Vol. II: Male Bodies and the 'White Terror'*. Minneapolis, Minnesota: University of Minnesota Press.

Thompson, E.P. (1967) 'Time, work-discipline and industrial capitalism', *Past and Present*, 38: 56–97.

Thompson, E.P. (1980 edition) *The Making of the English Working Class*. Harmondsworth: Penguin.

Tijssen, L. van Vucht (1991) 'Women and objective culture: Georg Simmel and Marianne Weber', *Theory, Culture and Society*, 8: 203–218.

Tom, G. (1995) 'Classical conditioning of unattended stimuli', *Psychology and Marketing*, 12: 79–87.

Tomas, D. (1995) 'Feedback and cybernetics', *Body and Society*, 1 (3/4): 21–43.

Toole, M. (1998) 'Overreaching and overtraining in endurance athletes', in R. Kreider, A. Fry and M. O'Toole (eds), *Overtraining in Sport*. Champaign, IL: Human Kinetics.

Toulmin, S. (1990) *Cosmopolis: The Hidden Agenda of Modernity*. Chicago: University of Chicago Press.

Toynbee, P. (2003) *Hard Work*. London: Bloomsbury.

Trevarthen, C. (1988) 'Universal cooperative motives: How infants begin to know the language and culture of their parents', in G. Johoda and I. Lewis (eds), *Acquiring Culture*. London: Croom-Helm.

Tseelon, E. (1995) *The Masque of Femininity*. London: Sage.

Turkle, S. (1995) *Life on the Screen*. New York: Simon and Schuster.

Turner, B.S. (1984) *The Body and Society*. Oxford: Blackwell.

Turner, B.S. (1986) 'Simmel, rationalization and the problem of money', *Sociological Review*, 34: 93–114.

Turner, B.S. (1991a) 'Recent developments in the theory of the body', in M. Featherstone, M. Hepworth, and B.S. Turner (eds), *The Body: Social Process and Cultural Theory*. London: Sage.

Turner, B.S. (1991b) *Religion and Social Theory*. London: Sage.

Turner, B.S. (1991c) 'The discourse of diet', in M. Featherstone, M. Hepworth, and B.S. Turner (eds), *The Body: Social Process and Cultural Theory*. London: Sage.

Turner, B.S. (1992) *Max Weber: From History to Modernity*. London: Routledge.

Turner, B.S. (1993) 'Outline of a theory of human rights', *Sociology*, 27 (3): 489–512.

Turner, B.S. (1995 2nd edition) *Medical Power and Social Knowledge*. London: Sage.

Turner, B.S. (1996) 'Introduction to the second edition: The the embodiment of social theory', in B.S. Turner, *The Body and Society*, 2nd edition. London: Sage.

Turner, B.S. (2003) 'Biology, vulnerability and politics', in S. Williams, L. Birke and G. Bendelow (eds), *Debating Biology*. London: Routledge.

Turner, B.S. and Rojek, C. (2001) *Society and Culture*. London: Sage.

Turner, B.S. and Wainwright, S. (2003) 'Corps de ballet: the case of the injured ballet dancer', *Sociology of Health and Illness*, 25 (4): 269–288.

Turner, J.H. and Maryanski, A.R. (1988) 'Is "neofunctionalism" really functional?', *Sociological Theory*, 6: 110–121.

van Maanen, J. and Kunda, G. (1989) '"Real feelings": Emotional expression and organizational culture', in L. Cummings and B. Straw (eds), *Research in Organizational Behaviour*, Vol. 11. Greenwich, CT: JAI Press.

Venable, V. (1945) *Human Nature: The Marxian View*. New York: A.A. Knopfy.

Verroken, M. (1996, 2nd edition) 'Drug use and abuse in sport', in D. Mottram (ed.), *Drugs in Sport*. London: E. and F.N. Spon.

Vetinsky, P. (1994) 'Women, sport and exercise in the nineteenth century', in D.M. Costa and S.R. Guthrie (eds), *Women and Sport: Interdisciplinary Perspectives* (2000). Champaign, Il: Human Kinetics.

Virilio, P. (1986) *Speed and Politics*. New York: Semiotext.

Virilio, P. (2000) *Polar Inertia*. London: Sage.

Visser, M. (1991) *The Rituals of Dinner*. New York: Grove Weidenfeld.

Wacquant, L. (1992) 'Toward a social praxeology: The structure and logic of Bourdieu's sociology', in P. Bourdieu and L. Wacquant, *An Invitation to Reflexive Sociology*. Chicago: The University of Chicago Press.

Wacquant, L. (1995) 'Pugs at work: Bodily capital and bodily labour among professional boxers', *Body and Society*, 1 (1): 65–93.

Wainwright, S. and Forbes, A. (2000) 'Philosophical problems with social research on health inequalities', *Health Care Analysis*, 8: 259–277.

Walby, S. (1986) 'Gender, class and stratification', in R. Crompton and M. Mann (eds), *Gender and Stratification*. Cambridge: Polity Press.

Walby, S. (1997) *Gender Transformations*. London: Routledge.

Walton, J. (1992) *Fish and Chip Shops and the British Working Class, 1870–1940*. Leicester: Leicester University Press.

Walvin, J. (1975) *The People's Game: A Social History of English Football*. London: Allen Lane.

Warde, A. and Hetherington, K. (1994) 'English households and routine food practices: A research note', *The Sociological Review*, 42 (4): 758–78.

Warde, A. and Marteens, L. (2000) *Eating Out*. Cambridge: Cambridge University Press.

Washburn, S. and Lancaster, J. (1968) 'The evolution of hunting', in S. Washburn and P. Jay (eds), *Perspectives on Human Evolution*. New York: Holt, Rinehart and Winston.

Watson, J. (2000) *Male Bodies: Health, Culture and Identity*. Buckingham: Open University Press.

Weber, M. (1948 [1919]) 'Science as a vocation', in H. Herth and C. Wright Mills (eds), *For Max Weber*. London: Routledge.

Weber, M. (1991 [1904–05]) *The Protestant Ethic and the Spirit of Capitalism*. London: HarperCollins.

Weinberg, K. and Arond, H. (1952) 'The occupational culture of the boxer', *American Journal of Sociology*, 5: 460–469.

Weinberg, R. and Gould, D. (1995) *Foundations of Sport and Exercise Psychology*. Champaign, Il: Human Kinetics.

Weiner, N. (1948a) 'Cybernetics', *Scientific American*, 179: 14–19.

Weiner, N. (1948b) *Cybernetics: Or Control and Communication in the Animal and the Machine*. New York: John Wiley.

Welton, D. (ed.) (1998) *Body and Flesh: A Philosophical Reader*. Oxford: Blackwell.

Wharton, A. (1993) 'The affective consequences of service work: managing emotions on the job', *Work and Occupations*, 20 (2): 205–32.

Wheelock, J. (1990) 'Consumer attitudes towards processed foods', in J. Somogyi and E. Koskinen (eds), *Nutritional Adaptation to New Life-Styles*. Basel: Kruger.

Whitehead, T. (1984) 'Sociocultural dynamics and food habits in a southern community', in M. Douglas (ed.), *Food in the Social Order*. New York: Russell Sage Foundation.

Wickes, P. (1992 2nd edition) 'The role of rock music in the political disintegration of East Germany', in J. Lull (ed.), *Popular Music and Communication*. London: Sage.

Wiggins, D. (1977) 'Good times on the old plantation', *Journal of Sport History*, 4 (3): 260–84.

Wiggins, D. (1979) 'Isaac Murphy: Black hero in nineteenth century American sport', *Canadian Journal for the History of Sport and Physical Education*, 10 (1): 15–33.

Wiggins, D. (1986) 'From plantation to playing field', *Research Quarterly for Exercise and Sport*, 57 (2): 101–116.

Wilbur, S. (1997) 'An archaeology of cyberspaces', reprinted in D. Bell and B. Kennedy (eds), (2000) *The Cybercultures Reader*. London: Routledge.

Wilkinson, R. (1996) *Unhealthy Societies*. London: Routledge.

Wilkinson, R. (2000) *Mind the Gap: Hierarchies, Health and Human Evolution*. London: Weidenfeld and Nicolson.

Williams, S. (1996) 'The vicissitudes of embodiment across the chronic illness trajectory', *Body and Society*, 2 (2): 23–47.

Williams, S. (1999) 'Is there anybody there? Critical realism, chronic illness and the disability debate', *Sociology of Health and Illness*, 21 (6): 797–819.

Williams, S. (2000) 'Emotions, social structure and health: rethinking the inequalities debate', in S. Williams, J. Gabe and M. Calnan (eds), *Health, Medicine and Society: Future Agendas*. London: Routledge.

Williams, S. (2003a) 'Beyond meaning, discourse and the empirical world: Critical realist reflections on health', *Social Theory and Health*, 1: 42–71.

Williams, S. (2003b) *Medicine and the Body*. London: Routledge.

Williams, S., Birke, L. and Bendelow, G. (2003) *Debating Biology*. London: Routledge.

Williams, W. (1997) 'The equality crisis', in L. Nicholson (ed.), *The Second Wave: A Reader in Feminist Theory*. London: Routledge.

Willis, P. (1977) *Learning to Labour*. Farnborough: Saxon House.

Willis, P. (1978) *Profane Culture*. London: Routledge.

Willson, M. (1997) 'Community in the abstract: a political and ethical dilemma?', reprinted in D. Bell and B. Kennedy (eds), *The Cybercultures Reader* (2000). London: Routledge.

Wilson, J. (1988) *Politics and Leisure*. London: Unwin Hyman.

Wilson, J. (1994) *Playing by the Rules: Sport, Society and the State*. Detroit: Wayne State University Press.

Wilson, N. (1988) *The Sports Business*. London: Piatkus.

Winston, B. (1998) *Media, Technology and Society, a History: From the Telegraph to the Internet*. London: Routledge.

Winston, R. (2002) Review of M. Warnock 'Making Babies: Is There a Right to Have Children?', *The Sunday Times*, 4 August, pp. 33–34.

Wittig, M. (1992) *The Straight Mind and Other Essays*. Boston, MA: Beacon Press.

Wolf, N. (1990) *The Beauty Myth*. London: Vintage.

Wood, R. (1995) *The Sociology of the Meal*. Edinburgh: Edinburgh University Press.

Woolgar, S. (1998) 'A new theory of innovation?', *Prometheus*, 16 (4): 449–53.

Woolgar, S. (2002) *Virtual Society? Technology, Cyberbole, Reality*. Oxford: Oxford University Press.

Wrong, D. (1961) 'The oversocialised conception of man in modern sociology', *The British Journal of Sociology*, 50 (4): 543–562.

Wyatt, S., Thomas, G. and Terranova, T. (2002) 'They came, they surfed, they went back to the beach: Conceptualising use and non-use of the Internet', in S. Woolgar (ed.), *Virtual Society? Technology, Cyberbole, Reality*. Oxford: Oxford University Press.

Yamamoto, D. (2000) *The Boundaries of the Human in Medieval English Literature*. London: Oxford University Press.

Ye, S. (1997) 'Unfair competition', *Heat*, 6: 123–138.

Yelanjian, M. (1991) 'Rhythms of consumption', *Cultural Studies*, January: 91–7.

Young, I.M. (1998) '"Throwing like a girl": twenty years later', in D. Welton (ed.), *Body and Flesh: A Philosophical Reader*. Oxford: Blackwell.

Zapf, D. (2002) 'Emotion work and psychological well-being', *Human Resource Management Review*, 12 (2): 237–68 (page numbers refer to online edition).

Zapf, D., Seifert, C., Schmutte, B., Mertini, H. and Holz, M. (2001) 'Emotion work and job stressors and their effects on burnout', *Psychology and Health*, 16: 527–45.

Zapf, D., Vogt, C., Seifert, C., Mertini, H. and Isis, A. (1999) 'Emotion work as a source of stress', *European Journal of Work and Organizational Psychology*, 8: 371–400.

Zillman, D. and Gan, Su-lin (1997) 'Musical taste in adolescence', in D. Hargreaves and A. North (eds), *The Social Psychology of Music*. Oxford: Oxford University Press.

Zurcher, L. and Meadow, A. (1967) 'On bullfights and baseball', *The International Journal of Comparative Sociology*, 8 (1): 99–117.

Author Index

Subject Index